CHARLES VERNON EDDY
GRAND MASTER OF MASONS IN VIRGINIA
(1937-1938)
GRAND HIGH PRIEST, R. A. M. (1941-1942)
GRAND COMMANDER, K. T. (1925-1926)

FREEMASONRY

IN

WINCHESTER, VIRGINIA

1768 - 1948

By

WILLIAM MOSELEY BROWN, P. G. M.

PUBLISHED BY AUTHORITY OF
Winchester Hiram Lodge No. 21, A. F. & A. M.
John Dove Chapter No. 21, Royal Arch Masons
Winchester Commandery No. 12, K. T.

1949

McClure Printing Co.
Staunton, Virginia

Second Edition 1979

COPYRIGHT 1949

By

The Trustees of

Winchester Hiram Lodge No. 21

A. F. & A. M.

All rights reserved

Second Edition
Updated 1949-1979
Published December, 1979

CONTENTS

Chapter		Page
	Charles Vernon Eddy	7
	Foreword	9
I	The Background	11

PART ONE

THE LODGE

II	The First Lodge in the Shenandoah Valley	19
III	Seven years of Progress (1771-1777)	31
IV	The Post-Revolutionary Period	47
V	From Pennsylvania to Virginia	61
VI	First Years Under Virginia Jurisdiction	65
VII	Two Score Years of Active Service	79
VIII	War and Reconstruction	95
	Appendix I to Chapter VIII—Degrees Conferred during Federal Occupation	111
	Appendix II to Chapter VIII—Abstract of Documents Conferring Right to Meet in the Winchester City Hall	119
IX	The Years of Recovery (1871-1900)	121
X	Hiram Lodge After 1900	131
XI	Winchester's Grand Masters	143
XII	Notes on Other Winchester Lodges	147
	Masters, Treasurers, Secretaries, and Trustees of Winchester Lodge No. 12 and Winchester Hiram Lodge No. 21	152

PART TWO

THE CHAPTER

XIII	The Pre-Grand Chapter Period	161
XIV	Winchester Chapter and the Grand Chapter of Virginia	173

CONTENTS (Continued)

Chapter		Page
XV	The First Forty Years Under Virginia's Jurisdiction	179
XVI	The War of 1861 To the End of the Nineteenth Century	185
XVII	John Dove Chapter Since 1900	193
	High Priests, Treasurers, and Secretaries of Winchester Chapter No. 12 and John Dove Chapter No. 21	200

PART THREE
THE COUNCIL

XVIII	Winchester Council, Royal and Select Masters	207

PART FOUR
THE COMMANDERY

XIX	Winchester Encampment and the Grand Encampment of Virginia	217
XX	Winchester Encampment Becomes Dormant	227
XXI	The Years of Uncertainty	233
XXII	The Reconstruction Period and After	235
	Commanders, Treasurers, and Recorders of Winchester Encampment No. 1 and Winchester Commandery No. 12	242
	Charters of the Masonic Bodies of Winchester	245
	Acknowledgements	254
	Rosters of the Masonic Bodies of Winchester (1949)	256
	Index of Names	265
	Index of Subjects	279

PART FIVE
1949-1979

Winchester Hiram Lodge No. 21	254-3
Winchester Commandery No. 12	254-17
John Dove Royal Arch Chapter No. 21	254-25
McKinley Chapter No. 19, Order of Eastern Star	254-A

LIST OF ILLUSTRATIONS

Charles Vernon Eddy .... *Frontispiece*

                                                                              Facing Page

Portrait of Dr. John Dove 16

Masonic Temple, Winchester 32

Market House, Winchester 33

Alexander Mantz Baker 48

Detail of East End of Lodge Room Ceiling 64

Lodge Room from the West 65

Lodge Room from the East 80

Detail of West End of Lodge Room Ceiling 81

Tablet to Revolutionary War Heroes 111-a

Tablet to Dr. Robert Jonston 111-b

Chapter and Commandery Room 128

Loudoun Street as McKinley Knew It 142

McKinley Visit and Portrait 143

Judge Richard Parker 158

Frank Talbot McFaden, D. D. 159

TO
CHARLES VERNON EDDY
Man and Mason
Citizen and Friend
For his fiftieth Masonic
Birthday

CHARLES VERNON EDDY

Charles Vernon Eddy was born at Winchester, Virginia on September 13, 1877. He received his education in private schools in that city and, from 1896 to 1912, he was engaged in the business of printing and publishing. In 1913 he became the Librarian of the public library of the city of Winchester, known as The Handley Library, which position he has held to the present time. This library is a part of the service contributed to the people of Winchester by the Handley Trust, a city Trust with a corpus in excess of one and a quarter million dollars. In 1921 Brother Eddy became secretary to the Handley Board of Trustees, and he has held that position also to date, becoming ten years later the treasurer of this Board as well. He served two terms as President of the Virginia Library Association; is chairman of the Park Commission of Winchester; became a charter member of the Winchester Rotary Club 27 years ago and has retained his membership in that organization continously to the present. He has also served constructively the Boy Scouts of America; the American Red Cross; and the Historical Society of his county and community.

The Masonic record of Charles Vernon Eddy is a truly remarkable one. He was raised April 11, 1899 in Winchester Hiram Lodge No. 21; exalted and greeted in John Dove Chapter No. 21, Royal Arch Masons; and knighted in Winchester Commandery No. 12, Knights Templar, one year after his raising. He is a member of the Scottish Rite bodies of Richmond, and, in 1947, he received the rank and decoration of Knight Commander of the Court of Honor by vote of the Supreme Council in Washington. He was Grand Master of Masons in Virginia in 1937; Grand High Priest in 1941; and Grand Commander of Knights Templar in 1925. In 1929 he became Grand Recorder of the Grand Commandery, Knights Templar, of Virginia and still serves in that office.

He is also Grand Sentinel of the Grand Imperial Council, Red Cross of Constantine; Celebrant of Virginia College, Societas Rosicruciana in Civitatibus Foederatis; Deputy for Virginia of the Royal Order of Scotland; and a member of the Board of Directors of the National League of Masonic Clubs. In 1947 he was appointed Grand Captain of the Guard of the Grand Encampment, Knights Templar, U. S. A., and in 1948 he became Sovereign Grand Master of the Grand Council, Allied Masonic Degrees, U. S. A. He has also served as Grand Master General, Knights of the York Cross of Honor, and Prefect of the Great Priory of America, Chevaliers Bienfaisants de la Cité Sainte. He is likewise a Past Preceptor of Gethsemane Tabernacle, No. 2, Ordo Sacerdotalis Templi. He holds honorary membership in a large number of Masonic bodies and is universally regarded as a man and Mason with whom his Brethren like to be associated. It is a pleasure to do him honor in dedicating the present volume to him on the occasion of his fiftieth Masonic birthday. He is one of that small group of Masons, who hold that every Masonic honor carries with it corresponding responsibilities. And Vernon Eddy is perfectly willing, without urging, to step in and do the task which goes with every honor he receives.

THURMAN CROSSLIN, Worshipful Master
Winchester Hiram Lodge No. 21

JACK K. JENKINS, High Priest
John Dove Chapter No. 21

ROBERT A. WHITTEN, Commander
Winchester Commandery No. 12

FOREWORD

The story of Freemasonry in Winchester, Virginia is a fascinating one. The present volume represents the first attempt in the direction of setting forth the facts concerning *all* of the Winchester Masonic bodies in a reasonably comprehensive way. So far as the writer has been able to determine, there has never been a history of any of these bodies previously prepared except the relatively short sketch of Winchester Hiram Lodge No. 21, which was prepared by Judge Richard Parker before 1894. This sketch was published in the Proceedings of the Grand Lodge of Virginia and there were also a number of off-prints, some of which are still in the possession of the Lodge. Judge Parker was Master of Hiram Lodge in 1868-1869, Grand Master of Virginia in 1876-1877, and had won fame by being designated to preside over the trial of John Brown in December, 1859. But there is no reference to the Chapter or the Commandery in this brief sketch.

Hence, it is particularly fitting, that the story of Winchester Masonry should be compiled at this time. For not only the Lodge, but the Chapter and Commandery as well, have played remarkable roles in Virginia Masonic history. We know of no other community in the commonwealth, where all three of these York (or American) Rite bodies were in existence prior to 1815, all being self-congregated and self-constituted before receiving warrants or charters from any sovereign body, and all being in existence today. True it is, that there were lapses occasionally in the existence of one or another of these bodies, but these were due to the advent of war or other similar exigencies of the times. And there was always sufficient life and vigor to insure the revival of Lodge, Chapter, or Commandery when more auspicious circumstances arose.

Furthermore, Winchester was the first Virginia city to be established west of the Blue Ridge mountains. It was also the first community west of the Blue Ridge to have a Masonic Lodge. It thus became the center of Masonic influence for all the lower Shenandoah Valley, and the message of Masonry was carried from the Winchester bodies not only to the immediately surrounding territory but also to what is now West Virginia and doubtless to other states in the Mid-West as well.

There is the further important fact, that Masonry in Winchester did not come from the older Lodges in Tidewater Virginia but from Pennsylvania, more particularly from Philadelphia, with which the people of Winchester had at that time very strong business and cultural ties. The Winchester Lodge was warranted by the Provincial Grand Lodge of Pennsylvania in 1768 and was one of three Lodges in Virginia, which owed their existence to Pennsylvania, the others coming later and being located at Alexandria and Portsmouth. Not only did Winchester's symbolic Masonry come from the Quaker state, but so did its Capitular and Templar Masonry as well. It was not until 1807 that the Lodge severed the tie, which had bound it to Pennsylvania for nearly forty years, and even today the Winchester Brethren point with pride to their Pennsylvania Masonic heritage.

We mention only one other fact, which makes Winchester Masonry noteworthy, namely, the organization of the Grand Encampment (now Grand Commandery) of Virginia Knights Templar there in 1823. Hence, from the standpoint of Templary, there is no doubt that Winchester is the most important locality in the commonwealth. The fact of its relatively early organizaion in comparison with the other Grand Commanderies of the United States makes the Grand Commandery of Virginia the third oldest in the country.

It will be seen, therefore, that the Masons of Winchester were men of vision and of foresight, especially in those early days when there were manifold difficulties to be overcome, which we of the twentieth century do not know. It is fitting that their story should be set forth in the following pages not only as a memorial to those, who have gone before, but as an inspiration and guide to those, who come after them and who are endeavoring to follow in their footsteps.

THE AUTHOR

Winchester, Virginia
January, 1949

CHAPTER I

THE BACKGROUND

The background, against which Freemasonry in Winchester, Virginia, developed, is one of the most fascinating in American history. Thus the heritage, which the Winchester Brethren of today enjoy, entails more than an average amount of responsibility. There is a disposition to take things for granted, not only among Masons but among Americans generally; to assume, that the history and the traditions, which we enjoy, came to us by a veritable dispensation of an over-ruling Providence, who somehow decided that America should become the promised land of the seventeenth through the twentieth centuries; that the rest of the world should come to us in these present days, like the sons of Jacob in early Biblical times, to "buy corn", so to speak, while famine and drought and despair stalked in nearly all other countries. Many of us feel, that the liberties, which are ours, came from this same divine cornucopia, whose bounties shall never end and whose abundance is a sort of "magic quality" which exists entirely above and apart from our own determination and endeavors.

But none of this is true and every Mason knows, that it is only through devotion and self-sacrifice, that the Masonic institution, along with every other democratic organization, has survived and flourished through the years since the first speculative Grand Lodge was organized in London on June 24, 1717. And it was precisely the same kind of spirit, which made America and Virginia and Winchester possible in days when savages and the howling wilderness greeted every man, who dared to invade their precincts at any point along the Atlantic seaboard. Add to these the difficulties of passing first the foothills and eventually the mountain ranges, which we now call the Blue Ridge, the descent into the great Valley of Virginia amidst the frequent attacks of Indians, the extreme scarcity of the means of making a livelihood, and the terrible loneliness and the fears, which so constantly beset our pioneer forefathers. The responsibility of such a heritage bears doubly upon us in these days of the twentieth century, when we are called upon to discharge the duties of citizenship in one of the few democratic countries still left in the world. In the opinion of the present writer, there are few places in our entire United States, where so many streams of influence, historically speaking, at least, come together, intermingle, and then roll on in an even mightier current than at Winchester. Among these important streams of influence not the least important was that of Freemasonry, and it is this phase of the community's history, which forms the subject of the present volume.

Every Winchester citizen knows (or should know), that he resides in the oldest Virginia city west of the Blue Ridge mountains. Originally called Fredericktown, this name seems to have been given to the settlement because of the fact, that it was the county seat and that Frederick County was authorized in 1738 and was sliced from Orange County in 1743. Nothing was more natural, therefore, than to assign the same name to both county and town, especially since the latter had its beginning six years after the county was named. For in 1744 James Wood laid out on the site of the present Winchester a courthouse square and 26 lots. He also built a log house at the present Glen Burnie, in which the first court of Frederick County was held. If Lord Fairfax had had his way, the county seat would have been established at Stephens City. According to tradition, however, James Wood outwitted him by serving to one of the justices enough toddy to induce him to cast the deciding vote in favor of Fredericktown. In 1752, just eight years after the first settlement, the town was laid out and named for Winchester, England, the two cities being on especially friendly terms today.

Though many of the first settlers in Winchester were English, there were also many Germans, who came from the northern colonies, especially Pennsylvania. In 1732 Joist Hite (whose influence came eventually to be felt throughout the entire Shenandoah Valley) crossed the Potomac River at Pack Horse Ford, near the present Shepherdstown in West Virginia, bringing with him 16 families from Pennsylvania. These all settled at Opequon, five miles south of Winchester. From Isaac and John Van Meter, Hite purchased lands, which formed a part of the Northern Neck proprietary of Lord Fairfax.

In 1748 another historic event of great importance to Winchester took place, for it was in that year, that George Washington, then a red-headed, freckle-faced lad of sixteen, paid his first visit to the town. Washington was then engaged in his first job, that of surveying the vast holdings of Lord Fairfax. He wrote of this particular area that he "went through ye most beautiful groves of Sugar Trees and spent ye best part of ye Day in admiring ye Trees and richness of ye Land". After General Braddock's defeat in 1755, Colonel Washington was placed in command of the frontier forces and came to Winchester again. He writes of this visit, that he "rid post to this place.....and found everything in the greatest hurry and Confusion, by the back Inhabitants flocking in, and those of the town removing out......No orders are obey'd, but what a Party of Soldiers, or my own drawn Sword, Enforces". He set about quieting the people and building Fort Loudoun for their protection.

In the Revolutionary War the men of Winchester played an important part also. We shall find in the following chapters of this volume, that the membership of the Masonic Lodge became so depleted by this fact, that it was forced to suspend its activities for a period of approximately eight years and that some of its members were among those, "who never returned". The leader of the Winchester men was Daniel Morgan, who had moved there from New Jersey in 1753, just one year after the town had been laid out and renamed. After the Battle of Bunker Hill he organized a company of northern Virginia riflemen and was commissioned a captain of militia under General Benedict Arnold. Morgan led his company as far north as Canada, was held prisoner in Quebec, fought in both battles of Saratoga, and became the hero of the battle of the Cowpens, where he defeated

Colonel Tarleton on that memorable occasion. Morgan spent the last ten years of his life in Winchester.

One of the important reasons for Winchester's growth was its location "at the crossroads", for here was the intersection of two old trails, leading respectively north-south and east-west. Their origin went back to the times before the advent of the white man and the two modern highways, which are their lineal descendants, contribute greatly to the prosperity of the Winchester of today. During the Revolutionary War (1779) the General Assembly authorized the incorporation of the community as a town. Early in the nineteenth century stage lines began to operate between Winchester and Harpers Ferry and the Winchester and Potomac Railroad was completed between the same two points in 1836.

When the War Between the States broke out, Winchester was a thriving business center for the entire lower Valley. During the whole period of hostilities it was also the scene of all kinds of military activities. At the beginning it was an important requisitioning point for the Confederacy because of its mills and factories and of the crops and cattle which abounded in the surrounding area. When General Thomas J. Jackson took command of the Department of the Shenandoah in October, 1861, he proceeded at once to clear Winchester of the invading Federal forces. In March, 1862, however, General Banks took the town, but did not remain for long, since Jackson moved in again on May 25th of that year. Until the summer of 1864 Winchester changed hands many times, but was finally taken by the Union forces, who remained in possession until the end of hostilities. It was during this period of Federal occupation that Hiram Lodge enjoyed one of its most prosperous epochs. The story of those months, when the Lodge resumed its workings with the permission of the occupying authorities, forms an episode, which is almost without parallel in American Masonic history. Numbers of the Federal officers received their degrees in the Lodge, among them Capt. William McKinley. But of this we shall have occasion to speak later in some detail.

When the war was ended, Winchester speedily returned to its normal state. It became rapidly an important marketing center for the rich agricultural district surrounding it and especially does it owe its recent prosperity to the near-by orchards. For more than twenty years this fact has been celebrated in the annual Apple Blossom festivals, at which a new "Queen Shenandoah" is crowned each year. Winchester became a city in 1874 and established the city manager form of government in 1915. Throughout their long history the Masonic bodies of Winchester have been closely indentified with the business, cultural, and religious life of the community and have made a contribution, which it would be indeed difficult to overestimate. The fact, that the Chapter and Commandery have held their meetings for many years in the market house and later in the City Hall under a mutually satisfactory arrangement existing between them and the public authorities bears eloquent testimony to the esteem in which the Winchester Masons are held. The city's associations with the name and work of George Washington, "the greatest Mason of them all," and many another Mason of distinction make it extremely important that the story of Freemasonry in Winchester be recorded in some adequate manner, so that it will be available not only to the Brethren of the present generation but also to those, who will become in time their successors in venerating the memory of those gone before and in perpetuating their contribution as long as our noble fraternity shall last.

We close this chapter by calling attention to the most tangible evidence still in existence, proving the presence of Masons in the town of Winchester prior to the date of warranting Lodge No. 12 (October 1, 1768). This indisputable evidence is in the form of a tablet, which without doubt formerly marked the grave of the Brother, whose name is engraved thereon. About 1900 Brother Alexander M. Baker, one of Winchester's most prominent Masons, found this marker in the basement of Christ Episcopal Church. A diligent search on his part failed to disclose the original source, whence the stone had been removed. Noting the square and compasses at the top of the tablet, he suggested to the vestry of the church, that it be presented to Winchester Hiram Lodge No. 21, and the presentation was accordingly made. The tablet is now mounted near the entrance of the dining room in the Masonic Temple at Winchester and is in a good state of preservation. There is no reference to Masonry in the inscription other that the very prominent position given to the Masonic emblem at the top. The remainder of the epitaph reads as follows:

> Sacred to the Memory
> of
> DR. ROBERT JONSTON
> Who departed this Life
> October 8th 1763
> Age 27 Years
> Come hither Mortals, Cast an Eye
> Then go thy way, prepare to die
> Here read thy Doom, that die thou must
> One Day like me, be turn'd to dust.

From this tablet it will be seen, that Dr. Jonston died almost exactly five years before the date of Lodge No. 12's original warrant. If, as we may suppose, he had resided in Winchester for several years prior to his death, we may then state with assurance, that there were Masons in Winchester before 1760. Our guess is, that they were there at least as early as 1750—and with this we leave the matter to the reader's own determination.

Let us now return to the year 1768, when *organized* Masonry made its first appearance in the community. It is almost certain that the Brethren had been holding informal assemblies even before they decided to organize formally and to request a warrant from the Provincial Grand Lodge of Pennsylvania meeting at Philadelphia. This decision was reached some time in the year mentioned and certainly prior to October of that year. The sequel to this important action on the part of the early Winchester Brethren is set forth in the following pages.

PORTRAIT OF DR. JOHN DOVE
Personally Approved by Him and now a prized
possession of John Dove Chapter No. 21, R. A. M.
(See page 189)

PART ONE
THE LODGE

CHAPTER II

THE FIRST LODGE IN THE SHENANDOAH VALLEY

From the facts as set forth in the preceding chapter it will be seen that the following results came as a natural consequence: first, that Freemasonry came into the lower Shenandoah Valley shortly after the middle of the eighteenth century with settlers migrating from Pennsylvania; second, that Winchester, being then a town of some importance and rapidly becoming even more so, became the seat of the first organized group of Masons in that entire section of the Colony of Virginia; and third, that the spread of Freemasonry throughout the lower Valley was due to the prominence and influence of Winchester Lodge No. 12. From 1768, the date of its warrant, until 1784 this Lodge was the *only* Lodge in Virginia west of the Blue Ridge Mountains. In the latter year Staunton Lodge No. 13 was organized and received its charter in 1786 from Edmund Randolph, Grand Master of Virginia. But Winchester Lodge still retained the honor of being the only pre-Revolutionary Lodge in Virginia west of the Blue Ridge, also of being one of the ten Lodges existing in Virginia at the time of the organization of the Grand Lodge in 1777-1778. Two other Lodges were warranted in Virginia by Pennsylvania *after* the close of the Revolutionary War—No. 39 at Alexandria (now Alexandria-Washington Lodge No. 22) and No. 41 at Portsmouth, which has long since ceased to exist.

Since Winchester Lodge (as will be seen later in this narrative) decided to maintain its allegiance to the Grand Lodge of Pennsylvania, refusing to leave its "first love" until 1807, this Lodge did not participate in the organization of the Grand Lodge of Virginia.

Let us now take a look at the earliest records of Winchester Lodge No. 12.

The original minute book of the Lodge contained a copy

of the warrant granted by the Grand Lodge of Pennsylvania under date of October 1, 1768 (Sachse says the date is October 4th but this is apparently a mistake). However, the loss of several pages at the beginning of this book as well as of the original document itself have rendered it impossible for us to reproduce the wording of the warrant here in full. We give the sole surviving lines of this important document herewith. The reader must remember always, that the term "warrant" was used in those days in exactly the same manner as we use the word "charter" today.

.....as Free Masons and such Successors in like manner shall Nominate Chuse and Install their Successors &c &c &c: such Installation to be upon (or near) every St. John the Evangelist Day, during the continuance of this Lodge for ever PROVIDED the above Named Brethren and all their Successors Pay due Respect to the Right Worshipfull Grand Lodge from whom they have this Authority Otherwise this Warrent [*sic*] to be of no Force or Virtue. GIVEN under our hands, and Seal of the Grand Lodge in the City of Philadelphia and Province of Pennsylvania the 1st day of October in the Year of our Lord 1768, and in the Year of Masonry 5768.

JNO. WOOD G. Secretary
[Seal of the
Grand Lodge]

To the above the Lodge secretary of that day (possibly John Lewis—the record does not show positively) has appended the following:

The Coppy of the Warrent Granted by the Grand Lodge of Philadelphia To the Town of Winchester in the County of Frederick and Colony of Virginia.

1768

On the very next page following the copy of the warrant appears the first set of by-laws for the new Lodge with the following interesting "preamble":

The By Laws of No. 12 of Ancient Free and Accepted Masons for the Town of Winchester County of Frederick and Colony of Virginia by Virtue of a Special Warrent to Brother James Gamul

The First Lodge in The Shenandoah Valley

Dowdall Master Brother James Lindsay Sen'r. Warden Broth'r. Samuel Dobie Junior Warden and their Successors being duly Congregated for ever Granted by the Grand Lodge of Antients in the City of Philadelphia and Province of Pensylvania The Right Worshipful William Ball Esq'r. Grand Master Blackwaite Jones Esq'r. Deputy Grand Master M'r. David Hall Sen'r. Grand Warden M'r. Hugh Lennox J. G. W. with the Consent of the Lodge Baring Date the 1'st. Day of October In the Year of our Lord 1768 and in the Year of Masonry 5768.

The first list of members of the Lodge appears a few pages farther along in this same minute book and with the following caption:

A List of the Brethren of the Most Antient & Honorable Fraternity of Free and Accepted Masons of Lodge No. 12 in the Town of Winchester.

Then comes the list of 22 Brethren, though the name of John Howard has been crossed out for some reason. The other 21 names are as follows:

James Gamul Dowdall	Morgan Alexander
James Lindsay	Edmund Taylor
Samuel Dobie	Edward McGuire
Peter Helphinstine	Robt. Russell
Joseph Beeler	Isaac Leen
Dorcy Penticost	Thom's. Craig
John Lewis	John Timberlake
Samuel May	Benj'n. Ashby
Angus McDonald	Willm. Campbell
David Kennedy	George Rootes
John Humphreys	

It is to be noted, however, that not all of the Brethren listed here were members of the Lodge at the beginning or even during the first year of its existence. The list seems to have been augmented from time to time over a period of at least several years. Then, at a still later date, the list was corrected, eight Brethren are noted as "dead" and two (Joseph Beeler and Dorcy Penticost) as "gone over the mountains", probably signifying that they had migrated westward.

The first recorded minutes of the Lodge under its warrant

(though, as has been stated, it undoubtedly existed for some time previously on a more or less informal basis) are incomplete because of damage to this page of the minute book. The date of this meeting is not certain but it occurred apparently on November 8, 1768. The Lodge was opened "in due form" with James Gamul Dowdall in the chair, James Lindsay as Senior Warden, Samuel Dobie as Junior Warden, and Peter Helphinstine as the only other member present. The remainder of the proceedings are recorded in the following words:

> Opened our Lodge and proceeded to Business. Read over our Warrent from the Right Worshipfull Grand Lodge of Philadelphia To the Town of Winchester County of Fred'k. & Colony of Virginia. Next our by Laws and had an Entered Aprentices Lecture. Lodge Closed till the 2'd tuesday in December Extra Lodg[es] Excepted.

These minutes are certainly brief enough and we might wish that they were in somewhat greater detail. But the entry for the next meeting is still more brief:

> December 13th Brother James Lindsay S. W. Brother Samuel Dobie J. W. & Brother Peter Helphinstine. Mett according to Appointment. Did no Business that night our Master being gone to WillmsBurgh.

We can only conjecture the reasons for the absence of James Dowdall in Williamsburg at that time. He was hardly there on Masonic business, however, since the Grand Lodge of Virginia was not in existence as such until ten years later. It is possible that he may have made contact with Peyton Randolph, however, since Randolph was Provincial Grand Master of Virginia at the time and remained so, from all we can gather from the meagre Masonic records of the time, until his death in 1774. But there was never a Provincial Grand Lodge in Virginia and thus there could have been no question as to the allegiance of the new Lodge in Winchester to Virginia or Pennsylvania. Note also, that the Grand Lodge of Pennsylvania is mentioned as the *Grand Lodge of Philadelphia* in certain of the earliest Winchester Lodge records.

By St. John the Evangelist's Day of 1768, however, James Dowdall had returned from Williamsburg and we find the following recorded of the meeting held on that date:

[Dec.] 27th [1768]

Lodge held tonight at John Sexton's James Dowdall Master in the Chair Brother James Lindsay S W Brother Sam'l Dobie J W Brother Peter Helphinstine M[ember]. Agreed in Open Lodge that the Same Officers shall act till next St. John the Evangelist Except in case of Misconduct and the Lodge to be held at John Sexton's as long as it proved agreeable to the Body then assembled or any part should hereafter join us.
Capt'n Joseph Beeler and M'r. Dorcy Penticost proposed themselves to be Ballotted for on next Lodge Night. Lodge was closed till the 1st Tuesday in January Extra Lodges Excepted.

These first two petitioners were ballotted for and unanimously admitted on January 3, 1769 but "being found clandestine were entered past & raised to the Degrees of Master Masons". On February 7th William Little petitioned but there is no immediate record of what disposition was made of his petition. The first mention of any visiting Brethren is to be found in the minutes of April 4, 1769 when John Hay and Alexander Woodrow were admitted to visit the Lodge "after a just exam'n." The name of William Little now reappears in the minutes of "Munday May 1st", 1769. and we are told that he "sent a reasonable excuse for his not attending to be balloted for now three Nights since his desire to be Entered on our Lodge Books". The last we hear of his case appears in the minutes of September 4, 1769 as follows:

Agreed that Mr. W'm. Little a Petitioner on our Books should be deemed Unworthy of Our Society by his Neglect of Attending since his petittioning & his Contempt of us in Sending no Reasonable Excuse since the 1st of May, now four Lodge Nights since.

Let us return for another look, however, at the minutes for May 1, 1769. They contain an important reference to a communication received from Temple Lodge, of Lancaster, Pennsylvania, "with the Laws of Charity inclosed therein", all of which were read in open Lodge and "it was agreed that they should be Copy'd off and added to our By Laws and that the Thanks of this Body should be returned to our Worthy & Well Beloved Brethren of the Town of Lancaster for their care of us".

At the meeting of June 5th Peter Helphinstine was appointed Junior Warden "in the room of Br. Saml. Dobie removed to Fredericktown in Maryland". Further it was "agreed upon that Br. John Lewis should act as Secretary (on it being first proposed & his being pleased to accept the Office)". On July 3d John Hay, who had been admitted as a visiting member on April 4th (see above), asked again for the same privilege and he was "refused on his not complying with our desire & his promis (on April 4th and May 1st Lodge Nights) of applying to No. 2 of Philadelphia for a certificate where he on the first of the above nights gave his voluntary oath that he was made a Master Mason (on our examining before he got admittance) and likewise for behaving so much out of Character in town on Different Times as it put it out of our power to support our character as Free Masons in shewing him any futher Countenance and therefore deemed him unworthy."

At all of these early meetings there was usually a "short lecture" in some one of the Masonic degrees before closing. Business was always transacted in a Lodge opened on the first degree and this continued to be the custom in all Virginia Lodges for many years and until well into the nineteenth century. The minutes are usually very brief and are signed by neither the Master nor the Secretary. In fact, only one set of minutes is signed by the Secretary prior to December 27, 1774, after which date the minutes are regularly signed by the Secretary upon the "order of the Master". The first regular election of officers took place on St. John's Day, December 27, 1769 (the officers under the original warrant having served until that date, as previously mentioned) and James Gamul Dowdall was re-elected Master. He then designated the remaining officers for the ensuing year, namely, James Lindsay as Senior Warden, Peter Helphinstine as Junior Warden, and John Lewis as Secretary.

This marks the first time that a secretary was formally designated, Lewis having served previously in that office by informal appointment since June 5, 1769. From time to time additional Brethren, who had been made clandestinely, petitioned for membership in the Lodge and were, if accepted, entered, passed, and raised usually on the same evening. Occasionally a petitioner of this type was refused. The reference to clandestine Masonry was doubtless an aftermath of the contest between the "Antients" and the "Moderns", since the first Grand Lodge in Pennsylvania was styled the "Moderns" (1731-1760), but a Provincial Grand Lodge of the "Antients" seems to have been organized about 1760 or 1761, of which William Ball, who granted the warrant to Winchester Lodge No. 12, was Provincial Grand Master 1761-1782. Reference to Ball is made frequently in the early minutes of Winchester Lodge and there was considerable correspondence between him and the Lodge upon several occasions, copies of some of the letters, which were exchanged, having been incorporated into the Lodge minutes.

The question of clandestinism was not disposed of for some years, however. The Winchester Brethren held obviously to the "Antients", this being a part of their very birthright. But the "Moderns" rose up to plague them from time to time and especially in 1771. For example, in the minutes of September 2d of that year (or rather as a footnote to these minutes) we find this *"rara avis"* so far as recorded Lodge minutes are concerned:

> N. B. A Body of the Clandestine Masons of the Lower part of this County Applyed to us for a Coppy of Our Bye Laws which was refused and their Application Treated with Contempt.

It is also interesting to note, that the minutes of these first meetings are exceedingly brief. Sometimes they consist of only three or four lines; sometimes they are somewhat longer. In most instances the minutes of three, four, or even five Lodge meetings will be found recorded on a single page of the record book. The by-laws were required to be read at regular intervals, usually once or twice each year, so that the members might be reminded constantly as to what was required of them as Freemasons. On February 10, 1770 an applicant for the degrees handed in his petition a second time, he having been rejected previously. The Lodge agreed to "give him a second chance", but again he failed of acceptance, the record stating that "three Blacks appeared, therefore deemed him unworthy of ever bein admitted into our Society". The minutes of April 2d of this same year contained an unusual entry:

> Most of the present Brethren begged to be Excused from Sitting to-night their Family being down in the Small Pox. Received an Appology from Br. James Lindsay to the same purpose. Adjourned to the first Munday in May at the house of John Sp (?) where it was unanimously agreed to hold our Lodge for the Future, John Sexton having quit tavern keeping.

The first observance of St. John the Baptist's Day is recorded as having taken place on June 24, 1770. Only five members are listed as being present—the three stationed officers, the Secretary, and a Fellow Craft. "The Lodge being called and no Immediate Business lying before them, after the usual Toasts on the Occasion, closed Till Lodge in Course". On October 6th following James Lindsay was excused for non-attendance on account of long-continued ill health, also Joseph Beeler and Dorcy Penticost because they had "removed out of our Country". These last were the same two Brethren who were indicated as being "over the mountains" in the first membership list of the Lodge as indicated above.

The minutes of November 5, 1770 have another "N. B." attached to them as follows:

> N. B. Broth'r. May and B'r Howell not Paying the Hon'r due to the Lodge, the Reason their being so long without being Raised to the Degree of Master Masons.

At the very next meeting, however (December 3d), Brother Howell announced through Brother May, that he would no longer attend Lodge because of "some ill treatment he said he had rec'd of B'r. Jas. Gam'l. Dowdall. The Brethren concluded on sending him a summons on which he Appeared. Both Parties being heard it was unanimously agreed that B'r. Dowdall was not in Falt and Proposed a Reconciliation which they consented to after Receiving the Bennefit of a Lecture".

On December 10th an "Extra Lodge in proper form" was held for the consideration of the following important business:

> B'r. Dowdall informed the Lodge of his receiving a Message from the R. W. G. Lodge of Pensylvania the 8th Inst. by M'r. Whitehead (who says he was Made Mason there) that they desired we should send them a Coppy of our Transactions. The Members present taking it into Consideration the Shortness of the Time between this & next St. John's day and that we had so long defer'd that part of our Duty for want of being propperly acquainted with it in ourselves and thro' the neglect of M'r. Whitehead not acquainting us sooner Agreed that B'r. Dowdall Should in the Name of the Whole Write such Facts as we hope would Apoligize to B'r. David Hall to Forw'd. [same] to the Grand & That B'r. Lewis Should Coppy of the Transactions to be Inclosed in said Letter as soon as possible.

It was accordingly so done. Two days later the following letter was dispatched to Brother David Hall, Senior Warden of the R. W. G. Lodge of the Province of Pennsylvania:

> Winchester 12th December 1770
>
> B'r. Hall:
> In the last letter I was favor'd with of yours you gave me to understand that the Grand would expect a Coppy of the Transactions No. 12 which Slip'd my Memory 'till the 8th Inst. M'r. Whitehead told me he was Desired to Acquaint this Lodge of the Same. He has not been here since his being admitted a Member of the Antient Craft in Philadelphia 'till that Day. On the 10th we Called an Extra Lodge on the Occasion Where it was Unanimously Agreed to Inclose a Coppy to the R. W. G. as soon as possible and to Intreat they will not Impute our not sending sooner to the least Disrispect in us rather our not being Acquainted with that particular part of Our Duty and Request if there be any thing Impropper in the Form of Entring Our Transactions or Mode of Proceedings we may be set right by them Whome only we Choose to Coppy after in Points of Masonry. We likewise plead for a Book of Constitutions the want of which has been an Unknown Loss to this little Body since their being Favoured with a Warrent. The R. W. G. may think

strange at our being so Few in Number. The Reason is we have not a Man in the Lodge that is not an Ornament to the Society nor will we suffer any other to Enter in among us. There are Severall Clandestines in this Neighborhood that we are Informed intend to apply to the Grand for a Warrent. Most of them the Vilest Scum of the Earth which gives an Indifferent Oppinion of Masonry in general to some Worthies that are Seemmingly Inclined to become Acquainted with Our Misteries. We hope by our Steady Perseverance to Remove the False Odium they are Prejudiced with and Earnestly Entreat your presenting the Inclosed to the R. W. G. Lodge in behalf of the Brethren of No. 12 Who joyns in Love and Gratitude to the R. W. the Grand Master Wardens and Brethren of the Grand Lodge of the Province of Pensylvania &c, &c. With, Dear David,
Your Faithful B'r.
& sincere Friend
JAM'S. GAM'L. DOWDALL

The record of the year 1770 ends with the usual celebration of St. John the Evangelist's Day on December 27th. No program of the ceremonies is given, however, but certain business was transacted, including the required election and installation of officers. James Dowdall was re-elected Master for the ensuing year, the election taking place in a Master Mason's Lodge and not that of an Entered Apprentice. Then the record sets forth this magnanimous action on the part of Brother Dowdall:

B'r. Dowdall Represented to the Lodge the Unjustice they unknowingly did themselves in keeping him so long in the Chair, that thereby they were deprived of Arriving to the Degree of an Excellent Mason and the Valuable Secrets thereto belonging and after thanking the Brethren for the Hon'r. they Confered upon him Begg'd they would Chuse one who had not served, after said request was allowed to resighn [sic] and B'r. Angus McDonald elected in his room and by him Install'd.

At this same meeting John Lewis was made Senior Warden, Peter Helphinstine Junior Warden, James Lindsay Treasurer, and Samuel May became Secretary. A "genteel supper" was held with the usual toasts and it was voted to change the bylaws of the Lodge so that each Brother would pay five shillings per quarter for the support of that body.

We thus come to the close of what may be regarded as the beginning period of the history of Winchester Lodge No. 12. It had now been in existence for more than two years, during all of which time the venerable James Gamul Dowdall had served as Master. He had now retired from this office at his own request and Angus McDonald had succeeded him as the second Master of the Lodge. The fee for filing a petition for the degrees with the Secretary had been set at two shillings, for which the Secretary was expected to make out the petition for the candidate. The fees for the degrees were "forty shillings to the Box & five shillings & sixpence toward Cloathing the Lodge". As stated previously, the annual dues had been set at five shillings per quarter or one pound for the year. At that time, of course, there were no "dollars" and "cents," and the English method of reckoning currency did not finally go out until well into the nineteenth century.

The Treasurer's ledger shows, too, that the Lodge had paid £5/10/0 for its warrant, £9/14/1 for a complete set of jewels purchased through David Hall (before-mentioned as Senior Grand Warden of the Provincial Grand Lodge of Pennsylvania), six shillings for a Bible, three shillings for paper for the "Transaction Book & Book for the By Laws," and twelve shillings for a Book of Constitutions (this last being purchased later in accordance with James Dowdall's letter to David Hall). Thus it was now well on its way in the long and important career, which it has had under both the Pennsylvania and Virginia Grand Lodges and which has made it one of the most historic Lodges now on the rolls of the Grand Lodge of Virginia.

We cannot conclude this chapter without quoting from Judge Parker's readable sketch of the Lodge (published in 1894) as to the character of James Gamul Dowdall, its charter Master:

> As learned from an aged resident of Winchester, Brother Dowdall, the first Master, was a most estimable gentleman, possessed of ample means, including a considerable and valuable real estate in the town. His occupation was that of a merchant, which he conducted on an extensive scale, and what seems scarcely credible (such is the change which time has wrought in our smaller Vir-

ginia towns), he was an importer from foreign countries of many of the articles needed in his business, and at the same time was an exporter to them of the products of our own soil.

The proceedings of No. 12 show plainly how he was regarded by his Masonic Brethren. So valuable were his services that they continued him in his honorable office until December 27, 1770, when he was again elected, but, at his own request, was permitted to resign, and Angus McDonald was made Master. As early thereafter as March 2, 1772, he was again restored to his former position, and served until December 27th of that year, when Samuel May succeeded him; but he was once more elected on December 27, 1773, and continuously thereafter, with the exception of a single year, until December 27, 1785, when he was a second time succeeded by Samuel May, and thereafter, as the proceedings prove, he was again and again entrusted with various matters of importance to his Lodge.

Surely Winchester Lodge, first as No. 12, then as No. 21, has become in a very real sense over the years the lengthened shadow of James Gamul Dowdall. The regret is, that he did not become active in the affairs of the Grand Lodge of Pennsylvania or, later, in those of the Grand Lodge of Virginia. To our way of thinking he would have made almost an ideal Grand Master.

CHAPTER III

SEVEN YEARS OF PROGRESS
(1771-1777)

By the beginning of the year 1771 Winchester Lodge was well under way. Meetings were held regularly once each month and sometimes, when the occasion required, there was a so-called "Extra Lodge" held. Usually these extra meetings were for the purpose of conferring degrees and the by-laws required, that the candidates should bear the expenses of the night in such cases, including both refreshments for those present and the Tyler's fee.

The meetings of January 7, February 4, and March 4, 1771 were occupied with only routine business. On April 1st an apology was presented from David Kennedy for non-attendance since the preceding St. John's night, this being the fourth successive meeting which he had failed to attend. The Brethren "agreed to excuse him and concluded that he should not be subject to the law for excluding members on the fourth night for non-attendance as he lived at a great distance from us." On May 6th George Pearis made application for admission as a "V. B." (visiting Brother), but he had to present a certificate, stand a thorough examination, and receive the approval of the Lodge before admission. Every "V. B." was required, incidentally, to pay his share of the evening's expenses, amounting to one shilling, sixpence, also to show that he was a "Lawful Antient Mason", and even then he was not admitted "if any one or more of the Brethren have any Doubt and cannot get them Solved." It might be well for us of the present day to take our Masonic responsibilities equally as seriously.

At the meeting of July 1, 1771 this enlightening entry occurs concerning a candidate, who was rejected:

Mr. W...... S...... at his request was ballotted for, his petition lying on Our Books Three Lodge Nights tho' his character

[had] been made propperly known by a B'r. present it was Agreed he should have a Chance. Accordingly was Bll'd. for. On Five Black Balls appearing a Messenger was sent to him to prevent his wating so long in Suspence.

At the following meeting (August 5, 1771) there was no business to transact, so this was the entry: "Read the By Laws, Went threw a Lecture, Loge Closed to the 1st Munday in September, Extra Lodges excepted." (The reader will note, that the word "Monday" was spelled "Munday" nearly always in these early minutes.) Then, at the September 2d meeting, John Humhreys "returned from Carolina, who pray'd to be made a Memb'r. of our Most Antient & Honorable Society on this Night, his petition standing on our Books since May, 1770", was elected and made an Entered Apprentice. It was at this meeting also, that the request of a clandestine Lodge in the lower part of Frederick County for a copy of Winchester Lodge's by-laws was refused and treated with such contempt, as previously indicated in this volume.

The last important business of the year 1771 took place on December 27th. It was the time for the annual election of officers, but, as the Master, Angus McDonald, was absent, James Dowdall "took the chair" and the election was deferred until the next meeting. But it was "ordered that the Secretary copy of[f] the Transactions to be in Readiness to send of[f] to the Grand Lodge the first Opportunity". Angus McDonald was absent from the meeting of January 6, 1772 also, as well as from the Extra Lodge on January 15th. Nevertheless, it was agreed at this latter meeting that the election of officers should be held at the next regular meeting and that Brother McDonald should be notified of this action. But the fates were against this decision, for February 3d saw only four Brethren present on account of a deep snow. Angus McDonald was on hand but James Dowdall was in Falmouth on business and could not return in time for the meeting. Hence, the election of officers was again postponed. Then, at long last, officers were finally chosen for 1772 on March 2nd of that year, at which time it was announced that

MASONIC TEMPLE, WINCHESTER
HOME OF WINCHESTER HIRAM LODGE No. 21, A. F. & A. M. (1949)
116-120 N. Loudoun Street

MARKET HOUSE, WINCHESTER (1821-1899)
LODGE, CHAPTER, AND COMMANDERY MET IN THE SECOND FLOOR ROOM TO EXTREME RIGHT IN THIS VIEW.

John Lewis, Senior Warden for the preceding year, had removed to South Carolina. The applications of Phillip Pendleton, Edward McGuire, and Robert Russell for the mysteries of Masonry were received at this same meeting and the minute covering the election of officers is in the following language:

> Next Ballotted for Master to serve for the year after the Antient Custom. B'r. Jam's. Gam'l. Dowdall elected, who chose B'r. Sam'l. May S. W., B'r. Peter Helphinstine J. W., B'r. Jam's. Lindsay Treasurer, B'r. Edm'd. Taylor Secretary, B'r. Morgan Allexander Sen'r. Deacon, B'r. John Humphreys J. Deacon.

On April 2d an Extra Lodge was held, at which David Karr (or Kaar—both being probably misspelled forms of Kerr), a visiting "Entered Prentice" of Fredericksburgh Lodge, was admitted to the meeting on the recommendation of James Dowdall, who had met him previously. The records goes on to say:

> A Motion was made that B'r. David Kaar begg'd to be Hailed by our Advancing him a Degree further in Masonry and on the Brethren present being well assured from the Chair that he was a Worthy Brother of unexceptionable Character was advanced to the Degree of a Fellow Craft.

This action on part of Lodge No. 12 in conferring the Fellow Craft degree on an Entered Apprentice of Fredericksburgh Lodge was entirely lawful and proper at that time. The doctrine of "continuing jurisdiction" over a candidate elected by one Lodge, which had also given him the degree of Entered Apprentice, and the requirement of a "waiver of jurisdiction" before another Lodge could confer a subsequent degree on the candidate, had not been developed then. Thus Lodge No. 12 broke no regulations and disregarded no Masonic landmarks by taking the action, which it did in the case of David Karr.

On April 29, 1772 an Extra Lodge was "summoned on account of a Number of the Brethren being in Town; Mett by Unanimous Consent at the house of B'r. Edw'd. McGuire". The Lodge was opened on the first degree (as usual) and the presence of nine Brethren, including the officers, was noted. Two of these were Entered Apprentices, one being none other than Edward McGuire, at whose house the Brethren were assembled. It seems that there had been some complaint about the payment of so large a sum as five shillings per quarter (£1 per year) for the support of the Lodge. After due discussion and a motion, which was made, seconded, and thirded, it was voted to cut this amount in half and to make the quarterly contribution two shillings, sixpence, the by-laws being changed accordingly. At the May meeting only four Brethren appeared and the Lodge was "closed till Lodge in course". Six members attended the June meeting but only four were present for the July session, James Dowdall being absent in Baltimore and the other Brethren pleading that they were "busy attending their harvest" and asking to be excused for this reason.

The meeting of August 3d was out of the ordinary and we give an extract of some length from the minutes of that date:

A Motion was Handed to [the] Chair in Writing which after being perused was handed to the Sen'r. Warden (the Sec'y. being absent) who read the same. The Contents was that Severall of the Brethren Complained of the Inconveniency of attending on the first Munday of the Month being allways Court Week, that the Breth'n. of the Town suffered by Quitting their Business in the evening of that day and the Breth'n. of the County most commonly had a good dale [deal] of other Business to mind at these times & would rather Chuse to attend on any other Week [that] might be agreed upon. Besides finding that they could not be altogether so privit[e] as they chose, the house being generally throng[ed] on s'd. [said] times. The Motion being seconded & Thirded the Question was Putt. The whole Lodge Concluded on Holding the Lodge for the Future on the Third Tuesday of the Month. They next unanimously agreed upon fineing each Member the sum of Three Shillings every of the s'd. nights he absented himself from the Lodge Without sending in a Reasonable Excuse for his absence over and above the sum of Eighteen Pence which is to be p'd. on every night by every Brother absent as well as by those present, being their proportion of each night's expences. It was next proposed to forward the Two E. P. [Entered Apprentices] then present, who both requested to be excused 'till next Night when they might have more Leizure, the house being throng[ed] & [they] had Business to attend [to]. On which the Lodge Closed 'till the Third Tuesday of this Month. B'r. Lindsay excluded for absenting [himself] three nights according to Rule.

It will be recalled, that James Lindsay was the Treasurer of the Lodge at the time of his unceremonious exclusion, but he received apparently no consideration whatsoever on this account. Presumably he did not attempt to gain reinstatement or to send in any excuses for his absence, as his name seems to disappear from the Lodge records entirely after this date (August 3, 1772) and the ledger shows no charges against him after June 1st of that year, when he was charged with two quarterly payments of two shillings, sixpence each. From April 1, 1771 to June 1, 1772 he had been charged with 25 shillings, against which the ledger shows no credits whatever. This may have been another reason for the lack of leniency which characterized the Lodge's action in Brother Lindsay's case. No indication can be found, that he even troubled to turn over to his successor the funds in his hands, or even that any successor was chosen by the Lodge until the following December 27th, when James Dowdall was elected Treasurer, as he appears to have been the member, in whom the Lodge had the most confidence, and Samuel May was chosen as the Lodge's third Master.

On August 18, 1772 the roll was called half an hour after the opening of the Lodge and four Brethren were found to be absent in addition to Past Master Angus McDonald, who was in Maryland on business and sent an apology for his absence. No fines were imposed on the other four, however, until they had received an opportunity of appearing before the Lodge in person and making their excuses. At the next meeting (September 15th) John Humphreys offered the excuses for himself and Morgan Alexander with reference to their absence on August 18th. But he appears to have pleaded very well for Brother Alexander and not well enough for himself, since the Lodge fined him (John Humphreys) five shillings and charged him, in addition, the specified eighteen pence for the night's expenses. Morgan Alexander was absent from the September meeting, also from that of October 20th, being marked "excused" in the latter case. Edmund Taylor, the Secretary, was also absent from the September meeting, having "gone to Falmouth". He recorded the minutes of the October meeting and signed them, this being the first time in the records of Winchester Lodge that the minutes carry the signature of the Secretary or of any other officer. Following these minutes we find the following important entry:

Coppy of a Letter sent to B'r. David Hall Inclosing a Coppy of the Transactions of No. 12 from the 12th December 1770 to the 21 October 1772 to be lay'd before the R. W. G. Lodge of Pensylvania.

Winchester 21st October 1772
B'r. Hall
  The Brethren of No. 12 presents their Respects to the R. W. Grand Master Ward's. & Brethren of W. Grand Lodge of Pensylv'a., Humbly offers a Coppy of their Transactions [to] be laid before them, Which I take the Liberty to Inclose you for that Purpose. The Brethren grieves that they received no Acc't. or advice from the W. G. Lodge since they sent them the last Coppy. We apply'd for a Book of Constitutions but have the Mortification to find we are taken so little notice of. You'll receive this from the Hand of B'r. Rob't. Russell, a Worthy Member of No. 12, a Fellow Craft. I am
    Dear David in the Name of the Whole
    Your Faithful Bro'r.
    & Most Ob't. Hbl. Serv't.
    J. G. D.
(Note: The initials are obviously those of James Gamul Dowdall.)

The same Robert Russell, who was the bearer of this letter, was raised a Master Mason on December 15, 1772 as was also Edward McGuire, in whose house the Lodge was holding its meetings. Brother McGuire was ordered "to prepare a supper for as many of the Members as should attend on St. John's Night, the expenses to be paid out of the Box", i. e., out of the Lodge treasury. This program was accordingly carried out on December 27th, at which time Samuel May was chosen Master; John Humphreys, Senior Warden; Peter Helphinstine, Junior Warden; Edward McGuire, Secretary; and James Dowdall, Treasurer. We read further that Brother May was "installed by B'r. Dowdall according to the Antient Custom and rec'd. the Complim'ts. of the Lodge in the Master's Chair", referring, of course, to the ceremony of communicating the "secrets of the chair", now done in most American jurisdictions by conferring the degree of Past Master. In Virginia at the present time both the Senior and the Junior Wardens must receive the Past Master's degree prior to installation on the theory that either one of these officers may be called upon to preside over the Lodge in the absence of the Master. With the exception of the candidate, of course, no Brother is permitted to be present at the "communicating of the secrets of the chair" except those, who have previously received them.

The Lodge began the year 1773 with a new rule regarding absentees. On January 19th it was voted

> ...... that all or any of the Brethren who shall or may absent him or them[selves] three Nights successively from the Lodge, he or they living more than nine miles from Winchester, shall pay a fine of Ten Shillings for every such Night for the Benefit of this Lodge provided he or they cannot give a Sufficient and Lawful excuse for such absence.

No further meeting is listed until April 20th when it was "agreed that every Visiting Brother after the first Visit shall be at Liberty to pay his Club at every time of meeting". In other words, visiting Brethren were expected to pay their share of the evening's expenses if they visited the Lodge on two or more successive occasions. On May 18th the Lodge "having but a thin company did no business" and on the following meeting night (June 15, 1773) it was noted that "all the Brethren being busily engaged cou'd not attend, consequently no business was done."

The meetings for the remainder of the year 1773 were largely routine when held. There was no meeting in August because of the "thin company" in attendance, and none in October, "the weather being bad and but few of the Members attending." A number of petitions for the degrees were received, of which three were rejected, the minutes stating very specifically that six black balls appeared against one and seven against each of the other two. The usual election was held on December 27th, when James Dowdall again became Master; Angus McDonald, Treasurer; and Benjamin Ashby, who had been passed to the degree of Fellow Craft just three days previously, was made Secretary. The record shows that he received his Master's degree six months later (June 10, 1774).

The minutes of January 10th and February 15th of the year 1774 show only routine entries but on March 15th we find that George Rootes "desiring to become a Member of this Worshipful Lodge, on paying the Pecuniary Fee for initiation specified in the Bye Laws, was admitted by the unanimous consent of the Lodge." Two candidates were passed to the Fellow Craft's degree on April 19th, but it is noted that they "had no lecture, it being late before the ceremony was performed, so by the unanimous consent of the Lodge [it] was omitted for the Night." We know of many instances in far more recent times when the Master would have liked to omit the lecture pertaining to the degree conferred that evening but dared not do so because of Grand Lodge regulations. Another case when it was "neither the time nor the place" for such an omission!

Only two members appeared on May 13, 1774, so no Lodge was held. On June 10th two candidates received the degree of Master Mason, then no meetings were held until October 21st, when one petition was received. Again no further meetings were held until St. John's Day (December 27, 1774), when officers for the ensuing year were elected, James Dowdall again becoming Master, when "after supper and the usual toasts for the night adjourn'd till Lodge in course, Extra Lodges excepted." But how true it is, that "man proposes but God disposes", for there was a period of almost fourteen months before the Brethren again assembled in a formal Lodge meeting. The minutes do not contain the slightest hint of what happened, Masonically speaking, in Winchester during those months. Silence, however, is sometimes more eloquent than words and we may be sure that the Brethren were occupied with their personal affairs and with the promotion of the public welfare so far as the future of the community in particular and of the Colonies in general was concerned. Doubtless the actual outbreak of hostilities at Lexington and Concord in April, 1775 and the necessity of all possible patriotic endeavor in behalf of the cause of American independence added to the reasons for the prolonged intermission in the Lodge's affairs. When labor was eventually resumed, it was to be for little more than a year, for after December 5, 1777 there is a hiatus in the records for more than seven years. And lean years they were so far as the formal activities of No. 12 were concerned, but there can be no doubt, that the Brethren were living and practicing the tenets of their profession in every imaginable way during those years of "storm and stress." The story of this period is told in the record of the first Lodge meeting held in 1785, of which we shall have much more to say later.

We return to the minutes of February 23, 1776, when the Brethren assembled after a lapse of nearly fourteen months. Seven members only attended. Samuel May was in the chair *pro tem.*, it appearing that he had been requested by James Dowdall, the last elected Master, to preside, since the latter would have much to say during the evening. We let the minutes speak for themselves:

> Lodge being opened the Members proceeded to business, when B'r. Dowdall made a sensible & Judicious speech on the present unhappy contest between Great Britain & the Colonies, intimating this to be the cause of the Lodge's long recess, as many of the Brethren were withdrawn in defense of our Rights & Privileges. A Motion was made whether the Lodge should be dissolved during the public calamity or renewed & continued on its former establishment. The same being considered, a Majority were for continuance.

In spite of this brave and determined decision, however, no meeting could be held in March, for "several of the few remaining Brethren who reside in Town being absent on occasional Business, it was adjudged by the rest unnecessary to sit for the night, as there was nothing material to transact". On April 5, 1776 only five members were present and the "evening was far advanced before the Brethren could attend", therefore it was "adjudged too late to have a Lecture". It was ordered that James Dowdall serve as Master, Thomas Craig as Senior Warden, and William Campbell as Junior Warden until next St. John's Day.

Still the Lodge continued to have its difficulties, for there is no record of further meetings until September 6, 1776, when only three of the Brethren were present, "the rest being abroad", so no meeting was held. On October 4th seven members attended and "matters [were] adjusted relative to future proceedings, the absenting Brethren having given satisfactory reasons for their non-attendance on the stated nights before mentioned." At the November 1st meeting seven members were again present; there was "an apprentice's lecture to the entire satisfaction of the whole; after receiving some necessary & seasonable directions from the Worshipful Master, adjourned till the first Friday in December, Extra Lodges excepted." However, on December 6th, "it being late before the Brethren attended no business was entered upon." Then on St. John's Day following, the annual election of officers was held, James Dowdall was again chosen Master, the by-laws were read ("some of which were repealed and others enacted"), but there appear to have been no supper and no toasts.

The next meeting of record was not held until May 2, 1777, when the Brethren "enter'd upon Business by settling their respective Accts. with the Treasurer, and paying off their arrears". Meanwhile, there had developed a growing sentiment in Tidewater Virginia looking toward the establishment of an independent Grand Lodge for the new Commonwealth. The first meeting for this purpose was held in Williamsburg on May 6, 1777, when a committee was appointed to draft a letter setting forth the reasons for the formation of an independent Grand Lodge in Virginia. The report of this committee was submitted on May 13th, one week later, in the form of a letter, copies of which were ordered to be sent to all regular Lodges in the Commonwealth. The copy sent to Winchester Lodge No. 12 arrived in time for consideration at the meeting of the latter held on June 6th, at which six members and one visiting Brother were in attendance. The sole business transacted at this important and historic

SEVEN YEARS OF PROGRESS 41

meeting was the reading of the letter from Williamsburg and the consideration of the reply thereto. The full text of this Williamsburg letter, which may be termed the "declaration of Masonic independance" for Virginia, is included in the minutes of No. 12 and reads as follows:

> To the Right Worshipful Master, Worshipful Wardens and Worthy Brethren of the Winchester Lodge:—
>
> In consequence of a proposition of the Williamsburg Lodge inviting all the regular Lodges in Virginia to attend at their Lodge on the 5th of May, 1777, for the purpose of electing a Grand Master of Free Masons for the said Commonwealth of Virginia, five regular Lodges appeared by deputation on the 7th instant, viz: Norfolk, Kilwinning Port Royal Crosse, Blandford, Williamsburg, and Cabin Point Royal Arch, and thence by adjournment to the 13th instant, when taking the subject of meeting into consideration, are unanimously of opinion that a Grand Master is requisite in this state for the following reasons, founded on the principles of necessity, convenience, and right, to-wit:
>
> First. We find that the Lodges in this state hold their charters under five distinct and separate authorities, viz: The Grand Masters of England, Scotland, Ireland, Pennsylvania, and America (the last at second hand). Of course all have an equal right to appoint their deputys, who can claim no authority over those not holding of his principal. Therefore, any difference arising between Lodges holding differently cannot be settled for want of a common Tribunal. For the same reason the Craft can never meet in annual communication, manifesting that brotherly love and affection, the distinguishing characteristic of Masonry, from the beginning. Such divided and sub-divided authority can never be productive of any real good to the Craft.
>
> Secondly. We cannot discover, upon strict enquiry, that Masonry has ever derived any benefit from the foreign appointment of a Grand Master in this country, they being little known, and as little acknowledged.
>
> Thirdly. Being at this time without a supreme and so circumstanced as to render it impossible to have recourse to the Grand Lodge beyond the sea, should any abuses creep into the Lodges, or should any body of the Brotherhood be desirous of forming a new Lodge, there is no settled authority to apply to. In this case we are of opinion that a Grand Lodge is a matter of necessity.

Fourthly and lastly. We find upon record that the Grand Lodges of England, Scotland and Ireland founded their original right of election upon their sole authority, by mutual consent, distinct and separate from all foreign power whatsoever. We therefore conclude that we have and ought to hold the same rights and privileges that Masons in all time heretofore have confessedly enjoyed.

We, the deputys aforesaid, for ouselves and our respective Lodges, humbly beseech and desire that you will be pleased to take the foregoing reasons into consideration, and that you will favor us with your attendance by deputation in the Lodge for the purpose of electing a Grand Master for this state, on the 23d day of June next, ensuing at 10 o'clock, in the forenoon for the first time, and ever after at such time and place as the Grand lodge shall determine. We having signified this our desire to all others, our regular and loving Brethren in like manner, as we have done to you, hoping to see you on the day appointed, and we have caused these our proceedings to be signed by our loving Brother, Duncan Rose, our President, & attested by our worthy Brother, James Kemp, Secretary, this 13th day of May, A. L. 5777, A. D. 1777.

JAMES KEMP, Sect'y.   DUN: ROSE, Pres't.

The Lodge's action upon this important matter is thus recorded in the minutes of this same meeting (June 6, 1777):

The preceeding Letter being thus openly read, was order'd for a small space of time to lie on the Table for the Consideration of the Brethren. The time being expired, it was RESOLVED Unan., That an Answer be sent to said Letter as soon as Convenient, & that Broth'r. Craig be appointed to make out one for that purpose, the time of notice being too short for a Deputy to attend. It being too late to enter upon other Business, Lodge adjourned till the 24th Inst. being St. John's.

Meanwhile the convention at Williamsburg met on June 23d, the day before the next scheduled meeting of Winchester Lodge, so that no reply was available to the Williamsburg meeting from Winchester. None the less, the Brethren meeting at Williamsburg went ahead with their plans for the organization of a Grand Lodge, inasmuch as representatives from not less than five Lodges were present and in accordance with a Masonic custom then beginning to be recognized, only three Lodges were necessary for the formation of a soverign body. Henceforth, Winchester Lodge No. 12 does not appear either in the correspondence or the proceedings of the Grand Lodge of Virginia until 1807, when the Lodge surrendered its Pennsylvania charter (which, incidentally, was its *second* charter or warrant from Pennsylvania, as we shall see later) and, in return, received a charter from the Grand Lodge of Virginia.

Let us now return to the meeting of Winchester Lodge No. 12 on June 24, 1777. There were eight of the Brethren present, including one visiting Brother. It is evident that Thomas Craig, who was the Lodge Secretary, had done his work well in composing a reply to the communication received from the Williamsburg convention, for we read:

> In pursuance of an order of the foregoing Lodge [No. 12] B'r. Craig intimated that he had framed an answer to the Letter from the convention of Masons at Williamsburg & begg'd permission to read the same, which was accordingly granted, & being approv'd of was order'd to be enter'd, viz:
>
> To the Right Worshipful the President of
> the Conven'd Lodges at Williamsburg:—
> Right Worshipful and Worthy Brethren,
>   The particular honor you have done us by informing us of your proceedings demand our warmest acknowledgements. We sincerely thank you for the Brotherly invitation given us, but are sorry to inform you that the notice was too late for this Lodge to attend (as desir'd by Deputation). We however most cordially approve of your meeting & hope it will tend to the honor & glory of the Craft, the promotion of virtue, & those generous purposes of Benevolence that first gave birth to Masonry. We also rejoice that the Brethren in Virginia have set the Laudable example of denouncing foreign authority, & hope the Fraternity in the other States will adopt the like conducive measures. The distance of our residence from the Capital would render an annual meeting extremely inconvenient to us, & more especially as there are none of the Members of this Lodge who have any particular connection or concerns in that part of the country. Moreover we hold at present our Charter from the Grand at Philad'a. whom we are bound to honour & esteem, notwithstanding would rejoice to be in

brotherly communication with the worthy part of the Craft residing in this State. And as we could not possibly attend will be glad to be furnished with a copy of your proceedings together with such Laws & regulations as are adopted & made on the occasion. It is however the opinion of this Lodge that should a Grand Master be elected for the Common Wealth & should it appear conducive to join with the body which we much wish for, we know of none so worthy or deserving of that Office as his Excellency General George Washington. Therefore could we attend would give him our vote.
We are, Right Worshipful & Worthy Brethren
                    Your sincere well Wishers
                          & true and faithful Brethren
                              J. GAM'L DOWDALL, M [aster]
THOMAS CRAIG, Sec.

This important item of business having been disposed of, the Brethren felt free to pass to the usual program for St. John's Day as follows:

B'r. McGuire haveing prepar'd a decent & genteel Supper (after business) the night was spent to the entire satisfaction of the Communication, the usual Toasts being drank according to the good old custom of Masons, also several Constitutional & sentimental ones suitable to the times, the sons of Salem clos'd the Lodge in harmony & love till Friday, the 5th day of July, extra Lodges excepted.

It is important to note here, that it is on the basis of the suggestion contained in the above quoted letter, that George Washington be chosen the first Grand Master of Virginia, that Winchester Lodge claims the honor of having been the first Lodge in the commonwealth to make such a nomination. However this may be, the minutes of the Williamsburg convention of June 23d also contain a reference to George Washington as the only person mentioned by name for the office of Grand Master, though provision was made for the election of someone else in case such election became necessary. Washington is said to have declined the office when it was tendered to him, his reason being that he was then serving as commander-in-chief of the American Army. There was also the other reason, which has been advanced by some, namely, that he was not a Master or Past Master of any

Lodge, but we do not believe that this fact carried any weight with him or with the other Virginia Brethren. Warner Lewis, of Gloucester, was the second choice of the convention, but he also declined. Thus John Blair, acting Governor of the commonwealth, became Virginia's first Grand Master by being the third choice of the Williamsburg convention. He was elected on October 13, 1778 and installed into office on October 30th following.

Winchester Lodge met again on July 5, 1777 and again on August 1st, September 5th, and November 7th without transacting any business of note or receiving any petitions for the degrees. Finally, on December 5, 1777 the Lodge held its last meeting for that year and for seven years to come. There was no action taken at this meeting looking toward the suspension of operations, however. Circumstances simply arose to make it either undesirable or even impossible to meet under the prevailing conditions incident to the prosecution of the Revolutionary War. Undoubtedly the Brethren expected to continue their meetings from time to time, even if not regularly each month, for we find the following entry in the minutes of this date:

> A motion being made by B'r. May that the stipulated expence of the nights of meeting & also the quarterly Payments had for some time past appear'd inadequate either to prepare proper refreshment or support the fund owing to the excessive rise of every necessary of life, the same being seconded it was unanimously
> RESOLVED, that the expence of each Member of this Lodge be Three Shillings a Night for the future, till such time as they see cause to dissolve the same & that every quarterly payment from this Resolution be Six Shillings which sum shall continue to be paid till otherwise order'd.
> RESOLVED also, that every Person becoming a Member of this Lodge shall pay to the Master or Treasurer the sum of Three Pounds Ten shillings before initiation.
> Order'd that B'r. McGuire prepare a supper the 27th Instant being the anniversary of St. John the Evangelist. Lodge clos'd till St. John's.
> THOMAS CRAIG, Sect'y.

Here there is a change from one minute book to another and between the last leaf of the old book and the first leaf of the new there is, as has been stated previously, a hiatus of more than seven years. It is possible that a few leaves have been lost or destroyed but hardly probable that the entire proceedings for seven years are missing, especially in view of the references made in the minutes of February 2, 1785 to the lapse, which had occurred and the reasons therefor, all of which are set forth at length in the following chapter of this volume. So we find it necessary to content ourselves with the thought, that old No. 12 was 'put to sleep" (to use a very modern expression derived from the French) because of the fact, that most of its members were far from home, doing their part in the great national emergency, as has been traditional with Masons both before and since that day. Yet withal, there must have been attempts to revive the activities of the Lodge from time to time even during that eventful period and especially after the surrender of Cornwallis at Yorktown on October 19, 1781. For it is reasonable to suppose that James Dowdall, the Masonic patriarch of Winchester in that important era, must have taken steps sooner than 1785 to congregate the Brethren and get them started as an active Lodge again. However, we have been able to find no evidence to show that he was even remotely successful, at least until the war had been over for more than three years and conditions, even if not normal, were, to say the least, not as chaotic as they had been during the years of active warfare.

As has been proved on so many occasions in our own time, such is the vitality, such the appeal of Freemasonry, that it is like "truth crushed to earth"—it rises again with the first dawn of individual liberty and the earliest withdrawal of the frosts and cold of tyranny and oppression. Thus Winchester Lodge, after having been dormant for seven years, became once again an active force in the life of Winchester and the entire community, of which it was the center. This story we shall read in the pages following.

CHAPTER IV

THE POST-REVOLUTIONARY PERIOD

We have already noted that, for more than seven years after December 5, 1777, there is ominous silence so far as the records of Lodge No. 12 are concerned. We are left wondering what had happened to the Lodge and its individual members until we turn to the minutes of February 2, 1785, which contain a veritable "roll of honor" and a record of the contribution of Winchester Masonry to the struggle for American independence. These minutes are so important, that we give them here in full:

> At a Lodge summon'd by Br. J. Gamul Dowdall the second day of February 1785.
> Present: Br. Samuel May, Br. Edward Maguire, Br. David Kennedy, and Br. J. Gamul Dowdall attended in consequence of said Summons.
> With melancholy countenances in great distress we approached our once Agreeable Lodge room, where with poignant feelings we called to mind the many happy evenings we met, a numerous & very worthy number of Brothers assembled in order to do every Honor in their power to the Antient & Honorable Fraternity of Free & Accepted Masons. Finding ourselves reduced to the present few, could not help taking a retrospective view of our absent dearly beloved Brethren.
> The first presented to said view was our once worthy Bro. John Humphreys; he fell in Quebeck within a few paces of the Honorable Gen. Montgomery.
> Bro. Angus McDonald dyed by the fatigue of a severe campaign against the Indians.
> Bro. Peter Helphinstine, Dyed of wounds received in Carolina a few days after returning to his Family & Friends.
> Bro. Morgan Alexander, killed in Virginia.
> Bro. John Lewis, killed in Carolina.
> Bro. Thomas Craig, dyed of wounds received in an engagement under Colonel Thruston.
> Bro. Russell, dead.
> Bro. McBride, gone to Ireland.
> Bro. Samuel Dobie & Bro. John Howell, removed to Carolina.
> Bro. Edmund Taylor
> Bro. Dorcy Pentecost and
> Bro. Joseph Beeler, removed over the Alegany.

Bro. Benjamin Ashby
Bro. John Timberlake and
Bro. William Campbell, removed to different parts of the globe. We the remaining few of the once flourishing Lodge No. 12 requested Bro. Samuel May, Master at our last meeting, to assume the Chair and formed in as good order as was possible.
Worshipful Bro. Samuel May in the Chair, Bro. J. G. Dowdall P. M., Bro. Edward Maguire & Bro. David Kennedy, Wardens.
We came to the following Resolution:
That on account of the sincere affection we had to Masonry, for the good of the Craft we would receive the petitions of some worthy gentlemen, who had acquainted us of their having a great desire to have the secrets of Masonry made known to them in an Honorable way, that we could meet hereafter regularly on the stated nights, and conform ourselves to the Antient rules & regulations as formerly, in hope to raise a new and reputable number of Brethren to supply the places of them, who, alas! to us is no more. We comforted ourselves with the blessing that those, who Honorably dyed, in the defence of their country, were only removed from us while we remained Mortals and that we shall hereafter meet them, in the First great Grand Lodge cloathed in white raiment in the presence of our first great Grand Master, the Maker of us all.

We have seldom read a more moving account of a Masonic gathering of any kind. The story of how the Lodge erected, many years later, a bronze tablet to the memory of the six Brethren, who gave their lives in the Revolutionary War, is told in a later chapter of this narrative. A copy of these minutes, however, was sent to the Grand Lodge of Pennsylvania and read to that body at an "Extra Grand Lodge" held on October 8, 1785, upon which Grand Lodge took appropriate action. We quote the following extract from the Grand Lodge minutes of that occasion:

Read a letter from the Worshipful Br. Samuel May and Br. J. Gamul Dowdall, Secretary of Lodge No 12, held at Winchester, inclosing the Minutes and Proceedings of said Lodge, and pointing out the Numerous Difficulties under which they have laboured, in consequence of the Death and Departure of many of their Brethren from that Body, which having been taken into consideration
Unanimously Resolved, That this Grand Lodge approve in the strongest manner of the Conduct and Proceedings of Brothers Samuel May, Edward Maguire, David Kennedy, and J. G.

ALEXANDER MANTZ BAKER
Grand Commander, Knights Templar of Virginia
(1912-1913)
At the laying of the cornerstone of the Handley Library, May 28, 1908

Dowdall, of their Zeal and Attention to the interests of Masonry, and of their Exertions on the 2d of February last; and this Grand Lodge do also highly approve of the Conduct of the Brethren of Lodge No. 12, and are of opinion that the said Lodge merit the Thanks and Respect of all regular Masons, and recommend to them a continuance of their Zeal.
Ordered, That the Thanks of this Gd. Lodge be transmitted by the R. W. Gd. Master to Lodge No. 12, and that said Lodge be assured of all the Protection and Advice this Grand Lodge can afford.

Thus did Lodge No. 12 resume its labors after the Revolution with a nucleus of only four Brethren. They did not wait to hear from the Grand Lodge in answer to their communication, however, but continued their efforts without delay toward the rehabilitation of Masonry in the Winchester community. Thus we find, that these four Brethren met again on March 4, 1785, read the by-laws, went through the E. A. lecture, and received the petitions of two merchants residing in the town—John Kean and Daniel Norton. On March 15th both of these petitions were acted upon favorably, both candidates received the E. A. degree the same evening, and both received the necessary charges, heard the by-laws, and received a "short lecture". On April 1, 1786 there was still another meeting, at which we note that the "Lodge was in as good form as so few members could make it". The same two candidates were examined on their proficiency in the first degree and we read: "The Master Masons were Agreeably surprised at the rapid progress our late Apprentices had made in the knowledge of Masonry, which they convinced us. Owing to great industry, close application, and a very sincere Love to the Antient Craft, we therefore at their request, after ordering them to a drawing room, prepared our Lodge to received them and passed them separately to the Second Degree of Masonry." Three more petitions were received at this meeting, one from Archibald Magill, of whom we shall hear more in these pages. He was destined to become the first member of Lodge No. 12 (later Winchester Hiram Lodge No. 21) to be made Grand Master of Masons in Virginia. These three petitions were duly "ordered to lye on ye books", but some time between then and May 6th the candidates all received the E. A. degree, though we have no record of the meeting, at which this took place. This becomes obvious when we read the following extract from the minutes of May 6th:

> The last three after going through a Strict Examination in which they acquitted themselves so much to the Satisfaction of the Lodge were at their Request Separately Passed to the Second Degree. Had a Craft's Lecture after Reading the By-Laws. A motion was made to the Chair, that it was Exceedingly Inconvenient to the Whole of the present members to attend Lodge on the first Friday of the Month, being the court week and held in this County in this Town, that three of the present Members were Magistrates & Had to set on the Bench most part or the whole of the week, the Rem'r were all Storekeepers living in Town & were Commonly Fattigued or so hurried in the day that they wished to rest themselves in the Evenings, and moved that the Lodge Night be altered to some day in any other Week of the Month that might be judged most Conven't. The Motion being Seconded, it was Concluded upon to hold the Lodge for the Future on the Second Tuesday in each Month. Then by Order of his Worship, Lodge Closed unto the 2d Tuesday in June, Extra Lodges excepted.

On June 14, 1785 (the second Tuesday) the Lodge met as agreed and there were eight Brethren present (including the Fellow Crafts). The chief business of this occasion was the discussion of plans for observing the ensuing St. John's Day (June 24th), when they "met at their Lodge room at five o'clock A. M. [evidently intended for P. M.]......put on the proper ornaments belonging to their Lodge, had a genteel supper and spent the evening in Innocent Mirth until the Hour of Ten Approached, then parted true friends, each Br. returning to his Home or Lodgings to Cheer his Wife or mistress."

Additional meetings were held in 1785 on July 12th and 20th (at this latter meeting Archibald Magill and William Maguire were raised), August 9th, September 13th, November 8th, and December 18th and 27th. At the September meeting Brother Dowdall stated, that he intended to leave shortly for Philadelphia and was requested to take with him a copy of the minutes since February 2, 1785 and

...... humbly to lay the same before the Worshipful Grand Lodge in Philadelphia, Hoping they will not impute the Unfortunate Distressing Situation they were reduced to, occasioned by the Unforeseen powers and fortune of War, to any neglect in them, and Praying the Worshipful Grand Lodge will Honor them with what Commands they may Judge Expedient as a Rule for their future Conduct, as nothing can be more Comfortable to them in their present growing situation than being taken under the Patronage & Guidance of so Worthy and Reputable a Body as the Grand Lodge of Pennsylvania, &c, &c from whom they hold their Charter & whom they Revere, Respect and Esteem in preference to any Lodges in the Known World.

By the time of the November meeting Brother Dowdall had returned from carrying out his mission and made a report thereon, stating that he had received very polite treatment at the hands of the R. W. Grand Master and that a special meeting of Grand Lodge had been called for hearing the report of the representative from No. 12. Brother Dowdall then read the following letter, which he had been instructed to bring back to the Winchester Brethren:

To the Master & Brethren of No. 12, at Winchester, Virginia
Dear Brethren:
This serves to cover a resolution of the Grand Lodge of Pennsylvania directed to your Lodge at Winchester. The late war has caused great troubles amonge Masons, of which you have had more than Common Share, and Certainly you deserve great Credit for the care and attention you have paid in Raising your Lodge to the flourishing state it is now in, for which I beg you to accept my Warmest acknowledgement. May that bright spark of harmony continue among you, which will make you a lasting band of Brothers is the sincere wish of
Your affectionate Brother
WILL ADOCK, G. M.

The Lodge minutes further state, that Brother Dowdall then presented to the Lodge the new Book of Constitutions and several printed copies of two sermons, one preached on December 27, 1783 by Dr. Samuel Magaw, Vice Provost of the University of Pennsylvania, and the other preached on December 27, 1784 by Dr. William White, rector of Christ Church and St. Peter's Church in Philadelphia. We read further:

On receiving the Above Honors the Master & Brethren of No. 12 Resolved, That from the Sincere Love and Respect they allways bore to Masonry & the Happiness they felt on being promised the protection & advice of the R. W. Gd. Lodge (which they so ardently wished for) and not only like a tender parent overlooking their failings but honoring them with their thanks, the Effects of which by every Grateful Heart can be easyer felt than described and very Visible & Expressively appeared in the Countenance of all then Present. That hereafter they would to the Utmost of their Abilities Continue that Zeal so much Approved of by the R. W. Grand Lodge.
It is further Resolved, That the thanks of this Lodge be Unanimously given to Br. J. G. Dowdall for acquitting himself so much to the satisfaction of its present members as its Representative in the R. W. Gd. Lodge.

The story of how the Lodge got its first Tyler after the Revolution is a most interesting one as appears from the following entry in the minutes of December 18th:

On a Motion from the W. M. in the Chair, that a Stated Tyler was much wanted, that he had with the Advice of the present members Applied to a Certain John Crockwell, a Man well known to most or all present, of a fair Character, had been advanced in Masonry to the degree of F. C. under a travelling Warrant in Braddox War, was an industrious good Carpenter, but became infirm by sickness & age, was then in the House & Willing to serve us, provided we advanced him in Masonry, w'd give him half a dollar a night & a drink of toddy. The Question being put, was received unanimously on his own terms.

The observance of St. John's Day following is recorded in this manner:

The Officers immediately put on the Ornaments of their office with new Aprons & Gloves and formed as near to the Order of Procession in the new Regulations as possible considering the deficiency in Number. Had prepared new Wands and new Pillars according to Order, tipp'd & guilt, with two new Velvet cushions.
1st. The Sword Bearer or Tyler.
2. Two Deacons bearing wands tipp'd with gold.
3. Treasurer & Secret'y bearing the Holy Bible and Book of Constitut'ns on 2 Crimson Velvet Cush'ns.
4. The Present Master with a new wand tipp'd with Gold.
5. The Past Masters.

6. The two Wardens with propper Pillars.
7, 8, &9. Members of the Lodge, two and two—& before twelve the procession [was] seated in the Isle near the Communion Table; every pew in the Church very full. Psalms were sung by a number of Boys & Girls genteely dressed (the first men's children of the Borough), each with a broad light blew [i. e., blue] sash in honor to Masonry, had been Instructed by a teacher for several days before and gave great Delight to the Audience. Had an elegant and enlightening discourse from the Pulpit, as suitable as possibly could be expected from a Gent'n wanting the Enlightening help of Masonry.

After service returned in same good order to our Lodge Room, regaled ourselves with an Excellent Dinner, Enjoyed a most pleasing Evening, and parted in hopes to meet again when the like happy Occasion offered.

The year 1786 opened with the Lodge holding its first meeting for the year on January 10th. A resolution of thanks was adopted with reference to the services of the retiring Worshipful Master:

This Lodge recurring to the care and attention of Br. May, our late Master, in conducting us to the present period and conceiving that to pass over the same in silence would render injustice to merit,
Thereupon, RESOLVED (*nemine contradicente*) [i. e., no one dissenting], that we have the highest sense of our obligations to our said Brother, and that he is justly entitled to our warmest thanks and acknowledgements.

On March 14th following the Lodge reaffirmed its allegiance to the Grand Lodge of Pennsylvania and, because of the difficulty of sending a representative to each Grand Lodge communication from Winchester, it was voted to elect George Hamilton, of Philadelphia, as the Lodge's more or less "permanent" representative and to send him the necessary credentials for this purpose. The entire text of this "power of attorney" is recorded in the minutes of the meeting of April 11th. The remaining meetings of the year were occupied with routine business, including the observance of the two St. John's Days and ritualistic work. It was also voted that a new set of jewels for the officers should be purchased. Then, for an entire year, the minutes are missing and we pick up the thread of our story again on St. John's Day, December 27, 1787. The usual procession (commencing at 10:00 A. M.), sermon, and dinner marked this occasion and we note from the record that

> ...... the Brethren having dined and sang a few songs, they retired to their different habitations with that perfect joy pictured in each countenance and that requisite decorum of manners that ever renders them respectable in the eyes of the populace.

During the year 1788 unexcused absences by various members from the Lodge meetings occupied the Brethren to a considerable extent. There was a roll call at each meeting and absentees, who had not sent in their excuses, were order to be fined according to the provisions of the by-laws unless suitable excuses were forthcoming by the next ensuing Lodge night. Receipts of fees and dues, as well as fines, were still recorded in pounds, shillings, and pence and continued to be so until well into the next century. On May 5, 1788 the record shows that no meeting was held because the "Worshipful Master and the most of the Brethren [were] necessarily absent from Town". Extra Lodges, as they were called in accordance with Pennsylvania nomenclature, were held from time to time and business was transacted at these special meetings just the same as at the regular ones. The Master did not have to watch his p's and q's in those days as much as is necessary today! Each Brother was required to pay his share of the "expences of the evening" and this included the cost of refreshments after the meeting as well.

The minutes of September 1, 1788 contain the text of a letter sent to Grand Lodge through George (or Gavin) Hamilton as follows:

> Friends & Brethren:
> With humility, meekness, and supreme felicity we do ourselves the honor of transmitting to your august and venerable Body the regular and minute proceedings of this Lodge, which for your all wise mature deliberation and discussion will be presented you in person by our well beloved Brother Gavin Hamilton. The height of our study and ambition is to merit your favor and patronage, and if we are so happy as to accomplish so desired an end,

Masonry will continue to flourish with all that lustre and dignity, that it hath hitherto done when so distinguished and honorable a Circle dart their rays on the Craft. We beg leave to remit you twelve pounds Virginia currency which will discharge the arrearages due. Our supplications are forcible, permanent, and sincere for a continuance of your esteem and protection. Indulge us with so estimable a Treasure as your salutary counsel, smiles, and admonitions, and this acquisition will cause every Member's cheek to glow with gratitude and joy. That the pleasures of imagination may speedily be realized is the constant and fervent wish of No. 12.

                Signed by order of the Chair:
                ALEX'R. KING, Secretary *pro tem.*

We have no doubt that the appeal of this communication was well nigh irresistible and that the desired objects were accomplished without trouble. The list of members for the year shows one Brother withdrawn, three Brethren removed, and one deceased.

By the beginning of 1789 Lodge No. 12 was back on its feet again and meetings were being held almost monthly, including the "extra Lodges." Occasionally a regularly scheduled meeting had to be omitted on account of the absence of so many of the Brethren from town. Later in that year the by-laws were amended so as to provide for regular monthly meetings to be held on the third Saturday of the month. Although this was the year when George Washington was inaugurated as first President of the United States, thus putting into operation our present Constitution, no reference to this event is made in the Lodge minutes. The year closed with the usual observance of St. John the Evangelist's Day. With the advent of more prosperous times and the increase in membership and in frequency of Lodge meetings, the old custom of having a lecture in one of the Masonic degrees or of reading over the by-laws gradually disappeared and we seldom find such notations in the minutes after the beginning of 1790. It may also be added, that the Secretaries began about this time to record the Lodge proceedings in much more abbreviated form, so that the minutes of eleven meetings in 1790 are somewhat sketchily recorded on less than eight pages in the large minute book. At the meeting of November 8th of that year, Brother John Service "wished to know of the Lodge whether it was their intention of continuing under the present Jurisdiction [and] was answered that no intention of the contrary had heretofore been urged or held in idea". Brother Service, it may be stated, had been sent down from Philadelphia to see how No. 12 was faring and to examine into the Masonic proficiency of its officers and members. We have no question as to the report, which he gave on his return home —entirely in the Lodge's favor.

We note nothing else of importance until April 21, 1792, when the Lodge voted to grant leave to Brother Cornelius O'Loughlin to "have recourse to the civil power for redress" in a matter of controversy with William Johnson, another member of the Lodge. Would that disagreements between Brethren might be handled in the same manner today! On August 6, 1792 the Lodge initiated three new members—two Army officers and a visitor from North Carolina—without requiring their petitions to lie over for the customary thirty days, since all three were about to leave town in pursuit of their respective professions. No dispensation was required from the Grand Master in those days when a Lodge wished to waive this and other requirements concerning petitioners! New by-laws were adopted toward the end of 1792, which were composed of seven sections under the caption: "The Bye Laws of Lodge No. 12 Ancient York Masons held in the Town of Winchester, Virginia under and by virtue of a Warrant from the Right Worshipful the Grand Lodge of Pennsylvania." Regulations were included governing the number of times a Brother might speak to any motion, the proper conduct of members in the Lodge room, the payment of expenses of the night, the admission of visiting Brethren, the reception of candidates, etc. Business was still transacted regularly in the Entered Apprentice's degree and thus all Brethren of whatever degree were permitted to participate.

The minutes of June 5, 1794 show that there were three visiting Brethren on that ocasion: Thomas Brooks, member of the Grand Lodge of Ireland; John Barclay of Lodge 479, County Tyrone, Ireland; and Thomas Jamerson of Lodge 39, Culpeper County, Virginia. They were very carefully examined beforehand and it required a vote of the Lodge, not merely the permission of the Worshipful Master, to admit these visitors. At several meetings in 1794 and 1795 the Secretary notes "no cash on hand." Once he records that the "Lodge closed as usual", and sometimes he uses the expression "with the usual good harmony".

In the minutes of March 5, 1795 we find the following significant entry:

> The Lodge being unanimously of opinion, that their Charter, which was obtained from the Grand Lodge of Pensylvania, ought to be relinquished and a Charter obtained from the G. L. of Virginia,
> ORDERED, that the sentiments of this Lodge be carried into effect and proper measures pursued for that purpose, and previous to an attempt of that nature the arrearages due the Grand Lodge of Pensylvania this Lodge are of opinion should be discharged.

The sequel shows, however, that it was more than a dozen years later, that this objective was finally accomplished, the Lodge requiring until 1801 to pay up its arrearages to Pennsylvania. This was the case in spite of the fact, that the initation fee was £3/2/6, a considerable sum in those days. Of this amount the Secretary's fee continued at two shillings, sixpence. In case an extra Lodge was called for degree work, it was the custom for those receiving the degrees to defray the expenses of the night. This same custom prevails today in most English Lodges. Frequently, too, if an applicant was not "in waiting" when his petition for the degrees was to be voted upon, the vote was postponed until some subsequent meeting of the Lodge, at which the applicant could be present in the ante-room. There seems to have been a decided feeling on the part of the Brethren, that they should be given the opportunity of interviewing an applicant personally, "giving him the once over" and asking him questions, before they approved his petition. A very good custom in our opinion!

On May 5, 1797 it was ordered that a committee be appointed to amend the by-laws so as to provide for 24 meetings each year instead of 12. It is not stated, whether all of these were to be considered as regular meetings or not, but the subsequent minutes seem to indicate, that both regular and extra Lodges were intended to be included in this total. On July 11, 1797 we note the first entry in the new decimal currency—"Brother Baily paid his initiation fee $10.50"—but, as indicated previously, this type of entry did not become the practice generally until after 1800. The Secretary elected the preceding December was Archibald Magill. He was so dilatory in his attendance and in the performance of the other duties of his office, that the Lodge voted to fine him 20 shillings on August 2, 1797 and to discontinue him from his office "unless he do arrange the transaction by next Lodge". But the transaction was not arranged and so, on October 4, 1797, the worthy Brother was relieved of his office and Frederick Hurst was elected to succeed him. And on November 7th following it was "ordered that the last Secretary do pay to the Lodge the sum expended in paying for having the books posted up." This amount was $20.00, a sum voted to Brother Hurst for bringing the Lodge books up to date. Luckily for posterity, this work was done promptly and the records of the Lodge for that period are, therefore, intact. At this same meeting one of the Brethren was expelled from the Lodge for "various crimes and misdemeanors", but he appealed to the Grand Lodge of Virginia later and Lodge No. 12 found it necessary to report to this Grand Lodge the finding in the case with the request that the Lodge be sustained in its action. We find no further reference to the matter, however, in either the Lodge or Grand Lodge proceedings, so its final disposition remains in doubt.

In 1798 we note, that the Lodge had a Standing Committee, to which were referred from time to time matters as amendments to the by-laws and other items of importance requiring special investigation and report before final action by the Brethren. On

July 3d of that year a visitor was refused admittance because, upon examination, he "proved insufficient to the task". On September 4, 1798 it is recorded, that the two Entered Apprentices of the night "returned the usual thanks to the Lodge". At another meeting (December 5th) of that year a Brother was fined $4.00 and reprimanded for "entering the Lodge in a state of intoxication". We also begin to note from time to time the presentation of cases for the relief of distressed Brethren and their families. There is, too, an occasional instance, where charges are preferred against a Brother and the matter dealt with by the Lodge as seemed to be appropriate.

On March 4, 1799 the Lodge voted to employ the Secretary, Brother Frederick Hurst, to ascertain the "true balance due to the Grand Lodge under which the Charter of this Lodge is held.. ..for which he is to receive a good and sufficient compensation". But the year closed without the completion of this matter, although Brother Hurst reported on June 3, 1799 a list of the "admissions, passings, and raisings" for the preceding ten years, whereupon he was voted the sum of $15.00 for this service. At this same meeting there was considerable division on the point of the dinner to be prepared on the ensuing St. John the Baptist's Day, some wishing to go to the tavern operated by Brother Angus McDonald, others preferring the house of Brother Peter Lauck. The Master gave his support to the latter proposal and his motion "was carried by a large majority—and it is ordered that we dine at Brother Lauck's accordingly". A considerable number of petitions was received during this year, among them being that of George Washington Timberlake, the first namesake of George Washington to be noted on the Lodge's roster. The number of rejections continued relatively large, as was the case in nearly every Lodge at that period. The standards for Masonic membership were, as a rule, much higher in that day than in our own, much to the disadvantage of present day Masonry.

At its meeting on November 4, 1799 the Lodge voted to recommend Brother John Hickman, of Front Royal, as a proper person to apply to the Grand Lodge of Virginia for the establishment of a Lodge at that place. The year 1799 closed with the usual celebration of St. John's Day on December 27th with a sermon at the Dutch Presbyterian Church by the pastor, Rev. Mr. Streit. George Washington had died on December 14th, but no mention of his passing is made in the minutes until the following February, a matter, which we shall consider more fully in the next chapter.

ORIGINAL SEAL OF WINCHESTER HIRAM LODGE No. 21
(Still in possession of the Lodge.)

CHAPTER V

FROM PENNSYLVANIA TO VIRGINIA

For Lodge No. 12 the year 1800 began with the regular meeting held on January 6th. The usual routine business was transacted and the Master's degree was conferred on one candidate. Nothing unusual happened at either the extra Lodge of February 1st or the regular meeting of February 3d. By February 15th, however, news of the passing of George Washington had reached Winchester through Masonic channels, though the secular press had carried this announcement some weeks before. But the following entry in the minutes of February 15th is significant:

> The Lodge being called for the purpose of taking into consideration the form of procession of the Brethren to take place on the 22d instant in honor to the memory of our late beloved Brother General George Washington and also to adopt a resolution of the Grand Lodge of Pennsylvania under which we hold our Charter respecting the mourning which said Grand Lodge wishes to have adopted by the subordinate Lodges on that day. . . It was ordered on the motion of Brother Wolfe, that the Treasurer do furnish to this Lodge forty mourning Aprons for the use of this Lodge and that each individual Brother do pay unto the hands of the Treasurer the sum of 1/6 on the delivery of each apron which will be on or before the 22d instant . . . It was also ordered, that the Brethren of this Lodge do proceed in Masonic procession from the Lodge room to the German Lutheran Church to hear a discourse to be delivered by the Rev'd Christian Streit in honor to our departed illustrious Brother.

On February 22d, Washington's birthday, the above-mentioned program was duly carried out and "the sermon having given such universal satisfaction, it was ordered, that a number of copies thereof be printed for the use of the Brethren". Later it was also "ordered that the bell ringer of the German Lutheran Church be paid one dollar for his services on the 22d instant", and that a painting or escutcheon depicting Washington and

61

mounted in a gilt frame be prepared for the use of the Lodge. The sum of $40.00 was appropriated for this purpose.

At the meeting of July 2, 1800 the Lodge voted an appropriation of $20.00 to relieve the distress of several mariners, who had applied for relief, Archibald Magill, the formerly inattentive Secretary, making the motion with this end in view.

The Lodge had still not settled its arrears with the Grand Lodge of Pennsylvania in spite of the fact, that, on April 21, 1800, that Grand Lodge had sent a letter to No. 12, notifying the members that they were in arrears for two (or more) years, and that "unless their dues were discharged by St. John's Day in December next or satisfactory reasons given why they are not discharged, their warrant will be considered as suspended". Mindful of this warning letter, Lodge No. 12 at its meeting on December 1, 1800 resolved, "that one of the Brethren of this Lodge do proceed to the Grand Lodge of Pennsylvania holden in Philadelphia and settle with said Grand Lodge its accounts with this Lodge, and pay any balance which, upon such settlement, may appear due from this Lodge to said Grand Lodge and draw from the Treasurer of this Lodge such balance." But the record does not indicate, that this was done, at least at this particular time, and this supposition is borne out by subsequent events, as we shall see.

On March 2, 1801 a Brother was passed to the Fellow Craft degree, he "wishing to become more bright in Masonry", and in the minutes of April 6, 1801 we find the first reference to the existence of the recently formed "Royal Arch Lodge." At this same meeting the Brethren in arrears were ordered to pay up at once, so that the back dues to the Grand Lodge of Pennsylvania could be paid. Apparently this effort met with some success, for, on May 4th it was voted, that "Brother Lewis Wolfe do proceed with one hundred dollars to the Grand Lodge of Pennsylvania and that the said Brother do carry with him a letter.... and the necessary credentials signed by the proper Officers of this Lodge and that he do proceed to said Grand Lodge as soon as possible therewith after June court next". (Lewis Wolfe seems to have had some connection with the Winchester judicial bodies.) The minutes of the quarterly communication of the Grand Lodge of Pennsylvania for June 15, 1801 show, that two letters were read to Grand Lodge from Lodge No. 12, one stating that "Brother Lewis Wolfe, S. W. of said Lodge", had been appointed to wait on Grand Lodge and to transact necessary business in behalf of No. 12. The other letter acknowledged the receipt of the letter from Grand Lodge, threatening the suspension of the charter, and added that, because of removals, deaths of members, and the delinquency of a Treasurer, the funds of the Lodge were greatly reduced and that it was impossible for the Lodge to ascertain what sum was actually due to Grand Lodge; furthermore, that they were determined to do all in their power to prevent any future delinquencies and that Brother Wolfe would pay Grand Lodge at this time the sum of $100.00 on account. In view of the contents of these two letters, Grand Lodge appointed a committee of three to make a settlement with Brother Wolfe, it being agreed that the amount of such settlement was to be final. On June 23, 1801 this committee, in a most magnanimous report too long to be included here, reported to an adjourned quarterly communication of Grand Lodge, that the sum paid by Brother Wolfe as indicated above had been accepted in full payment of all arrears and that the Lodge was "clear of the books", so to speak, so far as Grand Lodge was concerned. We hear of no more difficulties with Grand Lodge between that time and January 5, 1807, when Grand Lodge granted formal leave to Lodge No. 12 to resign its warrant and to accept a charter from the Grand Lodge of Virginia, on whose roster it then became Winchester Hiram Lodge No. 21.

This part of our story may well be concluded here by reference to the action of the Grand Lodge of Virginia taken in this connection on December 16, 1807:

RESOLVED, That a charter do issue for the permanent establishment of the Lodge formerly held in the town of Winchester, under the authority of the Grand Lodge of Pennsylvania, and that said Lodge be designated the Winchester Hiram Lodge No. 21, appointing Peter Lauck, Master; Wm. Silver, Senior Warden; and Lewis Barnett, Junior Warden.

Unfortunately the Lodge minutes are missing from August 5, 1802 to October 3, 1808, so there is little indication available as to what was actually done locally by the Winchester Brethren during this time. We do know, however, that there was a period of some six years after the settlement with the Grand Lodge of Pennsylvania before final action was taken by No. 12 looking toward affiliation with the Grand Lodge of Virginia. There is no reason to suppose, that any more arrearages accrued to Pennsylvania during that period and the immediate cause of the transfer of allegiance is, so to speak, anybody's guess. Apparently the change was never regretted by the Winchester Brethren, though they still point with pride to their Pennsylvania Masonic heritage—and, we think, rightly so.

The reader of the present day will no doubt learn with some satisfaction, that Brother Lewis Wolfe was later voted the reimbursement of all his expenses in making the settlement with the Grand Lodge of Pennsylvania in 1801 and, as a further evidence of their esteem for his financial skill, the Brethren elected him Treasurer of the Lodge on January 7, 1802. That year closed with a rather distressing incident involving the Worshipful Master, who was eventually expelled from the Lodge and the proceedings in his case were duly reported to Grand Lodge.

In the following chapter we shall see something of the activities of Winchester Hiram Lodge No. 21, bidding now an affectionate farewell to Lodge No. 12 and acknowledging with deepest gratitude the contribution made through it by our early Pennsylvania Brethren to Freemasonry in the Old Dominion.

DETAIL OF EAST END OF CEILING, WINCHESTER HIRAM LODGE,
No. 21, A. F. & A. M.

LODGE ROOM OF WINCHESTER HIRAM LODGE NO. 21, A. F. & A. M.
(as seen from the West).

CHAPTER VI

FIRST YEARS UNDER VIRGINIA JURISDICTION

It has already been noted that the Lodge minutes for the first few months of its existence under the jurisdiction of the Grand Lodge of Virginia have been lost. The record of the meeting of Winchester Hiram Lodge No. 21 for October 3, 1808 is the earliest one now extant under the new régime. We note, that the names of James Gamul Dowdall, Samuel May, Daniel Norton, and other earlier stalwarts have disappeared from the minutes and little or no indication is given as to what became of these founders of Winchester Lodge. In 1808 we note especially the names of Peter Lauck, Conrad Kremer, William Silver, Daniel Walker Thomas, Joseph Sexton, Joseph Sittler and others, who carried over from the Pennsylvania to the Virginia jurisdiction and who played prominent parts not only in symbolic Masonry in Winchester, but in the organization of the Chapter, Council, and Commandery as well.

At the very outset we note at the meeting of October 3d that charges were preferred against Daniel Walker Thomas for "robbing the funds of the Lodge". It appears, however, that this charge had been preferred in malice by Brother William Hines, for the Lodge voted to suspend the latter while it was unanimously declared that Brother Thomas was entirely innocent of the charges against him. Thomas was then the Lodge Secretary. He also became in time the organizer and head of Winchester Encampment, Knights Templar and was the first Grand Master of the Grand Encampment (now Grand Commandery) of Virginia when it was organized in 1823. The Lodge went even farther in the matter of the charges against Thomas and directed the officers to furnish him with a certificate signed by them and testifying to his innocence of the charge alleged against him.

In the minutes of November 28, 1808 we note that Lewis Wolfe was elected representative to the Grand Lodge of Virginia and ordered to be furnished with the necessary credentials, also to take with him the sum of $20.00 to be paid to the Grand Treasurer as the amount of Winchester Hiram Lodge's dues to Grand Lodge for the year 1808. Thus Wolfe became the first representative ever to be chosen by the Lodge to represent it in the Grand Lodge of Virginia. At the meeting of December 5th officers for the ensuing year were elected, Peter Lauck being continued as Master, William Silver as Senior Warden, and Daniel W. Thomas as Secretary. John S. Williams became Junior Warden and Lewis Barnett Treasurer. The Lodge still transacted most of its business on the E. A. degree and did not hesitate to act upon a petition the same night it was received if there were cogent reasons for doing so.

From this point on most of the Lodge minutes are of a very routine nature, dealing with petitions, the conferring of degrees, and the financial affairs of the Craft. Hence, we shall not attempt to record in the remainder of this narrative anything but the more interesting and outstanding items mentioned in the record. The names of many visitors are listed from time to time but there is little indication as to the Lodges from which they hailed. This fact is to be regretted, since identification of these Brethren is made much more difficult than would otherwise be the case.

On April 3, 1809 the Lodge ordered a new jewel to be made for the Secretary and that the silver in the old jewel be used towards making the new one. At the following meeting Brother Abraham Baker, in consideration for services rendered the Lodge (we are not told what they were, however), was relieved of further payment of dues and became the *first* honorary member of Winchester Hiram Lodge No. 21. In the minutes of June 6, 1809 we find the second reference to the existence of a Royal Arch Chapter in Winchester, when a committee was appointed to invite the Chapter members to join the Brethren of the Lodge in the celebration of St. John the Baptist's Day of that year.

For his services on that day, the bell-man received $1.00 and for the sermon he preached the Rev. Christian Streit received an honorarium of $10.00. The organist of the occasion refused compensation, so he was given a vote of thanks by the Lodge.

The minutes of July 3, 1809 contain the first reference to the erection of a Masonic Hall in Winchester. Previously, it will be recalled, the Lodge meetings had been held usually in the home of one of the Brethren, or in a tavern, or in a room rented for the purpose. Now, with the increase in membership and influence in the community, the Brethren began to think in terms of a permanent home for the Lodge. Hence the adoption of the following resolutions:

> On motion made, it was unanimously agreed to build a Masonic Hall over the addition directed to be built (by the Common Hall of the Corporation of Winchester) to the North end of the Market-house in said Corporation.
>
> Bro's. Peter Lauck, Lewis Barnett, William Doster, and William Ball are appointed a committee to make application to said Common Hall for the priviledge of building said Masonic Hall, and also to contract with a fit person or persons to undertake and compleat said Hall.

On July 31, 1809 another very interesting resolution was adopted concerning the liquid refreshments supplied to the Lodge by the bar-keeper:

> On motion, ordered that the Bar-keeper shall deliver no liquor of any kind to any Bro'r. for the use of the Lodge, unless upon an order from the Secretary, stating the quantity and kind of liquor; and any liquor delivered contrary to the above order, shall not be paid for at the expense of the Lodge.

Since the cost of these liquid refreshments was included regularly in the "expenses of the evening", it is apparent that some of the more temperate Brethren had complained of the fact, that they were paying for liquor, which they did not themselves consume.

Further reference to the building of a Masonic Hall is found in the minutes of October 2, 1809:

The Lodge Taking under consideration the proposition for building a Masonic Hall in this Town were of opinion that the FOUNDATION STONE thereof ought to be laid agreeable to ancient custom. Whereupon Bro's. Peter Lauck, William Silver, and William Doster were appointed a committee to meet in session with that appointed by Union Lodge No. 66 to make the necessary arrangements for laying said STONE.

Here we find also the first reference in the minutes of Winchester Hiram Lodge to the existence of Union Lodge No. 66, a brief sketch of which will be found elsewhere in this volume.

The December meeting for 1809 was advanced to November 18th "for special reasons appearing to the Lodge" and the Brethren were notified of this change through the "publick papers". The election of officers was held at this meeting and Lewis Wolfe was chosen again as the Lodge's representative to Grand Lodge. Delinquent members were giving considerable trouble about this time and there are several references in the minutes as to the disposition of their cases. There were two kinds of delinquency, to which reference is made frequently: non-payment of dues and non-attendance on the Lodge meetings without sufficient excuse. In February, 1810 a committee was appointed to handle such cases and empowered to summon before the Lodge all those Brethren, who persisted in their delinquencies. It will be seen, therefore, that present day Lodges are no different from those of a century or more ago as regards the negligence and indifference of some of their members. The name of Archibald Magill now reappears frequently in the Lodge minutes and it appears that he was also very active in the affairs of Union Lodge No. 66. It will be recalled that this same Brother was disciplined by the Lodge for neglect of his duties as Secretary in 1797, though the minutes of that year do not indicate the ultimate outcome of the matter. And even more important and astonishing is the fact, that this Brother became, on December 9, 1817, Grand Master of Masons in Virginia and served two years in that office. We shall have more to say of him later.

In the minutes of April 2, 1810 it is noted that "the petition of Jesse Brown was discarded, he not having paid attention thereto." The nature of this inattention on the applicant's part is not disclosed, but we surmise, that he did not present himself for possible interview by the Brethren before his petition came up for ballot. At the meeting of June 4, 1810 arrangements for the celebration of St. John the Baptist's Day were made and a committee was appointed to arrange with the Brethren of Union Lodge for the dedication of the new Masonic Hall on that day. Although the minutes of the ensuing meeting (July 2, 1810) do not so state, it is to be inferred that the Hall was dedicated according to schedule, for Brother Lewis Barnett presented at this time a bill for his expenses in building the Masonic Hall but the amount involved is not stated nor are we told that it was paid. The mere notation, that it was "ordered to be registered in the Treasurer's book", would seem to indicate, that the Lodge did not have the full amount available and that Brother Barnett had to content himself with payments on the installment plan. At this same meeting Matthew Thomas was made an honorary member of the Lodge "so long as he complies with the bye laws." Since no copy of these "bye laws" is available, we are unable to state the provisions governing honorary membership at that period.

The question of refreshments at Lodge meetings came up again on August 6, 1810 when a committee of five was appointed to "form rules with respect to furnishing the Lodge with refreshment". Lewis Wolfe was again chosen as representative to the sessions of Grand Lodge held in 1810 and Peter Lauck was continued as Master for the ensuing year. And we now have evidence, that Archibald Magill dimitted from Winchester Hiram Lodge No. 21 in favor of membership in Union Lodge No. 66, for he is listed from time to time in the minutes of No. 21 as a visitor and also as W. M. of Union Lodge. More trouble with Lodge officers arose in 1811, when the Treasurer, Philip Hoff, began to absent himself from meetings. Hence, on April 1, 1811, the Lodge voted that he should be deprived of his office and some other Brother appointed in his stead if he did not attend the next meeting. Brother Hoff paid no attention to this admonition, however, and Hugh T. Rose was appointed to succeed him as Treasurer on May 6, 1811. On June 13th of that year the Secretary was ordered to purchase blue ribbon "sufficient to trim the jewels of this Lodge against St. John's Day next", and it was ordered for that day, "that no spirituous liquor of any kind be brought into the Lodge room 'till after sermon". On August 5th three Brethren were suspended and one expelled for un-Masonic conduct, and on September 2d a "traveling Brother" was also expelled for writing a letter, which was highly derogatory to the character of Brother Peter Lauck. Disputes between Brethren sometimes required the appointment of committees to intervene between them, and other committees were appointed as occasion required to investigate and determine charges preferred against some Brother for an alleged breach of Masonic propriety. Nor did the Lodge hesitate to order Brethren to be summoned to testify in any matter, which concerned the good name of the Lodge and of the Masonic fraternity in the community. If a Brother disregarded his obligation to the extent of disobeying a summons served on him, the Lodge punished him accordingly, usually by suspension during the pleasure of the Brethren. To cover at least a portion of these cases, an amendment to the by-laws was adopted on December 2, 1811 as follows:

> If any Brother shall hereafter be guilty of drunkenness or other un-Masonic conduct, he shall be suspended or expell'd at the disgression [discretion] of the Lodge.

At the same meeting it was ordered "that the Secretary do buy two Choir [quires] of paper for this Lodge and render his bill at the next stated meeting", also that the Treasurer "do furnish a load of hickory wood for the Lodge and have the same cut up and safe stowed away for the use of this Lodge".

Beginning about this time more and more of the Lodge business was transacted on the M. M. degree. However, the complete transition did not take place for a decade or more, perhaps after 1820 or even later. The Lodge minutes show, that the E. A. Lodge was opened "in form", the F. C. Lodge "in due form", and the M. M. Lodge "in ample form". On January 6, 1812 an account of 75 cents was allowed to Jonathan Foster "for advertising the anniversary of St. John the Baptist last". This is evidently an error on the part of Daniel W. Thomas, the Secretary, since it was the anniversary of St. John the Evangelist (not St. John the Baptist), which was observed on the preceding December 27th. Suspensions for non-payment of dues now begin to appear in the minutes also, but Brethren, who paid up promptly after suspension, seem to have experienced no trouble in getting reinstated. The usual observance was held on June 24, 1812 with the collaboration of the "H. R. A. [Holy Royal Arch] Chapter and Union Lodge No. 66."

We give here in full the short but interesting minutes of the meeting *supposed to have been held* on July 6, 1812:

> July 6th   Anno Lucis 5812   past 9 o'clock
> *Present*
> Only Conrad Kremer S. W., Daniel W. Thomas Secretary, James Foster Treasurer, Bernard Jackson, Anthony Whitehall Tyler, John Frederick.
> Visiting Brethren, Robert L. Beaty, Lazarus Pine.
> It is to be lamented that Brethren are so negligent in attendance that there are not a sufficient number of members present to open a lodge.
>   D. W. THOMAS, Sec'y.

We are at a loss to understand why eight Brethren duly assembled were unable to open Lodge that night. But we do know of many Lodges in our own day, which have held frequent meetings with fewer than this number in attendance. The commentary of Daniel W. Thomas on non-attendance might well have been lifted from a minute book of 1949 instead of one of 1812!

On July 13, 1812 charges were preferred against two of the Brethren "who have been represented as guilty of un-Masonic conduct in quarelling and fighting with each other on the public race field to the disgrace of the Fraternity and wounding of the feeling[s] of all true Brethren". Both parties were reprimanded on their plea of intoxication and confession of guilt. Another

Brother was summoned to appear before the Lodge at its next meeting to "shew cause (if any he can) why he pleaded the act of limitation against the accompt [account] of said Bro'r. Daniel W. Thomas when the said account was duly proven to be just, which is a disgrace to any man, more especially one professing to be a Mason". We could wish that the same high standards of conduct in such matters might be applied to the members of the Masonic fraternity in the present day.

Under date of July 15, 1812 we find the first reference to the holding of a Lodge of Past Masters, at which Archibald Porterfield and Alexander Stephens received this degree. A similar Lodge of Past Masters was held on December 20th of that year, when the newly elected officers of the Lodge were duly "lectured". Thomas C. Wyndham succeeded Daniel W. Thomas as Secretary at this time. The following significant entry is found in the minutes of January 4, 1813 (probably due to the outbreak of the War of 1812 shortly before):

> A motion was made and seconded that Brothers Seevers, Swearingen, and Wyndham be a committee to consider and report against the next regular night whether that clause of the charge of the first degree, which reads "true to your Sovereign and the Kingdom in which you live" shall be altered or stand as it now reads.

This committee did not make its report, however, until May 31, 1813, when it recommended that the following words be added to the above statement in the charge of the E. A. degree: "without your conforming to the rule of Sovereigns".

Reference is made again in the minutes of February 1, 1813 to Brother George Washington Timberlake, who seems to have gone to Kentucky and to have affiliated with St. Andrew's Lodge No. 18 of that jurisdiction. It will be recalled, that this Brother was the first namesake of George Washington to be made a member of old Lodge No. 12. And on May 31, 1813 (the same date as the above mentioned action on the charge of the E. A. degree), the Lodge took vigorous and emphatic action on Grand Lodge's alleged failure to recognize the Lodge officers:

FIRST YEARS UNDER VIRGINIA JURISDICTION   73

Ordered, that Brother Daniel W. Thomas do write to the Secy. of the Grand Lodge on the subject of the Master of this Lodge not being acknowledged by the Grand Lodge in two circular letters.

Ordered further, that the Secy. do write to the Grand Secy. to know the reason why the Officers of this Lodge are not acknowledged by the G. Lodge.

The results of this protest to Grand Lodge do not appear in subsequent minutes of the Lodge nor is any reference to the matter to be found in the Grand Lodge minutes for 1813.

On July 5, 1813 it was ordered that "Mr. Williams, an officer in the 12 months' service" be allowed to apply for initiation at any time before he left Winchester and receive the E. A. degree. At the August meeting a committee was appointed to file all loose papers belonging to the Lodge, but these, unfortunately, have not survived the ravages of the years. At this meeting also Brother Nicholas Cox, of Trenton Lodge No. 5 (New Jersey), "passed the chair", i. e., received the degree of Past Master.

In the minutes of October 4, 1813 we find the first reference to the existence of the Knights Templar in Winchester. Because of the importance of this entry, we think it desirable to quote it in full.

> Ordered, that the petition of sundry members of this Lodge praying that the Knight Templars Lodge may have leave to sit in this Hall, so that they do not interfere with any Entered Apprentice's, Fellow Craft's, Master's, Past Master's, Mark Master's, or Royal Arch Lodge be granted— and that the petition in the words following be recorded.
>
> The Standing Committee of the Assembly of Knight Templars held in the Town of Winchester, State of Virginia, on behalf of the Excellent Captain General and the rest of the Officers and Brethren of said Encampment—To the Worshipful Master, Officers and Brethren of Hiram Lodge No. 21
> ### SEND GREETING
> Worthy Brethren:
> For the unauthorized Liberty that we have taken as Knights of the Temple (tho' Masons) of meeting in the Masonic Hall, we

feel ourselves bound to apologize. We assure you, Brethren, that it was not through arrogancy but through inadvertency that we took that liberty. We wish to cultivate harmony and brotherly love. We have not the most distant idea of contemning those different degrees, through which we have passed; but on the contrary we revere them, and pledge ourselves that we will use our utmost endeavors to support Ancient Masonry, in all its various degrees, agreeable to the Usages and Customs thereof: and that we will not at any time make or cause to be made or suffer to be made (if in our power to prevent the same) any inroads or innovations thereon; but will aid and assist our Brethren in restoring that Sublime Order to its primeval Beauty and Glory. Now, worthy Brethren, we have given you some of the outlines of our Order, which we are determined (and bound) with the help of God to pursue (*ne varietur*) and upon those terms & principles we hope to be patronized by your Worshipful Lodge in assembling in the Masonic Hall as Knight Templars—which if granted will be considered a fraternal favour conferred on your Brethren, who wish you Grace, Mercy and Peace through God the Father and our Lord Jesus Christ. Amen.

Signed in behalf of our Assembly the 28th day of the ninth month (Called September) in the Era of Knight Templars 779.

    SIGNED   CONRAD KREMER, President
    CHRISTOPHER WETZEL, Secretary

JAMES FOSTER
ROBT. L. BEATY
HENRY SEEVERS
D. W. THOMAS
} MEMBERS

The further story of Templary in Winchester will be found in another section of the present work.

Archibald Magill was chosen to represent Hiram Lodge at the Grand Lodge of 1813, he being District Deputy Grand Master that year. The Grand Lodge proceedings show, that he represented the Lodge accordingly but no representative of Union Lodge is shown for that annual communication of Grand Lodge. We assume, therefore, that Union Lodge was already becoming inactive or was actually dormant and that Archibald Magill had renewed his membership in Hiram Lodge. Nevertheless, the Lodge minutes of No. 21 are silent on this point. However, we find that Brother Magill, at the meeting of Hiram Lodge held on

August 1, 1814, "gave notice, that he should visit this Lodge at the next stated meeting as D. G. Master". The reference is obviously to the office of District Deputy Grand Master, since Charles H. Graves was the Deputy Grand Master of the Grand Lodge of Virginia at that time. The record of the meeting of October 3d following shows that

> Brother Archibald Magill took the chair as Deputy Grand Master, and requested the Records, which were accordingly shewn, of which he took a memorandum. He then inquired into the prosperity of the Lodge and was answered by the Senior Warden 'that it was in a declining state on account of the non-attendance of the members'. An appropriate charge was then delivered by the D. G. Master.

The year 1815 began with Lemuel Bent, active in all branches of Winchester Masonry at that time, as Master and Edmund Pendleton as Secretary of the Lodge. On January 2d the axe fell on 28 Brethren, some of them Past Masters, who had "forfeited their seats by the non-payment of dues for two years" We know of no similar case in Virginia Masonry of that era. On March 6, 1815 some of the Brethren complained about the lack of cleanliness in the Lodge room and the Tyler was ordered, therefore, "to clean the Hall once every two months, for which he shall be paid out of the funds of the Lodge". On June 5th Daniel W. Thomas was voted the sum of $5.43 for boarding another Brother "two weeks and five days while sick". During the next few months various Brethren, who had been suspended on January 2d, were reinstated. On March 5, 1815 we find the first reference to the Lodge's being in mourning because of the death of one of its members. The Brethren were ordered "to wear crape around their hats for thirty days in token of respect of his memory". The reader can easily imagine the picture of all Winchester Masons appearing in such attire on the streets of the town during the period indicated. Archibald Magill was again chosen to represent Hiram Lodge at the Grand Lodge of 1815 and, on November 25th of that year, the Lodge rescinded its action of January 2d and restored all the Brethren affected by that order to their previous standing in the Lodge.

On March 4, 1816 the fee for the degrees was increased from $11.00 to $12.00 "that the Steward may have one dollar as a compensation for his services". And at the meeting of July 1st of that year it was "ordered, that Brothers Lauck, Thomas, Kremer, & Pendleton wait on Parson Reck and request a copy of his sermon (delivered on St. John's Day) for publication". The parson also received $5.00 for his services on that occasion, and the printer was paid $15.00 for publishing it. On September 30th 23 members were suspended at one time for non-payment of dues and reference is made to the petition of Jacob Buzzard for initiation, which was later withdrawn. We wonder if some of the Brethren had a slight prejudice against this worthy gentleman's name! At the instance of Grand Lodge, Brother Cyrus Baldwin, Master-elect of the Lodge at Front Royal, was installed by Hiram Lodge after receiving the degree of Past Master at the hands of the Winchester Brethren. On October 2, 1817 a previously expelled Brother was "reexpelled", so to speak, because of further enormities charged against him and he was "solemnly pronounced" as "unworthy the countenance of all regular Masons, he having violated every principal of the Order". The Grand Secretary was also to receive a copy of the proceedings in this case.

Frequent appeals from traveling Brethren in distress were received and their pleas were answered in truly Masonic fashion. For example, there were two visiting Brethren present on March 10, 1818, Augustine Mayer, a member of Stella Diana Lodge No. 4, Italy, and Francis Rawpe, whose Lodge is not indicated. It was ordered, that the Treasurer "pay the above visitors $10.00 each to relieve their necessities and that Brother Brown go around amongst the Brethren for further assistance". There is not a word of detail as to the nature of the distress, in which these two Brethren found themselves. But the reasons assigned by them for asking assistance were entirely satisfactory, we may be sure, to the Brethren, and their response was to the limit of their ability. At the meeting of April 5, 1818 the Secretary was allowed 50 cents for the repair of his jewel and it was ordered, "that Judge Carr have leave to hold his court in this Hall for the present session". The Tyler of the Lodge at that period was Brother A. Witherall. He was in very straightened circumstances, apparently, for we find a number of entries in the minutes indicating that the Lodge not only paid the greater portion of his board with a private family but also purchased numerous articles of clothing for him as occasion required.

On November 30, 1818 Lemuel Bent declined re-election as Master of the Lodge and Conrad Kremer, also very active in all branches of Masonry in Winchester, was chosen to succeed him. Philip A. Klipstine became Secretary and Adam Brown was made Treasurer. It was Conrad Kremer, with whom the Tyler boarded and Brother Kremer was voted $2.00 weekly in payment for this service. Brother Witherall soon had to give up the duty of tiling the Lodge, however, and James Foster was appointed as his successor. At the meeting of February 12, 1819 the Lodge voted a donation of $20.00 to Brother Roger Hammel "a distressed worthy Brother for the purpose of assisting him to bring his family from Ireland to this country and that he be recommended by this Lodge to other Lodges to procure means for that purpose". At the same meeting the managers of the Polemic Society (a local literary and debating group) were warned, that they would lose the privilege of meeting in the Masonic Hall "unless they keep the Hall in better order". The death of Brother Witherall is reported in the minutes of March 1st and the Lodge made the necessary arrangements to pay the expense of his funeral. At the same meeting it was voted to amend the by-laws "so as to initiate the candidate if the dissenting Brother fail to give good & sufficient reasons for rejecting him". It was likewise ordered "that the Common Council of this town have leave to hold their meetings in this Hall". On May 3d it was voted to amend the by-laws further by providing that every member of the Lodge should pay his monthly dues of 25 cents, whether he attended the Lodge meetings or not. Other amendments were adopted on July 5th, including one, which increased the fee for the degrees from $10.00 to $15.00 and another, which fined each officer, who received compensation, each time that he was guilty of a "default of duty".

On October 15, 1819 a committee was appointed "to wait on Brother Archibald Magill to consult him on the propriety of petitioning the next General Assembly of Virginia (also to draw a petition) to incorporate Hiram Lodge No. 21", an action which is quite illegal under present Grand Lodge law. And at the following meeting (November 1, 1819) we find the first mention of the reading of the minutes before the closing of the Lodge, a practice, which was to be followed regularly from that date. The year 1820 began with a complete revision of the Lodge by-laws, which now comprised thirteen articles and were transcribed in full into the minute book. Further amendments made during the year set up a permanent fund and prohibited the Treasurer and the Secretary from accepting "due bills" from any members in payment of their dues. A mild scandal was caused when some Brother divulged some of the secret transactions of the Lodge, so that they became matters of public knowledge and comment, but this soon subsided and there is no reference to any report from the committee appointed to investigate the matter.

Thus ends the period from 1807 to 1820 and, after approximately thirteen years under the jurisdiction of the Grand Lodge of Virginia, Winchester Hiram Lodge found itself in a rather flourishing state despite certain problems, which have been common to all Lodges almost since the establishment of Masonry as a speculative science. Lemuel Bent was made Master for the year 1821 with Peter Lauck as Treasurer and Francis M. Beckwith as Secretary. Our story will be continued in subsequent Chapters but not in the same amount of detail as we have employed up to this point.

CHAPTER VII

TWO SCORE YEARS OF ACTIVE SERVICE

The Lodge held its first meeting of 1821 on New Year's day. The Brethren adopted an appropriate New Year's resolution, as it were, in the nature of another general revision of the by-laws. This time there were 30 articles and the regulations were much more extensive and complete than any, which the Lodge had employed previously. On February 24th the following action was taken with reference to the Masonic Hall:

> Ordered, that Brothers Lemuel Bent and Peter Lauck be appointed a committee on the part of this Lodge to confer with the committee of the Common Council of the Corporation of Winchester or with the committee itself on the subject of removing the Hall &c. and building a new one. Also ordered that Brother Alfred H. Powell, former Master of Lodge No. 66, be requested to cooperate with said Committee.

These Brethren evidently did their work well, for we find the following entry in the minutes of July 20, 1821:

> Ordered, that Brothers Peter Lauck, Conrad Kremer, Townsend W. Thomas, and Francis M. Beckwith be appointed a committee to make arrangements for laying the cornerstone of the new Masonic Hall, and that Brothers George Reed, Daniel W. Thomas, and Lemuel Bent be a committee to make arrangements for the procession and to invite the authorities of the Town, the Clergy, &c, & to regulate the proceedings of the day.

The cornerstone was accordingly laid with full Masonic ceremonies on July 31, 1821 but we have no reference to the details of the occasion in the minute book. On March 2, 1900 this same cornerstone was opened. Among its contents were two remarkable documents bearing upon the early history of Winchester Encampment of Knights Templar. These are reproduced in full in the Commandery section of this book (see page 237). We are not told when the Hall was completed and dedicated but it is presumed that this was done some time early in 1822. At the end of the year 1821 Moses T. Hunter was recommended to Grand Lodge for appointment as District Deputy and William Byrd Page, who had been raised only a few weeks before, was chosen to represent the Lodge at the Grand Lodge session that year.

On July 17, 1822 we find the first record of an "extra communication" called for the purpose of conducting Masonic burial services, the deceased being Brother Edward Slater, Sr., who had left the special request that he "be returned to his mother earth with Masonic honors". On August 6, 1822 a committee was appointed to make final settlement for the expenses incident to the completion of the new Lodge room and authority was granted to this committee to borrow sufficient funds to make the necessary payments in this connection. At the meeting of February 3, 1823 the petition of Benjamin Bushnell, who was to play an important part in the future history of the Lodge, was presented and it was resolved, "that the Master of this Lodge offer to Chancellor Carr the use of this hall for the purpose of holding his court". On November 17th of that year the Lodge declined to approve the establishment of a Lodge at Luray on the ground that the request was presented orally and not in writing, but made it clear, that such a request would be approved when properly presented.

We find, that James Cushman, Grand Lecturer of the Grand Lodge of Virginia, was a visitor on April 5, 1824 and presided during the conferring of the Fellow Craft degree that evening. Cushman probably remained in Winchester for some days, instructing not only the Lodge but the Chapter and Commandery (called Encampment at that time) as well in the work of the various degrees. Committees of inquiry were regularly appointed to investigate all petitions for the degrees during this period, a practice, which is forbidden by the Grand Lodge of Virginia today on the theory that the entire membership of a Lodge should constitute itself a committee of investigation on *every* petition offered. Cushman was present again on December 5, 1824 and at a number of meetings during the ensuing four or five years. He

LODGE ROOM OF WINCHESTER HIRAM LODGE NO. 21, A. F. & A. M. (as seen from the East).

DETAIL OF WEST END OF CEILING, WINCHESTER HIRAM LODGE,
No. 21, A. F. & A. M.

eventually returned to Connecticut, where he died about 1831. He had caused great consternation among the Knights Templar of Winchester by insisting that they were of irregular origin. This subject is treated more fully elsewhere in this volume.

The following interesting and important resolution was adopted by the Lodge on November 1, 1824:

> Whereas, the members present feeling an anxious desire to join with their Brethren and fellow citizens in other parts of the country in testifying their fraternal regard and grateful recollection of the distinguished worth of Gen'l. La Fayette and of his eminent services in the cause of our beloved country in its struggle for independence, RESOLVED therefore, That in order to evince to him and to our fellow citizens the high respect and brotherly affection that we feel for that great and good Mason and friend of man, that Bro's. Lemuel Bent, S. H. Davis, W. G. Singleton, S. Heister, R. W. Barton, W. B. Page, I. Tooley, and Peter Lauck be a committee to confer with Lodges No. 66 and 117, Winchester Encampment of Knight Templars, and the Winchester Chapter of Royal Arch Masons and request their cooperation to invite Gen'l. LaFayette to visit this Town and partake of a repast to be provided for him by his Masonic Brethren and that said committee in conjunction with such committees as may be appointed by the above-named Lodges, Encampment, and Chapter do convey to him this invitation in the most respectful and affectionate terms and make such arrangements for his reception as the said committees may deem advisable and ask the cooperation of our fellow citizens if it should be thought proper.

At the same meeting a committee was appointed to investigate the conduct of Brother William B. Whitney, charged with un-Masonic conduct in setting himself up as a sort of Masonic authority and lecturer and conferring various degrees upon susceptible members of the fraternity "for a price". This was the Brother, who presented to Hiram Lodge the request for approval of the establishment of a Lodge at Luray as mentioned above. The report of this committee was submitted on November 19th and the Lodge found Whitney guilty of "several flagrant instances of pecuniary fraud in this town & other un-Masonick conduct". He was ordered to be reported to the Grand Lodge as a "base imposter" and all Lodges in the surrounding territory were to be warned against him.

On April 4, 1825 steps were taken by the Lodge to obtain the cooperation of the other Winchester bodies "on the subject of finishing the Master's Chair & carpeting the Hall". Also a committee was appointed "to make the best possible bargain with some printer for the printing & half-binding of the by-laws of Hiram Lodge No. 21".

During the years 1824 and 1825 the Lodge was in a very prosperous condition. There were many petitions and degrees were conferred at almost every meeting. An occasional instance of difficulty between Lodge members or of charges growing out of alleged un-Masonic conduct occupied the attention of the Brethren but, for the most part, the fortunes of Hiram Lodge were decidedly on the up-grade. Once there was considerable difficulty with some of the members residing in the vicinity of Millwood, but this also was amicably adjusted. In 1826, however, the minutes of the fourteen meetings held are quite brief and the amount of work done by the Lodge slowed down considerably. Approximately the same number of meetings was held in 1827, all of which were of more or less routine character. In one or two instances, in fact, no meeting was held because of the small number of members present. The cornerstone of the new Episcopal church was laid on June 24, 1828 with the cooperation of the neighboring Lodges. District Deputy Grand Master Timothy Carrington paid an official visit to Hiram Lodge on October 6th, at which time the Brethren "shewed themselves to be accomplished Masons".

On November 5, 1828 Samuel H. Davis retired from the office of Master after occupying the chair for the preceding five years. Solomon Heister was elected to succeed him. James Cushman visited the Lodge on November 26 and 27 as Grand Lecturer and received $5.00 each night for his services. Twelve meetings were held in 1829, none of them eventful. The Lodge was occupied with regular business and with several items of new furnishings for the Lodge room. The old chairs were removed and replaced with "handsome settees" if we are to believe the account given in the record. When there was no work, Lodge usually closed by nine o'clock, otherwise not later than ten o'clock. In 1830 eleven meetings were held. One Brother (Fellow Craft) was expelled during the year and his expulsion announced in the public press. Brethren were rather delinquent in the payment of their dues and, toward the end of the year, a collector was appointed at a salary of 15% of all he collected. Levi L. Stevenson, of Staunton, was chosen to represent Hiram Lodge at the 1830 Grand Lodge communication. No meetings at all were held in January and February, 1831. But on March 9th the Lodge was called to make plans for attending the funeral of Judge Robert White, one of its members, on the day following. Suitable resolutions were adopted and it was arranged, that the local band should furnish the music for the occasion. Another Masonic funeral was conducted by the Lodge on March 19, 1831. On October 31st of that year we find that, as there was no further business before the Lodge, "it was adjourned untill Thursday evening, Nov. 3, at early candle light for the purpose of initiating W. Andrews". (Note that Lodges could be "adjourned" in those days!)

At its meeting on February 6, 1832 a committee was appointed by the Lodge to plan for participation in the centennial anniversary of the birth of George Washington, which was accordingly done on the ensuing February 22d. During this period Edmund Pendleton Hunter, a future Grand Master of Masons in Virginia, became a member of Hiram Lodge and the Lodge voted to recommend him for the office of District Deputy Grand Master for the Masonic year 1833. On August 5, 1833 C. A. B. Coffroth, who was later to serve the Lodge and other Winchester bodies for many years in various capacities, received the degree of Entered Apprentice, being passed and raised later in due course. During the year the Lodge took action opposing the proposed distribution of the Charity Fund of the Grand Lodge of Virginia and made arrangements for improved lighting in the Lodge room with the financial collaboration of the other bodies. On March 31, 1834 James Foster was removed from his office as Tyler because of his laxity in performing the duties of that office. William Jenkins was appointed in his stead and a committee was designated "to wait upon the old Tyler and inform him of the proceedings of the Lodge".

The observance of St. John's Day on June 24, 1834 was a memorable occasion, being marked by a procession with the local band and light infantry companies participating. The oration was delivered by Edmund P. Hunter and was afterwards ordered printed at the expense of the Lodge, each of the other Lodges in the district being presented with 25 copies of this address for distribution among its members. The by-laws were again revised toward the end of 1834 and, on March 9, 1835, the sum of $12.00 was appropriated "for the purpose of defraying the expense attending the folding, printing, and stitching of the By-laws of this Lodge". The case of James Foster, former Tyler, came up again at the meeting of October 8, 1835 and a committee was appointed to wait upon him "informing him of the steps intended to be taken by the Lodge, to wit: giving him the privilege of selecting his own boarding house and the Lodge pledging themselves to defray all necessary expenses over and above his pension, which he at present receives". At the following meeting it was resolved, "that the Standing Committee of the Lodge be authorized to draw upon the Treasurer" for all funds necessary to carry out this arrangement.

The year 1836 passed so uneventfully, that there was some talk of surrendering the charter. At its meeting on November 9th (which was the date for the annual election of officers) the following question was debated in open Lodge: "Is it the pleasure of this Lodge to surrender the charter thereof?" After a lengthy discussion, the vote was in the negative and officers were chosen with Nathaniel Seevers as Master and representative to Grand Lodge. The thanks of the Brethren were also tendered to Brother William Anders "for his humane and benevolent conduct towards our aged and infirm Tyler, Bro. James Foster, and for his general zeal on behalf of the Institution". Union Lodge No. 66 seems to have become completely dormant by this time, for Hiram Lodge adopted a resolution on May 11

1837 petitioning Grand Lodge for the jewels of Union Lodge. Conrad Kremer, mentioned many times previously in this narrative and for many years a member of Hiram Lodge, died on May 29, 1837 and was buried with Masonic honors on the day following. Again on November 27th of that year Hiram Lodge adopted strong resolutions against the proposed distribution of the Grand Charity Fund to the several Lodges of the state and in favor of the use of this fund for the establishment of a manual labor school.

In 1838 more stringent regulations were adopted against intoxication in the Lodge room and the Lodge participated officially in the celebration of July 4th of that year on the invitation of town officials. The most important event recorded in 1839 was the passing of Peter Lauck, whose funeral the Brethren attended to the number of 21. The obsequies took place on October 3d and fulsome resolutions were adopted on the death of this esteemed Brother; from them we think it appropriate to quote as follows:

> Early in life when it was found necessary for the people of this country to take up arms in defense of their dearest rights, our deceased Brother volunteered his services in Morgan's celebrated company of riflemen, shouldered his rifle, and marched to the scene of action near Boston and from thence through a trackless wilderness in the cold month of December to Quebeck, where the gallant Montgomery fell and where our Brother, with a number of others, were taken prisoners and remained in rugged confinement for some months until he was exchanged, when he returned to Winchester. As a Mason he was pre-eminent. To him this Lodge is indebted for much of its usefulness. He was indeed its father. Presiding over it as Master for a number of years, he was indefatigable in his zeal to promote the object of the Institution.

The matter of absentees was still a bugbear so far as the Lodge was concerned and, at its first meeting in 1840, it voted to amend the by-laws so as to suspend automatically any Brother who was guilty of absence from three successive meetings. During this year Henry H. Goertz, who was listed as a "musical master", was elected to receive the degrees and the year ended with thirteen meetings to the credit of the Lodge. The general situation had shown material improvement as compared with that of the four previous years. The question of the disposition of the Grand Charity Fund continued to be agitated during 1841. On November 1st of that year a convention of representatives from the various Lodges of the district met at Winchester at the instance of Hiram Lodge. Resolutions were adopted unanimously in favor of the establishment of a manual labor school and copies ordered to be sent to Grand Lodge. A committee from the membership of the several Lodges was also appointed to promote this idea and the expenses of the committee were to be borne equally by each Lodge in the district.

On June 24, 1843 Hiram Lodge joined with George Washington Lodge No. 51, of Berryville, in the observance of St. John's Day, and on July 3d, Philip Hoff, who had been suspended in 1812, was reinstated at his own request after a suspension lasting more than thirty years. Another convention on the matter of tht Grand Charity Fund was held at Charlestown during that year and still another at Woodstock in 1844. On April 10, 1844 the Lodge was visited by Levi L. Stevenson in his capacity as Grand Lecturer. The use of his services was optional, since his expenses and an honorarium were to be paid by the Lodge inviting him. The action taken was unanimously in favor of inviting Brother Stevenson to instruct the Lodge and he remained in Winchester for that purpose for approximately two weeks, presiding over special communications of the Lodge on April 15th, 16th, 17th, and 22d. There is no record as to the amount paid by the Lodge for his services. On November 4, 1844 the Lodge approved a proposal submitted by Marshall Lodge, of Lynchburg, that the use of spirituous liquors be excluded from the periods of refreshment at Grand Lodge, but amended the proposal to the effect "that all sorts of refreshments be excluded".

The Masonic Hall required a new roof in 1845 and a committee was appointed by the Lodge to act with the committee appointed by the Common Council for this purpose. The Lodge's share of this expense was the large sum of $30.43, which was paid in due course. On June 30, 1845 the Brethren adopted suitable resolutions on the passing of ex-President Andrew Jackson, these being published in the Winchester press. A memorial service for General Jackson was held by the Lodge on July 26th following. Various other repairs were made to the Lodge room during the year and the former resolutions relative to the abolishing of the use of spirituous liquors at Grand Lodge, also to the reduction of the salaries of the Grand Lodge officers, were readopted.

In February, 1846 the Lodge adopted resolutions looking toward the erection of another story on the Masonic Hall, so that the Lodge and Chapter might have separate meeting rooms. On July 6th of that year the Brethren refused to permit the Lodge room to be used by another (non-Masonic) organization and adopted a resolution "that this Lodge room shall not hereafter be used for any other than Masonic purposes unless by the unanimous consent of the Lodge". The most important event of 1847 was the Lodge's vigorous denunciation of the efforts of a group of Masons to revive Union Lodge No. 66 without obtaining first the consent of Hiram Lodge No. 21. The following action was taken in this case:

> Whereas, it has been reported to this Lodge that, since our last regular communication, certain Brethren have made application to the G. M. for a dispensation to open or revive No. 66 without having made application to this Lodge for the recommendation required by the Laws of the Grand Lodge; and Whereas, it is reported that such dispensation has been actually granted and the Lodge opened; therefore, be it RESOLVED, That this Lodge cannot recognize No. 66 as a Lodge of Masons, regularly and legally constituted as such, and that we hereby solemnly protest against the same.

Copies of this resolution were broadcast throughout the entire state. Meanwhile, the Tyler, who had accepted the same office in No. 66, was notified that he must withdraw from Hiram Lodge if he continued to tile for No. 66. He promised to withdraw from the latter and to accept no office or emoluments from No. 66 until the matter in controversy was finally settled. Later the Tyler decided otherwise and resigned his office in Hiram Lodge, whereupon the Master called a special communication on September 11th (the original action had been taken on September 6, 1847), at which the previously adopted resolutions were re-affirmed and a new Tyler was chosen. This subject also occupied the attention of the Brethren on September 22d, at which certain correspondence with the Grand Master was read, and his reply to the Lodge's protest was "deemed altogether unsatisfactory". There was a "free interchange of sentiments by the members and the committee was further instructed to embody the sentiments of the Lodge fully". We believe, however, that no further action was taken by the Grand Master at that time.

The Lodge membership at this time numbered 25 and the annual contribution for each member was $2.00 with the proviso, "that, whenever at the end of any fiscal year, the surplus on hand shall exceed the sum of fifty dollars, that from that time, the annual contribution of each member shall be only one dollar, until the necessities of the Lodge shall require it again to be increased".

At its final meeting of the year 1847, the Lodge heard and adopted a long report on the matter of the revival of Lodge No. 66, this report occupying some five pages in the minute book and protesting further to Grand Lodge on the grounds, that practically all the activities preliminary to the revival of No. 66 were conducted surreptitiously and "not above board". This report was ordered to be transmitted to Grand Lodge by Hiram Lodge's representatives that same month. In spite of the refusal of Grand Master Sidney S. Baxter to recall the dispensation in question, the matter was taken to the floor of Grand Lodge by Hiram Lodge's delegates, Past Master J. B. T. Reed and Brother J. I. Smyth. On their return to Winchester they reported complete success in their efforts and made a formal report to the Lodge at its first meeting in 1848 (January 3d), the purport of which was, that Grand Lodge had recalled the dispensation previously issued to Lodge No. 66 and refused to grant this Lodge a charter. Brother Reed then climaxed his report by moving "that a committee be appointed to prevent any other surreptitious procurement of a charter or dispensation by Union Lodge No. 66", and this motion was adopted unanimously.

It is interesting to note that, at this particular period, balloting for candidates was conducted for each degree separately just as is done in Virginia today. The petitioner was expected to make his request known to the Lodge at the time that he desired to receive each degree. Ballots were recorded as "coming up fair" or "coming up foul" and petitioners were notified accordingly. Communications were received from the Grand Secretary an average of once or twice each year and were read in open Lodge. Sometimes these communications (or "circulars" as they were often designated) were posted in the Lodge room after reading, so that the Brethren might have the opportunity of reading them again at leisure.

On September 4, 1848 the Lodge adopted a resolution calling upon the Secretary, Brother L. T. Moore, to attend more regularly or to resign his office. But this resolution was "toned down" before final adoption, so that the Secretary was requested to furnish a proxy when he could not attend in person. On October 2nd of that year, the spectre of Lodge No. 66 again bobbed up and it was reported that the Grand Master had "granted a charter for the revival of No. 66." It was the same Grand Master as before, Sidney S. Baxter, who was determined, apparently, that Grand Lodge should not impose its will in the matter upon him. Baxter had been elected to serve his second year in that office as was more or less customary at that time. Of course, he could not grant a *charter* but he had every right, if he chose to do so, to grant another *dispensation* to the petitioners in question. Hiram Lodge still stood its ground, refused to withdraw its protest previously registered and voted to request the District Deputy to correspond with the Grand Master and ascertain the facts in the case.

At the end of 1848 the Lodge had 31 members on its roster after deducting the names of three Brethren, who had removed during the year. A committee of three members was appointed to "collect facts with regard to No. 66 to be laid before the Grand Lodge at its annual communication" (December, 1848). Past Grand Master J. Worthington Smith visted Hiram Lodge on December 4, 1848 and again on December 22d following. At the latter meeting Brother J. H. Carson "narrated the proceedings of the Grand Lodge in relation to No. 66" but it was resolved "that all motions in relation to No. 66 be laid upon the table for the present". It is unfortunate that the minutes do not contain the slightest indication as to the nature of Brother Carson's report. But the general trend of his remarks on the subject may be inferred from this entry in the minutes of February 5, 1849:

> The Worshipful Master laid before the Lodge a communication signed "William Jenkins, Master", in reference to which on motion
> RESOLVED, That this Lodge decline acceding to this or any similar request. Bro. Wm. Anders was directed to inform those interested of the decision of the Lodge. The following resolutions were then offered:
> 1. RESOLVED, That while we feel all due respect for the authority of the M. W. Grand Lodge, we yet recognize a higher authority. We deny that it is in the power of any man or body of men to make any innovations in the body of Masonry. Such we conceive has been done by the Grand Lodge of Virginia in chartering a Lodge in this Town with a Mason suspended from this Lodge as Master, & whose suspension took place before the application for a charter was laid before the Grand Lodge.
> 2. RESOLVED, That it is an innovation upon the body of Masonry to publish the name of .... in the Proceedings of the G. L. as a Past Master in regular standing in Union Lodge No. 66, while the said .... is under charges preferred against him before the said Union Lodge had an existence. A warrant to try the said charges regularly issued by the M. W. Grand Master being now, and was before the meeting of the G. L., in the hands of the Brethren appointed to investigate the case. The said charges being for ...... un-Masonic conduct.

It was ordered that these resolutions be laid on the table and the Lodge apparently took no further action regarding them. But this did not end the matter by any means, for we find that the Master was directed on June 4, 1849 to correspond with the Grand Master "on the subject of the promised committee to examine as to the state of things between Hiram and Union Lodges". At the same meeting a visiting Brother from St. George's Lodge, London, was received. He was granted certain financial assistance but was later repudiated because he was seen drunk on the streets of Winchester. The minutes of July 3d contain lengthy resolutions on the passing of former President James K. Polk, which were ordered to be printed and transmitted to neighboring Lodges. On September 3d a committee was appointed to prepare a circular setting forth the facts of the controversy between Hiram and Union Lodges for distribution to the Lodges of the state. Copies of this circular are still in existence and it is most certainly an *emphatic* protest in which the position of Hiram Lodge is set forth in no uncertain terms. In the minutes of November 1st there is also a lengthy memorial to Grand Lodge on this subject.

In 1850 the Lodge was invited to join with Grand Lodge in the laying of the cornerstone of the Washington monument in the grounds of the state capitol at Richmond. On February 2d of that year, one member of the Lodge was excused of charges of intemperance in view of the fact, that he had promised a reformation and had joined the Sons of Temperance as evidence of his good faith. Lewis Wolfe, whom we have mentioned a number of times in this narrative, died on June 11, 1850 and the Lodge adopted appropriate resolutions in his memory. He was buried the day following, the Lodge conducting the Masonic funeral service at the grave. On August 3, 1851 the Lodge held an election of officers out of the usual time simply by suspending the section of the by-laws requiring the election to be held in November. At this time it was also voted to "procure the services of P. M. Jno. B. T. Reed to lecture before the Lodge". At the beginning of the year 1852 the Lodge had 25 members, three having withdrawn during the preceding year. On April 7, 1852 Grand Lecturer Levi L. Stevenson visited the Lodge and assisted in settling a disagreement existing between two of the Lodge members. The election of officers had now been changed to June instead of November. On June 5, 1852 Brother L. T.

Moore was elected Master but declined the office and William Anders was chosen instead.

On January 1, 1853 the Lodge appropriated $20.00 "for the benefit of Winchester Encampment" (of Knights Templar). On February 5th a former member of Lodge No. 66 applied for membership in Hiram Lodge. There is the further notation in the minutes, that the charter of Union Lodge "had been revoked". We are certain that this fact gave every possible satisfaction to the Brethren of No. 21. On June 18th the Lodge voted to request its members to participate in the laying of the cornerstone of the new Masonic Hall in Staunton, the ceremonies to be conducted by the Grand Lodge of Virginia. The cornerstone of the Methodist Episcopal church of Winchester was laid on September 21, 1853 with Grand Master Edmund P. Hunter, a former member of Hiram Lodge, as one of the distinguished visitors of the occasion. By June 1, 1854 the membership of the Lodge had grown to 44 and its finances were reported as being in very satisfactory condition. The balance in cash in the Treasurer's hands was $121.88 and the Lodge owned twelve shares of stock in the Valley Fire Insurance Company. On September 12th of the same year a lengthy memorial was adopted on the passing of Grand Master Edmund P. Hunter, who was Virginia's first Grand Master to die in office. On November 18th it was reported to the Lodge, that its members had voluntarily "taxed themselves $1.00 each to assist in relieving the necessities of the family of our beloved Grand Master deceased", and the Brethren voted to request Grand Lodge to take action with a view to having all the Lodges in the state do likewise. Past Grand Master J. Worthington Smith, in his capacity as District Deputy for the Winchester District, visited the Lodge on June 2, 1855 and "delivered a most forcible lecture on the duties of Masons generally both in and out of the Lodge". It may be stated here, that M. W. Brother Smith had been made a Mason in Staunton Lodge No. 13, had served as Grand Master in 1842-1844, and had gone to Missouri in 1844 at the invitation of the Grand Lodge of Missouri for the purpose of establishing there the first so-called

Masonic College in the United States. After some years he had returned to Virginia and was now District Deputy Grand Master of the District in which Hiram Lodge was included.

On August 17, 1855 Hiram Lodge laid the cornerstone of the new Capon Chapel at Capon Springs with a large number of Brethren from this and other Lodges in attendance. During that year various appropriations were made for relief of distressed persons both in Winchester and in several other localities. On August 2, 1856 it was voted that "it is expedient that the Lodge provide itself with a copy of the *Universal Masonic Library* as soon as the funds of the Lodge will justify". In January, 1857 Henry Seevers, one of the Lodge's most venerable members, died and was buried with Masonic honors. The membership as of June 1st of that year was 46 with a loss of four members noted for the preceding twelve months. On October 16th a silver goblet was presented to Past Master William Anders with the following inscription: "Presented to Brother P. M. William Anders, as a testimonial of its confidence and regard, by Hiram Lodge No. 21, F. & A. M., Winchester, Va., A. L. 5857". On October 8, 1858 the cornerstone of the new Methodist Episcopal Church (South) was laid and the Brethren wore new aprons and gloves purchased for the occasion.

The year 1859 passed uneventfully and in February, 1860 the Lodge recommended to the Grand Lecturer the appointment of "Past Master Jno. B. T. Reed as an Assistant Grand Lecturer for the Western District of Virginia". Later in the year an effort was made by some of the Brethren to bring about the resignation of the then District Deputy on the grounds that he was unable to perform the duties of his office because of physical infirmities and intemperate habits. This motion was defeated, however. William H. Harman, Grand Senior Warden of the Grand Lodge of Virginia and a member of Staunton Lodge No. 13, was chosen to represent Hiram Lodge at the Grand Lodge communication in December, 1860. Colonel Harman later became a distinguished officer in the Confederate Army and was killed at Waynesboro on March 2, 1865 while attempting to escape from enemy forces.

He was Grand Master at the time of his death and was the second of Virginia's Grand Masters to die in office.

By the close of the year 1860 the Lodge had a membership of 35 Master Masons, four Entered Apprentices, and two Fellow Crafts. There was a balance of $127.33 in the treasury and the Lodge owned 25 shares of the Valley Fire Insurance Company's stock. All business was now transacted on the M. M. degree, dues not being chargeable against any but Master Masons and they alone were permitted to hold office. The Grand Lodge Proceedings were regularly reported to the Lodge by committees appointed for that purpose from year to year. The order of business for the stated and special communications was virtually the same as that which is familiar to every Virginia Mason today. The term "extra Lodge", which had been inherited from Pennsylvania, had now disappeared and the expressions "special communication" or "called meeting", and "regular communication" or "regular meeting" were now used entirely. There are frequent entries in the minutes covering "letters of dimission" and "traveling certificates" and Brethren so requesting are noted as being "given leave to withdraw", i. e., to become non-affiliates, though this privilege was so abused that Grand Lodge had to take action against it in the 1850's. Suspensions for non-payment of dues and charges growing out of alleged un-Masonic conduct were fairly frequent. The Lodge regularly conducted Masonic rites at the funerals of deceased Brethren when requested to do so. In one instance, these rites were conducted for a Brother, who committed suicide under questionable circumstances, but the mantle of charity was thrown over his memory and no investigation into the matter was held.

There is no indication whatever in the Lodge minutes as to the storm, which was then brewing between the North and the South. All the affairs of the Lodge were conducted in the utmost harmony and we do not find the slightest allusion of a hostile character in remarks, resolutions, or any other item recorded in the minutes. Thus the Brethren adhered rigidly to the ancient Masonic custom, that no discussion of race, religion, or politics should be permitted in the Lodge room.

CHAPTER VIII

WAR AND RECONSTRUCTION

Hiram Lodge began the year 1861 with great plans for the future. Among other things, the Brethren proposed to hold a great celebration on St. John the Baptist's Day (June 24th) and to invite all the neighboring Lodges to participate. At the same time the representatives of the several Lodges were to meet in convention to make plans for petitioning Grand Lodge for the appointment of a District Lecturer, also for working out an agreement respecting the appointment of the District Deputy for the district each year. This convention was to be held on the day following St. John's Day "at early candle light". The entire proposal is set out in full in the minutes of April 2, 1861. But there is still no reference to the impending conflict which we know as the War Between the States. Then, on April 9th, came the attack on Fort Sumter. One week later the Lodge met again in stated communication and we find that the entire matter of the district convention was *"indefinitely postponed"*. No reasons are given—the reader must surmise these for himself. But the Secretary, C. A. B. Coffroth, has underlined these words in the minute book—and there the matter rests.

Then, on July 17, 1861 there was a special communication, whose purpose is recorded as follows:

> P. M. Carson announced the death of our Brother, Lieut. Wm. Patten, of the Rockbridge Grays, and a member of Lodge No. 67, and that the Lodge was specially convened for the purpose of attending the funeral of our departed Brother.

There were twelve visitors on that occasion, many of whom were doubtless comrades in arms of the deceased. Three of these visitors are listed as coming from Lodge No. 67, which was located at Lexington.

No further meetings were held until October 1, 1861, at which time new officers were elected and installed. Brother J.

B. T. Reed, one of the Lodge's oldest and most venerated members, was made Master, doubtless because of the thought, that most of the younger members had already entered the Confederate service or would soon do so. The financial report of October 2d shows a balance of $71.08 in the treasury in addition to the ownership of 25 shares of stock in the Valley of Virgihia Insurance Company and two shares of stock in the Winchester Gas Company. On October 25, 1861, under a dispensation from the Grand Master, the degrees of Fellow Craft and Master Mason were conferred on Brother J. H. Funk, who was doubtless about to enter the armed services. Then, because of the presence of so many Confederate units in the vicinity, the Lodge adopted the following resolutions on December 3, 1861:

> 1. RESOLVED, That the Lodge hold its meetings weekly during the sojourn of the Army in our midst; and that at each of these meetings the W. M. and other qualified Brothers be selected to exemplify and lecture in the several degrees of Masonry.
> 2. That P. Masters Ginn, Carson, and Brent be requested to exemplify the work on the several degrees of Masonry on Tuesday evening next.
> 3. That P. M. Jno. B. T. Reed be requested to exemplify and lecture on the 1st degree of Masonry on Tuesday night, the 17th inst.

It was accordingly so done and Past Masters Ginn and Brent, at the meeting of December 10th, exemplified the work of the first degree. But there is this interesting notation in the minutes of that meeting: "R. W. Deputy Grand Master Harman and R. W. Grand Junior Warden Terry also lectured in the same degree". These Brethren were thanked and the Lodge resolved, that Brothers Colonel Harman and Captain Terry be requested to lecture on any branch of Masonry they chose on December 24th "if within the length of their cable tow to be present". These programs were carried out accordingly and Brothers Harman and Terry exemplified the Fellow Craft and Master Mason degrees on Christmas eve of 1861 as requested. They were asked also to lecture the Lodge again on Tuesday, January 7, 1862, but the sequel of events decreed that it was not "in the length of their cable tow to be present". Hence, the only business transacted by the Lodge on the latter date was the reading of the minutes of the previous communication.

It is clear, that events were taking place swiftly in the Winchester area at this time, since no more Lodge meetings were held after February, 1862 for considerably more than a year. The town was in the hands of the Federal forces for much of that period and Lodge meetings (as well as other assemblies of the local citizens) were forbidden without express permission. An attempt was made to hold a communication of the Lodge on February 5, 1862, but the brief minutes of that occasion state merely the following: "This being the regular meeting of the Lodge. No quorum present". On March 12, 1862 occurred the first occupation of Winchester by Federal forces during the War Between the States. General Banks was the commander of the occupying forces this time and there was consternation among the inhabitants as he approached, no one knowing just what fate the town would meet while in the hands of the enemy. Some presumed that it would be burned and all expected that private business would come to a virtual standstill through confiscation of public and private property and other extreme war measures.

The Bank of the Valley, one of several financial institutions in Winchester, sent its cash and some of its records to a bank in Baltimore just prior to the arrival of the Federals. Baltimore was at that time located in neutral territory and Brother Edwin S. Brent, a bookkeeper in the Bank of the Valley, was entrusted with this important mission. Brother Brent was likewise Junior Warden of Hiram Lodge during that year. The significance of this event will appear later in our story.

The reader is now asked to pass in his imagination from March, 1862 to April, 1863, during all of which time there were no formal Masonic activities of any kind in Winchester. Then, on April 20, 1863 the Lodge suddenly resumed its labors, *undoubtedly with the permission of the Federal authorities*, though we are not told in the minutes exactly how this permission was obtained. On the date mentioned, however, John B. T. Reed presided as Master and there were two visiting Brethren, L. Moss, of Lodge No. 2, Philadelphia (a very historic Lodge), and P. Coborne, of Lodge No. 105, Sharpsburg, Maryland (where a terrific battle had been fought between the Federals and Confederates on September 17, 1862, called by some historians the "bloodiest single day's battle of the entire war"). These two visitors were examined at the altar in the presence of the Lodge (only eight of the Winchester Brethren were in attendance) and were admitted to visit. The following resolutions were then adopted unanimously:

> RESOLVED, That we hail all Ancient, Free & Accepted Masons in regular standing as *Brothers* and that the members be authorized to invite any such to visit any future meeting of this Lodge ......
> RESOLVED, That, until further order, the regular communications of this Lodge shall be held on every Tuesday and Friday night.

A committee was appointed to provide better lights for the Lodge room and the Secretary was ordered to furnish a list of the Lodge members to the Tyler, who was directed to give them all proper notice of the meetings as far as this might be possible under prevailing conditions. This and subsequent meetings were held in a room rented for the purpose somewhere on Loudoun Street, as far as is now known. At any rate, they were not held in the Mason Hall, since this and the entire Market House had been commandeered by the Federal authorities.

It will be seen that the Brethren had set for themselves a very heavy schedule, which required the holding of two meetings weekly. For the most part this program was carried out as planned until June 12, 1863, when the work of the Lodge was again interrupted and there was no further meeting until November 28, 1864. The Secretary during the 1863 period of activity was Alfred P. White and he has left a fairly accurate record of what took place at the 30 meetings held during the months of April, May, and June of that year. We give herewith a summary of these meetings as follows:

War and Reconstruction

Date	Winchester Brethren	Visitors	Work
April 20	8	2	None
April 21	8	1	Lecture on E. A. degree
April 24	9	5	E. A. degree (1)
April 28	8	5	M. M. degree (1)
May 1	8	13	None
May 8	7	11	E. A. degree (7)
May 9	8 (also others)	7	F. C. degree (1)
May 11	7	0	F. C. degree (2)
			M. M. degree (2)
May 12	8	8	F. C. degree (3)
May 13	7	0	F. C. degree (1)
			M. M. degree (1)
May 15	4	3 (also others)	M. M. degree (1)
May 19	5	3	M. M. degree (1)
May 20	3	5 "	E. A. degree (2)
			M. M. degree (1)
May 21	6 (also others)	5 "	E. A. degree (1)
			M. M. degree (1)
May 22	3 (also others)	4	E. A. degree (1)
May 23	4 " "	2 "	E. A. degree (2)
			F. C. degree (4)
			M. M. degree (1)
May 25	7 " "	4 "	F. C. degree (2)
			M. M. degree (2)
May 25 (second meeting)	3 " "	4 "	M. M. degree (3)
May 26	5 " "	3 "	E. A. degree (1)
			F. C. degree (1)
			M. M. degree (2)
May 27	2	4	E. A. degree (1)
			F. C. degree (1)
			M. M. degree (1)
May 28	?	?	E. A. degree (1)
			F. C. degree (1)
			M. M. degree (1)
May 29	?	?	E. A. degree (1)
May 30	2 " "	3	F. C. degree (1)
			M. M. degree (1)
June 1	4 (also others)	2 "	F. C. degree (1)
			M. M. degree (1)
June 2	5 " "	3 "	None (election of officers)

June 5	4	7	E. A. degree (1)
			F. C. degree (1)
			M. M. degree (1)
June 8	10	19	E. A. degree (2)
June 9	6	11	E. A. degree (1)
			F. C. degree (2)
June 10	5	10	E. A. degree (1)
			F. C. degree (2)
			M. M. degree (2)
June 12	4	6	M. M. degree (2)

The totals for the period are as follows: E. A. degree, 23; F. C. degree, 23; M. M. degree, 25.

An interesting item in the minutes of May 1st was the presentation of a handsome copy of the Holy Bible to the Lodge by Brother J. B. McDonald, a resident of Columbia City, Indiana and a native of Virginia. On May 21st Brother J. B. T. Reed was voted an honorarium of $50.00 for his zeal in carrying on the work of the Lodge under very trying circumstances. The total receipts of the Lodge during this brief period of activity amounted to $445.00. Most of the members of the Federal forces receiving degrees at this time requested to be allowed to withdraw when they left Winchester and this permission was granted. Fifteen of these are listed in the minutes of May 26th, all being officers except two.

This happy sequence of events was rudely interrupted by the approach of the Confederate forces under the leadership of General R. S. Ewell, who took the town on June 14th and marched into it in triumph on the day following (June 15, 1863).

The town continued to change hands during the ensuing months and the condition of affairs was so uncertain, that no work was done by the Lodge. Finally, the Federals took Winchester for the last time on September 19, 1864 and held it until well after the close of the war. Their hold was threatened only once (in October, 1864) when the Confederates under General Jubal A. Early came as far as Cedar Creek but were repulsed—an incident made famous in the poem, "Sheridan's Ride", which does not adhere strictly to the facts, however.

Following the battle of Cedar Creek conditions in Winchester become once more relatively quiet. They remained so, in fact, until the end of the war, since, as already stated, the

Confederates never again threatened the Federals in their Winchester stronghold. Edwin S. Brent, who had remained in Baltimore for most of the preceding two years and more, now returned to Winchester. He and several other members of Hiram Lodge, particularly George Legge (or Legg), the Secretary, endeavored to get permission to open the Lodge, which had been closed since June of 1863. General Phil Sheridan was in command of the town at that time and it was extremely difficult to obtain an interview with him.

Remembering that he had had some business acquaintance with the Honorable Montgomery Blair in Baltimore, while a sojourner there, Brother Edwin S. Brent now wrote to Mr. Blair for a letter of introduction to General Sheridan. Mr. Blair was a Marylander by birth and was then Postmaster General in President Lincoln's cabinet. The letter came in due course and proved an "open sesame" for Brothers Brent and Legge. They were ushered without delay into Sheridan's presence in the northeast room of the Federal headquarters, formerly the residence of Mr. Lloyd Logan, a tobacconist, now the Elk's Home. General Sheridan was surrounded by orderlies and members of his staff. After presenting their credentials, the two Brethren stated, that their mission was to request permission to re-open the Masonic Lodge. The request was refused peremptorily by Sheridan, which was not surprising in view of his known religious and political affiliations.

At this point a surgeon on Sheridan's staff, Dr. C. H. Allen, a member of Aurora Lodge of Vermont, espoused the cause of the visitors and told General Sheridan, that he thought it would be a wise move to allow the re-opening of the Lodge, since it would permit many of the officers and soldiers in his army, which was encamped just to the south of Winchester, to mingle in a fraternal way with the local people and thereby remove some of the bitter feeling, which was being manifested by the townspeople toward the Union forces. Dr. Allen further stated, that he himself was a Mason and Past Master of his Lodge in Vermont, promising that he would be present at every

Lodge meeting and would see that nothing inimical to the government of the United States would occur at these meetings. In addition he ventured the belief, that some of the officers of Sheridan's army were desirous of receiving the Masonic degrees while encamped in the Winchester vicinity. Thus the desired permission was obtained, though very reluctantly, and Dr. Allen never had occasion to report to the General, that his confidence had been violated in the slightest degree.

We now come to one of the most interesting periods of the history of Hiram Lodge. The first meeting held under the permissive order issued by General Sheridan took place on November 28, 1864. The minutes of this meeting and of all others between that date and June 24, 1865, when the Union occupation was virtually concluded, are fortunately still in existence. A complete list of the Brethren receiving degrees in the Lodge between these two dates is appended to this chapter. The list contains 231 names and is its own best commentary. Nearly all of these candidates came from the Federal forces, though some from Winchester and Frederick County are included. Most of those belonging to the Union army naturally requested their dimits as soon as they were raised, although a few waited until long afterwards to do this. We include the dates of raising and of dimitting, also the home addresses so far as these are available. By far the most prominent and important name in the list is that of William McKinley, at that time a Captain, later a Major, and still later President of the United States. An account of his visit to Winchester while he was President will be found in a later chapter of this book. He received the E. A. degree as one of five candidates on May 1, 1865, the F. C. degree as one of four candidates on May 2d, and the M. M. degree as one of four candidates on May 3, 1865. The degree was conferred on May 3d by Brother John B. T. Reed, who had been Master of the Lodge during the entire war (at least at such periods as it had worked) and who little realized on that eventful evening, that he was raising a future President of the United States, a Brother who was also destined to fall a martyr to an assassin's hand.

WAR AND RECONSTRUCTION 103

One further comment should be made at this point concerning the list appended to this chapter. In the Lodge minute book of that period every Brother, who received one or more degrees from Hiram Lodge, was required to subscribe his name and address. In many cases the candidate also gave his rank as well. There are in this same minute book the signatures of many of the visiting Brethren, most of whom came from the North, of course, and many of them added the names of the Lodges from which they hailed. Since all of the meetings of these unsettled months were occupied with receiving and ballotting upon petitions and with conferring degrees, we do not attempt here to include further details regarding them. The full story can be easily inferred by the reader if he will take the time to study carefully the list at the end of this chapter.

By St. John the Baptist's Day in 1865 the affairs of the Lodge began to show signs of resuming their normal course. There are few names of visiting Brethren and most of the Federal soldiers, who had received degrees in the Lodge, had departed. The annual election of officers was held but there was no other business of importance transacted at this meeting. Of course, there was no procession or other public observance of the day. At the immediately following meetings more petitions were received from local candidates than at any time for several years and there was, naturally, considerable degree work. At the meeting of July 31st a long report was presented by the committee previously appointed to "invest the surplus funds of the Lodge", of which committee Judge Richard Parker, a future Grand Master of Virginia, was a member. In this report it is noted, that the Lodge had received between November 28, 1864 and June 26, 1865 some $4044.00 in United States funds in addition to $40.00 in Virginia bank notes and $60.00 in Confederate currency. We shall see, that it was from these funds that the Brethren were able largely to finance the erection of the present Masonic Temple in Winchester, an account of which will be given shortly.

On November 6, 1865 it was voted, that the dues of the

Lodge members commence with January 1, 1866. As of January 22, 1866 there were 62 members on the rolls and on February 5th we find the first reference in the minutes to the proposal to erect a new Masonic Hall. On that date a committee reported in favor of having the Common Council of Winchester erect a new Lodge room on the second story of the market house and outlined the conditions, under which this objective could be attained. The report was adopted, a building committee was appointed, and another committee was designated to "collect funds to beautify our new Hall". However, the project does not seem to have made much progress, for, on July 2, 1866, resolutions were offered with a view to continuing the use of the old hall and of making the necessary alterations for that purpose. In opposition to these resolutions William R. Denny, Master of the Lodge at that time, suggested, that it might be for the good of Masonry in Winchester for the Brethren to consider the purchase of an independent site for the erection of an entirely new building; and further, that "the property of Mrs. Richardson, occupied as a store by Bro. H. C. Krebs, could be purchased for the sum of $3,000.00, also the building we now occupy at the sum of $3,500.00". The reference to the latter building should be explained by stating, that the Federal authorities had commandeered the market house during their occupancy of the town and the Lodge meetings had been transferred to the building now numbered 172 North Loudoun Street. It was at this location, that William McKinley received the Masonic degrees as previously mentioned. After considerable discussion it was voted to appoint a committee, with the Master as chairman, to examine further into the possibilities of his suggestion.

On July 6th, four days later, this committee made a lengthy report to the Brethren, upon which both propositions (remaining in the old hall or erecting a new one) were discussed at some length and, apparently, with considerable feeling. The votes on both proposals are recorded by names and the motion to remain in the old hall was lost by a vote of 14 to 11. But by the same division the motion to purchase the property of Mrs. Richardson was also lost. Thus the entire matter was left for the time being *in statu quo*, so to speak. Nothing further was done until September 3d, when a resolution was offered, "that a committee of five be appointed......to consider and determine upon providing a comfortable hall for the use of this Lodge"— a very diplomatic way of re-opening a subject so full of dynamite, we think—and this resolution was adopted. On November 5th the report of this committee was called for but, upon vote of the Lodge, it was given further time in accordance with the request of its chairman. Meanwhile, there was another element injected into the situation by a suggestion, that a new stairway be erected to the old hall, so that it could be used at once. From the entries in the minutes it would appear that the Lodge was meeting at the "wigwam" of the Shawnee Tribe of Red Men, since there is reference to the suggested removal of the Lodge furniture from the old hall to the new Red Men's hall in return for the fact, that Hiram Lodge had permitted the Red Men to use the Lodge room for some time past. However, the exact status of this particular phase of the matter is not altogether clear.

By March 4, 1867 the Brethren must have tired of discussing a matter, which was getting them nowhere, for at that meeting there was an attendance of 38 members, 35 of whom voted for and 3 against the adoption of the following proposal, which was submitted by the Master, Brother W. R. Denny, and Brother T. B. Wood:

> Brethren: We have bought the Miller lot on Loudoun Street for Hiram Lodge No. 21 conditionally as follows, subject to the approval of the Lodge. It has 32 feet front, depth 189 feet—it includes the Ware House, a wide alley back, and egress from Market Street. The price is $110 per front foot, making the entire cost $3520. Payment as follows: as much cash as we can pay down, the balance of one-third in 90 days, one-third in six months, and the remaining third in twelve months. On the two last payments longer time can be had if desired; interest on deferred payments from the day of purchase.
>
> We have obtained a substantial subscription of gifts to the Lodge of sufficient amount in connection with what we have in money, notes, and stocks to pay for the lot.

Brother Thos. B. Wood proffers us a loan of Four Thousand Dollars, to be furnished through the summer as we may want it, to build the Temple—he to have a lien on the premises and to receive the income from the building until he is paid.

The $4,000 will be ample in connection with private gifts, the cornerstone and dedicatory services, and what may be received from new members—Initiations, Passing, and Raising.

It is supposed by competent judges that the income from the building in five years will pay the entire debt.

Therefore, we move that Hiram Lodge No. 21, A. F. & A. Masons, accept and approve the purchase of the lot at the price named for the purpose of building thereon a Masonic Temple to belong to and owned by said Hiram Lodge No. 21 forever. Said Temple to be built as soon as practicable.

A building committee was appointed consisting of five members to carry out the terms of the above letter and was empowered to utilize the assets of the Lodge in so doing, but only after the employment of a competent architect to prepare a "full draft of a plan of the building and all the proper specifications". Another committee was appointed to "procure furniture and fixtures for the new hall". Thus the movement leading to the erection of the present temple was now well under way. At the same time, the Lodge gave its assent to the Royal Arch Chapter "to fit up and take possession of the old hall if they should deem it necessary for the accommodation of the work of the Chapter". The reader is referred to page 119 for a full discussion of the Lodge's rights in this matter.

As soon as the intentions of the Lodge to erect a new building got about town, there was great interest manifested on every hand and applications for the leasing of space began to come in. Nor was that all. At the meeting of April 1, 1867 nine petitions for the degrees were received and six other applicants received the E. A. degree that evening. Thirteen petitions were presented on May 6th and there was already discussion at this same meeting as to arrangements for laying the cornerstone of the new structure. It was announced that Brother William H. Travers, of Charlestown, was to be the orator of the occasion, and that

Lodges in Baltimore, the District of Columbia, and the surrounding Virginia territory would be invited, likewise all the other Masonic bodies of Virginia. The date set for the occasion was May 29, 1867. Various committees were appointed to make the necessary preparations, the business men of the town were asked to close their establishments between the hours of 10:00 A. M. and 2:00 P. M., and several special communications of the Lodge were held during the preceding week for the purpose of conferring the degrees on the large number of candidates already elected.

The program was carried out as planned and eight pages of the large minute book are given over to a minute description of the ceremonies. Elaborate printed programs had been prepared and the minutes contain minute descriptions of the order of procession, scene at the temple, and the address of Brother William H. Travers. More than twenty Lodges from half a dozen states were represented as well as Royal Arch Chapters and the Winchester Commandery of Knights Templar. It was without doubt one of the greatest celebrations ever held in the town of Winchester up to that time. As of June 1, 1867 the roster of members of Hiram Lodge contained 117 names, the largest number in its entire existence to that date, thus reflecting the tremendous amount of interest, which the building of the new temple had created. At the meeting of June 3d, seven new petitions were presented, various resolutions of thanks were adopted, and the bills incident to the cornerstone laying were presented and ordered paid. These amounted to $183.68. New officers were elected on June 22d with Joseph M. Ginn as Master, Richard Parker as Senior Warden, and Thomas B. Moore as Junior Warden. Brothers John Kerr and C. A. B. Coffroth were re-elected Treasurer and Secretary respectively. No special observance of St. John's Day was held, due, we suppose, to the fact, that the cornerstone laying ceremonies had been held so recently.

The minutes of several meetings held at this period contain grateful acknowledgements to various Lodges in other jurisdictions, which had contributed to the temple fund of Hiram Lodge in response to a printed appeal broadcast some time previously. A Lodge in Louisiana is noted as contributing $50.00 and many other Lodges sent in smaller amounts. The remainder of the year 1867 was occupied with the usual regular (also many special) communications, at nearly all of which there was work in one or more of the degrees. At the meeting of January 6, 1868 Brother W. R. Denny presented to the Lodge two gavels, two snuff boxes, a rough ashlar, and a perfect ashlar, which he had brought back from the Holy Land. Mark Twain, incidentally, had been in the same party and recounts his experiences in this connection in *Innocents Abroad*. He mentions Brother Denny at least once in this narrative, a fact of which the latter was very proud.

Suitable thanks were returned to Brother Denny for his valuable gifts and it was proposed (with his consent) to dispose of the two snuff boxes for the benefit of the Lodge by means of a lottery. Tickets were sold at $1.00 each and a total of $61.00 less approximately $5.00 for expenses was realized from the transaction. At the meeting of May 4, 1868 the building committee reported that the new building had been mortgaged in the course of construction for a total of $9,307.57. It was voted at this time to hold the dedication and centennial ceremonies (1768-1868) combined on some date in the month of July following. At this same meeting (May 4th) a beautiful copy of the Oxford edition of the Holy Bible was presented to Hiram Lodge by Maryland Lodge No. 120, of Baltimore.

The dedicatory ceremonies were held on July 22, 1868 as planned. However, the full account of the occasion is not to be found in the Lodge records unfortunately, but we know from other accounts that the celebration was in every respect a most successful one. In the minutes of this same period we find only the briefest references to the beautiful paintings, which adorn the walls of the present Lodge room. It is to be regretted that the story is not more fully recorded. We quote from the minutes as follows:

(January 6, 1868) The Chairman of the committee for furnishing the new Hall reported that the workmen to frescoe the room had arrived, and asked authority of the Lodge to negotiate a loan to provide furniture, &c.

(February 3, 1868) Ordered, That the Secretary correspond with Prof. Knapp of the Peabody Institute, requesting him to extend the leave of absence granted to Mr. Ango, artist, at work on the Masonic Temple.

(August 3, 1868) On motion of Bro. Wm. R. Denny, the Chairman of the Building Committee be and he is hereby authorized to pay Mr. Cebring(?) the balance of his bill for frescoing the temple building.

This is all we have been able to find regarding this matter so far as the actual Lodge records are concerned. It is reported, however, that the artist (Mr. Ango) was sent to Winchester under arrangements made by the Lodge with the Peabody Institute of Baltimore. He was either so careless in the amount of time spent on the work or was so addicted to the use of intoxicants, that the project required a much longer time than was originally estimated. Finally, various members of the Lodge made it their business to escort the artist from his room each morning, see that he had his breakfast and then reported to the Lodge room, locked him in the room, carried his noon meals to him there, and escorted him to his supper and then to bed at night. It was only in this way that the work was finally completed after arrangements were made with Professor Knapp, of the Peabody Institute, to grant further time for this purpose. It is stated, that the artist in question was allowed a certain amount of liquid refreshment while he was actually at work, this being apparently necessary to furnish him with the requisite inspiration to enable him to carry on his labors. At any rate, the final results proved to be of such a marvelous character, that the paintings remain to this day the admiration of all visitors to the Lodge room. We believe, that they constitute one of the most unique collections of its kind to be found anywhere. Illustrations of some of these paintings will be found elsewhere in this volume.

The year 1869 passed without events of great significance.

The Master, Dr. William S. Love, was chosen as the Lodge's representative to Grand Lodge that year with Brother Richard Parker as his alternate. Judge Parker was one of the Lodge's most distinguished members of his day and became Grand Master of Virginia Masons in 1876. On January 3, 1870 the Royal Arch Chapter was granted the use of the new Lodge room for the purpose of holding a special convocation, and on January 31st the same privilege was extended to Winchester Commandery also. It would appear from the record, that both of these bodies were in process of reorganization at that time following the inactivity caused by the War Between the States. They naturally wished to avail themselves of the use of the new Temple's facilities for this purpose. On June 23, 1870 the annual election of officers was held and Dr. William S. Love was continued in the office of Master for another year. The usual public observance of the St. John's Days seems not to have been resumed after the war and there is little further reference to these anniversaries in any of the subsequent Lodge minutes until our own time. On December 5th the Lodge voted to send a committee of five to a convention to be held at Martinsburg, W. Va. for the purpose of establishing a Masonic Benefit Association if the convention should deem this to be advisable. The object of this association was the relief of the widows and orphans of Master Masons. We suspect that the need was becoming more and more acute at the time, particularly as one of the after-effects of the war. The last meeting of the year 1870 was held on December 16th, at which time Judge Parker made a full report to the Lodge as to the proceedings of Grand Lodge, from which he had just returned.

APPENDIX I TO CHAPTER VIII
DEGREES CONFERRED IN WINCHESTER
HIRAM LODGE NO. 21
UNDER FEDERAL OCCUPATION

GROUP I
(April 20-June 12, 1863)

NAME	DATE RECEIVED			DATE
	E. A.	F. C.	M. M.	DIMITTED
James Adair	(Gettysburg, Penna.)		May 23	May 26, 1863
H. L. Baker	May 23	May 23	May 25	May 26, 1863
F. L. Ballard	May 28	May 28	May 28	
Lampson P. Bryant	June 9	June 9	June 12	
†C. F. Eichelberger	June 5	June 5	June 5	August 5, 1870
Milton A. Ellis	May 23	May 23	May 26	May 26, 1863
Charles Green	May 20	May 30	May 30	
Hamilton L. Karr	May 21	May 23	May 25	May 26, 1863
William M. Kerr (Lt.)	May 8	May 12	None	
†Isaac Krebs	(E. A., April 2, 1861; F. C., April 16, 1861)		April 28	*July 1, 1884
J. Lowry McGee	May 8	None	None	
Thornton Malory	May 27	May 27	May 27	
James W. Moffett	(Clarksburg, Va.)	June 9	June 12	
Thomas Morley	June 8	June 10	June 10	
William T. Morris (Major)	May 8	May 12	May 20	May 26, 1863
William L. Moseley	May 8	May 12	May 19	May 26, 1863
Mark Poore	May 8	May 9	May 15	May 26, 1863
Harvey R. Reakirk	June 10	June 10	June 10	
Hiram L. Sibley (Lt.)	(Pomeroy, Ohio)		May 21	May 26, 1863
†John Stephenson	April 24	May 25	May 25	June 5, 1870
B. F. Stivers	May 29	June 1	June 1	

(†) Indicates petitioner resided in Winchester or near-by Virginia.

NAME	DATE RECEIVED			DATE
	E. A.	F. C.	M. M.	DIMITTED
Albert B. Teeters	May 8	May 11	May 11	May 26, 1863
James Washburn (Col.)	May 8 (?)	May 13	May 13	May 26, 1863
John F. Welch	May 20	May 23	May 25	May 26, 1863
‡Alfred P. White	(Affiliated June 9)			
Charles W. White (Capt.)	May 26	May 26	May 26	May 26, 1863
Thomas S. Wildes (Lt. Col.)	May 8	May 11 (?)	May 11(?)	May 26, 1863
A. W. Williams	May 22	May 25	May 25	May 26, 186.

(†) Indicates petitioner resided in Winchester or near-by Virginia.

(*) Isaac Krebs died on July 1, 1884. He is the only one listed above (except those Federal soldiers, who may have been killed in action or died from wounds or disease), who clung to Winchester Hiram Lodge "until death us do part".

(?) This mark following a date indicates that the actual date cannot be proved from the extant records. The Lodge minutes, however, do prove that the degree was conferred and the dates given are such as are not only probable but offer a reasonable explanation of the usually accurate Brother Alfred P. White's lapse in recording the events indicated.

(‡) Brother White, as is quite evident from the records, was a member of the Federal forces and not a local Brother. He served as a Secretary for all the meetings held from April 20 to June 2, 1863 with a few exceptions. At the election of officers held on the latter date he was elected Junior Warden and occupied that station on June 8th and 9th (he was absent at the June 5th meeting). At the meeting on June 9th he applied for membership (by affiliation) in the Lodge and was elected; whereupon, another election was held to fill the office of Junior Warden and he was elected unanimously again to that office. At that time it seems, that the Secretary was remunerated by receiving 10% of all moneys he collected. At any rate, it was moved at the June 9th meeting, that Brother White be paid the customary 10% of all funds, which he had collected while serving as Secretary *pro tem*. A Brother Kern objected to this proposal, upon which the proposer reduced the amount to 8%, which was passed with all but Brother Kern voting in the affirmative. There is no further record of Brother White's connection with Hiram Lodge. It may be conjectured whether General Ewell "bagged" him and many others of the Northern Brethren when Winchester fell into Confederate hands on June 14 and 15, 1863.

Further Comment on Group I—It may interest the reader to know, that one other local man petitioned Hiram Lodge during this period, namely, John S Lupton. He presented his petition on May 21, 1863, was initiated an E. A. on July 17, 1865, received the F. C. degree on July 31, 1865, and was made a M. M on August 7, 1865. He received his dimit on February 17, 1871. It is quite probable that he submitted a second petition in 1865 due to the lapse of approximately two years after the first was presented.

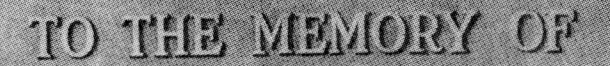

BRONZE TABLET TO THE MEMORY OF THE BRETHREN OF WINCHESTER LODGE NO. 12, ANCIENT YORK MASONS, WHO FELL IN THE WAR OF AMERICAN INDEPENDENCE. (See page 47)

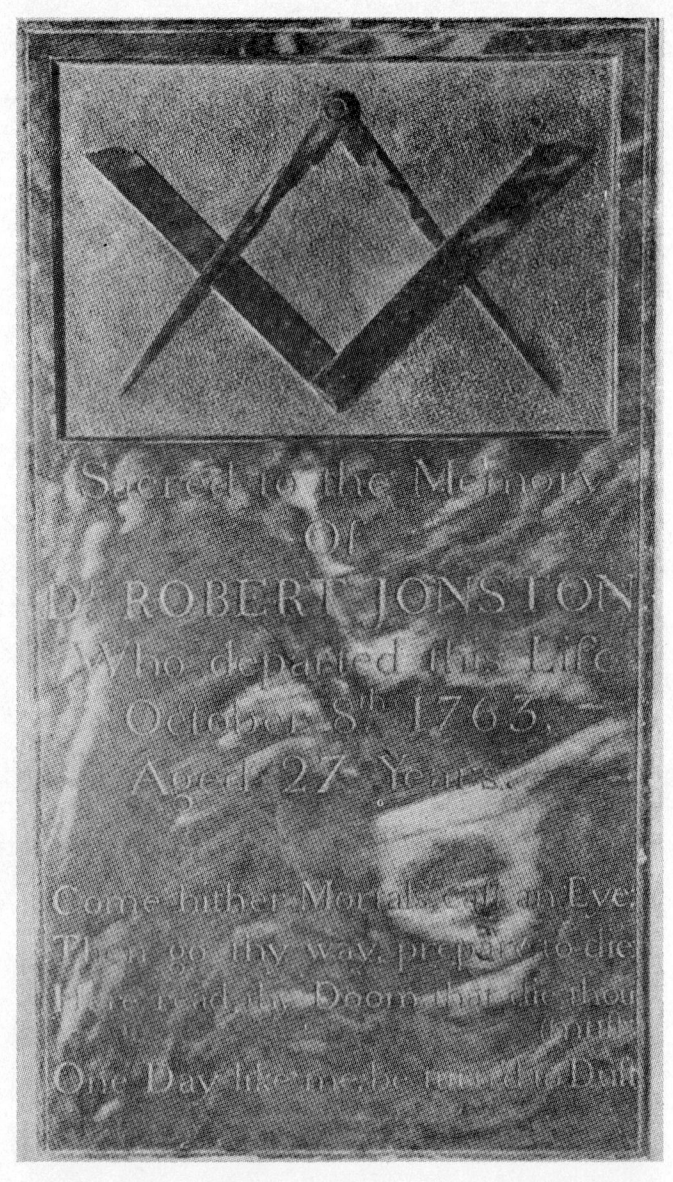

TABLET TO DR. ROBERT JONSTON ERECTED IN 1763 AND THE EARLIEST EXTANT EVIDENCE OF THE EXISTENCE OF FREEMASONRY IN WINCHESTER. (See page 16)

FREEMASONRY IN WINCHESTER VIRGINIA 111-b

GROUP II
(November 28, 1864 to June 24, 1865)

NAME	RESIDENCE	RECEIVED M. M. DEGREE	DIMITTED
†Rev. Jas. B. Averitt	Winchester	Mar. 24, 1865	
D. H Armstrong	Reed Creek, Wayne County, N. Y.	Dec. 24, 1864	
LeGrand Abbott	Brocklyn, N. Y.	Jan. 5, 1865	Jan., 1865
Moses Anker	Baltimore, Md.	Feb. 10, 1865	Feb. 18, 1865
Liberty C. Abbott	Jamestown, N. Y.	Mar. 30, 1865	Apr. 1, 1865
Simon S. Andrews	Biddeford,, Me.	Apr. 7, 1865	Apr. 7, 1865
O. W. Armstrong	Richfield Springs,, N. Y.	Apr. 8, 1865	
S. C. Atkinson	Salem, Washington County, Ind.	Apr. 14, 1865	Apr. 14, 1865
I. N. Broach	Brooklyn, N. Y.		
Rev. Wm. Brown— (Re'd. from Ioa Hill Lodge No. 63)		Dec. 2, 1864	Died Dec. 12, 1864
Edwin A. Bean	Norristown, Pa.	Dec. 7, 1864	Feb. 22, 1865
A. W. Bradberry		Dec. 17, 1864	Feb. 22, 1865
Joseph E. Barrett		Dec. 9, 1864	Jan. 22, 1865
W. R. Brownell		Dec. 9, 1864	Feb. 22, 1865
Herman Bendell	Albany, N. Y.	Dec. 12, 1864	Jan. 2, 1865
Daniel Brundage	Wayne County, Pa.	Dec. 20, 1864	Jan. 2, 1865
Dr. Geo. M. Burdett	Wilkes County, Pa.	Dec. 20, 1864	Sep. 11, 1865
Theo. W. Bean	Norristown, Pa.	Jan. 6, 1865	Jan. 2, 1865
John S. Brigham	Boston, Mass.	Jan. 10, 1865	Feb., 1865
†Oliver M. Brown	Winchester	Jan. 25, 1865	
†Robert L. Baker	Frederick County, Va.	Apr. 8, 1865	
Seth Bonney	Sterling, Mass.	Jan. 26, 1865	Feb., 1865
N. A. Branson	Baltimore, Md.	Feb. 3, 1865	Feb., 1865

(†) Indicates petitioner resided in Winchester or near-by Virginia

NAME	RESIDENCE	RECEIVED M. M. DEGREE	DIMITTED
W.m. W. Blackmer	Boston, Mass.	Feb. 14, 1865	Feb., 1865
Wm. P. Brown	Memphis, N. Y.	Mar. 11, 1865	Mar. 13, 1865
Geo. A. Burtis	Syosset, Queens County, N. Y.	Mar. 17, 1865	Mar. 13, 1865
J. H. Brock	Brooklyn, N. Y.	Mar. 25, 1865	Mar. 28, 1865
James W. Brown	Winthrop, Me.	Apr. 3, 1865	
Henry Burnett	New York City	Apr. 4, 1865	Apr. 4, 1865
W. A. Baldwin	Brooklyn, N. Y.	Apr. 3, 1865	Apr. 3, 1865
Horace Binney	Philadelphia, Pa.	May 5, 1865	May 13, 1865
W. A. Belcher	Ironton, Ohio	May 13, 1865	
†Albert L. Barrett	Winchester	May 13, 1865	
†Dr. Daniel Conrad	Winchester	Dec. 7, 1864	
T. G. Colt	Pittsfield, Mass.	Dec. 12, 1864	Jan. 2, 1865
John Canfield	Newton, Md.	Jan. 2, 1865	Feb. 16, 1865
Warren Chapman, Jr.	New York City	Jan. 14, 1865	Feb. 22, 1865
James C. Cooley	Long Meadow, Mass.	Jan. 13, 1865	Feb., 1865
W. H. Clinton	Baltimore, Md.	Jan. 19, 1865	Feb., 1865
A. I. Coope	Cayensca, N. Y.	Feb. 2, 1865	
L. W. Clarke	Winchester, Conn.	Feb. 16, 1865	
Jerome E. Cross	Methuen, Mass.	Feb. 21, 1865	Feb. 24, 1865
L. D. H. Currie	New York City	Feb. 3, 1865	Mar. 2, 1865
†P. A. Clark	Frederick County, Va.	Mar. 23, 1865	
L. F. Cummings	Portland, Me.	Mar. 30, 1865	Apr. 1, 1865
E. R. Clarke	Lowell, Mass.	Apr. 3, 1865	Apr. 4, 1865
†Meredith Capper	Frederick, County, Va.	Apr. 19, 1865	
James Cahill	San Antonio, Texas	Apr. 23, 1865	Apr. 2, 1866
John R. Craig	Cincinnati, Ohio	May 3, 1865	May 3, 1865
P. D. Cox	New Harmony, Ind.	Apr. 12, 1865	
J. R. Capron	Warren County, Pa.	Apr. 12, 1865	May 3, 1865
†Chas. L. Crum	Winchester	May 19, 1865	
Edward G. Dike		Dec. 1, 1864	
Geo. W. Divinger	Port Jervis, N. Y.	Dec. 8, 1864	Feb., 1865
Coe Duland	Cambridge, Mass.	Dec. 12, 1864	Jan., 1865

(†) Indicates petitioner resided in Winchester or near-by Virginia

Appendix 1 to Chapter VIII 113

NAME	RESIDENCE	RECEIVED M. M. DEGREE	DIMITTED
†Joseph S. Denny	Winchester	Jan. 6, 1865	
†James H. Denny	Berkeley County, Va.	Jan. 23, 1865	
D. H. Darling	Painesville, Ohio	Jan. 17, 1865	
D. H. Dickinson	New York City	Apr. 4, 1865	Apr. 4, 1865
Jabis T. Denning	Machaic Falls, Me.	Apr. 7, 1865	May 18, 1865
Owen Edwards		Dec. 7, 1864	Jan. 2, 1865
William Egan		Feb. 20, 1865	
James D. Earles	Grand Rapids, Mich.	Feb. 21, 1865	Feb. 23, 1865
Owen Emmitt	Hammondsport, N. Y.	Apr. 15, 1865	Apr. 15, 1865
James F. Fitz	Niagara Falls, N. Y.	Jan. 13, 1865	Feb., 1865
Chas. E. Fisher	N. Attleboro, Mass.	Dec. 17, 1864	Feb. 2, 1865
Herbert Fearn	Brooklyn, N. Y.	Jan. 2, 1865	Jan., 1865
Gen. Jas D. Fessenden	Portland, Me.	Jan. 13, 1865	
F. M. Fordyce	Morgantown, W. Va.	Feb. 17, 1865	Feb. 18, 1865
Eugene W. Ferris	Lowell, Mass.	Feb. 14, 1865	Feb., 1865
Chas H. Ferrell	Washington, D. C.	Feb. 21, 1865	Feb. 25, 1865
F. M. Frame	Elam, Pa.	Mar. 25, 1865	
D. M. Fraleigh	Catskill, N. Y.	Apr. 4, 1865	Apr. 4, 1865
David R. Goetchius	New York State	Dec. 10, 1864	Jan. 2, 1865
†Joseph M. Ginn	Winchester	Jan. 2, 1865	
Richard H. Goodall	Stafford, N. Y.	Feb. 24, 1865	Feb. 24, 1865
Adelbert E. Gould	Rushford, N. Y.	Feb. 27, 1865	Feb. 27, 1865
†Chas. L. Ginn	Winchester	Mar. 25, 1865	
Reed Gleason	Morrisville, N. Y.	Mar. 23, 1865	Jun. 10, 1867
Reed B. Grainger	Eastport, Me.	Apr. 7, 1865	May 29, 1865
Gilbert G. Green	Tarrytown, N. Y.	Apr. 7, 1865	
John C. Gray	Belmont, Me.	Apr. 7, 1865	Apr. 7, 1865
Elwood Grist	Lancaster, Pa.	May 5, 1865	
Dr. T. V. Hayden		Dec. 6, 1864	Mar. 10, 1865
C. I. Hackett		Dec. 20, 1864	Jan. 2, 1865
A. F. Hayden	Buffalo, N. Y.	Jan. 2, 1865	Jan. 2, 1865
E. D. Hoffman	New York City	Jan. 10, 1865	Apr. 10, 1865
J. W. Havener	(E. A.)	Feb. 9, 1865	
E. L. Hamilton	Rochester, N. Y.	Mar. 7, 1865	Mar. 8, 1865

(†) Indicates petitioner resided in Winchester or near-by Virginia

NAME	RESIDENCE	RECEIVED M. M. DEGREE	DIMITTED
Russell Houghten	Lunenburg, Mass.	Feb. 17, 1865	Mar. 30, 1865
Joseph W. Hayden	Northport Island, N. Y.	Mar. 17, 1865	Mar. 20, 1865
Edward Harbison	Lainesville, Ind.	Apr. 12, 1865	Apr. 12, 1865
Edward S. Hay	Mt. Vernon, Ind.	Apr. 14, 1865	
Wm. H. Hudson	Coryden, Ind.	Apr. 14, 1865	
William Howard	Philadelphia, Pa.	May 8, 1865	May 9, 1865
K. Hester	(E.A.)	May 6, 1865	
John A. Irwin	Winchester	Jan. 6, 1865	
†Geo. E. Jenkins	Winchester	Jan. 10, 1865	
†Chas. S. Jenkins	North Chatham, Mass.	Feb. 16, 1865	Feb. 23, 1865
Amos G. Jones	Methuen, Mass.	Mar. 21, 1865	Apr. 8, 1865
Thos. B. Johnston	Lowell, Mass.	Apr. 7, 1865	Apr. 8, 1865
Jno. E. Jewett	Zanesville, Ohio	Apr. 15, 1865	Apr. 15, 1865
Daniel W. Jones	North Weave, N. M.	Apr. 26, 1865	May 6, 1865
Robert Kay	Lainesville, Ind.		
G. E. Kibbe	New York City	Dec. 12, 1864	Jan. 2, 1865
Geo. Knowlton (by request of Mt. Vernon Lodge No. 3, Albany N. Y.)	Albany, N. Y.	Dec. 29, 1864	Jan. 2, 1865
†Henry Kinzel	Winchester	Jan. 6, 1865	
Horatio C. King	New York City	Jan. 6, 1865	Jan., 1865
†Y. A. Kirwan	Harpers Ferry, Va.	Jan. 4, 1865	Feb. 2, 1865
Chas. King	Washington, D. C.	Jan. 30, 1865	Feb. 26, 1867
Robert Kelly	Monroe, Michigan	Feb. 24, 1865	Feb. 24, 1865
Thos. D. Kneeland	S. Randolph, Mass.	Mar. 11, 1865	Apr. 1, 1865
I. C. Kilingsmith	Frederick, Md.	Mar. 25, 1865	Mar. 25, 1865
Jos. H. Kinsley	Boston, Mass.	Apr. 3, 1865	May 1, 1865
Jos. Klenfield			
H. L. Knorr	Scranton, Pa.	May 8, 1865	May 9, 1865
Jno. L. Lupton	New York City	Dec. 17, 1864	Jan. 2, 1865
Geo. F. Linquist	Yonkers, N. Y.	Dec. 14, 1864	Feb., 1865

(†) Indicates petitioner resided in Winchester or near-by Virginia

Appendix 1 to Chapter VIII

NAME	RESIDENCE	RECEIVED M. M. DEGREE	DIMITTED
George Lloyd	New York City	Dec. 17, 1864	Jan. 2, 1865
Wm. R. Lamb		Feb. 2, 1865	
Wm. H. Lannis	York, Pa.	Feb. 17, 1865	Mar. 13, 1865
W. B. Laithe	Troy, N. Y.	Apr. 6, 1865	Apr., 1865
Geo. W. Lamb	Crawfordsville, Ind.	Apr. 15, 1865	Apr. 15, 1865
Wm. H. McKele	New York City		
Rev. Frank C. Morse		Dec. 2, 1864	Jan. 2, 1865
Henry Miller	New York City	Dec. 15, 1864	Jan. 2, 1865
R. K. McMurray	Baltimore, Md.	Dec. 14, 1864	Dec. 29, 1864
Thos. W. Moore	Staten Island, N. Y.	Dec. 29, 1864	Jan. 2, 1865
Myron D. Mather	Castleton, Vt.	Jan. 5, 1865	Feb., 1865
Robert McElroy (Elected Honorary Member Jan. 13, 1865)	New York City	Mar. 24, 1865	Feb. 22, 1865
†P. M. McGraw	Harpers Ferry, Va.	Jan. 14, 1865	Feb. 22, 1865
John P. Morris	New York City	Jan. 24, 1865	Feb., 1865
Frank McConaughty	Philadelphia, Pa.	Feb. 3, 1865	May 7, 1865
J. L. McGee		Feb. 8, 1865	
Geo. W. McVicker	Morgantown, W. Va.	Feb. 14, 1865	
†Archibald McCarroll, Jr.	Brucetown, Frederick County, Va.	Feb. 22, 1865	
†Jas. N. McKericher	Winchester	Mar. 18, 1865	
Wm. A. Mallery	Baltimore, Md.	Apr. 14, 1865	
John McIllwain	Washington, D. C.	Mar. 21, 1865	Apr. 4, 1865
A. B. Mead	Bridgeport, Vt.	Mar. 21, 1865	
†F. E. Meredith	Winchester	Mar. 25, 1865	
Isaac N. Mead	Amenia, N. Y.	Apr. 20, 1865	Apr. 21, 1865
Frederick Maes	Williamsburg, N. Y.	Apr. 4, 1865	
Edward Mahon	New York City	Apr. 7, 1865	
L. Murrin	Cincinnati, Ohio	Apr. 15, 1865	Apr. 15, 1865
William McKinley	Poland, Ohio	May 3, 1865	May 3, 1865
Alexander Moore	Galena, Ill.	Jun. 24, 1865	Jun. 24, 1865
N. M. Nowland	Washington, D. C.	Jan. 2, 1865	Feb. 22, 1865
Jas. N. Nunsbach	Baltimore, Md.	Jan. 21, 1865	
Andrew Naphier	New York City	Apr. 7, 1865	Apr. 17, 1865

(†) Indicates petitioner resided in Winchester or near-by Virginia

FREEMASONRY IN WINCHESTER VIRGINIA

NAME	RESIDENCE	RECEIVED M. M. DEGREE	DIMITTED
Geo. H. North	Philadelphia, Pa.	Apr. 12, 1865	Apr. 12, 1865
Thos. C. Neat	New York City	Mar. 11, 1865	Mar. 14, 1865
Patrick Oates	New Albany, Ind.	Apr. 14, 1865	
†Dr. Thos. Page	Winchester (Received)	Nov. 28, 1864	
†R. E. Parker	Winchester	Dec. 7, 1864	
O. C. Potter		Dec. 9, 1864	Feb., 1865
H. W. Pearsing	(E.A.)	Dec. 7, 1864	Jan. 2, 1865
Geo. B. Pommeroy		Dec. 7, 1864	Jan. 2, 1865
Wm. H. B. Post	New York City	Jan. 5, 1865	Jan. 5, 1865
Col. Lewis M. Peck	Brooklyn, N. Y.	Jan. 21, 1865	Feb. 16, 1865
Elias P. Pillett	Norwich, N. Y.	Feb. 3, 1865	Mar. 18, 1865
Chas. W. Patrick	Albany, N. Y.	Feb. 3, 1865	Feb., 1865
H. M. Pollard	Milwaukee, Wis.	Feb. 16, 1865	Mar. 9, 1865
Stephen D. Purdy	Detroit, Mich.	Feb. 10, 1865	Feb., 1865
Wm. B. Perkins	New Bedford, Mass.	Feb. 14, 1865	Feb., 1865
Wm. B. Porter	Brooklyn, N. Y.	Mar. 17, 1865	Mar. 20, 1865
L. F. Packard	Ischua, N. Y.	Mar. 21, 1865	Mar. 22, 1865
Geo. C. Pitcher	Jefferson, Me.	Apr. 3, 1865	Apr. 3, 1865
Byron I. Preston (Member of Valley Lodge No. 109, Rochester, N. Y.)	Rochester, N. Y.	May 19, 1865	Aug. 1, 1865
†Theo. Reed	Winchester		
Uriah Rorapaugh	Green County, N. Y.	Feb. 3, 1865	Mar. 20, 1865
Wm. W. Root		Dec. 26, 1864	Feb., 1865
Henry Rittenburg (By request of National Lodge No. 12, Washington, D. C.)	Washington, D. C.	Jan. 2, 1865	Jan. 2, 1865
Augustro Randell	Oshkosh, Wisc.	Apr. 4, 1865	Apr. 4, 1865
Geo. W. Rodgers	Brooklyn, N. Y.	Apr. 3, 1865	Apr. 3, 1865
W. F. Randolph	Philadelphia, Pa.	Apr. 8, 1865	Apr. 8, 1865
Geo. W. Riddle	Leavenworth, Md.	Apr. 12, 1865	Apr. 12, 1865

(†) Indicates petitioner resided in Winchester or near-by Virginia

Appendix 1 to Chapter VIII 117

NAME	RESIDENCE	RECEIVED M. M. DEGREE	DIMITTED
Robert Ray	Lainesville, Ind.	Apr. 14, 1865	Apr. 14, 1865
Byron L. Rolf	Albany, Green County, Wis.	Apr. 23, 1865	Apr. 23, 1865
William Russell, Jr.		Apr. 16, 1865	
Geo. E. Stone (Died at Harpers Ferry, April, 1865)		Dec. 1, 1864	Jan. 2, 1865
E. Smidt.		Dec. 15, 1864	Jan. 2, 1865
Dr. Arnold Steele	New York City	Dec. 17, 1864	Feb., 1865
Elijah Swift	Falmouth, Mass.	Dec. 12, 1864	Feb., 1865
Theo. M. Swift	Seymour, Conn.	Dec. 17, 1864	Jan. 2, 1865
John C. Shroeler	Sheneyville, Iowa	Jan. 5, 1865	Jan. 5, 1865
N. W. Schermerhorn	Chenango Couty, N. Y.	Feb. 16, 1865	Mar. 20, 1865
Jno. Scofield	Lubee Mill, Me.	Apr. 7, 1865	Mar. 20, 1865
Chas. B. Stone	Roxbury, Mass.	Apr. 3, 1865	Apr. 11, 1865
Wm. I. Stewart	New York City	Apr. 4, 1865	Apr. 4, 1865
Chas. C. Sawyer	West Cambridge, Mass.	Apr. 8, 1865	Apr. 8, 1865
H. B. Spencer	New Albany, Ind.	Apr. 13, 1865	Apr. 14, 1865
Jno. W. Slocum	Christiana, Pa.	Apr. 26, 1865	
Alfred M. Shegoge	New York City	May 5, 1865	May 13, 1865
George W. Seibert	Philadelphia, Pa.	Jun. 7, 1865	Aug. 8, 1865
R. W. Thomas	Oak Hill, N. C.	Dec. 26, 1864	
W. C. Thomas	New Bedford, Mass.	Dec. 27, 1864	Jan. 4, 1865
†James H. Triplett	Frederick County, Va.	Feb. 6, 1865	
James Thompson	Shelbyville, Ind.	Jan. 5, 1865	Jan., 1865
Anson K. Tower	Rochester, N. Y.	Feb. 3, 1865	Feb., 1865
A. F. Tremain	Gloucester, Mass.	Feb. 16, 1865	Mar. 9, 1865
Wm. Thompson		Feb. 23, 1865	
Richmond R. Titus	Groton, Mass.	Mar. 17, 1865	Mar. 20, 1865
John Thiel	New York City	Apr. 4, 1865	Apr. 11, 1865
H. Thompson		May 1, 1865	
Walter Url		Dec. 15, 1864	Jan. 2, 1865
E. E. Vaile	Richmond, Ind.	Mar. 30, 1865	Apr. 1, 1865
Frank Volker		Jun. 7, 1865	Jun. 24, 1865

(†) Indicates petitioner resided in Winchester or near-by Virginia

NAME	RESIDENCE	RECEIVED M. M. DEGREE	DIMITTED
Elisha M. White	Washington, D. C.	Dec. 2, 1864	Jan. 2, 1865
W. A. Weidenstine	Philadelphia, Pa.	Jan. 12, 1864	Jan. 2, 1865
Geo. S. Wicks	Caine, Green County, N. Y.	Jan. 14, 1865	Feb. 22, 1865
Thomas Worthey	Providence, R. I.	Feb. 6, 1865	Feb. 6, 1865
G. D. Weekes	Brooklyn, N. Y.	Feb. 17, 1865	Apr. 17, 1865
Jas. M. Willman	Lyndeborough, N. H.	Feb. 17, 1865	Feb. 18, 1865
Rev. B. F. Whitemer	Roxbury, Mass.	Mar. 7, 1865	Mar. 8, 1865
Frank T. Wilson	Lowell, Mass.	Apr. 3, 1865	Apr. 4, 1865
Artemus Witherly	Rochester, N. Y.	Apr. 4, 1865	Apr. 4, 1865
Geo. R. Whitmer	Warren, Pa.	Apr. 6, 1865	Apr. 6, 1865
Albert C. Wright		Apr. 7, 1865	Apr. 7, 1865
John H. Wright	Camden, N. Y.	Apr. 8, 1865	Apr. 8, 1865
J. P. Wallis	(E.A.)	Apr. 17, 1865	
John F. White	(E.A.)	Apr. 18, 1865	
Maurice Watkins	Newark, Ohio	May 3, 1865	May 3, 1865
Jno. B. Warrick	Ohio	May 13, 1865	Jun. 1, 1865
James M. White	Greenville, Ohio	May 19, 1865	Jun. 1, 1865
Eugene T. Buck	Carthage, N. Y.	Feb. 21, 1865	
R. W. Moore			Jan. 2, 1865
Chas. C. Graves			Feb. 2, 1865
H. K. Rehart			Apr. 4, 1865
L. W. Clark			Mar. 3, 1865
B. F. Stover			Feb. 24, 1865

Note: This list contains 231 names. Those designated thus (†) were petitioners residing in Winchester and near-by Virginia communities, a total of 24. The remaining 207 candidates were presumably connected with the Federal troops occupying Winchester, most of those listed being officers. William McKinley's name appears as number 146 on the list. Many of the Brethren listed above corresponded with the Lodge in after years, some of this correspondence being still extant. It is not known how many of them are still living as of this date (1949).

APPENDIX 2 TO CHAPTER VIII

Abstract of documents confirming the rights of the Masonic bodies of Winchester, Virginia to meet in the City Hall (or Municipal Building). (Note: This abstract is based on certain researches made in 1947 by Mr. W. W. Glass and reported to the Common Council of Winchester in that year.)

December 7, 1865—Common Council received a communication from a committee consisting of J. B. T. Reed; John Kerr, and Wm. R. Denny on behalf of the order of Free Masons, having reference to the improvement of the Market Square and erecting a building thereon. (See Council minutes, vol. 1857-1870, p. 218).

January 8, 1866—Common Council approved the report of its committee appointed to confer with a committee from the Masonic Fraternity. This report provided, that the Masonic Fraternity should convey to the city all rights and title to the premises occupied by the Fraternity in the Market House, in return for which Common Council agreed to make certain improvements to the Masonic section of the building, to permit the Masonic Fraternity to add certain structures of their own for their own use, the stairs of the building to be for the joint use of the city and the Fraternity, etc., and this arrangement was to continue in perpetuity. (See Council minutes, vol. 1857-1870, pp. 220 ff.)

January 20, 1866—A deed was executed and recorded in the clerk's office of the Corporation Court of the City of Winchester carrying out the provisions of the above-cited action of the Common Council on January 8, 1866. (See Deed Book No. 11, Clerk's Office of the Corporation Court, Winchester, pp. 226 ff.)

May 2, 1866—A memorial was presented to Common Council from Hiram Lodge No. 21 "respectfully requesting the deeds passed between the Council and Hiram Lodge in relation to a transfer of halls be rescinded". (See Council minutes, vol. 1857-1870, p. 234.)

May 11, 1866—Common Council took action assenting to the memorial of Hiram Lodge No. 21 with the proviso, that "the expense incurred, or to be incurred, be paid by Hiram Lodge No. 21". (See Council minutes, vol. 1857-1870, pp. 237, 238.)

May 15, 1866—A deed was executed and recorded in the clerk's office of the Corporation Court of the City of Winchester carrying out the provisions of the above-cited action of Common Council and annulling the deed executed and recorded on January 20, 1866. This left the matter exactly where it had been previously to December 7, 1865 and it is so acknowledged to be by the following statement in the deed of May 15, 1866: "....so as completely and in every respect to reinstate all the said parties to the condition they were in before the said deed was executed". (See Deed Book No. 11, Clerk's Office of the Corporation Court, Winchester, pp. 252 ff.)

The action of Hiram Lodge, therefore, in transferring to Winchester Chapter the Lodge's rights to meet in the City Hall (or Municipal Building) was entirely within the prerogatives of the Lodge.

CHAPTER IX

THE YEARS OF RECOVERY (1871-1900)

Like other institutions in the community, Hiram Lodge No. 21 endeavored to re-establish itself as rapidly as possible after the worst of the Reconstruction period had passed and to contribute to the progress of the town in every possible way. The erection of the new temple had given a great impetus to the Lodge and the Brethren found, that this fact aided them in attracting some of the most promising of the younger men of town and country to apply for the Masonic degrees. Judge Richard Parker continued his active interest in the affairs of the fraternity, both locally and throughout the state. It is certain that he did not neglect his Lodge even in the face of pressing professional and other demands upon his time and energies. We find, for example, that this distinguished Brother, on February 17, 1871, "addressed the Lodge......in a chaste and eloquent [manner] concerning the pure teachings of Masonry and in a forcible manner explained the solemn obligation resting upon every Master Mason". At some of the subsequent meetings for that year other lectures were delivered by some of the better informed Brethren also. At the election in June of that year Dr. Love expressed the desire to be relieved of the office of Master but his plea went unheeded and he was duly re-elected for the year 1871-1872.

Toward the end of the year 1871 the Lodge became once more greatly concerned with the question of its finances. There was still considerable indebtedness on the new building and various methods of raising funds were discussed, such as staging a series of entertainments, increasing the annual dues, etc. It appears that the dues were actually increased but the minutes do not indicate the amount. Judge Parker, in addition to his office in Grand Lodge, was also District Deputy for 1871 and made his official visit to Hiram Lodge on December 4th, when he was received with all honor, and, after examining the Lodge records and inquiring as to membership and attendance, addressed the Lodge "on subjects pertinent to the general good of the Craft". On January 19, 1872, the financial condition of the Lodge was such, that it was deemed expedient to negotiate a loan to take care of current operations. The amount of this loan is not stated, but the acuteness of the financial embarrassment of the body was accentuated by the listing of some fifteen Brethren, who were decidedly in arrears in the payment of their dues. One Brother made a donation of $100.00 on June 3, 1872, which was ordered to be applied on the Lodge's note at the bank. Again Judge Parker visited the Lodge on December 2d of that year in his capacity as District Deputy and, at the same meeting, the Lodge voted to recommend to Grand Lodge his appointment to this office for another year. Brother William R. Denny was made "Receiver" to receive and disburse the funds of the Lodge during its financial crisis.

The minutes of March 22, 1873 show that Alexander M. Baker was elected on that date to receive the E. A. degree. Judge Parker was chosen as the Lodge's representative to Grand Lodge that year and Dr. Love was continued as Master. At the election of June 1, 1874 Dr. Love again besought the Brethren to relieve him of the duties of the chair, but his plea went again unheeded and he was re-elected. Brother Baker was chosen as Senior Warden at the same time. Brother Henry Kinzel now succeeded Brother William L. Bent as Treasurer, Brother C. A. B. Coffroth continued as Secretary, and Brother George E. Bushnell was re-appointed Organist, a position he had held for some years. By October 4, 1874 the remaining indebtedness to the banks had been paid off and the finances of the Lodge showed a decidedly improved condition, this being due to an increase in the amount of work done during the preceding months. The Receiver's report for the year showed a balance of $244.96 on hand and the outstanding debt on the temple to be $6,225.00. Considerable trouble was still being experienced with delinquent Brethren, so that, on April 5, 1875, the Secretary was ordered to prefer charges against nine delinquents, who had failed to obey the summons of the Lodge to appear and show cause why they should not be suspended for non-payment of dues. On June 21, 1875 Winchester Commandery of Knights Templar paid a formal visit to Hiram Lodge on the occasion of the installation of the Lodge officers for the ensuing year. Dr. Love still continued in the office of Master and, on the occasion of his reinstallation this time, Judge Parker presented him with "a magnificent gold Past Master's jewel" appropriately inscribed. On October 4, 1875 a communication was read from Grand Lodge calling attention to the recently organized "Masonic Widows' and Orphans' Home" and asking for the Lodge's support of this endeavor (which was not finally consummated, however, until after 1890). Brother John Kerr, for many years Treasurer of the Lodge, was buried with Masonic ceremonies on November 17, 1875.

At the annual election held on June 5, 1876, Dr. Love was finally relieved of the office of Master and Alexander M. Baker was chosen to succeed him. The new officers were installed on the "eve of St. John's Day", June 23, 1876. Brother William Anders, long an active member of the Lodge, and later a member of B. B. French Lodge No. 15, Washington, D. C., was honored on that date by having appropriate resolutions on his death spread upon the Lodge minutes. On June 4, 1877 Brother William R. Denny was made Master of the Lodge, largely, we believe, because he had been acting as "Receiver" for the Lodge funds and the Brethren were looking to him to bring the body back to a state of solvency in the near future. At this same meeting permission was granted for the use of the Lodge room by the Chapter and the Commandery on the request of Judge Parker, who was at that time Grand Master of Masons in Virginia. He presided over the Lodge at its meeting on June 23d and installed the officers-elect for the year 1877-1878. On this date the Receiver reported a balance of $13.68 and the Treasurer a balance of $7.21 respectively. Nineteen Brethren were reported on the delinquent list of July 2, 1877 and four of these were suspended on the following September 3d. On December 31st the salary of the Secretary was reduced from $50.00 to $25.00 per annum as an emergency measure. At the meeting of April 1, 1878 a "neat and handsomely finished 'Charity Box' with scriptural mottoes thereon" was presented to the Lodge and placed in charge of the Senior Deacon, who was ordered to circulate it among the Brethren on every Lodge night.

On January 6, 1879 a beautiful memorial was adopted to the memory of Past Master William L. Bent, who had passed away on the preceding December 16th. By March 31, 1879 the indebtedness of the Lodge had been reduced to $5,115.00, but there was still a long list of delinquent members, who could not be prevailed upon to pay up. In order to take care of this indebtedness some of the Brethren now came forward with the idea of selling part of the temple and retaining only the Lodge room and such other space as was needed for Masonic purposes. This idea was vigorously opposed by Judge Parker and several others and, at the meeting of June 10, 1879, the proposal was unanimously defeated. During these years the Lodge proposed several times to Grand Lodge, that the latter pay the expenses of the Grand Officers and of one representative from each Lodge in attending the annual communications of Grand Lodge, but this measure was never adopted by the latter. The obvious reason for Hiram Lodge's suggestion in this regard was, of course, the Lodge's own difficulty in meeting the expenses of its representative to Grand Lodge each year.

By January, 1880 the Lodge's indebtedness had been still further reduced and now stood at $4,574.21. On November 7th of that year the Brethren made another move to conserve their financial resources by adopting a resolution petitioning Grand Lodge to reduce the *per capita* tax from 50 cents to 25 cents per member, but we believe that this proposal also failed of adoption by the Grand Lodge. On January 11, 1881 occurs the first reference to a project for compiling a history of Hiram Lodge. A Historical Committee was appointed for this purpose, consisting of Judge Parker and five other Brethren. The report of this committee, however, was never published as such and, some twelve years later, Judge Parker wrote a sketch of Hiram Lodge, which was published in the Grand Lodge Proceedings. This is the only history of the Lodge ever prepared, so far as the records show, until the present work was undertaken in the fall of 1948. On May 10, 1881 Brother Wm. R. Denny was appointed a committee "to gather up the pictures belonging to Hiram Lodge, have them framed and hung in the ante-room". The Brethren were informed on August 19, 1881, that the Grand Master would pay an official visit to the Lodge on the following Tuesday, August 23d. It was voted that an entertainment be given for the Grand Master, Peyton S. Coles, and the necessary committees were appointed for this purpose. The program was carried out according to schedule and a "sumptuous entertainment was provided" in the banquet hall of the Taylor Hotel. The Grand Master granted a verbal dispensation while he was in Winchester for the conferring of the M. M. degree on a Brother, who had just received the F. C. degree that evening, but ordered, that this Brother receive instruction on the F. C. degree later and that a report of his progress be made in writing to the Grand Master. Further action with regard to enlarging the powers of the Receiver was considered on May 8, 1882 at the request of Brother W. R. Denny, who still held this office. Final action on this set of proposals, however, was deferred several times and the matter was not completed until January 9, 1883. On May 31, 1883 the Lodge laid the cornerstone of the new public school building of Winchester with Judge Richard Parker presiding at the ceremonies. This is now known as the John Kerr School.

On June 12, 1883 Brother C. E. Hoover was appointed a committee "to procure camphor and tobacco to sprinkle the carpet so as to prevent the injury of it by moths". The Secretary was also requested to "deliver his lecture on 'Brotherly Love, Relief, and Truth' at such time as he may designate, and that the families of the members and lady friends be invited to be present; also, that the W. M., Sr. and Jr. Wardens, and Bro. C. E. Hoover be appointed a committee to solicit contributions from the members to prepare an entertainment on this social reunion". On November 20, 1883 the Lodge was notified of the passing of Brother C. A. B. Coffroth, who had been its Secretary for a number of years, and suitable resolutions were adopted in his memory, these being published at length in the Winchester papers. Brother Coffroth was buried with Masonic honors the following day. Brother C. E. Hoover was designated to fill out the unexpired term until the next annual election of officers.

By January 3, 1885 the entire debt of the Lodge had been reduced to $3,029.46 and on February 10th of that year Brother W. R. Denny, for reasons, which do not appear in the minutes, submitted his resignation from the office of Receiver and requested his dimit, which was granted. His letter of resignation states, that "this one of the great objects of my life has been frustrated. I assure you my sorrow and disappointment is extream". Very beautiful resolutions on Brother Denny's resignation and dimission were adopted by the Lodge at its meeting on March 10, 1885. The cornerstone of the new Baptist Church was laid by the Lodge on July 9, 1885 and an oyster supper was held on the anniversary of St. John the Evangelist (December 28, 1885).

On January 12, 1886 it was reported that the Lodge's indebtedness was now $2,800.00. At this meeting a committee was appointed to purchase a fireproof safe for the use of the Lodge at a cost not to exceed $50.00. Henry Kinzel, for some years Treasurer of Hiram Lodge, was buried with Masonic ceremonies on Feburary 24, 1886. Brother Henry Clay Krebs was elected on March 9th to succeed him. Past Master George W. Ginn was buried on April 2, 1887 with Brother John B. T. Reed officiating at the Masonic funeral service. On September 13th of that year District Deputy Grand Master George E. Bushnell, a Past Master of Hiram Lodge, paid an official visit to the Lodge. He was later recommended for reappointment to the office of District Deputy for the year 1888. On January 10th of that year Brother H. C. Krebs, who had been the representative of the Lodge at Grand Lodge the preceding month, reported that he had done all in his power to get Grand Lodge to pay the expenses of the Lodge representatives but without result. However, he had succeeded in getting "the old tax due by this Lodge to Grand Lodge reduced from $44.50 to $22.25". On February 14th Brother John B. T. Reed presented some old manuscripts to the Lodge bearing on its history as far back as 1769. On May 8th Judge Parker read his paper on the history of the Lodge to the Brethren. This

The Years of Recovery (1871-1900)

matter has already been mentioned in the preceding pages of this volume. By February, 1889 the total amount of the Lodge's indebtedness had been reduced to $1,700.00. On March 11, 1890 this amount had been further reduced to $1,182.30 with a balance in hand of $262.64 to apply on the debt. But by the end of this same year the report of the Treasurer shows that the actual debt was $1,709.68 instead of the figure previously mentioned. New by-laws were adopted in 1892 and the ladies of Winchester were very active during the spring of that year in behalf of the Masonic Fair held in Richmond in support of the then new Masonic Home of Virginia.

On February 14, 1893 steps were taken by the Lodge to provide a Masonic library and on June 13th of that year the Receiver reported the amount of debt due on the temple to be $359.74. The Lodge celebrated its 125th anniversary on October 17, 1893 with an address by Past Master Frank E. Conrad on the early history of Masonry in Winchester and Pennsylvania. Then, on Sunday, November 9th following, the Brethren conducted the last sad rites at the funeral of Judge Richard Parker and very fulsome resolutions were recorded in the minutes in memory of their distinguished departed Brother.

In the minutes of December 12, 1893 we find the first reference to the formal establishment of a committee on the investment of surplus funds, which had, in fact, existed more or less informally for some time previously. A resolution on this subject was offered as follows:

> RESOLVED, That the Worshipful Master of Hiram Lodge shall at the January communication of each year, appoint a committee of three Master Masons of this Lodge, who shall receive from the Receiver and Treasurer thereof from time to time the rents in his hands, after paying the insurance and necessary repairs, and carefully and safely invest the same in real estate loans or other sound securities.
> 2. The said committee shall continue to invest and reinvest as above provided said rents and the payments, interest, profits, and dividends of such investments, and hold the same as a reserve fund for the benefit of Hiram Lodge.
> 3. The said Committee shall make a report to the Lodge, at the

January and July communications of each year, of their proceedings and of the investments and other funds in their hands.

4. Any vacancy in said committee shall be filled by the Worshipful Master at any regular communication.

5. The investments and the fund above provided for shall be at the order of the Lodge.

These proposals were ordered to lie over until the next stated communication but final action was not taken until March 13, 1894, when the resolutions were adopted unanimously. The Master then appointed Brothers C. M. Gibbens, John Ray, and M. H. G. Willis as the first members of this committee on surplus funds, they thus supplementing, in effect, the regularly and formally appointed trustees of Hiram Lodge required by law. At the celebration of St. John's Day on June 24th of that year, a Masonic choir rendered musical selections under the leadership of Alexander M. Baker. The sermon for the occasion was preached by the Rev. Henry Branch, Grand Chaplain of the Grand Lodge of Maryland. A "committee on water closet and elevator" is mentioned in the minutes of January 8, 1895 and the committee on surplus funds, failing to make their report at this time, were directed to do so at the February stated communication. This was done and the committee reported the sum of $140.69 in its hands as of that date (February 12, 1895). Over one hundred visiting Brethren attended the St. John's Day services on June 23, 1895.

On March 10, 1896 Brother Charles W. Hensell presented to the Lodge a photograph of six prominent members of Hiram Lodge in 1862—Julius Waddell, Wm. R. Denny, David Barrett John Kerr, J. B. Tilden Reed, George W. Legg. This photograph is still one of the Lodge's treasured possessions. It may be added here, that by 1896 the members of the committee on surplus funds began to call themselves by the name and style of the "Trustees of the Reserve Fund" (they were not the legal trustees of the Lodge, however), and so rendered their report to the Lodge at the beginning of that year, showing a total of $581.61 in their

Room Used by John Dove Chapter No. 21, R. A. M. and Winchester Commandery No. 12, K. T. (as seen from the West)

The Years of Recovery (1871-1900)

hands. On July 14th of that year this amount had been increased to $599.11, and by January 12, 1897 the reserve fund had in- increased to $631.06. The original members of the committee on surplus funds were still serving in that capacity. At the end of 1897 82 members were shown in Hiram Lodge's returns to Grand Lodge. On January 11, 1898 the "trustees" reported $1,807.07 in the reserve fund, which was thus shown to be growing quite rapidly and satisfactorily. At long last Hiram Lodge's fundamental financial problems seemed to have reached a satisfactory solution. The original members of the reserve fund committee were still serving in this capacity. The "committee on the water closet" finally got in its report on September 13, 1898 and recommended a "walled pit" for this purpose at a cost of $15.00 or $16.00, which we consider cheap, though primitive, plumbing!

On April 11, 1899 a committee appointed to investigate the possibility of remodelling the store front on the first floor of the Masonic temple, recommended that the "safe and proper thing to do is to remodel and rebuild the whole front in a way that will give us a safe and ornamental building". The committee was ordered to look into the matter further and it reported on June 13th, that complete plans and specifications for an appropriate front could be obtained for $35.00. After discussion at several subsequent meetings, the Lodge voted on February 27, 1900 the suggested improvements to the front of the building and certain other repairs to be made at a cost of approximately $6,000.00 and that the committee having the matter in charge be empowered to draw on the "trustees" of the reserve fund for the payment of such sums as were needed in this connection. The Lodge was invited to lay the cornerstone of the new City Hall on May 15, 1900, at which ceremonies many visiting Brethren, also the local Chapter and Commandery assisted. At the June 12th meeting of this year, the same "trustees" were authorized to borrow up to $4,500.00 to be used in paying for the repairs and the new front to the temple, such loan to be secured by a mortage on the temple property to be obtained through the legal trustees. On July 10th the committee reported $2,081.18 in the reserve fund and, there being no indication of any change in the membership of this committee, we are left to assume that the originally appointed ones were still serving in that capacity.

Thus the nineteenth century closed with the Lodge actively at work, the morale of its members at a high level, and the Brethren respected throughout the entire community for their high standards of conduct and their contribution to the business, religious, and educational life of the town.

CHAPTER X

HIRAM LODGE AFTER 1900

The completion of the repairs to the building and the installation of the new front augured well for Hiram Lodge at the beginning of a new year and a new century. For at the very first meeting of the year 1901 (January 8th), the committee on repairs submitted its report, showing that this work had been practically completed at a cost of nearly $8,000.00.

Although there is no record of it in the Lodge minutes, the most important event in the history of Hiram Lodge in the year 1901 (and indeed in its entire history) was the visit of President William McKinley to Winchester in May of that year. At that time he had just begun his second term in that office and the Masons and other citizens of Winchester welcomed him most heartily. The situation was such, that Hiram Lodge was not able to hold a meeting in honor of its former member—the most prominent Brother ever to sign his name on its roster. However, the Lodge has many mementoes of the occasion, including photographs of the President standing just outside the Masonic Temple with the crowds surrounding him just as he is about to enter the building. He climbed the steps to the Lodge room and stood near the spot where the present Treasurer's desk stands. There followed a public reception in his honor, which many of the present members of the Lodge recall very vividly. The one regret is that the Secretary of that day did not include in the Lodge records something of a printed or written character as a permanent evidence from the Masonic standpoint, that McKinley came back to the meeting place of his "Mother Lodge" on this one occasion after he was raised. We suspect, that the Secretary would have done this, had he had even the slightest suspicion of what proved to be a tragic sequel to this visit.

On September 7, 1901 Worshipful Master Harry M. Baker sent the following telegram to President McKinley's secretary,

George B. Cortelyou, at Buffalo, New York upon receiving the news of the President's assassination:

> In their extreme misfortune and present hour of suffering Winchester Hiram Lodge No. 21, A. F. & A. M. expresses her heartfelt sympathy and concern to President and Mrs. McKinley. Her sincerest hopes are for his speedy recovery.

To this telegram the following reply was received:

> The following bulletin was issued by the President's physicians at 9:30 P. M.: condition continues much the same. The President responds well to medication, pulse 132, temperature 102.5, respiration 25. All temperatures reported are taken in the rectum. The physicians in attendance wish to say that they are too busily engaged to reply to individual telegrams.

Upon the death of the President, the Master of Hiram Lodge called a special communication on September 16, 1901, at which lengthy and beautiful tribute was paid to their departed Brother in resolutions spread upon the minutes and ordered to be sent to Mrs. McKinley. The President had intended to visit the Lodge again in October of that year but the dispositions of an all-wise Providence prevented. Thus the Brethren of Winchester bade farewell to the most distinguished Brother, whose name had ever been entered upon the Lodge rolls, and his memory is still one of the proudest of Hiram Lodge's possessions.

The cornerstone of the Memorial Hospital of Winchester was laid on November 8, 1901 and the "trustees" of the reserve fund reported on January 14, 1902, that they held a balance of $2,206.63 to their credit. The "trustees" are now listed as Brothers John Ray, George R. Blake, and J. C. Smith. On June 20, 1902 there was a public installation of officers, the ceremonies being conducted by Past Grand Master R. T. W. Duke, of Charlottesville. On January 13, 1903 the same "trustees" reported a balance of $1,233.70 in hand after the payment of $1,500.00 on the bonded debt of the Lodge during the year. The balance of the bonded debt on that date amounted to $4,500.00. On April 14, 1903 the committee appointed to procure a photograph of the late President McKinley reported progress and was granted further time. This photograph was duly obtained and is now one of the Lodge's prized possessions. It is reproduced opposite page 131 of this book.

On August 25, 1905 Hiram Lodge met in special communication to receive Grand Master Thomas N. Davis (known affectionately as "King Solomon" by his Brethren), who conferred the M. M. degree on Brother A. C. Slonaker for the edification of the members present. On January 28, 1907 the Lodge conducted a Masonic funeral for Brother David Petrie Cruickshank, who was born in the Isle of Man on April 21, 1848, receiving the Masonic degrees there in 1877. After having been a member of several other Lodges, both in the British Isles and in America, he had affiliated with Hiram Lodge on December 13, 1904.

New resolutions were adopted regarding the functions of the Lodge's legal trustees on February 13, 1906 and the Tiler was made the collector of all rents due the Lodge and the supervisor of all repairs to the temple building under orders from the trustees. In May of the same year came the California earthquake and the Lodge contributed $100.00 in currency (forwarded by express) to the Grand Master of California to be used in Masonic relief work among the victims of the disaster. C. Vernon Eddy served the Lodge as Master in 1907 and has been its Secretary (with the exception of one year when he was Grand Master) since 1918. On May 28, 1908 Hiram Lodge laid the cornerstone of the Handley Library and about the same time charges were preferred against a certain Brother for discussing political matters in the Lodge room and refusing to stop such discussion when admonished by the Master to do so. He was later declared not guilty after investigation by a commission. Brother C. W. Wilson, long the Secretary of the Lodge, died in September, 1909 and was buried by the Lodge with appropriate ceremonies.

In the minutes of June 14, 1910 we find that final disposition was made of the recommendations of the "committee on the water closet", which were ordered to be carried out. It would seem that there had been some question in the minds of the Lodge members, as to the exact location of this proposed improvement.

It was finally voted to place the closet "where Bro. C. F. Barr now has his coal bin." The Lodge held a sumptuous banquet on November 24th of that year and each member was *presented* with two tickets for himself and lady. In 1911 we note at various times, that Hiram Lodge was visited by members of Love Lodge No. 311, which had been chartered recently by Grand Lodge. It was named in honor of Dr. William S. Love, still living at that time and long a beloved and active member of Hiram Lodge. During that same year Hiram Lodge lost two of its most prominent members—Judge William Mayo Atkinson and Solomon Hable. In January, 1912 the Lodge's reserve fund showed a balance of $5,417.08 on hand.

On May 10, 1912, Henry Baetjer passed to his reward. He was a German by birth and had located in Winchester in 1865, receiving the degrees in Hiram Lodge two years later. He had served the Lodge many years as one of its legal trustees. Brother William E. Cooper was appointed to fill the vacancy in the trustees caused by the death of Brother Baetjer. Dr. William S. Love was buried by the Lodge with Masonic honors on December 15, 1912.

On March 13, 1913, the trustees, at the request of the Lodge, presented a detailed statement of the amount of indebtedness then being carried by the Lodge—a total of $6,300.00 requiring the payment of interest charges in the amount of $338.00 annually. We find that there were four trustees at this time, namely, H. B. McCormac, G. H. Kinzel, W. G. Conway, and William E. Cooper. On August 12th of that year, the trustees and the reserve fund committee jointly presented a lengthy report to the Lodge with detailed recommendations as to ways and means for paying off the Lodge's indebtedness. This report was adopted unanimously and its provisions were subsequently carried out, much to the improvement of the Lodge's financial condition. The membership of the reserve fund committee at this time was as follows: J. E. Correll, W. Ray Smith, and A. C. Slonaker. At this same meeting (August 12, 1913) it was voted "that a night be set apart for reception and some entertainment for the

Masons that are here present during the encampment of the U. S. Cavalry near the city". Grand Master William L. Andrews, of Roanoke, paid an official visit to Hiram Lodge on January 10, 1914 and a very large assemblage of members and visiting Brethren greeted him on that occasion.

On March 10, 1914 the reserve fund committee made its final report, showing a balance in hand of $164.32. The committee was discontinued by the following action of the Lodge at that meeting:

> Moved by J. E. Correll "that the reserve fund committee be discontinued and that the resolution passed some years ago forming same be rescinded and that all moneys now in the hands of the reserve fund committee be turned over to the trustees, who shall hereafter collect all rents due the Lodge and pay same out according to their orders". Motion carried.

The cornerstone of the Methodist Episcopal Church, South, at Stephens City, was laid by the Lodge on May 19, 1914, and Division Grand Lecturer C. G. Davis visited the Lodge on June 2d of that year. In their annual report submitted on January 12, 1915 the trustees reported receipts of $1,001.13 and disbursements of $891.41 for the preceding year.

On December 13, 1916 Grand Master J. Alston Cabell visited Hiram Lodge officially and we have no doubt that his address was heard with rapt attention by the Brethren present. There has not been a more scholarly or eloquent Grand Master of Masons in Virginia than Brother Cabell, whom many of the Brethren now living still recall with deep affection and veneration. In the same year the Lodge voted to request Grand Lodge to eliminate the ballot on the moral qualifications of candidates after the E. A. degree, but this effort proved unsuccessful.

With the entry of the United States into World War I in 1917, the activities of the Lodge were stepped up so that we find a considerable increase in the number of petitions received and the amount of work performed during that period. Occasionally dispensations were requested from the Grand Master for the conferring of the degrees under emergency conditions. It was also during this same period, that the by-laws were amended so that the stated communications of the Lodge should be held on the second Tuesday of each month, a provision, which is still in force. Grand Master Earnest L. Cunningham visited the Lodge officially on April 23, 1918. He was accompanied by Past Grand Master R. T. W. Duke, Jr., both of these Brethren urging the support of the war effort and the purchase of Liberty Loan bonds. On July 2, 1918 Brother Charles M. Gibbens passed to his reward and was buried by the Lodge with Masonic honors. In the resolutions incorporated into the minutes on this occasion, we find the following poem quoted, of which Brother Gibbens was the author:

THE SOARER
Say, thou of strong and silent wing,
    That high above the peaks dost dare;
What power taught thee how to fling
    Thy will upon the subtle air;

That heedless seems—thee to obey—
    Of wonted laws of weight or form,
And bears thee toilless on thy way,
    Lone wanderer of cold and storm?

Or, art thou spirit, from the bourn
    Astray; or doomed the sky to roam—
Or till thy homing sense recall
    The lode-star to thy distant home—

What is it in me seems to fill,
    And, flutt'ring, longs to match thy flight?
Ah, is it dim remembrance still
    Of life before—beyond the night?

Yet oft in sleep, from half-loosed ties
    Of earth—that lightly cling until
I seem, yet all unwinged, to rise—
    I mount and poise me on my will.

A dream? Ah me, which is the dream?
    Perchance I've yonder fall'n on sleep
Uneasy, and its shadows deem
    Th' appointed round of life I keep;

Until the friendly touch shall shake
The pris'ning web of dreams apart,
And from the coil of flesh awake,
I back to life untrammeled start.

On reading this poem for the first time, we sensed strongly the influence of the English romantic poets—Wordsworth, Shelley, and Keats—and we were quite sure, that Brother Gibbens became steeped in their charm and magic during his years as a student at the University of Virginia, from which he was graduated with the M. A. degree in 1860. He was a true "gentleman and scholar".

With the outbreak of World War 1 in 1917 the Brethren of Hiram Lodge "rose to the occasion" in magnificent style. No less than 24 of its members responded to the call to the colors. There names are as follows:

C. R. Anderson	Claude M. Grim
L. W. Armentrout	Roger A. Kline
R. T. Barton, Jr.	J. H. Lacey, Jr.
C. R. Cammer	Fred M. Lemley
David C. Cather	Gervis E. Lemley
T. R. Cather	J. Alan Maphis
H. E. Clark	A. J. Novick
C. W. Cochran	R. H. Pope
F. A. Cochran	H. D. Robinson
E. W. Fansler	B. M. Roszel
G. E. Fansler	E. C. Shull
Allen B. Gray	E. C. Yost

All of these members returned home after the war was over.

In 1918 and 1919 the trustees invested heavily from their accumulated funds in Liberty Loan bonds. In the latter year, the dues were increased to 25 cents per month (it being the law of the Grand Lodge of Virginia that the Lodge by-laws must prescribe dues on a monthly basis). C. Vernon Eddy was elected Secretary of the Lodge on December 10, 1918 and has served continuously in that office to the present time with the exception of the year, in which he was Grand Master of Masons in Virginia. The Grand Lodge law does not permit a Grand Master to hold office in a subordinate Lodge; hence the break of one year in Brother Eddy's term as Secretary of Hiram Lodge.

On June 22, 1920 Grand Master William W. Galt paid a visit to a joint communication of all the Lodges in District No. 3. Hiram Lodge acted as host for this occasion. On November 15, 1921 the death of Brother E. S. Brent was recorded in the Lodge minutes. He lived to the ripe age of 92 years and was the senior Past Master of the Lodge at the time of his passing. He was buried the following day with the usual Masonic ceremonies. On December 13th of that same year the committee appointed for the purpose of preparing a group picture of the officers of Hiram Lodge at the time of the raising of William McKinley presented to the Lodge the results of its labors. The picture, handsomely framed, now hangs in the Masonic Temple at Winchester and forms an important item in the historical collection of Hiram Lodge. A duplicate of this picture was ordered prepared for presentation to William McKinley Lodge No. 431, of Canton, Ohio. This presentation was made on March 24, 1922, when a committee of Hiram Lodge, consisting of Brothers Stanley E. Harmer, C. Vernon Eddy, A. R. Breckenridge, R. Gray Williams, C. W. Trenary, and Richard Hunter Pope, visited McKinley Lodge for that purpose. When McKinley returned to Canton after the War Between the States, he became a charter member of Eagle Lodge No. 431, which was chartered on October 20, 1869. After McKinley's death the name was changed to William McKinley Lodge. On May 26, 1922 a delegation of Canton Brethren paid a return visit to Hiram Lodge and were received with the utmost courtesy by the Brethren of Winchester. On their return home, the visiting delegation reported that "southern hospitality had been lavished on them" and that they were charmed with the people of the Shenandoah Valley.

On October 3, 1922 a special joint communication of the Lodges of District No. 3 was held in the Masonic Temple, Winchester, for the purpose of receiving an official visit from Grand

Master James H. Price, who was accompanied by Grand Lecturer George W. Wright, P. G. M. The death of Brother Wright, which occurred less than a year later, was recorded in the Lodge minutes of June 12, 1923. In September of that same year Dr. Frank T. McFaden, a future Grand Master of Virginia, came to Winchester as pastor of the local Presbyterian church and affiliated with Hiram Lodge. He was soon appointed to the office of Chaplain in the Lodge, in which he served for some years thereafter.

Hiram Lodge held a special communication on May 1, 1924, which was attended by Grand Master Samuel M. Goodyear, of Pennsylvania, and Grand Master Charles H. Callahan, of Virginia. Brother Callahan visited the Lodge again on June 27, 1924. The year 1925 passed uneventfully except that the Lodge continued its activities enthusiastically and there was considerable work during that period. In 1926 the Lodge voted to erect a tablet in honor of the six members of old Lodge No. 12, who gave their lives in the Revolutionary War. The cost of this tablet is noted as $70.00 and it still occupies a prominent place in the Masonic Temple at Winchester.

The records of the meeting of July 13, 1926 contain the following interesting letter from Past Grand Master Joseph W. Eggleston, one of Virginia's outstanding Masonic scholars:

> Having read the record of the initiation, passing, and raising of our late beloved President of the United States, William McKinley, in your Lodge in May, 1865, I think that some record should be made of another fact in connection with such unique history, that future generations may know all of his connection with Virginia Masonry. On December 14th, 1899, he wore a Virginia Masonic apron in the Grand Lodge of Virginia at Alexandria, Virginia, and participated in the ceremony, making the formal address at the celebration of the one hundredth anniversary of the death of our first President, Brother and Worshipful George Washington. This was Brother McKinley's last Masonic act, so that he ended as well as began his Masonic life in Virginia.

The passing of Dr. Eggleston is noted in the minutes of Hiram Lodge for January 19, 1928.

The Lodge continued to enjoy prosperity during these years,

though it suffered somewhat during the depression of the early 1930's as did most other Lodges throughout the country. However, in the latter part of that decade, the membership again began to increase and the impetus given to it by the events of World War II is still reflected in its prosperity at the present time. Dr. Frank T. McFaden became Grand Master in 1930 and, seven years later, C. Vernon Eddy was also elevated to this important office.

In 1937 the trustees of the Lodge purchased the adjacent property known as the "Keller building" for the sum of $21,000. Considerable alterations were made, the second floor being made into a reception room and the third floor into a banquet hall, thus giving Hiram Lodge very commodious accommodations for the social aspect of its activities.

During World War II the Lodge made a notable contribution to the war effort both at home and abroad. In addition to investing some of its funds in government bonds to support the war effort, Hiram Lodge sent fourteen of its members into the armed services as follows:

Curtis Barr	William H. Heeps
Leroy Cahill	Charles P. McVicar, Jr.
David C. Cather	George F. Miller
Harry T. Denton	Vincent M. Noonan
John V. Eddy	George H. Snyder
George W. Good	George S. Taylor
R. M. Grimm	D. E. Wright

All of these Brethren returned home after the cessation of hostilities with the exception of Lt. Colonel George F. Miller, who gave his life for his country. Brother David C. Cather served in both World Wars.

At the annual election of officers in December, 1940 Brother William E. Cooper requested to be retired from the office of Treasurer after 28 years of service. Brother Claude M. Grim was elected to succeed him and still serves in this office. Brother C. Vernon Eddy is the present Secretary, having been first elected to the secretaryship in 1918 as noted above. At the present time (1949) Brother Thurman Crosslin occupies the office of Worshipful Master and the following are the Lodge trustees: Claude M. Grim, chairman, William E. Cooper, W. B. Goode, C. R. Cammer, and C. Vernon Eddy, Secretary-Treasurer. Many members of the Lodge are active in communities throughout the country as well as in Winchester, also Masonically in Grand Lodge and local Masonic affairs. The total membership is 242, the indications pointing to a probable passing of the 250 mark before the end of the current year.

We cannot close this story of Hiram Lodge without giving an account of an event of outstanding importance which took place on the evening of April 12, 1949. The honor guests of the occasion were C. Vernon Eddy, who had just passed his fiftieth Masonic birthday, and William E. Cooper, senior Past Master of the Lodge, for whom Brother Eddy had served as Senior Warden. There were in attendance 143 Brethren, including fourteen officers of the Lodge, fifteen of the Lodge's Past Masters, 36 members of Hiram Lodge and 78 visitors from other Lodges. Grand Master A. Douglas Smith, Jr. presided during the ceremonies and introduced the following officers of Grand Lodge: E. D. Flowers, Deputy Grand Master; Hugh Reid, Grand Junior Deacon; James N. Hillman, P. G. M., Grand Secretary; and Joseph H. Gasser, Grand Pursuivant; also Past Grand Masters Harry K. Green and Clarence D. Freeman. Each of these Brethren spoke in tribute to Brother Eddy, as did also Grand High Priest Charles M. Flintoff. Congratulatory messages were read from Past Grand Masters Earl C. Laningham, C. E. Webber, and others.

Brother William E. Cooper was presented to the Lodge by Brothers W. B. Goode and Thurman Crosslin. He was congratulated by the Grand Master, who presented him with the fifty-year emblem of Grand Lodge, after which Brother Goode commended Brother Cooper on his long service to the Lodge in many capacities, including 37 years as Trustee and 28 years as Treasurer, and presented him with a gift from the Lodge. Brother Eddy was then presented to the Lodge by Brothers Thurman

Crosslin and Lewis N. Barton, when he was escorted to the East, received and congratulated by the Grand Master, who presented him with Grand Lodge's fifty-year emblem. Brother Eddy then received from his Brethren of Winchester Hiram Lodge at the hands of Brother Barton a beautiful gold watch as a token of their affection and esteem. Both Brothers Cooper and Eddy responded to these presentations with appropriate remarks. Grand Master Smith then made the principal address of the evening after recognizing some of the other distinguished visitors present.

LOUDOUN STREET AS MCKINLEY KNEW IT (1865). DURING THE WAR
OF 1861-1865 HIRAM LODGE MET IN THE THIRD BUILDING SHOWN ABOVE

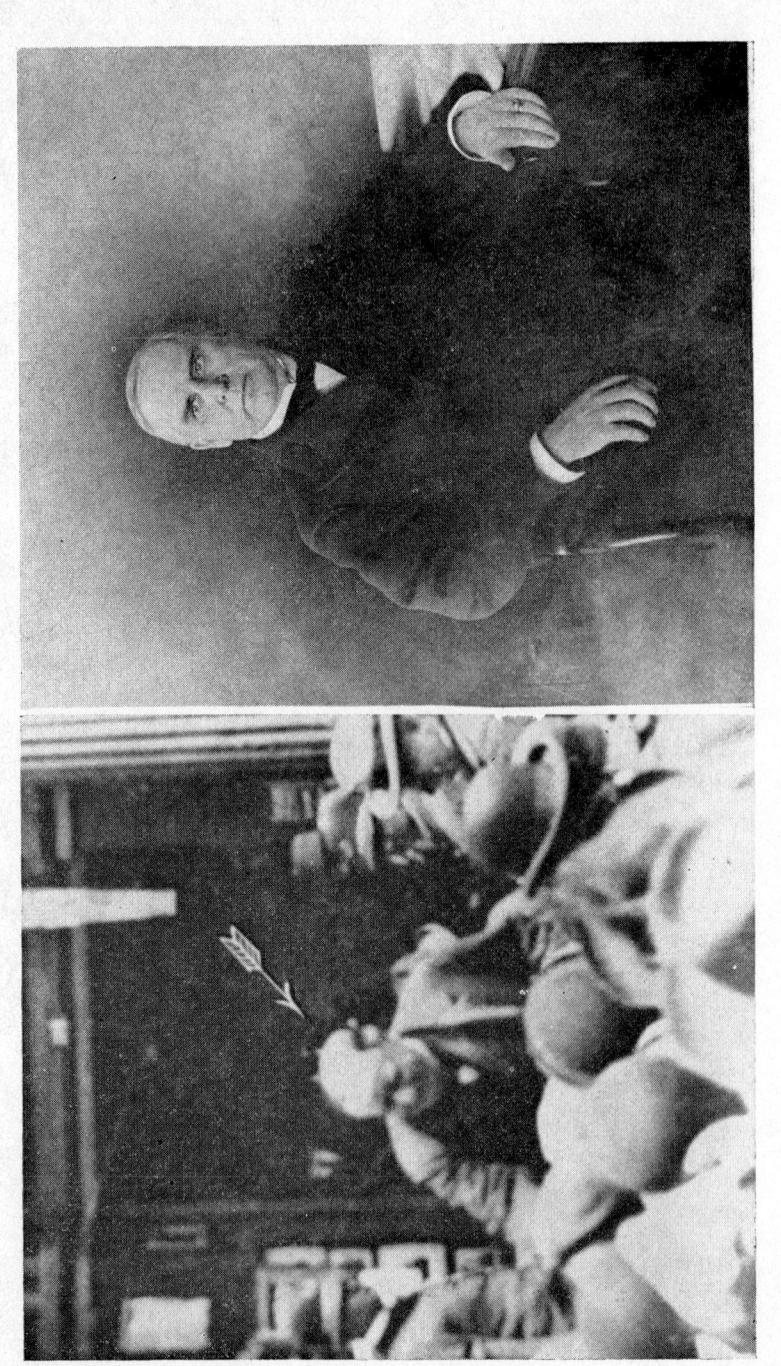

Scene in front of Masonic Temple, Winchester on the occasion of President McKinley's visit, 1901
(See page 131)

Portrait of President William McKinley, who received his degrees in Winchester Hiram Lodge No. 21 on May 1, 2, and 3, 1865
(See page 133)

CHAPTER XI
WINCHESTER'S GRAND MASTERS

The Grand Masters of Virginia, who were members of Winchester Hiram Lodge No. 21, were the following (the years are the dates of their service as Grand Master):

Archibald Magill	1817-1819
Richard Parker	1876-1877
Frank T. McFaden	1930-1931
C. Vernon Eddy	1937-1938

In addition to these, Edmund Pendleton Hunter, Grand Master in 1852-1854, was also at one time a member of Hiram Lodge (as previously mentioned in these pages) but had dimitted some years before he assumed the office of Grand Master. A sketch of the Masonic career of C. Vernon Eddy is to be found in the dedication of this book. We add by way of concluding this chapter brief sketches of Brothers Magill, Parker, and McFaden.

The facts here given regarding Archibald Magill are taken from Dr. J. R. Graham's *Sketches of the Magill Family* published in Winchester in 1908. Many members of the family both before and since the time of our particular Archibald Magill have borne the same name. It is important, therefore, to avoid confusing him with the others. The subject of this sketch was born near Winchester on March 20, 1764. In 1791 he was admitted a member of the Winchester bar but was also interested in general merchandising as well. His store was located on the corner of Loudoun and Water Streets and he acquired considerable wealth. He took an active interest in the affairs of the town, county, and state and became a very influential member of the Virginia legislature. He spent considerable time in Richmond, even when the legislature was not in session. On one of these sojourns he was badly injured in the burning of the Richmond Theatre on December 26, 1811, when a large number of persons lost their lives. He never recovered completely from these injuries, although he lived for ten years after receiving them. Magill was made a Mason in Winchester Lodge No. 12 and held several offices therein prior to becoming the charter Master of Winchester Union Lodge No. 66 in 1802. He apparently took his dimit from Lodge No. 12 about the same time, as he is shown on one or two occasions at that period as a "visitor" to No. 12. When Union Lodge went out of existence about 1811 or 1812, Magill appears to have reaffiliated with Winchester Hiram Lodge No. 21 (as it was now designated), and was a member of this Lodge when he became Deputy Grand Master of Virginia (1815-1817). In 1817 he was duly elevated to the office of Grand Master, in which he served for two years (1817-1819). His subsequent Masonic history does not appear in the records of either Hiram Lodge or of the Grand Lodge of Virginia. The exact date of his death is not known, but he apparently died in Richmond some time in 1821, leaving the request that his remains be interred in his beloved Winchester. He left no children.

Judge Richard Parker was the second Grand Master of Virginia Masons who was a son of Hiram Lodge. He was born in Richmond on October 22, 1810 and died in Winchester on November 10, 1893. He graduated in law from the University of Virginia and began the practice of his profession in Winchester soon after graduation. In 1849 he was elected a member of Congress from his district and, while serving in this capacity, he was also appointed Judge of the Circuit Court, whose jurisdiction embraced Winchester, Frederick County, and several adjacent counties likewise. It was thus that Judge Parker was called upon to preside at the trial of John Brown at Charlestown (now West Virginia) in 1859 and to sentence him to death. The eyes of the whole nation were upon Judge Parker during the entire period of that ordeal and at no time did he give the slightest cause for adverse criticism from any quarter. He was for many years a vestryman of Christ Episcopal Church, of Winchester, also superintendent of its Sunday School, and a trustee of the Virginia Theological Seminary. He received the Masonic degrees in Winchester Hiram Lodge No. 21 prior to the outbreak of the War Between the States, serving as Master of the Lodge in 1868-1869, also for several terms thereafter as District Deputy Grand Master. He represented the Lodge in the Grand Lodge of Virginia on numerous occasions and soon became an acknowledged leader in Grand Lodge affairs. He rose by regular steps to become Grand Master of Masons in Virginia in 1876-1877 and declined re-election to that office in spite of the insistence of his Brethren, that he serve a second term. He was High Priest of John Dove Royal Arch Chapter in 1873-1890, a period of seventeen years continuously. During this time he represented the Chapter at Grand Chapter on many occasions, where his ability and leadership were also recognized. Toward the close of his life Judge Parker became greatly interested in the early history of old Winchester Lodge No. 12 and its succecssor, Winchester Hiram Lodge No. 21. His sketch was read to the Lodge at one of its communications in the late 1880's and was also published as an appendix to the Grand Lodge Proceedings of 1894. It is the only attempt at the preparation of a history of this Lodge prior to the present work. This Brother was without doubt one of the most distinguished members of Hiram Lodge in its long history.

Dr. Frank T. McFaden became a member of Hiram Lodge by affiliation in 1923 when he became pastor of the Loudoun Street Presbyterian Church in Winchester. He was born in Salisbury, Maryland, February 5, 1864 and died in Marion, Virginia, on August 5, 1933. It was in the latter city that he was raised in Marion Lodge No. 31 on July 20, 1891. He later affiliated with Hill City Lodge No. 183, Lynchburg, then with Dove Lodge No. 51 and Meridian Lodge No. 284, of Richmond, serving both of these Lodges as Master simultaneously in 1920. He became a member of the Grand Lodge line in 1924, serving as Grand Master in 1930-1931. He was also Grand Chaplain of the Grand Royal Arch Chapter of Virginia for nearly 25 years. He was Grand Prelate of the Grand Commandery, Knights Templar of Virginia from 1898 to 1901, when he was started in the progressive line of Grand Commandery, becoming Grand Commander for the year 1907-1908. He was appointed Grand Prelate again in

1926 and held this office at the time of his death. He was also Prelate of Winchester Commandery No. 12 and a member of John Dove Royal Arch Chapter No. 21, of the Richmond Scottish Rite bodies, and of Acca Temple of the Shrine. No more popular or lovable Mason has served the Virginia Masonic bodies in our time than was Dr. McFaden.

CHAPTER XII

NOTES ON OTHER WINCHESTER LODGES

In addition to Winchester Lodge No. 12, now Winchester Hiram Lodge No. 21, two other Lodges existed in Winchester for short periods of time, though not simultaneously. Both of these were chartered by the Grand Lodge of Virginia, the first being established in the early nineteenth century and the other almost in our own day. Very little is known about either of these Lodges and we shall endeavor to complete the story of symbolic Masonry in Winchester by presenting in this chapter brief sketches of Winchester Union Lodge No. 66 and Love Lodge No. 311. No records of either Lodge are available locally and our information comes, therefore, from Grand Lodge sources, from various references to these Lodges in the minutes of Winchester Hiram Lodge No. 21, and from the recollections of some of the Brethren still alive and residing in Winchester.

WINCHESTER UNION LODGE NO. 66

Since none of the records of this early Lodge are available to the present writer, very little can be said about it in the present narrative. It is presumed, that the chief reason for the organization of this Lodge was the fact, that there was no Lodge in Winchester at that time (1802) working under the jurisdiction of the Grand Lodge of Virginia. Lodge No. 12, the original Winchester Lodge, was still holding to the Grand Lodge of Pennsylvania and did not come under Virginia jurisdiction until some five years after No. 66 was chartered.

It is presumed, that Lodge No. 66 was the child of No. 12 and this theory is supported by all the facts known in the matter. As has already been pointed out in the present volume, Lodge No. 12 was not able to withdraw from the Grand Lodge of Pennsylvania in the years immediately following the organization of the Grand Lodge of Virginia, this being due to the Lodge's inability to meet its arrearages to Pennsylvania. Finally this entire matter was cleared up in 1801 and Lodge No. 12 was certainly free to join the Grand Lodge of Virginia in that year in accordance with the terms of the resolution adopted unanimously by the members six years previously (1795). We find, that No. 12 was slow in taking this step, however, some of the older Brethren probably being reluctant to cut the ties, which bound them to Pennsylvania. It was at this juncture, that the movement for the establishment of Winchester Union Lodge No. 66 had its beginning.

The Grand Lodge of Virginia (according to Dr. Dove's reprint of the Grand Lodge Proceedings for 1777-1823) granted a charter to No. 66 on December 14, 1802. There is no reference to the matter in the proceedings of the day before. The record states simply the following:

> Whereas, a dispensation was issued by the Most Worshipful Grand Master, on May the 18th last, to authorize the opening of a Lodge in the town of Winchester, in the county of Frederick, by the name of the Winchester Union Lodge, appointing Archibald Magill, Master; John McDonald, Senior Warden; and William Maguire, Junior Warden; and the said dispensation having been returned, and ample testimonials of the regularity of their proceedings, and a petition for a charter:
>
> RESOLVED, That a charter do issue for the permanent establishment of a Lodge in the town aforesaid, by the name of the Winchester Union Lodge No. 66; appointing Archibald Magill, Master; John McDonald, Senior Warden; and James Chipley, Junior Warden.

At the annual communication of Grand Lodge held on December 12, 1803 we find that Lodge No. 66 was represented by Brother Hugh Holmes, who is listed as "Speaker of the House of Delegates". We find no further reference to No. 66 in the Grand Lodge Proceedings, nor does it appear to have been represented at Grand Lodge, until suddenly the name of Archibald Magill appears on December 9, 1811 as the representative of No. 66 to the Grand Lodge communication of that year. But on December 15, 1813 Archibald Magill is listed as the representative of Lodge No. 21, by which designation old No. 12 had been known since it joined the Grand Lodge of Virginia. Then, on December 14, 1818, he appears as Grand Master with no details in the Grand Lodge Proceedings as to how he was elected or any indication as to the Lodge, which he was representing at that time, although he had just completed two years as Deputy Grand Master.

All the indications support strongly the notion, that Lodge No. 66 had a very fitful existence of several years—perhaps less than ten—and that, when Lodge No. 12 came under the jurisdiction of the Grand Lodge of Virginia in 1807, all the grounds for the continuance of No. 66 disappeared. Hence, No. 66 faded rapidly out of the picture and its members became gradually absorbed by the older Lodge. It is unfortunate that the Grand Lodge Proceedings are themselves deficient in this matter, for they do not carry a list of dormant or extinct Lodges as of that period, so we do not know when No. 66 ceased to make its returns to Grand Lodge and was stricken from the rolls.

The abortive attempt of certain Brethren in 1847 to revive Winchester Union Lodge No. 66 has already been narrated in these pages. Hiram Lodge opposed this move vigorously and sent out a protest to all the Lodges in Virginia, setting forth the facts in the case. A controversy with Grand Master Sidney S. Baxter resulted, in which the Grand Master took the side of Lodge No. 66. However, we find that a former member of that Lodge petitioned Hiram Lodge for membership on February 5, 1853 and it would appear, therefore, that Union Lodge had gone out of existence before the end of 1852.

LOVE LODGE NO. 311

About the year 1908 serious disagreements arose between some of the members of Hiram Lodge as to the admission of certain applicants for the degrees. The difficulty became so great, that certain of the Brethren decided to confer with the District Deputy Grand Master and the

Grand Master regarding the possibility of establishing a new Lodge in Winchester. This seemed to offer the only adequate solution to the problem and the idea was apparently approved, for we find that, on September 22, 1909, Dr. Joseph W. Eggleston, Grand Master, granted a dispensation for the establishment of Love Lodge. The name was selected in honor of Dr. William S. Love, beloved Past Master of Hiram Lodge, whose name has already been mentioned several times in these pages. In his report to Grand Lodge in 1910 District Deputy A. G. Weaver stated, that "conditions have been much improved at Winchester as the result of the granting of the dispension for Love Lodge in that city".

As the result of this statement by the District Deputy and especially of the recommendation of Grand Master Eggleston, Grand Lodge voted on February 10, 1910 that a charter should be granted to Love Lodge, and it received the number 311 on the Grand Lodge roster. Dr. Love, who was still living and was one of Winchester's leading physicians at the time, had the signal honor of becoming the first Master of the Lodge under its charter. Harry M. Baker was named as Senior Warden and A. R. Breckenridge as Junior Warden in the charter.

The first returns of the Lodge were made to Grand Lodge for the year 1910. There was a total membership of 42 Brethren with seven new members raised during the year included in this number. These returns show the above-mentioned stationed officers, also C. L. Robinson as Treasurer and Isaac N. Good as Secretary. For the following year the returns show 43 members, including two raised during the year. Harry M. Baker had succeeded Dr. Love as Master and seven Past Masters are listed in the membership, only one of whom had actually served as Master of Love Lodge, namely, Dr. Love himself. The other six Past Masters had presided obviously over Hiram Lodge prior to the chartering of Love Lodge. The same Treasurer and Secretary continued to serve in their respective offices throughout the brief history of Love Lodge.

At the end of 1913 the membership of the Lodge stood again at 43 with C. R. McCann as Master for the year and eight Past

Masters listed in the membership. By that time, however, the situation, which led to the establishment of Love Lodge seems to have righted itself, for District Deputy W. Ray Smith reported to Grand Lodge in February, 1914, that Love Lodge had voted at its last meeting to surrender its charter, which would be mailed to the Grand Master "in a few days". Accordingly, the number 311 was immediately assigned to Mineral Lodge, which was chartered at this same Grand Lodge communication. Many of the members of Love Lodge had retained their membership in Hiram Lodge, so it was not difficult for the younger Lodge to pass out of the picture. Thus all became once more peace and harmony and Winchester Masonry has experienced no further disruptions down to our own time.

MASTERS OF WINCHESTER LODGE NO. 12 AND WINCHESTER HIRAM LODGE NO. 21
(1768-1949)

*James Gamul Dowdall 1768-1770
*Angus McDonald 1770-1772
*Samuel May 1772-1773
*James Gamul Dowdall.............................1773-1777
(No meetings) 1777-1785
*Samuel May (Acting) 1785
*James Gamul Dowdall 1785-1786
*Daniel Norton 1786-1788
*John Peyton 1788-1789
*John Kean 1789-1790
*Robert White 1790-1791
*John Conrad 1791-1792
*Hugh Scott 1792-1793
*Robert White 1793-1794
*John Peyton 1794-1795
*Richard Bowen 1795-1797
*John McDonald 1797-1798
*Richard Bowen 1798-1801
*Joel T. Gustine 1801-1802
(Minutes missing) 1802-1808
*Peter Lauck 1808-1811
*Henry Seevers 1811-1812
*Conrad Kremer 1812-1813
*Dolphin Drew 1813-1814
*Lemuel Bent 1814-1819
*Henry Seevers 1819-1820
*Lemuel Bent 1820-1823
*Samuel H. Davis 1823-1828
*Solomon Heister 1828-1832
*John R. W. Dunbar 1832-1833
*John B. Tilden Reed 1833-1834
*Nathaniel Seevers 1834-1837
*J. T. Randolph 1837-1839
*William Jenkins 1839-1841
*Benjamin Bushnell 1841-1842
*G. W. Grim 1842-1843
*John B. Tilden Reed 1843-1846
*William Y. Rooker 1846-1847

*Deceased.

Worshipful Masters

*Michael Danner 1847-1848
*Joseph S. Carson 1848-1850
*James H. Carson 1850-1851
*Robert W. Reed 1851-1852
*L. T. Moore 1852-1853
*Henry W. Thorpe 1853-1854
*L. T. Moore 1854-1855
*J. Carson Watson 1855-1856
*William L. Bent 1856-1858
*George W. Ginn 1858-1859
*Benjamin Miller 1859-1860
*E. S. Brent 1860-1861
*John B. Tilden Reed 1861-1866
(The Lodge was only partially active during these years.)
*William R. Denny 1866-1867
*Joseph M. Ginn 1867-1868
†*Richard Parker 1868-1869
*William S. Love 1869-1876
*Alexander M. Baker 1876-1877
*William R. Denny 1877-1878
*H. Clay Krebs 1878-1880
*R. M. Hunter 1880-1882
*George E. Bushnell 1882-1883
*W. W. Faulkner 1883-1885
*George E. Bushnell 1885-1887
*S. B. Baker 1887-1890
*William S. Love 1890-1896
*J. Clinton Smith 1896-1898
*M. H. G. Willis 1898-1899
*William S. Love 1899-1900
*M. H. G. Willis 1900-1901
*Harry M. Baker 1901-1902
*B. M. Knight 1902-1904
William E. Cooper 1904-1906
†C. Vernon Eddy 1906-1907
*H. R. Homer 1907-1909
*W. Ray Smith 1909-1911
H. C. Sheetz, Sr. 1911-1912
*Hollie B. McCormac 1912-1913
*A. C. Slonaker 1913-1914
*W. B. Wagner 1914-1915
*T. Russell Cather 1915-1916
*C. H. Schenk 1916-1917
*Philip Klompus 1917-1918

*Deceased.
† Also Grand Master.

*C. B. Stickley, Jr. 1918-1919
J. B. Beverley, Jr. 1919-1920
Richard H. Pope 1920-1921
*A. R. Breckenridge 1921-1922
C. S. Hartman 1922-1923
D. R. Slonaker 1923-1924
Lewis N. Barton 1924-1925
Walter M. Shade 1925-1926
Claude R. Cammer 1926-1927
*E. D. Calvert 1927-1928
W. B. Goode 1928-1929
Dudley C. Lichliter 1929-1930
M. V. B. Snoke 1930-1931
H. M. Seabright, Jr. 1931-1932
*Frank H. Dorsey 1932-1933
Harry L. McCann 1933-1934
O. C. Cassell 1934-1935
Harvey F. Carper 1935-1936
Claude M. Grim 1936-1937
Roy A. Larrick 1937-1938
Herbert W. Harmer 1938-1939
*Brady W. Largent 1939-1940
Wilbur E. Hewitt 1940-1941
Mifflin B. Clowe 1941-1942
J. Lee Miller 1942-1943
Douglas O. Grimm 1943-1944
Sebert J. Smith 1944-1945
John H. Fisher 1945-1946
Philip N. Hunter 1946-1947
Laurens P. Jones 1947-1948
Thurman Crosslin 1948-1949

*Deceased.

Note: The names of Archibald Magill (Grand Master 1817-1819) and Dr. Frank T. McFaden (Grand Master 1930-1931) do not appear in the list given above for the reason, that neither of these Brethren ever served as Master of Hiram Lodge. Archibald Magill apparently served as Master of Winchester Union Lodge No. 66 when it was chartered in 1802. Dr. McFaden served as Master of Dove Lodge No. 51 and Meridian Lodge No. 284, both of Richmond, at the same time. Both of these Brethren were members of Hiram Lodge *at the time* that they occupied the office of Grand Master of Masons in Virginia. One other Grand Master, Edmund Pendleton Hunter, was also a member of Hiram Lodge for a short time *before* he became Grand Master, but he is not claimed as one of the Grand Masters supplied by Hiram Lodge to the Grand Lodge of Virginia, since he was not a member of that Lodge *while* he was serving in that office.

TREASURERS

*Dorcy Penticost	1769-1770
*James Lindsay	1770-1772
*James Gamul Dowdall	1772-1773
*Angus McDonald	1773-1776
*Edward Maguire	1776-1790
(No meetings)	1777-1785
*John Kean	1790-1795
*William Maguire	1795-1796
*John Kingan	1796-1798
*Peter Lauck	1798-1801
*Lewis Wolfe	1801-1802
(Minutes missing)	1802-1808
*Lewis Barnett	1808-1809
*Philip Hoff	1809-1811
*James Foster	1811-1812
*Solomon Hollingsworth	1812-1813
*Peter Lauck	1813-1817
*Adam Brown	1817-1819
*Edmund Pendleton	1819-1820
*Peter Lauck	1820-1823
*Jacob Harmer	1823-1825
*William Powell	1825-1827
*Benjamin Bushnell	1827-1828
*William Jenkins	1828-1830
*Charles H. Clark	1830-1831
*Robert Barr	1831-1832
*John Kerr	1832-1835
*Benjamin Bushnell	1835-1841
*William Anders	1841-1842
*Michael Danner	1842-1843
*H. H. Conway	1843-1845
*John Kerr	1845-1869
*William L. Bent	1869-1874
*Henry Kinzel	1874-1885
*H. Clay Krebs	1885-1897
*John Ray	1897-1904
*T. Y. Kinzel	1904-1912
William E. Cooper	1912-1940
Claude M. Grim	1940-

*Deceased.

SECRETARIES

*John Lewis	1769-1770
*Samuel May	1770-1771
*Edmund Taylor	1771-1772
*Edward Maguire	1772-1773
*Benjamin Ashby	1773-1776
*Thomas Craig	1776-1777
(No meetings)	1777-1785
*James Gamul Dowdall	1785
*John Peyton	1785-1786
*John Kean	1786-1788
*Alexander King	1788-1789
*John Peyton	1789-1790
*Daniel Norton	1790-1792
*Francis Raworth	1792-1793
*John Peyton	1793-1794
*Archibald Magill	1794-1795
*James Gibbs	1795-1796
*Archibald Magill	1796-1797
*Frederick Hurst	1797-1801
*Daniel Sittler	1801-1802
(Minutes missing)	1802-1808
*Daniel Walker Thomas	1808-1810
*Conrad Kremer	1810-1811
*Daniel Walker Thomas	1811-1812
*Thomas C. Wyndham	1812-1814
*Edmund Pendleton	1814-1817
*Edward Slater	1817-1818
*Philip A. Klipstine	1818-1819
*F. M. Beckwith	1819-1821
*Thomas Hollis	1821-1822
*Samuel H. Ball	1822-1823
*Edward Slater	1823-1824
*John Wilson	1824-1828
*Samuel H. Davis	1828-1829
*Benjamin Bushnell	1829-1830
*William Shepherd	1830-1831
*William Jenkins	1831-1832
*George A. Reed, Jr.	1832-1833
*John W. Hollis	1833-1834
*C. A. B. Coffroth	1834-1836
*John W. Hollis	1836-1837
*Thomas W. Edwards	1837-1838
*D. Barnett	1838-1839

*Deceased.

Other Officers of Winchester Lodge

*William Towers 1839-1844
*C. A. B. Coffroth 1844-1848
*Charles Tucker 1848-1849
*C. A. B. Coffroth 1849-1863
*Alfred P. White (*pro tem.*, served April 20th to June
   9th only) 1863
*William McP. Fuller 1863-1864
*George W. Legge 1864-1866
*C. A. B. Coffroth 1866-1883
*C. E. Hoover 1883-1890
*Richard L. Gray 1890-1899
*J. E. Correll 1899-1904
*C. W. Wilson 1904-1909
*Isaac N. Good 1909-1918
C. Vernon Eddy 1918-1936
Harvey F. Carper 1936-1937
C. Vernon Eddy 1937-

TRUSTEES

*William R. Denny 1867-1888
*George W. Ginn 1867-1887
*John Kerr 1867-1875
*William L. Bent 1867-1878
*Thomas B. Wood 1867-1871
*George F. Glaize 1888-1896
*George E. Bushnell 1888-1898
*William S. Love 1888-1912
*Henry Baetjer 1888-1912
*H. Clay Krebs 1888-1911
*S. H. Hable 1900-1911
*A. M. Baker .... 1900- (?)
*Thomas N. Lupton .... (?)-1911
*W. G. Conway 1912-1917
*H. B. McCormac 1912-1937
*George H. Kinzel 1912-1914
W. E. Cooper 1912-
*J. E. Correll 1914-1915
C. Vernon Eddy 1914-
*A. C. Slonaker 1915-1928
*T. Russell Cather 1922-1944
*B. M. Knight 1929-1937
Claude M. Grim 1937-
Wendell B. Goode 1938-
Claude R. Cammer 1944-

---

*Deceased.

Note: The first trustees of Winchester Hiram Lodge No. 21 were appointed at the June term of the Circuit Court of Frederick

County in 1867. Their function was to hold title to the present Lodge property and any other real estate, which might be acquired by the Lodge subsequently. For many years their duties were merely nominal and the "Reserve Fund Committee" handled most of the funds of the Lodge until 1893 when a committee on investment of surplus funds was appointed. This latter committee also performed some of the functions ordinarily performed by trustees. Finally, on March 10, 1914, the "Reserve Fund Committee" was abolished by formal action of the Lodge and its duties were ordered to be performed by the trustees, who have obeyed this mandate from that date to the present. The present method of selecting a trustee to fill a vacancy is, that the Lodge selects a Brother by ballot for recommendation to the Corporation Court of the city of Winchester after the Lodge is informed by the trustees, that there is a vacancy in their number. Previously the Master made the appointment without reference to the Lodge. The present trustees are as follows:

    Claude M. Grim, Chairman
    William E. Cooper
    W. B. Goode
    Claude R. Cammer
    C. Vernon Eddy, Secretary-Treasurer

JUDGE RICHARD PARKER
GRAND MASTER OF MASONS IN VIRGINIA
(1876-1877)

FRANK TALBOT McFADEN, D.D.
GRAND MASTER OF MASONS IN VIRGINIA
(1930-1931)
GRAND COMMANDER, K. T. OF VIRGINIA
(1907-1908)

PART TWO
THE CHAPTER

CHAPTER XIII

THE PRE-GRAND CHAPTER PERIOD

The Grand Chapter of Royal Arch Masons of Virginia was organized at Norfolk in May, 1808. The first steps looking toward its establishment were undertaken by correspondence several years previously and the first convention with this object in view took place, also in Norfolk, on May 3, 1806. So far as is now known, there were five independent Chapters located at as many different places in Virginia prior to the calling of this first convention. There may have been others but, if so, their existence has not been brought to the attention of the present writer. These five "pre-Grand Chapter" Chapters were the outgrowth, of course, of the local Lodges, which had been established in the same localities, namely, Norfolk, Richmond, Staunton, Winchester, and Dumfries. All of them originated as incidental groups, which met at first informally and conferred the Royal Arch degree upon Brethren, who were *invited* to become Masons of that degree. The close relationship between the symbolic degrees and the Royal Arch in England is well known and it was but natural that the same sort of tradition (though it was hardly old enough at that time to be called a "tradition") should be carried over to Masonry in the American colonies. Virginia has at least two claims to distinction in this regard: first, Fredericksburg Lodge No. 4 (Washington's "Mother Lodge") has the oldest extant record of the conferring of the Royal Arch degree anywhere in the world (December 22, 1753 on three candidates); second, Cabin Point Royal Arch Lodge, located on the south side of James River a few miles below Richmond, was warranted by Joseph Montfort, Provincial Grand Master of North Carolina, on April 15, 1775. This Lodge undoubtedly chose its name to indicate its pride in the fact, that the Royal Arch degree was attached to it.

Of the five Chapters in existence as separate bodies prior

to the organization of the Grand Chapter of Virginia, the one at Dumfries is long since extinct. The Chapter at Winchester was apparently too remote from Tidewater Virginia to participate in the organization of Grand Chapter, and thus the remaining three Chapters (Norfolk, Richmond, and Staunton) were exactly the minimum number (three) required by Masonic usage and custom to institute a sovereign Grand Body. It is certain that all of the five Chapters mentioned were organized before 1800. It is also entirely probable, that Norfolk Chapter, which was the oldest, came into existence as a separate body before 1790, for we know definitely, that Staunton Chapter was organized in that year and Richmond Chapter in 1792. The date of the establishment of Dumfries Chapter will probably never be known, as no records whatever have survived from that body. Finally, the Chapter at Winchester dates from August 26, 1799 and we have, fortunately, the brief minutes of the organization meeting. Like the other four Chapters, Winchester Chapter was self-organized and self-constituted. The same was true, as we have seen, of the original Winchester Lodge No. 12. That was quite usual in those days due to the prevailing conditions, the lack of adequate means of transportation and communication, and the absence of sovereign Grand Bodies, to which applications for warrants could be transmitted.

Because of their extreme importance we quote here from the record the complete minutes of the organization meeting of Winchester Chapter.

> AT A MEETING of several R. A. M. agreeably to the Ancient Constitutions held at the Room of Lodge No. 12 in the Town of Winchester, Virginia, the 26 day of August, A. L. 5799, and it appearing to the Companions assembled, that great advantages would result to Free-Masonry by the establishment of a R. A. C. in this Borough—
>
> THEREFORE RESOLVED, That we, the following Companions here present, viz., James G. Dowdall, Richard Bowen, Edwd. Slater, Peter Lauck, Anthony Weatherall, Jno. Peyton, and Thomas Purse, do form ourselves and are hereby formed into an R. A. C. of the most sublime degree of R. A. Masonry.

RESOLVED, That this C. do proceed without delay to appoint officers to preside over the same until a Code of Laws be formed for the future Government of the said R. A. C. The following Companions appeared by a majority of votes duly elected, viz.
  James G. Dowdall, M. E. H. P.
  Edward Slater, 1st C.
  Anthony Weatherall, 2d C.
  Thomas Purse, 1st S.
  Richard Bowen, 2d S.
  Peter Lauck, T.
  John G. Crockwell, G.

The reader who is acquainted with the terminology of present day Royal Arch Masonry will note at once several titles used in the above minutes, which are not employed in our own country today. Hence, we give them in full here in the order, in which they are used above as follows: Most Excellent High Priest, 1st Chief, 2d Chief, 1st Scribe, 2d Scribe, Treasurer, Genitor (i.e., Janitor whose function was also that of tiling the Chapter as well as of keeping the meeting room in order). It will be noted also that John G. Crockwell, Tyler of Lodge No. 12 and the first man to hold the office of Genitor in Winchester Chapter, was not even a member and was probably not a Royal Arch Mason. However, as may be surmised, this was no great obstacle to his serving in that capacity. The titles originated, of course, in the particular form of ritual used by the Winchester Companions (probably the Irish ritual). This was all changed, when James Cushman came to Virginia in 1820 and persuaded the Grand Chapter of Virginia to adopt the Royal Arch ritual, which we use at the present time and which shows marked differences from the Irish ritual, not only in the list of officers of the Chapter but also in the content of the degree itself.

We call attention also to the fact, that James Gamul Dowdall, the "father of Winchester Masonry" and, as we have already seen, the first Master of Lodge No. 12, was chosen also as the first High Priest of Winchester Chapter. It is also an interesting fact, that, while the minutes of this organization meeting are not signed, a number of the subsequent early minutes, beginning with the very next meeting of the Chapter held on the same day

(August 26th), are signed by both the 1st and 2d Scribes.

Before proceeding with the discussion of Winchester capitular Masonry in detail, we think it pertinent here to quote a paragraph from John Dove, for whom the revived Winchester Chapter was named many years later:

> Royal Arch Masonry was taught and practiced in this State during the latter part of the last century under the authority of a Master's Warrant, until the want of some specific legislation seemed evidently indicated for the internal government of the Royal Arch Chapters, which were then growing in number and increasing in members; and taking the hint from movements in the Northern States, as well as our sister State of Pennsylvania, a convention of Royal Arch Masons representing Chapters was held in the then Borough of Norfolk on the 3d day of May, 1806.

We now proceed with the subsequent history of the Winchester Chapter. At another meeting held the same day as its organization, the Companions "proceeded to form a Code of Laws for the government of this H. R. A. C. [Holy Royal Arch Chapter] and the same being examined and approved, they are ordered to be recorded in a book kept for that purpose". Unfortunately this book has not survived and we do not know what provisions were included in the Chapter's original "code of laws". We suspect, that these laws were modelled after those of some Chapter in Philadelphia, since the terminology "Holy Royal Arch Chapter", which is still used in Pennsylvania today, would indicate this. Winchester's symbolic Masonry came from Pennsylvania, as we have seen. There is no reason to suppose, therefore, that its capitular Masonry did not come from the same source.

The Chapter meeting scheduled for September 21, 1799 was not held because a sufficient number of the Companions was not present to open the Chapter. We do not know the minimum number required for this purpose at that time but the reader will have noticed already, that fewer than nine (the present day requirement) were at the organization meeting. On October 21, 1799 there were six Companions present, so the Chapter was opened by High Priest Dowdall. The following is the record of the proceedings on that occasion:

The Holy C. was opened with the usual ceremonies, the installation of officers was postponed on account of the absence of Comp's. Peyton and White. Read a petition B'r's. Seaton, Payne, Newman & Newby, who were all recommended by Comp's. Bowen, Lauck, and Slater, praying to become R. A. M. Ordered that they lie over. No other business, this H. C. was closed in due time and perfect harmony.

From a perusal of the subsequent proceedings of the Chapter, it is quite clear that one of its regulations provided for the election of officers every six months. This requirement was not observed very strictly, however, chiefly, we believe, due to the relative infrequency of Chapter meetings. However, the Winchester Companions were a law unto themselves at that time and, by mutual consent, they could do almost anything they wished, so long as the known landmarks of Masonry were not violated.

On November 27, 1799 another meeting was held, of which the following are the recorded minutes:

The Holy C. was opened with the usual Ceremonies, the list of members called, when Comp's. Peyton & White were absent. Ordered that they be fined *nisi*. The petition of Brother William Newby was taken up and ballotted for agreeably to the bye laws and accepted unanimously, after which a Past Master's Lodge was opened, Br. Newby rec'd. that degree. It was then closed. Br. Newby retired. The H. R. A. C. was again opened, Br. Newby brought in and rec'd. the Holy and Sublime degree. The petition of Br. Joel T. Gustine was then handed in—ordered to lie the usual time. Chapter then closed with good harmony.

In a note to these minutes we find that Brother Newby paid $7.00 for the two degrees, which he received, and the six other Companions present paid 25 cents each toward the expenses of the night. The Genitor received $1.00 for his services, which was taken out of Companion Newby's fee for the degrees. One other comment may be necessary here—the explanation of the use of the word *"nisi"* in the minutes quoted above. It indicates, of course, that the absent Companions were to be fined *unless* (this is what the word means in Latin) they could furnish good and sufficient excuses for their non-attendance.

The Chapter met again on December 16, 1799 and on January 20, 1800. Companion Dowdall presided at both of these meetings, at the latter of which three petitions were received, two being ordered to lie over and the third, being considered a case of emergency because the petitioner's residence was "100 miles distant from this Holy C.", was acted upon the same night, the applicant's prayer being granted. The next minutes are dated August 18, 1800, but a quorum was not present and no meeting was held. The two Scribes have inserted a note at this point reading as follows: "The Holy R. A. C. held no meetings in the months of February, March, April, May, June, or July, 1800". Certainly they were more thoughtful than many Masonic secretaries, whom we have known in our own time! On September 15, 1800 it is recorded that "a person of the name of H—— M—— certified from a C. of R. A. M. held in the town of Carlile, Cumberland County, Pennsylvania, was examined and found unworthy to be admitted". At the next meeting a visiting Companion was similarly examined and, being found worthy, "was admitted and took his seat accordingly". At this last meeting the petitions of several candidates, who had been previously rejected, were reconsidered. All were elected, exalted the same night to the Royal Arch degree, and "returned thanks accordingly". We suppose that these newly exalted Companions considered themselves extremely lucky in passing the scrutiny of their elders of that day.

On November 4, 1800 one candidate was exalted at an "extra Chapter" and on November 17th officers were chosen and installed for the ensuing six months with Richard Bowen as High Priest. Three petitions were accepted and one rejected at this meeting. At the meeting of December 14th a seal for the Chapter was ordered. In 1801 meetings were held on January 19th and 26th, February 16th, March 16th and 23d, April 2d and 20th, May 17th, June 5th and 15th, July 20th, August 18th, September 21st, October 15th, November 16th, and December 21st and 26th —a total of seventeen meetings for the year. The primary reason for this was the the fact that the members of Lodge No. 12 seem to have thought well of capitular Masonry from the beginning and a number of them decided to make application for the Royal

Arch during the first few years of the infant Chapter's existence. On March 23d Companion Purse presented to the Chapter a copy of the *Freemason's Monitor,* for which he received the thanks of the Companions, also the by-laws were "reconsidered" and certain amendments made, but we are not told in the minutes what these were. On April 2d the Chapter agreed to "remove to the stone house in Loudoun Street, in which Angus McDonald formerly resided, provided the B. Lodge do join with this C. in defraying the expenses of such removal, rent, &c." A committee was appointed to confer with the Lodge looking to the carrying out of this resolution. This meant, that the Chapter would leave the home of Peter Lauck, so it was unanimously voted to thank him "for his upright and zealous conduct as a Mason and a landlord and for his obliging and brotherly attention to us at all times". The Chapter at this period is always recorded as "opened with the usual solemnities and prayers read". New officers for the ensuing six months were elected on April 20th with Thomas Purse as the new High Priest.

A petitioner named Original Wroe (this is the name as recorded several times in the minutes) was elected on May 17, 1801 but a pencil notation states, that "he did not appear to be made a R. A. Mason". It was also voted at this meeting, that Companion Bowen be given an order for printing 500 summonses (Chapter notices) in accordance with such form as might be prescribed by the High Priest. On June 15th the Chapter voted to join with the Lodge in the celebration of next St. John's night, paying its proportionate share of the expenses of that occasion. On July 20th we note, that Brother Edward Christian (he was not a Royal Arch Mason) presented a "jewell" to the Chapter, which was accepted with thanks after the Companions had satisfied themselves that it was not intended for the Lodge but for the Chapter. In the minutes of this meeting we find the first reference to a candidate's being "admitted to the degree of an E. S. E. R. A. M." (Excellent and Super-Excellent Royal Arch Mason, as the degree was denominated in those days). One Companion, having "had grace granted him in Lodge No. 12" for the payment of his dues and "his suspension in this Chapter having taken place in consequence of his having been suspended in said Lodge No. 12, he is therefore reinstated in his office as Senior Scribe unanimously". A committee was appointed on August 18, 1801 to visit the Genitor, who is now listed as "Companion Genitor Crockwell", though his name is not shown anywhere in the preceding minutes as a Royal Arch Mason, and inquire into the nature of his indisposition with authority to draw on the Chapter funds for his relief, if necessary. At the meeting of September 21st, a visitor is noted in the person of Companion Arthur Clark "of Lodge No. 32, York County, Carolina" (evidently *South* Carolina), also two Companions requested and obtained "leave of absence for the remainder of the evening". On October 15th officers for the next six months were chosen with Edward Slater as High Priest. At the November meeting a committee was appointed to revise the by-laws and a rather unusual situation arose at the meeting of December 26th, when a certain Companion, who held an office in the Chapter was reported as having been installed shortly before as an officer in Lodge No. 12, all of which was a violation of the Chapter by-laws and obligation (we do not know why). Hence, this Companion was deprived of his office in the Chapter forthwith, was forbidden to march in the procession on St. John's Day wearing the Chapter insignia, and it was voted that charges be preferred against him for his action in the premises.

On January 18, 1802 several petitioners were elected, two of whom were required to pay $12.00 (instead of $6.00) for their exaltation fees, since they were not members of Lodge No. 12. On February 5th the request of a visiting Companion, that he be allowed to visit the Chapter, was refused after an examination by a committee, on the ground that the visitor was "an Excellent and not Super-Excellent R. A. M." We have often wished that the ritual of that day might be available to us now, so that Companions of the present time might be informed regarding this phase of early Virginia Capitular Masonry. The case of the Companion, who had violated his obligation as noted above, was discussed fully at the meeting of March 15th and he was permitted to make his defense in person. We then read: "A vote was taken whether he be expelled or not, which passed in the affirmative, whereupon he was desired to leave the room". Peter Lauck was then duly elected 2d Chief in place of the expelled Companion. There were evidently some long-winded Companions in the Chapter at that time, for we find an amendment adopted to the by-laws on April 19, 1802 providing that no Companion should be permitted to speak more than twice on the same question without special permission of the chair. Perhaps it would be a good thing for us to adopt such a rule in our Masonic bodies today!

On April 21, 1802 a special meeting was held to consider the report of the committee on the ailing Genitor and $6.00 was placed at the disposal of the committee members "to be laid out as they shall think best". In the minutes of May 17th we find this interesting entry:

> On motion it is ordered, that this Chapter pay a proportionable part of the expences for a sermon to be preached by the Reverend Christian Streit on St. John's Day; for playing the organ, & musick to and from Church.

At the next meeting (July 19, 1802) it was noted, that this sum amounted to $6.33, also it was ordered that Companion Purse should be reimbursed for "jewels, &c made and furnished by him for this Chapter". On October 18th the semi-annual election of officers was held, at which Peter Lauck became High Priest. We also note that, at this meeting, a certain Brother's petition "having lain before the Chapter the time prescribed by the Bye Laws and [he] not coming forward agreeable thereto, therefore ordered the same be throw'd out". On December 20, 1802 the by-laws were amended to "place the Winchester Union Lodge on the same footing with this Chapter that Lodge No. 12 stands with us", and a committee was appointed to cooperate with committees from the two Lodges in making plans for the celebration of St. John's Day following. Three Companions loom large in the proceedings of February 27, 1803, as their names are listed very prominently by the Scribes as "members who did not pay nightly expenses this night" in the amount of 25 cents each. In the minutes of March 21st two petitioners "were severally prepared, brought in, & received the Excellent degree of Arch Masons, and Super-Excellent Royal Arch Masons, for which thanks was returned in the usual manner". It is recorded that the Chapter had thirteen members on April 18, 1803.

On December 19, 1803 an interesting occasion arose when Companion William Ball was appointed to the office of 2d Chief and "took his seat as such—withdrew without leave from the Chair, was fined Two Dollars unless he can show cause approving of his conduct", also we note that "Companion Purse having left the room without leave was fined agreeable to the bylaws". We wonder what would happen if the same discipline were applied to our Lodges and Chapters today.

At the meeting of January 16, 1804 it was proposed to hold regular meetings of the Chapter quarterly but the matter was postponed for future consideration. It was also voted, "that the Chair of this chapter be repaired by Compn. Slater & that he be paid for the same out of funds". We find no further mention of the matter in the minutes of subsequent meetings, however, but the next "regular nights" seem to have been June 18th, August 20th, and December 17th, so the Companions evidently made some change in their by-laws to cover this subject. At the last-mentioned meeting new officers were chosen, including William Ball as High Priest for the next succeeding six months. At this time we also note the passing of Companion John Peyton, one of the first petitioners to receive the Royal Arch degree in Winchester Chapter. Philip Hoff and William Silver, both very active members of Lodge No. 12, received the Chapter degrees in 1805.

In the minutes of September 15, 1806 we note the first extant reference in the records of Winchester Chapter to the proposed organization of a Grand Royal Arch Chapter in Virginia. It reads as follows:

The committee appointed to take into consideration the constitution proposed for the government of the Grand Chapter not having performed their service therein are continued 'till the 22d instant, at which time they are to report, and the Scribes are directed to summons the members generally to attend at said time.

The further connection between the Grand Chapter of Virginia (then in process of organization) and Winchester Chapter will be presented in subsequent pages of our narrative.

CHAPTER XIV

WINCHESTER CHAPTER AND THE GRAND CHAPTER OF VIRGINIA

The affection of the Winchester Companions remained strong for Pennsylvania during 1806, and there was no hurry about ratifying the proposed constitution of the Grand Chapter of Virginia. Although Lodge No. 12 accepted a Virginia charter the year following (1807), the Chapter did not follow the Lodge's example in this matter until thirteen years later. It is our purpose in this chapter of our narrative to discover what happened to Capitular Masonry in Winchester during this formative and all important period from 1806 to 1820.

On September 22, 1806 the Chapter held an extra meeting for the consideration of the proposed Grand Chapter constitution but "after mature deliberation it was unanimously agreed that the ratification thereof should be postponed for further consideration". We would give a great deal if we could obtain a detailed record of the evening's discussion on this matter. On December 12th following, the committee in charge of reporting on the subject failed to make its report and an extra meeting was set for December 17th. In the minutes of that session we find the following:

> On motion made and carried, the Chapter formed themselves into a Committee of the Whole (Companion William Ball in the chair) in order to take into consideration the constitution framed by the United Chapter H. R. A. S. Masons at Norfolk in the State of Virginia. After sundry amendments being made to said Constitution the committee arose, and the Chairman reported the amendments to which the Chapter agreed.

Then, on February 24, 1807 the following significant action was taken:

> The Chapter on reconsidering the proposed Constitution for the Government of the Grand Chapter of this State, are unanimously

of opinion, that to agree thereunto would be involving themselves into difficulties, of which they are free in their present situation. Therefore do agree to send the following letter to the H. P. at Staunton:

Winchester, Feb. 24th, 1807

Worthy Companion,

The Chapter at this place having taken into consideration your highly esteemed letter, with documents accompanying it, and after the most mature reflection and respectful examination have determined on disagreeing to the proposed plan. Many reasons lead to this decision. To enumerate them would be an unnecessary consumption of time. Possessed as this body is of powers of the utmost extent and perhaps the oldest Chapter in Virginia, an addition to those powers is not desired, and a diminution could not be agreed to. I am directed in the name of the Chapter to notify their general dissent, and to return you their best thanks for your friendly communication.

This letter was signed by Lewis Wolfe, High Priest at that time. One error of fact is made in the letter namely the statement, that the Winchester Chapter was "perhaps the oldest Chapter in Virginia", since we have already shown, that it was antedated by at least four other Chapters. The reason for addressing the letter to the High Priest of the Staunton Chapter lies in the fact, that this was the nearest Chapter to Winchester, also that William Chambers, High Priest of Staunton Chapter for many years after its organization in 1790, was quite active in the proposal to organize a Grand Chapter for Virginia and was made its "Most Excellent Supreme Grand Captain of the Host" (second ranking officer in those days) when Grand Chapter was finally organized in May, 1808. Thus ended the matter for the time being, at least so far as Winchester Chapter was concerned.

The year 1807 saw the election of Archibald Magill (a future Grand Master of Virginia) to the office of High Priest of Winchester Chapter (June 15th), also the decision of the Companions to the effect, "that no Mason shall be hereafter exalted to the degree of R.A. in this chapter unless he at the time thereof is actually a member of some Master Mason Lodge". It was also voted, that membership in the Lodge should be required as a prerequisite for the continuance of membership in the Chapter.

The matter of the Grand Chapter of Virginia came before the Chapter again on April 23, 1808. We read in the minutes of that date that "the communication from the United Chapter of Norfolk was laid before this Chapter, the subject of which being of great importance, the Chapter was adjourned until Monday, the 25th instant, for the consideration of the Companions". At the meeting on the 25th a committee consisting of Peter Lauck, William Ball, Daniel W. Thomas, William Silver, and Archibald Magill was appointed to make the necessary amendments to the proposed constitution. It was also ordered that a letter be written to the High Priest of the Norfolk Chapter, thanking him for his communication and stating "that at the present period no decisive answer could be given" to his proposals.

In the minutes of May 5, 1808 it is noted that there was "lent out of the funds of this Chapter to Hiram Lodge No. 21, July 10th last, four dollars ($4)". On September 26th of that year a new code of by-laws was adopted and the Treasurer was ordered to have the candlestick repaired before the next meeting. It was likewise ordered, "that Companions Kean & Clare be furnished with the necessary colours to finish the painting of the M. R. H. P.'s [Most Reverend High Priest's] Chair". The cost of repairing the candlestick is later noted at $1.00 but there is no indication as to the cost of the colours.

The subject of Grand Chapter was again scheduled for discussion on March 3, 1809, but too few Companions were present for so momentous a matter, hence it was continued to a subsequent meeting. At this point a number of pages have been removed from the minute book and we are led to believe that matters of importance were contained in them. These are followed by the minutes of a number of meetings dated "in the year of Royal Arch Masonry 2801". It is not clear what calendar year this indicates, since errors were apparently made by the Chapter Secretary in the utilization of such dates. It is quite apparent, however, that certain changes in the ritual had taken place, for the titles of the officers have been changed to Most Reverend High Priest, Most Excellent Captain of the Host, Excellent Captain of the Guard, Treasurer, and Secretary. The old style of two Chiefs and two Scribes had disappeared. With this change in the ritual we must assume also a change in the mode of reckoning the "year of Royal Arch Masonry" used in the dates given in the minutes. By a careful analysis of the matter, we are forced to the conclusion that the minutes for approximately five years have disappeared completely and that the first minutes dealing with the Chapter at the end of that period are concerned with a meeting held on December 18, 1814. Daniel Walker Thomas is still the Secretary, though he signs himself as "Grand Secretary", which was perfectly permissible for subordinate Chapters using certain rituals in that day. The next meeting was held on June 19, 1815, at which an election was held and Archibald Magill was returned to the office of High Priest. The meetings were apparently held quarterly at that time with as many "extra meetings" as might be necessary to transact the Chapter's business.

On March 2, 1816 we read that "a memorial was presented to this Chapter from the Assembly of Knight Templars requesting the privilege of holding their Assemblies in the Masonic Hall, which was accordingly granted". Then, following the minutes of this meeting (which were obviously transcribed into the minute book by a later hand) we find this notation:

> From a small piece of paper found in the chest of the Chapter it appears that James Hill was exalted to the degree of H. Royal Arch Masonry on the 21st of the 4th month called April, A. D. 1815, A. R. A. M. 2803.

By this time the meetings of the Chapter are designated as "regular" and "extra" *conventions*—the forerunner of our present term, *convocation*.

The minutes from August 5, 1815 to June 3, 1816 are also missing. On the latter date Lemuel Bent was elected High Priest and the Chapter voted to participate with Hiram Lodge No. 21 in the exercises of the succeeding St. John's Day. We now go to March 4, 1817, the minutes of the intervening "conventions" of the Chapter having been lost. At this meeting there were three exaltations, one more on June 7th, and another on June 17th. In the minutes of the last-mentioned meeting the date A. D. is given as 1817, hence we are once more on safe ground so far as our dates are concerned.

During the remainder of the year 1817 through 1818 and on into 1819 the meetings of the Chapter were held regularly and there was work at almost every meeting. George Reed was made High Priest on December 3, 1818 and was re-elected to that office on June 2, 1819. On New Year's day of 1820 we find the usual routine of the Chapter interrupted by the question of Grand Chapter again. The minutes on this point read as follows:

> This Chapter was convened in consequence of a letter from the Supreme G. Chapter of Va. directed to it, summoning it to attend a meeting of the said S. G. Chapter of Va. to be holden in the City of Richmond on the 17th day of the 1st month, called January, on business of importance to Masonry.
> RESOLVED therefore, That this Chapter, altho' it has never considered itself subordinate to the S. G. Chapter of Virginia, hath nevertheless thought proper to convene on the receipt of said summons and to commission Companion George Reed, M. R. High Priest thereof, to represent it in the said S. G. Chapter of Va. and to unite with the said S. G. Chapter of Va. if in his judgment it will comport with the interest of this Chapter & of Masonry in general.

This action on the part of the Winchester Companions proved to be more historic and more far-reaching than they could have supposed at the time it was taken. The sequel appears in the minutes of Winchester Chapter for February 1, 1820 as follows:

> This Chapter was convened for the purpose of taking into consideration the resolution of the Supreme Grand Chapter of Virginia, which is as follows:
> "A communication having been received from a Royal Arch Chapter now sitting at Winchester, Virginia, and working under a Charter No. .... from the Grand Lodge of Pennsylvania, praying to be associated with this S. G. Chapter and received into its jurisdiction for reasons set forth in that communication deemed sufficient by the G. Chapter, and in due consideration of the promptness with which that Chapter has attended this special

convocation,

"RESOLVED, that the said Chapter be and they are hereby received and that a charter do issue free of expense, appointing Companion George Reed, H. P.; Peter Lauck, King; and Lemuel Bent, Scribe.

"JOHN DOVE, S. G. S."

When it was resolved, that we entirely approve the measures adopted by them and hereby accede to this proposal.

The communication mentioned above as having been transmitted by George Reed in conformity to the authority granted to him by the Winchester Companions on January 1, 1820 is no longer extant. It is indeed unfortunate, that no copy of this letter has been preserved for our information today, especially since the reasons set forth therein are not available elsewhere so far as we know. Certainly the attitude of the Chapter had changed materially in the few years prior to this important step as compared with the formerly manifested intense loyalty to Pennsylvania.

Thus, after an existence of 21 years as an independent and sovereign local body (there is no evidence that the Chapter was ever connected in any formal manner with the Grand Chapter of Pennsylvania), Winchester Chapter cast in its lot with the other Chapters in Virginia and became a full-fledged member of the Grand Chapter of that commonwealth. We now turn to that part of our story, which deals with the Chapter in its new role as a part of the Virginia Capitular picture.

CHAPTER XV

THE FIRST FORTY YEARS UNDER VIRGINIA'S JURISDICTION

As has been previously mentioned in the section treating of Hiram Lodge, the year 1820 was an important one for all branches of Virginia Masonry. For it was in that year, that James Cushman arrived within the borders of the commonwealth and, among other things, persuaded the Grand Chapter of Virginia to adopt the Royal Arch ritual based upon the Zerubbabel legend rather than that of the Josiah legend of the rebuilding of the Temple at Jerusalem. Cushman also had himself elected in the same year to the office of Grand Lecturer of the Grand Chapter of Virginia, a position created especially at his instance, since he was the first Companion ever to exercise the functions of that office. Hence, in line with its action in joining the Grand Chapter of Virginia, the Chapter at Winchester (its name and number are not yet given in the minutes) changed its officers to High Priest, King, Scribe, Treasurer, Secretary, etc., about as we know them in Capitular Masonry today.

At the election of officers held on June 7, 1820, the three principal officers named in the charter (George Reed, Peter Lauck, and Lemuel Bent) were continued in office, Solomon Dodds was made Treasurer, Philip A. Klipstine Secretary, and James Foster Janitor. In the minutes of August 28th of that year we find the first mention of the new "year of Royal Arch Masonry", namely 2530. This change was also brought about by Companion Cushman, who paid the Chapter a visit "for the purpose of instructing it in the true and ancient mode of working". Cushman had evidently been instructing the Companions for some days previously, they being entirely "gullible" and accepting all that he taught them as truly Masonic gospel. On this particular evening they voted that "the sum of sixty dollars be paid to Companion Cushman in reward of his services". The following note is appended by

Secretary Philip A. Klipstine to the minutes of this *convocation* (the first use of this term in the Winchester Chapter minutes):

> In consequence of the union of this Chapter with the Grand Chapter of Virginia, the records of the subordinate degrees belonging thereto, viz. the Most Excellent Master, Past Master, and Mark Master, which heretofore have been kept separate and distinct, will henceforward be inserted in the records of the Chapter.

It appears that work in both the Mark Master's and the Most Excellent Master's degrees was held under Cushman's direction at this same convocation. He is listed as presiding at additional sessions of the Chapter "for work and instruction" on September 5 and 6, 1820, also at an extra communication of the Most Excellent Master's Lodge on the 4th day of that month. New by-laws had been adopted, under which an election was held on November 7, 1820. Philip A. Klipstine was made High Priest, Francis M. Beckwith King, and Lemuel Bent Scribe. Companion Klipstine was also chosen as representative to Grand Chapter, the first such representative ever designated by Winchester Chapter after receiving its Virginia charter. He submitted a bill for his expenses amounting to $22.50 after his return from Grand Chapter.

On November 2, 1824 there was a regular convocation of the Chapter, which was now designated as "Royal Arch Chapter No. 12". After working for some time, the Chapter was closed and the following notation appears in the minutes: "There being more business than can be done this evening, the Lodge is adjourned until tomorrow evening at 6 o'clock". The reference happens to be to the Lodge of Past Masters and it seems to us, that we have heard somewhere in our Masonic experience, that a Lodge cannot be *adjourned* and that this fact is taught in the ritual of the Past Master's degree. Yet we have here, on this particular occasion, the statement, that the Lodge in which this important principle is taught ritualistically, was itself *adjourned* by the presiding officer until the following evening. (Query: Did the candidate *adjourn* the Lodge this time—and get away with it?)

On November 3, 1824 the Chapter voted to join with Hiram Lodge in preparing for the proposed visit of LaFayette and officers were chosen for the ensuing year with Lemuel Bent as High Priest. The last minutes recorded in this particular minute book are dated January 19, 1825. After that there is complete silence until November 10, 1834, a period of nearly ten years. There is no reason, however, to presume that the Chapter was inactive during that period. On the contrary, all the indications point to the fact, that it was quite active, for a list of the members as of January 13, 1838 is included in the third minute book of the Chapter and there are 22 names in this list. On November 10th of that year there were 23 members and a year later there were 21, two having been lost during the year and none added.

We return now to November 10, 1834. George Reed served as High Priest *pro tem.* at this meeting, and it was voted to contribute $25.00 toward the expenses of the celebration held by Hiram Lodge the preceding June 24th. The minutes are signed by Benjamin Bushnell as Secretary. On February 4, 1835 it was ordered, that the members be required to attend on the second Tuesday of every month "for the purpose of receiving lectures and attending to such business as may come before the Chapter", also that $15.00 be paid to some one of the Companions, who would agree to "make fires and keep the room in order" (we assume that this last item was intended to cover the expense for the year). On June 22, 1835 the by-laws were ordered to be revised and it was voted that 100 copies be printed by Companion J. W. Hollis, who was then in process of receiving the Chapter degrees. He was given the Most Excellent Master's and the Royal Arch degrees without fee in return for this service.

On August 22, 1837 Lemuel Bent was re-elected High Priest and C. H. Clark Secretary. There is only one set of minutes extant between November 4, 1835 and August 22, 1837, but we believe the Chapter almost certainly held some additional convocations during that period. The by-laws were again revised on February 7, 1839 and ordered printed. On July 6th of that year charges were preferred against a Companion for un-Masonic conduct, the first time such an item has appeared in the minutes of Chapter No. 12. Companion Washington G. Singleton was elected High Priest on November 6, 1839 and he and John Dove were chosen to represent the Chapter at Grand Chapter the following month. At this early date the Companions must have learned to esteem and revere Dr. Dove, then Grand Secretary of Grand Chapter, for whom the Winchester Chapter was to be named at the time of its reorganization following the War Between the States. The Chapter pursued the even tenor of its way throughout 1840. The minutes of February 21 and March 3, 1841 are omitted. The Chapter met on May 4th that year for work and on November 17th for the annual election of officers. On March 2, 1842 the fees for the capitular degrees were set at the following amounts: Mark Master and Past Master, $5.00 Most Excellent Master, $5.00; Royal Master, $2.50; Select Master, $2.50, and Royal Arch, $10.00—a total of $25.00. This action was taken to meet the situation created by Grand Chapter, with which the Grand Council of Royal and Select Masters of Virginia was consolidated in 1841.

On March 6, 1844 the Secretary's salary was changed from $10.00 annually to 5% of all funds collected by him and, in addition, he was exempted from the payment of dues. At this meeting C. A. B. Coffroth was chosen Secretary in place of Companion William Towers, who had resigned. We assume, that the change in the Secretary's remuneration was made to meet the desires of Companion Coffroth. On February 3, 1846 a committee was appointed to cooperate with Hiram Lodge with "regard to the expediency of erecting an additional story upon the Lodge room for the use of the Chapter". On May 11th of that year Companion E. Smith Lee, of Michigan, visited the Chapter and, as he had not then received the degrees of Royal and Select Master, they were conferred upon him as a courtesy and without fee.

The meetings become more infrequent and the minutes somewhat more sketchy for the succeeding two years. Then, in 1848, the Chapter appears to be back once more "on an even keel".

On February 6, 1849 the Chapter did a most unusual thing. It voted to appropriate the sum of $20.00 for the purchase of a medal to be presented to Joseph S. Carson, one of the most prominent members of Hiram Lodge at that time, "as a testimony of the respect and esteem of this sublime body" (i. e., the Chapter). Brother Carson was so affected, that he immediately made application for the degrees of the Chapter and he was duly elected the same night. He received the degrees on March 7 and May 9 and 11, 1849. On November 1, 1850 there were 21 Companions belonging to Chapter No. 12.

During the years 1851 and 1852 Winchester Chapter held but few meetings. The total assets as of November 1, 1852 amounted to $37.82½ according to the report of William Anders, Treasurer. On May 10, 1853 the sum of $20.00 was ordered "placed in the school fund" (i. e., to be used to pay for instruction in the several degrees of the Chapter), and on November 16th another $20.00 was added to this fund and "on motion, Past M. E. High Priest John B. T. Reed was employed to deliver a course of lectures before this Chapter, at such compensation as the Chapter may determine hereafter". The fortunes of the Chapter seemed to be at a low ebb, however, for on November 8, 1854, the date for the annual election of officers, Companion William Anders "moved that we surrender the Charter of this Chapter. After some debate the motion was withdrawn", and the Companions proceeded to the election of officers with L. T. Moore as High Priest and the further decision, that a representative be sent to Grand Chapter in the person of John B. T. Reed. The convocations, however, became more and more infrequent until October 22, 1858, when the Chapter closed for the last time until March 6, 1861. John B. T. Reed was still the standby of the Companions, William Anders was Treasurer, and C. A. B. Coffroth was Secretary. The further fortunes of Chapter No. 12 will be described in the following chapter of this book.

CHAPTER XVI

THE WAR OF 1861 TO THE END OF THE NINETEENTH CENTURY

As suddenly as it had dropped from sight temporarily, Winchester Chapter bobbed up again on March 6, 1861 just before the outbreak of the War Between the States. Its minutes for that date show a full complement of officers headed by John B. T. Reed as High Priest. Four petitions were received and these were acted upon at the same meeting, the degrees of Mark Master and Past Master being conferred on the candidates immediately. Further meetings were held on March 12 and 18 and April 1, 1861, degrees being conferred at each of these meetings. Then, and just as suddenly as it had reappeared from oblivion, the activities of the Chapter ceased again, probably because of the prevailing emergency. No further meetings are recorded until February 28, 1868, almost seven years later. Again John B. T. Reed, who had also been a sort of "permanent Master" of Hiram Lodge during the war years, headed the Chapter and the former Secretary, C. A. B. Coffroth, was again at his desk in this capacity. The following action was taken at this meeting:

> Ordered, That all Royal Arch Masons present, and other absent members formerly belonging to the Chapter, be enrolled as members of Royal Arch Chapter No. 12 under the new organization.

> Whereas this Chapter, not having had a regular meeting since April, 1861, and there not having been an election of officers since the election preceding that date, the M. E. High Priest and the old officers holding over present, with the assistence of the *pro tem.* Companions, organized by opening the Chapter in due form, and doubts being expressed as to the legality of this proceeding: and the Chapter being desirous of doing nothing irregular or illegal and to conform in all respects to ancient usage; Ordered, That the Secretary be directed to certify the facts in the case to the M. E. G. H. Priest, with a request that he send such directions as the laws and usage of the order require; and that if a Dispensation be needed in order to put us again in regular working order, he be requested to send it at once, tendering at the same

time the charges against this Chapter on the books of the Grand Secretary, if any; and that the Secretary of this Chapter is authorized to draw upon the Treasurer for the said dues and other charges, if any, as soon as ascertained and remit the amount to the Grand Secretary.

At the same time committees were appointed to complete arrangements for the Chapter to resume labor on a permanent basis, including a committee to "report to the Chapter the probable estimate of repairing and refitting the old Masonic Hall over the Market House for Chapter and Commandery purposes exclusively, so fraternally tendered to our use by Hiram Lodge No. 21, and that the committee under this resolution take possession of the said Hall at once". (See page 119 for a full account of this matter.) It now appears that another Chapter had been organized in Winchester during the period when Chapter No. 12 was dormant, for, on January 12, 1870, due to the fact, that the latter Chapter had not done a great deal under the resolutions so bravely adopted in 1868, nine members of No. 12 Chapter requested dimits for the purpose of joining "John Dove Chapter". It is not certain from the records whether this new Chapter had already been chartered or was then (1869) in process of getting its charter. The present John Dove Chapter No. 21 does not go farther back than February 22, 1897 and the history of Capitular Masonry in Winchester during the years from 1870 to that date concerns itself solely with the original John Dove Chapter No. 21, whose dispensation seems to have been issued some time in 1869. From this point (January 12, 1870), old Winchester Chapter No. 12 fades out of the picture entirely after an existence of threescore years and ten (with certain lapses, of course), at first working under Pennsylvania, then, after 1820, under Virginia.

Some of the first minutes of the first John Dove Chapter No. 21 are definitely missing. It received its dispensation from the Grand High Priest in 1869, as stated above, and the first extant minutes are of a meeting held in September of that year (the date of this meeting is also missing). Companions H. M. Brent, Jr., Joseph M. Ginn, and E. S. Brent are listed as High Priest,

King, and Scribe respectively, and the fees for the six degrees were fixed at $30.00. At the convocation held on October 11, 1869, the meeting nights were set for the second and fourth Mondays of the month. Petitions began to come in from the very beginning and there was some kind of degree work at nearly every convocation for some time thereafter. On November 10, 1869 it is recorded, that six Companions were examined in open Chapter on the work of the preceding degrees before they were permitted to be exalted to the degree of Royal Arch Mason. On November 11th it was ordered, "that Companion S. M. Bowman be paid $35.00 for lecturing this Chapter". This Companion had evidently spent some time with the Chapter officers in order to acquaint them with the work and get them started under their dispensation. On November 23d $25.00 was appropriated to assist in paying the expenses of the Chapter's representative to the meeting of the Grand Chapter of Virginia to be held the month following. The charter was duly granted and the Chapter received the number 21 on the roster of the Grand Chapter of Virginia. We note, that Companion Bowman (who by then had been appointed Grand Master of the 2d Vail of Grand Chapter) was again present to instruct the Companions of John Dove Chapter in February, 1870. New officers were elected on February 14th, these being the first to be chosen under the charter: Henry M. Brent, Jr., High Priest; Richard Parker, King; and L. Campbell, Scribe. At this same meeting the following letter from John Dove, Grand Secretary of the Grand Chapter, was read and ordered to be spread upon the minutes:

By this express I send and present through you to John Dove R. A. C. No. 21 a seal and press, as a small testimonial of my appreciation of the high honor conferred on me by the Companions of that Chapter in giving it my humble name. I hope the device may please: after the waters of strife have subsided, the messenger of Peace shall return presenting in her bill the appropriate emblem, thus sealing her errand, and gazing through the azure *Blue* of Heaven, we see the Rainbow of Promise, by which we are assured against any repetition of like disaster. How grateful

should our hearts be to an all-wise and over-ruling High Priest for all his favours thus bountifully bestowed.
Very fraternally,
JOHN DOVE.

An appropriate letter of thanks was ordered to be sent to Companion Dove, the sum of $25.00 was voted to Companion Bowman for his additional services rendered, a committee was appointed to prepare by-laws for the new Chapter, and another committee was appointed to meet with a similar committee from Chapter No. 12 "to hear their proposition and report back to this Chapter". On March 14, 1870 it was voted to offer Hiram Lodge a rent of $60.00 for the use of its hall, the Chapter to furnish its own fuel and lights. For some reason, the committee to treat with Chapter No. 12 was discharged on April 11th without making any report. The new by-laws were finally approved on this same date and duly recorded in the minute book. New officers were elected on June 13th, the same three council officers remaining in their respective stations. High Priest Brent presented to the Chapter at this time a "beautiful representation of the burning bush". By June, 1870 the necessary arrangements had been made with Hiram Lodge to use its hall and one quarter's rent, amounting to $15.00, was ordered paid to the Lodge accordingly. It was also agreed to pay $1.00 per night for the lights used by the Chapter. On October 17th it was decided to invite the Rev. Mr. Brooke, of Alleghany City, Pa., to come to Winchester and deliver a lecture for the benefit of the Chapter and a committee on arrangements was appointed to make the necessary preparations for his coming.

In the minutes of January 14, 1871 are recorded the first resolutions adopted by John Dove Chapter on the passing of one of its members, Companion Thomas D. McCaw. The stated convocations of the Chapter were changed, on April 10th, to the first Tuesday night in each month. On March 5, 1872 it was decided to start a special charity fund for the Chapter by circulating the "charity box" at every convocation.

An interesting episode is recorded in the proceedings of John Dove Chapter for 1872. It appears that, since the Chapter had been named for this distinguished Virginian and Mason with his express permission, the Companions decided, that they would request Dr. Dove to honor the Chapter with his portrait. Hence, we find in the minutes of March 5th of that year the following item:

> On motion the M. E. High Priest and Secretary were directed to correspond with M. E. John Dove in regard to having his portrait, the same to be placed in the Hall.

The necessary letter was accordingly written, we suppose very promptly. The report is (though this is not recorded in the minutes), that no reply was received from the venerable doctor to the Chapter's request. After waiting what they considered a reasonable time, the members of the committee which had been appointed to handle the matter, decided to write to Dr. Dove again, but still no answer came. Finally a third letter was dispatched to him and, in a few days, along came Dr. Dove's portrait by express, charges collect, and this was followed by a bill submitted to the Chapter for $150.00 by the artist who made the portrait.

To say that the Companions were "flabbergasted" by this unexpected answer to their request is putting it mildly indeed. Their finances, at this early stage of their existence as a Chapter, were exceedingly limited, and they were much embarrassed by the entire matter. The committee reported the situation to the Chapter on May 27, 1872, and after full discussion (the details of which do not appear in the minutes), the following action was taken:

> The portrait of M. E. John Dove, Grand Secretary, was received, and, on motion, the portrait was accepted and ordered to be placed in the Hall. On motion the M. E. High Priest and Companion Hull were ordered to raise by subscription from the members of this Chapter only, and to borrow $150.00 at thirty days to pay for said portrait.

This portrait thus becomes one of the most historical and interesting in the annals of Virginia capitular Masonry, since, among other things, it was ordered by Dr. Dove himself and approved by him. A reproduction of it will be found elsewhere in this volume.

On May 23, 1873 Dr. Dove visited the Chapter, which had been named in his honor, and was given a royal welcome. So far as indicated in the records, this was the only time, that he was present at any of the Chapter convocations. He passed to his reward some three years later at the ripe age of 84 years after having served as Grand Secretary of the Grand Chapter of Virginia for 58 years consecutively.

Judge Richard Parker became High Priest of Dove Chapter on June 13, 1873 and served in that office continuously for the next seventeen years. By the end of 1873 the Chapter was meeting again in the Masons' Hall, though the minutes do not indicate the exact date when the change was made from the Lodge room. The Commandery of Knights Templar also changed to the Masons' Hall about the same time and, in 1874, the Knights of Pythias were granted permission to use the hall, provided they could obtain also the approval of the Common Council.

By the end of 1875 the new Chapter was well under way and the interest among the members continued on a high level. A very interesting proposal was accepted by the Companions on February 11, 1876, to the effect that seven Brethren from the Lodge at Hamilton would be permitted to receive the Chapter degrees with a reduction of $10.00 each in their fees. On October 10th the monthly dues were set at 15 cents ($1.80 per year) instead of 10 cents per month as formerly. At the end of the capitular year (June 8, 1877) the Treasurer reported a balance of $241.15 on hand. Companion S. M. Bowman had continued his interest in John Dove Chapter from the beginning and, on November 12, 1880, he paid the Chapter an official visit in his capacity as Grand High Priest for that year and "gave the Chapter some good and wholesome instruction". The request of a number of Companions at Front Royal, that John Dove Chapter give its consent to the formation of a new Chapter there, was granted at the meeting of November 18, 1881. On July 13, 1883 a previously adopted decision to invite Grand

Chapter to meet in Winchester in 1884 was rescinded, the reason not being given in the minutes.

The Chapter continued on the even tenor of its way for the next few years. In March, 1888 Grand Lecturer William H. H. Lynn, of Staunton, visited the Chapter and instructed the officers in the ritualistic work. Beginning about 1890, however, we find that there was a gradual decline in interest, fewer petitions were received, and, during the next six or seven years, there were a number of occasions when no convocation was held because of the lack of a quorum. As we read the minutes of the convocations held in 1895 and 1896, it is apparent, that there were certain difficulties, both financial and otherwise, besetting the Chapter, though these are nowhere specified in the minutes. At the final meeting recorded in this particular minute book under date of December 11, 1896, it was voted that "J. P. Hyde, C. W. Hensell, and J. C. Smith be named in the charter". What charter is meant is left to the reader to conjecture. The minutes of this and of the several immediately preceding convocations are recorded in pencil and are very carelessly written and we are left with the definite impression that some kind of reorganization of the Chapter was under way. This proved to be indeed the case, for Grand Chapter granted a new charter—or renewed the older charter—under date of February 22, 1897 (without change of name or number), and it is under this authority that the Chapter is working at the present time. At the meeting held on March 19, 1897, District Deputy T. E. Schwartz presided, presented the new charter, and installed the officers elected at that time, in addition to the three council officers named in the charter, these being the same as recommended by the old Chapter members on the preceding December 11th. At this time M. H. G. Willis became Treasurer and J. E. Correll Secretary. At the election on June 10, 1898 Companions Harry M. Baker, Charles W. Hensell, and Julius A. Bantz were chosen as High Priest, King, and Scribe respectively. At this same meeting Grand High Priest E. Louis Idé paid an official visit to the Chapter and installed the newly elected officers. On January 12, 1900

C. Vernon Eddy was exalted to the Royal Arch degree, and at the election of officers held on June 8th ensuing he was chosen to the office of King.

Thus Royal Arch Masonry in Winchester concluded its history for the period from 1860 to 1900. There had been many "ups and downs" during those forty years. Perhaps they might in some ways be likened to a sort of "forty years of wandering in the wilderness", since they saw the end of Winchester Chapter No. 12, the first chartering of John Dove Chapter No. 21 (1870), the decline of that Chapter under its first charter, and the eventual re-chartering of the Chapter with the same name and number in 1897. And thus, in Capitular language, the rubbish of the old temple (figuratively speaking) was cleared away preparatory to the building of the new—and this takes us into the twentieth century and the next chapter of our story.

Original Seal of Winchester Royal Arch Chapter No. 12. (Now in possession of John Dove Chapter No. 21.)

CHAPTER XVII

JOHN DOVE CHAPTER SINCE 1900

We find John Dove Chapter No. 21 beginning the new century with Judge William M. Atkinson as High Priest, thus continuing the tradition as to the high calibre of its presiding officers. Companion M. H. G. Willis continued as Treasurer and J. E. Correll as Secretary. It was reported at the convocation on January 11, 1901, that the Chapter rooms could be furnished comfortably for the sum of $580.00 and the committee in charge of the matter was given full power to have the work done. Grand High Priest J. E. Alexander was received on February 21st and, on May 8, 1902, Grand High Priest William J. Hubard paid an official visit to the Chapter. It is noted that the Chapter was "called off during the months of July, August, and September, 1902 on account of heat". Companion M. H. G. Willis died in March, 1903 and was succeeded as Treasurer by Companion Alexander M. Baker. On June 12th of that year, Companion C. Vernon Eddy was elected as High Priest and served for four successive terms. He was made Secretary of the Chapter in 1913 and has served in that office continuously since that date.

In 1904 the Chapter found it necessary to request a loan from Hiram Lodge No. 21. On February 12th of that year it was voted to present a "purse of gold" to Companion G. K. Fitch for the many services, which he had rendered to the Chapter on various occasions. This was done through the collecting of voluntary contributions from the members of the Chapter and a total of $50.00 in gold was raised for the purpose. Grand High Priest Ed. S. Conrad, accompanied by District Deputy John G. Yancey, visited the Chapter officially on September 9, 1904. Grand Lecturer William J. Hubard, P. G. H. P. visited and instructed the Companions in February, 1905. It is noted in the Chapter minutes for March 10th of that year, that Companion C. Vernon Eddy had received the Order of High Priesthood at Richmond, the ceremonies being held during the meeting of

Grand Chapter on November 9, 1904. Chapter pennies were reported as having been purchased in September, 1905. The indebtedness of the Chapter was still not paid and it was voted to join with Winchester Commandery (which was also in debt at that time) for making a loan of $600.00 from the bank in order to take up certain notes, which were then due. The difficulties of the Companions were increased, when it was reported on March 9, 1906, that "since the auditorium has been leased, we can get no light on second floor and have no gas in this room." A committee consisting of Companion J. E. Correll was appointed to have this situation remedied and to see to the placing of an electric light on the second floor. The installation of gas was omitted as being too expensive in view of the low state of the Chapter's finances. For this same reason the Companions were unable to send a contribution to the California earthquake sufferers in May, 1906. On February 8, 1907 we note that $15.00 was appropriated "to pay for heat for two years to March 1, 1907." Another appropriation of $6.00 was made on June 14th to "pay the discount" on the note mentioned above, which was then due. On November 8, 1907 Companion Eddy's letter was read, in which he regretted the necessity of declining reinvestiture as High Priest of the Chapter owing to change of residence to Philadelphia. Companion H. R. Homer was chosen to succeed him as High Priest as of the date of the election meeting in the preceding October. It is also noted, that Companion Homer received the Order of High Priesthood on March 6, 1908.

The Chapter had considerable trouble with delinquent Companions during this period and seven Companions were ordered suspended for non-payment of dues on April 8, 1910. This action seems to have had a salutary effect, for we note the collection of considerable amounts of dues listed in the minutes of January 13 and June 9, 1911. Then, at several subsequent meetings, the minutes state that "refreshments were served after the close of the Chapter," thus indicating that both finances and morale of the Companions must have been improved considerably. Grand High Priest Stanley W. Martin, of Danville, paid an official visit to the Chapter on May 24, 1912, addressing the Companions on ways to improve attendance at the meetings, also on the needs of the Masonic Home of Virginia. It was voted on December 13th of that year, that the Chapter send Christmas baskets or some other token of remembrance to the widows of deceased Companions. Companion Eddy had by this time returned from Philadelphia to make his permanent abode in Winchester, thus resuming his active participation in Chapter affairs. He was immediately (1913) made Secretary of the Chapter as previously noted. The salary attached to this office was increased in 1913 from $15.00 to $25.00 per year. The Chapter was called upon to mourn the passing of Companion George H. Kinzel on October 30, 1914 and Companion John T. Cochran, then Grand Master of the 3d Vail of the Virginia Grand Chapter, was present and assisted in the work on January 22, 1915. It was voted at this meeting to purchase a stereopticon outfit, which had been used that night for the first time, though four of the Companions voted against this measure. Three Companions were appointed to attend the Valley Royal Arch School to be held at Elkton in July of that year to "learn the correct R. A. work as taught in the school". On August 13th Companion Eddy turned over to the Chapter the old Chapter seal, which had been handed to him by the widow of Companion J. E. Correll, long the Chapter Secretary. A bill for $3.00 to the "Greek Restaurant" was approved on October 8, 1915.

On April 14, 1916 the Chapter voted to take out fire insurance on its furniture and other equipment and on June 8, 1917 we note the visit of Grand High Priest J. E. W. Timberman, who announced the appointment of Companion John T. Cochran to the office of Grand Lecturer in the place of William J. Hubard, who had just passed on. With the entry of the United States into World War I, two Companions, C. S. H. Campbell and Roger A. Kline, are noted in the minutes of November 9th as being already at training camps in the South. Copies of *How To Live at the Front,* by Hector McQuarrie, were ordered sent to these two Companions. It is noted in the minutes of April 16, 1918, that Companion Eddy presented to the Chapter an old minute book used by Winchester Royal Arch Chapter No. 12 from 1834 to 1870. The material contained in that minute book has been used freely, of course, in preparing the present volume. This same minute book was also used by the Chapter on May 9, 1919 in determining the membership status of Companion E. S. Brent, who had applied for reinstatement after the lapse of many years. In the years following the close of World War I there was a healthy increase in work and interest in the Chapter's affairs. By March 12, 1920 it was reported, that the body owned one $100.00 Liberty Bond and was now in position to purchase another bond of the same amount. Companion John T. Cochran, Grand High Priest and Grand Lecturer, paid an official visit to the Chapter on October 22d of that year.

By March 22, 1922 John Dove Chapter was in such excellent state, both financially and with regard to the work, that Companion John T. Cochran on a visit as Grand Lecturer "felicitated the Chapter on its splendid condition". Grand High Priest William Chapman visited the Chapter on May 17th of that year.

We find nothing of extraordinary importance in the Chapter proceedings for the next few years. Companion G. K. Fitch, then living at Luray, addressed a letter of greetings to the Chapter on January 19, 1926 and three months later the Companions were called upon to mourn his passing. He is the first member of the Chapter to have a page in the minute book set apart to his memory. It will be recalled, that he was the same Companion, to whom the Chapter presented a purse of $50.00 in gold some years previously. Dr. Frank T. McFaden, who had affiliated with John Dove Chapter soon after his arrival in Winchester in 1923, continued to served the Chapter as its Chaplain during all of this period. On April 16, 1931 Grand High Priest William L. Davis paid an official visit to the Chapter and was accompanied on that occasion by Grand Lecturer John T. Cochran. Grand High Priest P. M. Shirey visited the Chapter on December 9, 1932, also on April 6, 1933. On August 5th of that year Companion Frank T. McFaden passed to his reward and the members of his family presented certain of his Masonic books to the Chapter after his death.

For the next five years there is little of importance to report except that the Chapter continued active in spite of the falling off in membership due to the "depression". But on November 18, 1938 a large affair was held in the form of a "Ladies' Night", at which time Past Grand High Priests John T. Cochran, Edward A. Joachim, and Charles H. Ergenbright and their wives were present, also many other distinguished guests. An official visit was received from Grand High Priest Simon J. Sachs on March 8, 1940 and a large delegation of Companions from Arlington Chapter No. 35 visited Winchester on October 11th of that year. On the death of Grand High Priest A. S. Burnham in February, 1941, Grand King C. Vernon Eddy succeeded to that office automatically and was installed as Grand High Priest in John Dove Chapter on February 28th. On November 14, 1941 he was received again officially as Grand High Priest after his election to that office by Grand Chapter in the preceding month. Grand High Prist C. E. Webber visited the Chapter on April 9, 1943, and his successors in this office have also visited Winchester as follows: O. M. Miles, April 27, 1945; James N. Hillman on August 15, 1947; and Dan P. Sigourney on June 6, 1948.

The present High Priest of John Dove Chapter is Companion Jack K. Jenkins with Past High Priest Roy A. Larrick as Treasurer and Past Grand High Priest C. Vernon Eddy as Secretary. The membership totals 144 Companions as of the date of this writing and the last report of the Treasurer showed total assets of $2,061.65. The Chapter continues to play an important part in the affairs of Grand Chapter and in the upbuilding of Royal Arch Masonry throughout the entire jurisdiction of Virginia.

The only Grand High Priest from Winchester Chapter No. 12 or John Dove Chapter No. 21 during the entire history of these two Chapters was C. Vernon Eddy, a sketch of whom will be found elsewhere in this volume.

WINCHESTER MARK LODGE

We have already seen, that there was a separate Lodge of Master Mark Masons (or Mark Master Masons—both terms were used) in Winchester from about the same date as the original Chapter. From references to this subject already included in the previous pages of this book it will be seen, that the existence of the Mark Lodge was co-extensive with that of the Chapter up to about 1820, when, under the influence of James Cushman, the Mark Lodge became merged with the Royal Arch Chapter. A few minutes of meetings of the Mark Lodge are to be found in one of the minute books of Winchester Chapter, but the information contained therein is not sufficient to enable us to reconstruct, even in bare outline, the story of the Mark Lodge as a separate body.

WINCHESTER LODGE OF SUPER-EXCELLENT MASONS

There is also evidence among the existing records of Winchester Chapter, which indicates that there was likewise a Lodge of Super-Excellent Masons (or Excellent and Super-Excellent Masons) in Winchester for a number of years. The Excellent and Super-Excellent degrees may or may not have been the forerunners of our present degree of Most Excellent Master, though this is not clear. However, the information at present available regarding the Lodge of Super-Excellent Masters in Winchester is so meagre, that we can only call attention to the fact, that it existed some time prior to 1820 and that it worked closely with the Royal Arch Chapter and the Mark Lodge. Beyond this we are able to venture no opinion whatsoever. We do know, however, that this Lodge of Super-Excellent Masters (or what was left of it) also disappeared (like the Mark Lodge) after the advent of James Cushman and was probably absorbed into the new Capitular system as introduced by him into Virginia in the year mentioned.

SECRET MONITORS

In one of the minute books of Lodge No. 12 are listed the names of eleven Winchester Brethren, who had also received the degree of Secret Monitor. These were: John B. Tilden Reed, G. A. Reed, Jr., William Jenkins, George W. Kiger, C. C. Cameron, C. A. B. Coffroth, George R. Kiger, J. W. Hollis, George Smith, William Anders, and W. P. Shepherd. This degree is still conferred in the United States under the jurisdiction of the Grand Council, Allied Masonic Degrees. It was formerly given in Lodges of Secret Monitors located in various places throughout the country and was very extensively known half a century or more ago. There is no indication of the existence of a Lodge of Secret Monitors in Winchester. It is possible, that the degree was brought there by one of the Brethren from elsewhere and was communicated from time to time to certain others. We have not found such a list in existence in any other Virginia community.

KNIGHTS OF CONSTANTINOPLE

In the same minute book as the list of Secret Monitors we also find a list of Knights of Constantinople, consisting of eight names—all but the last three of those on the list of Secret Monitors. The Knight of Constantinople was a side degree formerly extensively conferred, the chief lesson of which was humility. It could be conferred by one Mason on another without the need of others to assist him. It was probably brought to Winchester from some other place and was conferred in time upon the eight Brethren listed in the minute book.

HIGH PRIESTS OF WINCHESTER CHAPTER NO. 12 AND JOHN DOVE CHAPTER NO. 21
(1799-1949)

*James Gamul Dowdall	1799-1800
*Richard Bowen	1800-1801
*Thomas Purse	-1801
*Edward Slater	1801-1802
*John Peyton	-1802
*Peter Lauck	1802-1803
*James Chipley	1803-1804
*Peter Lauck	-1804
*William Ball	1804-1805
*Lewis Wolfe	1805- (?)
(Minutes missing)	1805-1807
*Lemuel Bent	(?) -1808
*Peter Lauck	1808-1810
*Lewis Wolfe	1810-1811
*Archibald Magill	1811-1815
*Lemuel Bent	1815-1818
*George Reed	1818-1824
*Lemuel Bent	1824- (?)
(Minutes missing)	1824-1834
*W. G. Singleton	1834-1835
*John B. Tilden Reed	1835-1837
*Lemuel Bent	1837-1839
*W. G. Singleton	1839-1846
*John B. Tilden Reed	1846-1850
*George W. Ginn	1850-1851
*Robert W. Reed	1851-1852
*Joseph S. Carson	1852-1853
*E. C. Breedin	1853-1854
*L. T. Moore	1854-1855
*H. W. Thorpe	1855-1856
*A. B. Tucker	1856- (?)
(Minutes missing)	1857-1861
*John B. Tilden Reed	1861- (?)
(Minutes missing)	1861-1868
*John B. Tilden Reed	1868-1870
*H. M. Brent, Jr.	1870-1872

*Deceased.

High Priests of John Dove Chapter

*H. Clay Krebs	1872-1873
*Richard Parker	1873-1890
*John P. Hyde	1890-1898
*Harry M. Baker	1898-1899
*John P. Hyde	1899-1900
*William M. Atkinson	1900-1903
† C. Vernon Eddy	1903-1907
*H. R. Homer	1907-1908
*William L. Wood	1908-1909
William E. Cooper	1909-1911
*A. C. Slonaker	1911-1913
*W. Ray Smith	1913-1914
*Isaac N. Good	1914-1915
*William B. Wagner	1915-1918
*C. B. Stickley	1918-1919
*W. E. Coffman	1919-1920
Harold C. Sheetz, Sr.	1920-1921
C. S. Hartman	1921-1923
*William B. Wagner	1923-1924
D. R. Slonaker	1924-1925
Lewis N. Barton	1925-1926
J. B. Beverley, Jr.	1926-1927
Walter M. Shade	1927-1928
*Frank H. Dorsey	1928-1929
Dudley C. Lichliter	1929-1930
Allen B. Gray	1930-1931
Harold C. Jones	1931-1932
Wendell B. Goode	1932-1933
T. F. Jakimier	1933-1934
Roy A. Larrick	1934-1935
O. C. Cassell	1935-1936
W. E. Hewitt	1936-1937
Harvey F. Carper	1937-1938
M. V. B. Snoke	1938-1939
*Brady W. Largent	1939-1940
Douglas O. Grimm	1940-1941
Gus J. Kaknis	1941-1942
Claude M. Grim	1942-1943
Mifflin B. Clowe	1943-1944
J. Lee Miller	1944-1945
Harold C. Sheetz, Jr.	1945-1946
Matthew H. Ebersole	1946-1947
James R. Alexander, Jr.	1947-1948
Jack K. Jenkins	1948-1949

*Deceased.
† Also Grand High Priest.

TREASURERS

*Peter Lauck 1799-1802
*William Ball 1802-1803
*Peter Lauck ....   -1803
*Peter Elliott 1803-1804
*William Ball ....   -1804
*James Chipley 1804-1805
*Philip Hoff .... 1805- (?)
(Minutes missing) 1805-1807
*Adam Brown 1807-1810
*Philip Hoff 1810-1812
*Christopher Wetzel 1812-1817
*Adam Brown 1817-1820
*Solomon Dodds 1820-1824
(Minutes missing) 1824-1834
*C. H. Clark 1834-1835
*Benjamin Bushnell 1835-1841
*William Anders 1841-1857
(Minutes missing) 1857-1861
(No Treasurer listed) 1861-1870
*James W. Burgess 1870-1872
*George W. Ginn 1872-1874
*George F. Glaize 1874-1897
*M. H. G. Willis 1897-1903
*Alexander M. Baker 1903-1905
*George H. Kinzel 1905-1906
*F. S. Hunt 1906-1909
*C. L. Robinson 1909-1917
*Isaac N. Good 1917-1939
Roy A. Larrick 1939-

SECRETARIES

*Thomas Purse 1799-1800
*Richard Bowen 1799-1800

*William Newby 1800-1801
*Frederick Hurst 1800-1801

*Frederick Hurst   1801
*Nathaniel Kean   1801

*Frederick Hurst 1801-1802
*John J. Chinn 1801-1802

*Deceased.

Other Chapter Officers

*John Peyton 1802
*Nathaniel Kean 1802

*James Chipley 1802-1803
*John J. Chinn 1802-1803

*William M. Holliday 1803
*Daniel Sittler 1803

*William Newby 1803-1804
*Daniel Sittler 1803-1804

*William Newby 1804
*Peter Elliott 1804

*William Newby 1804-1805
*Nathaniel Kean 1804-1805

*William Newby 1805
*Nathaniel Kean 1805

*Daniel W. Thomas ....1805- (?)
*William Newby ....1805- (?)

*Edward Slater 1807-1808

(Minutes missing) 1808-1810

*Daniel W. Thomas 1810-1811
*William Newby 1810-1811

*Daniel W. Thomas 1811-1812
*Nathaniel Kean 1811-1812

*Daniel W. Thomas 1812-1817
*Edward Slater 1817-1819
*Philip A. Klipstine 1819-1820
(Minutes missing) 1820-1823
*Sutton I. Harris 1823-1824
(Minutes missing) 1824-1834
*Benjamin Bushnell 1834-1835
*C. A. B. Coffroth 1835-1837
*C. H. Clark 1837-1838
*William Towers 1840-1844
*George W. Ginn 1838-1840

---
*Deceased.

*C. A. B. Coffroth 1844-1870
*E. S. Brent 1869-1870
*H. Clay Krebs 1870-1872
*H. M. Brent, Jr. 1872-1873
*H. Clay Krebs 1873-1897
*J. E. Correll 1897-1903
*C. W. Wilson 1903-1909
*Isaac N. Good 1909-1912
H. L. Cather   1912
C. Vernon Eddy 1912-

*Deceased.

Note: The Chapter in its earliest years had, in effect, two Secretaries, who were designated as Senior Scribe and Junior Scribe respectively. The minutes were usually signed by both when both were present, otherwise by only one of the Scribes. Hence, where two names are listed above for the same period, this means that the first name occurring is that of the Senior Scribe, the second that of the Junior Scribe for the period indicated. After 1812 the Secretary (there was only one then) was designated as Grand Secretary or Grand Scribe until about 1817, after which the title is shown in the minutes as being simply that of Secretary.

There is also an overlapping in the years 1869-1870, when old Winchester Chapter No. 12 was in its last days and the new John Dove Chapter No. 21 was under dispensation.

In effect, then, we have listed in these lists the names of the High Priests, Treasurers, and Secretaries (or corresponding officers) of the original Royal Arch Chapter at Winchester, later Winchester Chapter No. 12, still later John Dove Chapter No. 21, and finally John Dove Chapter No. 21 under its renewal charter of 1897.

PART THREE
THE COUNCIL

CHAPTER XVIII

WINCHESTER COUNCIL, ROYAL AND SELECT MASTERS

Unfortunately for the Masonic historian, there are no extant records of Winchester Council of Royal and Select Masters. All the minutes of this Council have disappeared long since as have all correspondence and contemporary references of a local nature. In the extant records of the Grand Chapter, Royal Arch Masons of Virginia there is one letter; otherwise there is only an occasional reference to the Winchester Council, and that is all. We do not even know the precise name of this Council; hence, our discussion of it will be necessarily sketchy and, for want of a better name, we shall call it simply "Winchester Council". The account herewith is reconstructed from various sources and contains, we believe, such essential facts as will enable the reader to obtain a reasonably accurate picture of the establishment and very brief story of that body.

We know that Winchester Council was one of nine Councils established in Virginia by Jeremy Cross and James Cushman. Both of these men were New Englanders and both exercised a tremendous influence upon the Masonry of the early nineteenth century. With Thomas Smith Webb (also a New Englander) they determined largely the entire subsequent history of the Masonic ritualistic work in the United States, not only in the symbolic but in the so-called "higher" degrees as well.

In his capacity as General Grand Lecturer of the General Grand Chapter, Cross came to Virginia in 1817. Although Virginia did not adhere to the General Grand Chapter, this fact did not operate to prevent the Virginia Companions from giving Cross a most cordial welcome. During the winter of that year Cross conferred the degrees of Royal and Select Master upon several Royal Arch Masons living in Richmond. These two degrees then had a very uncertain status, being more or less in their infancy, so to speak. That of Royal Master is supposed to have originated in New York, while the degree of Select Master came from Baltimore. There is a long story back of both degrees, however, which does not need to be recounted here.

Among the Richmond Companions, who received these degrees from Jeremy Cross, was Dr. John Dove, who states in one of the surviving records that the charge for the two degrees was $5.00 and that this amount was paid to Cross by each person to whom the degrees were communicated. As soon as a sufficient number of Royal and Select Masters had been made in Richmond, Cross then stated, that he had received authority from the "Chief" (Joseph Eckel, of Baltimore) to grant charters for the holding of Councils of Select and Royal Masters. The Richmond Companions decided to accept Cross's offer and paid him $40.00 for a charter to establish Richmond Council (later Hiram Council) No. 1. The institution of this Council took place on Christmas Day, 1817, undoubtedly under Cross's direct and personal supervision. On January 6, 1818 Dumfries Council No. 2 was established at Dumfries. Soon thereafter, Cross left Virginia and apparently never returned. Dr. Dove then became the chief exponent of Cryptic Masonry in the commonwealth, though no further Councils were established during the ensuing two years.

However, in 1820 James Cushman, who was Cross's close associate and disciple, arrived in Virginia. He soon established himself in the eyes of the Virginia Masons as an authority on *all* the degrees of the York Rite (Lodge, Chapter, Council, and Commandery). His influence on Virginia Masonry cannot be over-estimated, though few of us today realize this fact. Cushman brought with him a "small pamphlet, containing a synopsis of the degrees of Select and Royal Master, and a list of charters granted by Cross in several states, at the head of which was the following certificate":

CERTIFICATE

I hereby certify, that having been duly authorized by the Grand Council of the State of Maryland, held in the city of Baltimore,

to establish and organize Councils of Select Masters in any State in the United States, where there was not already a Grand Council formed; I have, by the high powers in me vested by the aforesaid Grand Council, established the following Councils of Select Masters, and granted them a warrant of constitution.
JEREMY L. CROSS, D. G. P.

The reader will note, that this certificate refers only to the degree of Select Master, but Cross apparently extended his authority to include that of Royal Master as well. At any rate, Cushman so interpreted his prerogatives during his sojourn in Virginia. Thus, armed with the authority apparently conferred upon him by Cross, and exhibiting the printed ritual and list of regularly established Councils of Select Masters, Cushman had no difficulty in establishing "Councils of Royal and Select Masters" (note that *both* degrees were included) in Norfolk, Portsmouth, Petersburg, Lynchburg, Williamsburg, Staunton, and Winchester. Each of these Councils paid a charter fee of $40.00 together with $2.00 additional for each degree "conferred on the requisite number to form a Council". Thus by the end of 1820 there were nine Councils in all. Apparently the same type of charter was issued to each one of these Councils and we reconstruct the charter of Winchester Council as follows:

By the high powers in me vested by the Thrice Illustrious Deputy Grand Puissant, Jeremy L. Cross, I do hereby constitute and appoint the within named Companions to form themselves into a regular Council of Royal and Select Masters, and I do appoint my worthy Companions .... to be first Thrice Illustrious Grand Master, ... to be first Illustrious Deputy Grand Master, and ...., first Principal Conductor; granting them full power with their constitutional number, to assemble in the town of Winchester, by the name of Winchester Council No. 9; open, and confer the degrees of Royal and Select Master, and to do all other business appertaining to said degrees, they conforming in all their doings to the General Regulations of Select Masters.

Given under my hand and seal, the .... day of ...., A. L. 5820, A. D. 1820, and of the deposit 2820.
JAMES CUSHMAN, D. G. P.

The date of this charter was probably about the time of Cushman's first visit to Winchester, an account of which is given in the Chapter section of the present volume. The number of the Winchester Council was No. 9 as appears from George Reed's letter quoted below. Further conclusions will remain necessarily matters of conjecture until better evidence on these points is found than is now available. The reader will also note, that Cushman refers in this charter only to the "General Regulations of Select Masters", although it warrants a "Council of Royal and Select Masters". But this discrepancy apparently had no effect on the zeal, with which the Virginia Companions followed the suggestions of Cushman, who, in his travels throughout the state as Grand Lecturer of both Grand Lodge and Grand Chapter, was able to keep in close touch with the nine Councils operating within the jurisdiction.

The next step was, of course, to organize the Grand Council of Virginia. On December 8, 1820, therefore, with Cushman in attendance and undoubtedly playing the major role in the proceedings, the Grand Council of Royal and Select Masters of Virginia was organized. Levi L. Stevenson, of Staunton, became the first Thrice Illustrious Grand Master, and it is presumed, that all the Virginia Councils were represented on that occasion. With the exception of George Reed's letter (see below) the names of the representatives from Winchester do not appear in any of the records at present available. Nor has any list of the members of Winchester Council been found up to this time.

However, we do know that George Reed (mentioned previously) was a prominent Winchester Mason of that period and was active in the affairs of the Chapter and Council; and that it was he, who first proposed the organization of the Grand Council of Virginia. For he has supplied us with the one notable exception to the statement, which we have made previously, regarding the complete lack of records on the subject of Cryptic Masonry in Winchester. Some fifteen years ago the following letter was found by the writer in the archives of the Grand

Chapter of Virginia—a document, which is interesting in the extreme and is self-explanatory:

Winchester, November 10th 1820

T. I. Companion:

Having ascertained that there are nine Councils of Select Masters in the State of Va. and of course have it in their power to form a Grand Council, I have thought it advisable to open a correspondence with the other Councils informing them that our worthy Companion Philip A. Klipstine will be duly authorized by this Council to enter into any arrangement of this kind with the representatives of the other Councils. He will be in the city of Richmond during the sessions of the Grand Lodge & Grand Chapter of Va. at which time & place, if it meet with your approbation, you can appoint a representation with like powers. The advantages of having a Grand Council in our State have no doubt fully appeared to you; it is therefore unnecessary for me to say anything further on the subject.

You will please immediately on the receipt of this communicate your views on the subject to this and the other Councils.
Yours &c. with great respect,
GEO. REED

M. E. John Dove, T. I. G. M.)
Richmond Council No. 1   )

    Richmond No. 1—M. E. John Dove, T. I. G. M.
    Dumfries   2—   Philip D. Dawe
    Norfolk   3—   Richard Jeffery
    Portsmouth   4—   Robert B. Butt
    Petersburg   5—   John Bragg
    Lynchburg   6—   James Penn
    Staunton   7—   Samuel Clark
    Williamsburg 8—   Jesse Cole
    Winchester   9—   George Reed

It is presumed that these representatives met at Richmond according to Reed's suggestion and organized the Grand Council as related above. It is only through the existence of this letter that we have the complete list of numbers of the various Councils in the state. We know that the names, however, are not always listed correctly, though we have found no other designation for the Council at Winchester than "Winchester Council No. 9". From this point onward we have no further indications of this Council's activities. The name of Philip Klipstine, which appears in Reed's letter quoted above, is the only other name we have been able to identify positively thus far in connection with the history of Winchester Council. Like the other Councils in the state, this Council also must have had only a relatively short life. The same is true of the Grand Council itself, which appears to have had but few meetings after its organization. Eventually, in 1841, Grand Council merged with Grand Chapter by formal resolution and the Cryptic degrees have been conferred since that time by the various Royal Arch Chapters of Virginia. The order of conferring the degrees has been changed several times and at present they are conferred as follows: Mark Master, Past Master, Select Master, Royal Master, Most Excellent Master, and Royal Arch Mason. West Virginia inherited the Virginia system, of course, and these are the only two states, which confer all six of these degrees in the Royal Arch Chapter today.

We conclude this discussion with a quotation from Josiah H. Drummond, eminent Masonic authority of Portland, Maine in the last century:

> In December, 1817, Cross instituted a Council of Select Masters at Richmond; and the next month another at Dumfries. In 1820, Cushman, under authority from Cross, went to Virginia and instituted Councils at Norfolk, Portsmouth, Petersburg, Lynchburg, Staunton, Williamsburg, and Winchester. Thereupon, the same year, these Councils formed a Grand Council, which continued its labors till 1841, when it surrendered the jurisdiction of the degrees to the Grand Chapter, and disbanded, together with all its subordinates. The venerable John Dove was the first T. I. Grand Master of the first Council.
>
> We have seen the *Proceedings* of this Grand Council for 1828, 1829, and 1830. From them we learn that the *Proceedings* for 1820 were published, but not those of any of the intervening years. There was a special assembly for the election of officers in February, 1828, from which we infer, that the annual session in December, 1827 was not held. In 1828 there were fifteen Councils. We are unable to learn whether any *Proceedings* were afterwards published or not. Comp. Dove was present at all four of these

sessions. These *Proceedings* give some reason for believing that there was no session of the Grand Council between 1820 (or 1821) and 1828. A bill for printing the *Proceedings* of 1820, and another for advertising the meeting of 1821, were ordered to be paid in 1828. Cushman was ordered to pay the Grand Treasurer the charter fee for the five new Councils, "he having acknowledged the receipt of the same", but he dying in 1829, his bond given for those fees was cancelled and sent to his widow with a letter of condolence.

The subordinates in 1828 were ordered to return their charter or warrant (and again in 1829), and take a new one; and each Council was to pay five dollars in full of all arrearages to date.

We have given the story of Cryptic Masonry in Virginia and Winchester as set forth above for two reasons: first, the history of the Council degrees in the Old Dominion is largely that of the Grand Council, since the local Councils never assumed any great degree of importance, even in the larger cities where Councils were established; second, the lack of information regarding Winchester Council No. 9 as such makes it necessary for the reader to reconstruct, as best he may, the local picture from the facts set forth above.

(Note: We are unable to include the list of names of the Masters, Treasurers, and Recorders of Winchester Council No. 9 for the reasons set forth above, namely, that there are no records available containing this information. We also call attention to the statement of Josiah H. Drummond above, that there were *fifteen* Councils in Virginia in 1828 instead of *nine* as indicated by George Reed in 1820.)

PART FOUR
THE COMMANDERY

CHAPTER XIX

WINCHESTER ENCAMPMENT AND THE GRAND ENCAMPMENT OF VIRGINIA

In order to understand the story of Templary in Winchester the reader should bear in mind constantly the following: first, that almost all the records of Winchester Commandery prior to 1900 have disappeared, thus making it necessary for us to draw heavily upon contemporary documents outside of the original minute books for our information; second, that the story of the first few years is so closely interwoven with that of the organization of the Grand Encampment of Virginia, that the two are virtually inseparable; and third, that the designations "Encampment", "Grand Encampment", and "General Grand Encampment" were regularly used until 1856 for "Commandery", "Grand Commandery", and "Grand Encampment, U. S. A." respectively.

The evidence seems to indicate that there was an Encampment of Knights Templar at Winchester as early as 1812, which worked under the authority of Winchester Lodge No. 12. Like the Chapter, the Encampment came into being through the fact, that various members of the Lodge had received the Templar orders from time to time, beginning probably about 1810 or even earlier. In the course of two or three years there were enough Templars belonging to the Lodge to set up a separate body. The matter was doubtless discussed on a number of occasions, at first informally, then formally, and a decision was finally reached to form an Encampment of Knights Templar independent of the symbolic Lodge. No objection was registered on the part of the Lodge, since it was probably the leading spirits among the Brethren, who made up the Templar group. Thus, about 1812, as we have said, Winchester Encampment came into being as a self-constituted and self-congregated group. It worked the Order of the Temple primarily, the other orders being added later.

The source from which the Winchester Brethren and Sir Knights derived their Templar Masonry has not been definitely determined. However, it is most reasonable to assume, that it came to them from Pennsylvania as did the Lodge and Chapter degrees. If the date of organization of Winchester Encampment is set as 1812, which is as close as we can approximate from the extant evidence, this was four years before the organization of the General Grand Encampment, U. S. A. (1816) and St. John's Rising Star Encampment in Richmond. It was also eleven years prior to the formation of the Grand Encampment of Virginia (1823), of which we shall have considerable to say later. Within the decade following its establishment Winchester Encampment had not only made a real place for itself in local Masonic circles but had granted warrants for the formation of Warren Encampment at Harpers Ferry and Mt. Carmel Encampment, whose exact location does not appear from the available records but is supposed to have been Warrenton. Here again the assumption of such authority would not be tolerated under present day Masonic requirements, but the situation is explained in detail in a letter, which Daniel Walker Thomas, of Winchester, wrote to DeWitt Clinton, General Grand Master of the General Grand Encampment, under date of June 17, 1824. The purpose of this letter was to establish the regularity of the Grand Encampment of Virginia and to obtain Clinton's approval of what had been done up to that time. Thomas wrote in part as follows:

> Winchester Encampment was established some years before the General Grand Encampment, and through its zeal for the promotion of the orders of Knighthood, created a large number of Knights Templars, in the state of Virginia (there being no other Encampment in the state); and a large number of its members living at too great a distance to attend the assemblies of the Encampment, applied to us for leave to form local Encampments, and (there being no legally constituted source within the state from whence charters could be derived) we considered ourselves justifiable in granting their request, knowing that it would be for the benefit of the orders of Knighthood. Whereupon two more Encampments were formed, which being done, we thought it ad-

visable to form a Grand Encampment for the state of Virginia, in the same manner as all other states (wherein there are Grand Encampments) have done, and apply to the General Grand Encampment to be placed in the same situation as they are, we having followed their example step by step, in the formation and organization of our Grand Encampment. When organized, I was requested to write to you, Sir, to open a correspondence with the General Grand Encampment, which was accordingly done, and your friendly answer received, which we considered as fully sanctioning us; and [we] were about to make a communication to the General Grand Recorder of all our proceedings when Companion James Cushman, who says he has authority from the Deputy General Grand Master to create Knights and found Encampments, came to Winchester and condemned us and all our proceedings as illegal, and said that each Encampment must take a charter from the Deputy General Grand Master, as your letter was nothing but a complimentary one, and no guarantee, or sanction to us, or our proceedings.

M. W. Sir & Brother, I have now made a correct statement of our proceedings from the commencement of our first Encampment in the State of Virginia to the present time, and humbly request your decisive and explicit answer: whether we are a legal Grand Encampment or an illegal one; and whether you will recognize us or not; as Brother Cushman has thrown us all into confusion, and nothing has been done since he came here, or will be until we receive an answer from you (although an application has been made to us for the establishment of another new Encampment).

Cushman had made the same sort of statement to the members of St. John's Rising Star Encampment in Richmond. Technically, of course, he was correct in his assertion, but there was a questionable side to Cushman's Templar activities, since every application for a warrant had to be transmitted to the Deputy General Grand Master, Henry Fowle, of Boston, through Cushman. The cost of a new warrant (*charter of constitution*) was $90.00, while that of a warrant or *charter of recognition* was only $5.00 or $10.00. Cushman was more anxious to obtain the first mentioned sum, since it meant more to him personally, of course. We do not know exactly what financial arrangements had been made by him with Henry Fowle, but it is to be presumed that Cushman received the major portion of all sums collected, whether for warrants (charters) or for individual degrees. It was only in this way, that he was able to support himself and we have already seen to what extent he went in retaining the charter fees for Councils, which he organized in Virginia.

In the face of Cushman's assertions and also spurred by the fact, that St. John's Rising Star Encampment in Richmond had made some efforts to form an alliance with the Grand Encampment of Pennsylvania, thus leading the way for the establishment of that Grand Encampment as the sovereign body for Virginia Templary, the Winchester Templars decided to proceed with the organization of a Grand Encampment of their own. Cushman's claim, that Henry Fowle was the one person in the United States, who could issue lawful warrants for Virginia (in addition to DeWitt Clinton), did not make too great an impression on Daniel Walker Thomas, who was the head of the Sir Knights in Winchester. In fact, the presence of Cushman was actually resented and the only reply, which he received in reponse to his protests, was the decision to organize a Grand Encampment of Virginia. There were in existence three Templar bodies, which was the minimum number required under Masonic usage for the organization of a soverign body. On November 27 and 28, 1823 representatives of these three Encampments met at Winchester and organized the Grand Encampment of Virginia. Daniel Walker Thomas, for many years Grand Commander (as he was then called) of Winchester Encampment, became the first Grand Master and retained this office continuously until 1830. Numbers were assigned to the three participatin' Encampments as follows in the order of their establishment: Winchester Encampment No. 1, Warren Encampment No. 2, and Mt. Carmel Encampment No. 3.

The importance of the event and the outstanding part played by the Templars of Winchester in the formation of the Grand Encampment of Virginia make it desirable, we believe, to include here the brief minutes of the organization meetings in full:

At an Assembly of delegates from the several Encampments of Sir Knights Templars in the state of Virginia, held in the Masons'

Hall in the town of Winchester, on Thursday, the 27th of November, A. D. 1823, and in the era of Sir Knights Templars, 705.
Present the following delegates:
Winchester Encampment—Sir Knights Daniel W. Thomas, Warner Throckmorton, Conrad Kremer, Samuel H. Davis.
Warren Encampment—Jacob R. Thomas, John R. Hayden, Robert Blanchard, Timothy Herrington.
Mt. Carmel Encampment—Henry Seevers, William B. Whitney, Sutton I. Harris, William W. Blanchard.
Sir Knight Daniel W. Thomas was elected chairman, and Sir Knight Sutton I. Harris, secretary.

The object of the meeting was briefly stated by the chairman, who presented the following preamble and resolutions:

WHEREAS, There are now established (agreeably to ancient usage and custom) in the state of Virginia, three Encampments of Sir Knights Templars and the appendant orders, which are without any general head; and
WHEREAS, It is expedient and necessary that there should be some authentic source within the state from whence to derive charters and privileges, without the intervention of individuals licensed by the Grand Puissants of other states;
Resolved, Therefore, that a Grand Encampment of Sir Knights Templars (and the appendant orders) be established in the town of Winchester, for the state of Virginia. And for the government thereof,
Resolved, that the constitution heretofore framed by Winchester Encampment No. 1 (for the government thereof) be amended (where necessary) and adopted; which was accordingly done and ratified in convention on the 27th day of November, A. D. 1823, and in the era of Sir Knights Templars, 705.
Resolved, That this convention do adjourn until tomorrow evening, to meet at the Masons' Hall.

Friday, November 28, 1823.
The convention met agreeably to adjournment—all the members being present. Sir Knight Daniel W. Thomas was called to the chair, and Sutton I. Harris appointed secretary.
The convention, after examining, adopted the constitution in its present form, and ordered it to be recorded. They then proceeded to the organization of the Grand Encampment, and the following Sir Knights were appointed for the ensuing twelve months:
M. E. Sir Daniel Walker Thomas, Grand Master.
M. E. Sir Warner Throckmorton, D. Grand Master.
M. E. Sir Jacob R. Thomas, Grand Generalissimo.

M. E. Sir Henry Seevers, Grand Captain General.
Rev. Sir George Reed, Grand Prelate.
E. Sir Conrad Kremer, Grand Senior Warden.
E. Sir Samuel H. Davis, Grand Junior Warden.
E. Sir Sutton I. Harris, Grand Recorder.
E. Sir Peter Lauck, Grand Treasurer.
E. Sir Samuel H. Lauck, Grand Standard Bearer.
E. Sir Fountain Beckham, Grand Sword Bearer.
E. Sir Nahum W. Patch, Grand Warder.
E. Sir James Foster, Grand Sentinel.

Resolved, That Winchester Encampment No. 1 do continue to work as heretofore, until the meeting of the Grand Encampment.
Resolved, That the permits granted by Winchester Encampment No. 1 to form Warren Encampment No. 2 and Mount Carmel Encampment No. 3 be continued until the said meeting of the Grand Encampment.
Resolved, That each subordinate Encampment do pay into the hands of the Grand Treasurer any sum of money (not exceeding twenty dollars) when demanded, for the use of the Grand Encampment.
Resolved, That the Grand Encampment shall meet on the second Monday in November, A. D. 1824.
Resolved, That this convention be now closed *sine die.*

D. W. THOMAS,
Chairman

S. I. HARRIS,
Secretary

From an examination of the above minutes it will be seen that Winchester Encampment No. 1 not only played the leading part in the calling and the conduct of the convention proceedings but also received preferment at the hands of the official delegates present in that the four Winchester delegates were chosen to the offices of Grand Master, Deputy Grand Master, Grand Senior Warden, and Grand Junior Warden respectively. It was but natural that Daniel Walker Thomas, who seems to have been the leading spirit in this entire movement, should be elected to head the infant Grand Encampment, a fact which we have pointed out previously. The Rev. George Reed, Grand Prelate, and Peter Lauck, Grand Treasurer, were also members of Winchester Encampment as were Samuel H. Lauck, Grand

Standard Bearer, and James Foster, Grand Sentinel. Warren Encampment No. 2 and Mt. Carmel Encampment No. 3 likewise received representation in the Grand Encampment line, as was natural, but not by any means to the same extent as Winchester.

The sequel to this organization meeting of the Grand Encampment, Knights Templar of Virginia is so important and so largely indentified with the early history of the Winchester Encampment, that we feel justified in including some of the details here.

Immediately following the formation of the Virginia Grand Encampment, Grand Master (i. e., Grand Commander) Daniel Walker Thomas wrote to DeWitt Clinton, head of the General Grand Encampment, U. S. A., proposing a correspondence between the two bodies. The reply of Clinton was both courteous and encouraging, nor did he intimate in any way that he considered the action of Walker and his associates in forming the Grand Encampment of Virginia as irregular. We quote the following from Clinton's reply to Thomas:

> As your Encampment was established before the General Grand Encampment, I do not perceive the necessity of your taking out charters or dispensations; it would be, in my opinion, an unnecessary expense. If you have three Encampments I think it will be advisable for you to form a State Grand Encampment, and for that body to send me an instrument acknowledging the jurisdiction of the General Grand Encampment, in which case I will acknowledge you as a regularly constituted State Encampment, until the General Grand Encampment shall at their next meeting take order on the subject. This measure will save expense and trouble, and be in all respects proper.

This letter from Clinton seemed to settle the matter to the entire satisfaction of all concerned with the exception of one man—James Cushman. Before there could be any further action or correspondence on the subject, Cushman, acting again as the agent of the Deputy Grand Master of the General Grand Encampment (Henry Fowle), hurried again to Winchester and declared all the previous proceedings illegal, maintaining that, notwithstanding Clinton's statement to the contrary, every Encampment must have a charter (or warrant) from the Deputy Grand Master. Cushman's motives in insisting upon his particular point of view become particularly suspect at this point, for it appears, that, shrewd Yankee that he was, he was unwilling to allow possible remuneration accruing to him in the form of fees to slip through his fingers without a protest. We should remember, that Cushman was dependent upon such fees for his livelihood and that he is not to be too severely condemned for his insistence on this point.

It was at this juncture that Daniel Walker Thomas wrote the letter to Clinton, which has been quoted above, and which, in effect, requested a decisive and explicit answer to the question: "Is the Grand Encampment of Virginia a legal body, and do you, or do you not, recognize it as such?" This letter was written on June 17, 1824 and Clinton's answer was dated July 1st, stating, in effect: "If you will recognize the jurisdiction of the General Grand Encampment, I will recognize you as a regularly constituted Grand Encampment".

During the course of these proceedings, however, both Winchester and Warren Encampments, having been impressed by Cushman's claims, thought it best to "be on the safe side" and applied to the Deputy Grand Master for charters(or warrants), undoubtedly through Cushman. *Charters of recognition*, dated July 4, 1824, were issued accordingly. Note that the fee for such documents was not more than $10.00 each, while *charters of constitution* would have cost $90.00 each as already pointed out. This arrangement undoubtedly represents a compromise which was suggested by Cushman with a view to winning the members of Winchester and Warren Encampments to his viewpoint.

On August 11, 1824 a Special Assembly of the Grand Encampment of Virginia was held at Winchester to consider the proposal of General Grand Master Clinton and, if possible, to settle the matter once and for all. After due discussion,

...... The Assembly, taking into consideration the advantages to be derived from a union with the General Grand Encampment, *Resolved,* That this Grand Encampment do acknowledge the jurisdiction of the General Grand Encampment, and that it will obey, abide by, keep, and perform all the Constitutional Laws, Rules, and Regulations of the said General Grand Encampment.

The Annual Assembly of the Grand Encampment of Virginia took place according to schedule on November 22, 1824, when the final correspondence with Clinton was read and the outcome approved. But the representatives of Mt. Carmel Encampment, for some reason, dissented from this decision and declined to acknowledge the legality of the action of Virginia in becoming subject to the General Grand Encampment, U. S. A. It refused, therefore, to accept a charter from the new Grand Encampment of Virginia and resigned its dispensation, which had been granted one year previously when the Grand Encampment was organized. Therefore, Mt. Carmel Encampment became extinct and there is no further reference to it in the records. But an invitation was issued to the Richmond Encampment to affiliate with the Grand Encampment of Virginia and this invitation was accepted. As a consequence of the withdrawal of Mt. Carmel Encampment and the affiliation of Richmond Encampment, it was decided to hold another Special Assembly in Winchester, on March 23, 1825, at which there was a *pro forma* reorganization of the Grand Encampment of Virginia. At this time Daniel Walker Thomas was continued in the office of Grand Master and Dr. John Dove was made Deputy Grand Master. The Richmond delegates moved immediately to bring about a separation from the General Grand Encampment, U. S. A., actuated as they were by the still lingering resentment against Cushman, who had persuaded the Richmond Encampment to take out a *charter of constitution* in 1823, costing $90.00, a wholly unnessary step in the light of subsequent developments. The two other Encampments, although they had experienced similar difficulties with Cushman, were unwilling to prolong them at this time and declined to concur in the motion of Richmond Encampment on this subject. Therefore, Richmond sent neither returns nor representatives to the Assemblies for many years thereafter and continued, for the time being, independent of all other Templar bodies whatsoever. It did not affiliate again with the Grand Encampment of Virginia until 1845, when the Grand Encampment held an Assembly in Richmond on December 11th (at the time of the Grand Lodge sessions) after a lapse of some ten years.

Meanwhile, however, the Grand Encampment continued its activities without Richmond, holding its meetings annually in Winchester and granting charters from time to time for the establishment of new Encampments. James Cushman managed to continue his hold on the Virginia Templars and one item in the accounts of Grand Encampment indicates that Cushman was paid $12.50 toward his expenses in representing Virginia at the General Grand Encampment. Daniel Walker Thomas continued to serve as Grand Master until November, 1829, when he was succeeded by Charles A. Grice, who was "Grand Commander" (as he was then styled) of Portsmouth Encampment No. 5. This action was probably prompted by the fact, that Thomas removed from the state about that time, for he is noted as having been absent from the Annual Assembly of 1830, when it was voted to change the place of meeting from Winchester to Petersburg. Thus terminated the immediate influence and control of the Winchester Templars over the Grand Encampment of Virginia. In the next chapter we shall present certain additional facts relating to the history of Winchester Encampment No. 1 subsequent to the organization of the Grand Encampment of Virginia in 1823.

CHAPTER XX

WINCHESTER ENCAMPMENT BECOMES DORMANT

From the few available early records of the Grand Encampment of Virginia we learn some interesting facts regarding the first decade of Winchester Encampment under the new régime. Again the complete lack of Templar records in Winchester makes it necessary for us to confine ourselves to the meagre information available from other contemporary sources.

Fortunately the returns of Winchester Encampment No. 1 for the years 1823 to 1830 (with the exception of 1828) have survived the ravages of the years. From them we learn considerable about the officers and members of the Encampment from the beginning. The returns to the Grand Encampment for 1824-1825, which were the first required under the new organization, show the names of the following officers:

    M. E. Sir Daniel W. Thomas, Grand Commander
    M. E. Sir Lemuel Bent, Generalissimo
    M. E. Sir George Reed, Captain General
    Rev. Sir French S. Evans, Prelate
    Sir Samuel H. Davis, Senior Warden
    Sir Conrad Kremer, Junior Warden
    Sir Sutton I. Harris, Recorder
    Sir Solomon Heister, Treasurer
    Sir Peter Lauck, Standard Bearer
    Sir Samuel H. Lauck, Sword Bearer
    Sir John Frederick, Warder
    Sir James Foster, Sentinel

This return also contains the names of all the members, who ever belonged to Winchester Encampment up to September 7, 1825. There are certain discrepancies, however, since the return states that the Encampment has a total membership of 39, but there are various duplications, which reduce the number to approximately 25 after all those, who have withdrawn or have died, are eliminated. It is not clear where Daniel Walker

Thomas, Lemuel Bent, and George Reed received the orders, but there are certainly three additional members (Samuel Blair, Robert Beard, and William W. Blanchard), who had been created Knights Templar before they became affiliated with Winchester Encampment. There is a return for 1823-1825, which duplicates the preceding return in large measure and which likewise contains many discrepancies. One member, for example, is noted as having withdrawn in one return on September 10, 1825, but in the other he is listed as having been expelled on November 2, 1816. For this reason we cannot attach too much importance to the dates given.

However, we find that eight members withdrew in October, 1823, all of them residing at Harpers Ferry. This leads naturally to the conclusion, that these were the charter members of Warren Encampment, which was located at that place, and that the date of the charter (or warrant) was some time in October, 1823. Again it is noted, that first creations of Knights Templar in Winchester Encampment took place on May 4, 1813, when Robert L. Bealy and Robert Maloney were knighted. On May 24th of the same year Henry Seevers, of Frederick County was admitted. Other members received during the intervening years from 1813 to the date of the return came from such widely scattered places as Culpeper, Clarksburg, Romney, Shepherdstown, and Harpers Ferry, as well as from Winchester and Frederick County. Two members (William B. Whitney and Rev. French Strother Evans) are listed as "itinerant". There must have been a general purging of the rolls just prior to the submission of these two returns, since seventeen members are listed as "withdrawn" on September 10, 1825, one of these being only a "Knight Red Cross", and another is shown as having been "expelled".

There were few changes in the list of officers as given in the returns for 1826, 1827, 1829, and 1830. For these years the membership is given as 24, 25, 25, and 25 respectively. The following deaths are reported for this period:

Warner Throckmorton—March 13, 1826
Samuel H. Lauck—October 16, 1827

Two new members were knighted in 1827 and one in 1829. The return of 1830 shows Samuel H. Davis as "Grand Commander", Daniel Walker Thomas having withdrawn on September 2d of that year. The mystery of his whereabouts now becomes solved, since this return indicates that he had removed to Baltimore. This left Lemuel Bent in his usual place as Generalissimo, an office, which he had occupied all these years. There is no indication as to why he was not advanced to become the successor to Thomas as the head of the Encampment. Davis had been Senior Warden for the several preceding years and was evidently in high favor with the Sir Knights of Winchester. It is presumed, that the fact of his being Grand Recorder of the Grand Encampment of Virginia had much to do with Davis's elevation to the office of "Grand Commander" of Winchester Encampment. It may be added, that none of the returns after 1825 contains a list of the members, only the officers for the year being listed and the total number of members added at the end of the return.

The general conclusion which may be drawn from the returns cited above is, that Winchester Encampment had become somewhat inactive in line with the general tendency in the same direction so far as the Grand Encampment of Virginia was concerned. We know that the latter body held no Annual Assemblies between 1835 and 1838, also none between 1840 and 1844. The one Annual Assembly, which took place in that ten year period was in 1839, when no business of consequence was transacted. Then, too, there was trouble with the General Grand Encampment, which had granted a dispensation in 1838 for the formation of an Encampment at Wheeling, this being clearly an invasion of Virginia's jurisdiction. All of this caused more or less dissatisfaction and lack of interest and it remained for the Annual Assembly of 1845, which was held in Richmond, to effect a third re-organization of Virginia Templary—one which has continued until the present day.

The fate of Winchester Encampment No. 1 at this period

is revealed in a list published by the Grand Encampment of Virginia in 1865. This list shows that Winchester Encampment had been extinct since 1830, also that Warren Encampment at Harpers Ferry had ceased to exist in 1828. The last returns received from these two Encampments were for the years indicated and showed Winchester with 25 members and Harpers Ferry with 16, all of whom were included in the 419 members reported by the Grand Encampment of Virginia in 1855. Previously (in 1851) Winchester and two other Encampments had been warned by the Grand Encampment of the penalty of being declared extinct "unless they come forward by representation and pay up their dues at the next Grand Annual Assembly". Obviously the warning was not heeded, but the penalty was not imposed until four years later as already stated. Curiously enough, the list of Encampments under the jurisdiction of Virginia in 1855 shows both Winchester and Wheeling Encampments as being No. 1. And after the former was declared extinct, its number was not filled until Fredericksburg Commandery was chartered on October 18, 1875. The eventual loss of Winchester's two "daughter" Encampments, Warren No. 2 and Mt. Carmel No. 3, left these numbers also vacant. They were assigned respectively to Richmond Encampment (June 23, 1823) and Charlottesville Commandery (December 16, 1869). (The reader should be reminded here again, that the designation "Encampment" was changed to "Commandery" in 1856.)

Among the early members of Winchester Encampment, two served in the office of Grand Treasurer of the Grand Encampment of Virginia as follows: Peter Lauck (1823-1824), Solomon Heister (1824-1825), and again Peter Lauck (1825-1830). Two Winchester Sir Knights of that period also served as Grand Recorder: Sutton I. Harris (1823-1825) and Samuel H. Davis (1825-1830). Now, after the lapse of a century, the Grand Recordership has returned to Winchester, that office having been held by C. Vernon Eddy since 1929.

We conclude this chapter with the following letter, which furnishes some interesting sidelights on conditions prevailing in

Winchester Encampment and the Grand Encampment of Virginia in 1831:

Winchester, Nov. 29, 1831.
To Sir Wm. B. Hill, Grand Recorder of the Grand Encampment of Virginia:
Dear Sir and Brother:
I received some time since a letter from you asking for information respecting the funds of the Grand Encampment—to which I intended replying as soon as some matters connected with the funds could be settled. To prevent further suspense, I reply now, that my letter may be received before the annual meeting, although the matter is still unsettled. Two or three years ago, I was directed by the grand standing committee, to loan to Sir Knight George Reed, Grand Prelate, fifty dollars, for which he gave his note. The money was intended to relieve some person then in distress, and which was to be repaid as soon as he could obtain it. This, Mr. Reed assures me, he has not been able to do, but expects he will be during the present winter. Mr. R. is very responsible, and although slow, the debt is safe.

Though I have been the acknowledged Recorder of the Grand Encampment only, I have acted in fact as Treasurer, and it was not for me to decline obeying an order of the standing committee. I expected the delay which has arisen, but could not prevent it. It will be seen, that the balance in the treasury, according to the report of the committee of finance, presented at the last annual meeting, is thirty-nine dollars and eighty-eight cents ($39.88), from which take $2.25, for which I am accountable, for advertising the meeting this year in the Winchester papers, and the balance will be $37.43; so that $12.57 of the amount due by Mr. Reed belongs to me—a sufficient guarantee that I shall endeavor to collect the whole.

I gave to Sir Knight Cassell, of Portsmouth, last November, a portion of the records of the Grand Encampment. Neither the charter or the seal were taken. These, with whatever else may remain, I will endeavor to send to Richmond the present winter, so that you may be able to get them. I presume it would not be illegal, under the circumstances, to hold a meeting without the charter being present. I thought I had the record book, but do not find it—perhaps Mr. Cassell took it. The truth is I was more a nominal secretary than anything else—our Grand Master, Thomas, attending to all the business of the department, save the writing of charters, which was done by another person, to whom I gave the fee, and found the parchment in the bargain. We should never have had the Grand Encampment here, as nobody attended to it, but our worthy Grand Master, and he could not properly sustain it alone. Our subordinate Encampment, at Winchester, may be regarded as defunct. I trust your progress may henceforth be more prosperous than the past, and that the change will be promotive of good. We have a "cabinet", as it is termed, but which looks more like a clothes press than anything else—the property of the Grand and local Encampment jointly—which could not be sent to Petersburg without costing more than it is worth, and which, as perhaps the surviving heir of the concern, I may appropriate to my special benefit.

Fraternally yours,
SAMUEL H. DAVIS

P. S. The charter is sent by Mr. Parrott, the delegate from Ohio county; he will hand it to one of your delegates, who will send it by private conveyance to you.

CHAPTER XXI

THE YEARS OF UNCERTAINTY

When Daniel Walker Thomas changed the scene of his Masonic labors from Winchester to Baltimore in 1830 (as mentioned in the previous chapter), Templary in Winchester lost its mainstay. For some reason there was none to take his place and the history of Winchester Templary for the next forty years was one of extreme uncertainty. Like the trick penny, "first you see it, then you don't", the Commandery was "in and out", sometimes up and sometimes down. We shall now summarize briefly the story of its fitful existence, employing from this point in our narrative the term "Commandery" instead of "Encampment", the change in terminology becoming effective, as we have seen, by action of the Grand Encampment, U. S. A. in 1856.

After 1831 Winchester Commandery was completely dormant for two decades. Since the minute books are entirely missing, we depend for our knowledge of this period primarily upon the proceedings of the Grand Commandery of Virginia and of the Grand Encampment, U. S. A. We do not know the reasons for this long period of inactivity. We can only surmise that the two principal causes were the same as those we meet so frequently today in similar circumstances, namely, lack of leadership and lack of interest. For it was not until 1851 that Winchester Commandery was listed again in the Grand Commandery proceedings. As has been stated already Grand Commandery effected a reorganization in 1845, hence Winchester Commandery must have made an effort at revival some time about 1850. In the 1851 Proceedings the Commandery is still listed as No. 1 but the words "no return" indicate the precarious state of its existence at that time. In the Proceedings of 1852 Winchester Commandery is still carried but is listed as "extinct." and Wheeling Commandery appears as No. 1 in 1853 and 1854 with full returns for both years, though it is shown in 1855 as having made no return for that year.

For the succeeding five years there is no mention of Winchester Commandery at all and only 10 Commanderies are listed in the Proceedings of the Grand Commandery of Virginia for 1860. But Winchester Commandery appears again in the Proceedings of 1861, this time as No. 11 and with the words "no return" concluding its listing. The Proceedings for the war years (through 1865) carry the same listing of Winchester Commandery but with the notation "no return for two years", etc. successively. In 1866 the Commandery is shown as being "extinct" and it is omitted, therefore, from the Proceedings of 1867, 1868, and 1869. But in 1870 it reappears, still bearing the number 11 and reporting 11 members on its roster. John B. T. Reed is shown as Commander at this time, C. W. Reed as Treasurer, and C. A. B. Coffroth as Recorder. Then, in 1871, without warning, we find the listing of "Winchester Commandery No. 12" and no reason is given for the change in number. Since that time the Commandery has borne the number 12 without interruption. The 1871 returns show that Henry M. Brent, Jr. was Commander, William L. Bent Treasurer, and C. A. B. Coffroth continued in the office of Recorder. There were fourteen members that year and the *per capita* tax of 50 cents per member, totalling $7.00 in all, was paid in full.

Thus ends the all too short story of two-score years for Winchester Commandery. We might be inclined to speak of this period also as a sort of "forty years of wandering in the wilderness" for the Commandery (see similar comment on John Dove Chapter No. 21, page 192). At any rate as we have seen, returns were made to the Grand Commandery of Virginia for only two or three years between 1831 and 1871 and the Commandery winds up the period with only 14 members, including officers. The future did not look bright, and it was not until the advent of Alexander M. Baker as a member of the Commandery that the permanency of the body seemed to be assured. But of this we shall treat in the next chapter.

CHAPTER XXII

THE RECONSTRUCTION PERIOD AND AFTER

If the years following the War Between the States were characterized by political and economic reconstruction in the South, they were also years of reconstruction for Templary in Winchester. For, out of the uncertainties of the years from 1831 to 1871, there came a new order of things in the Commandery, this being brought about by Alexander M. Baker, who was a member of Winchester Commandery for almost fifty years, its Commander from 1899 to 1912, and Grand Commander of Virginia in 1912-1913. He died on June 19, 1931. His work was carried on by C. Vernon Eddy, who has been a member of the Commandery since 1900, was Commander in 1916-1917, Grand Commander of Virginia in 1925-1926, and became Grand Captain of the Guard of the Grand Encampment, U. S. A. in 1947. Thus we find, that the entire history of this Commandery centers around three men—the two just mentioned and Daniel Walker Thomas, to whom both Winchester and Virginia owe more than to any other one man so far as Templary is concerned. All three of these men served in the highest office attainable in Virginia Templary. With Dr. Frank Talbott McFaden, who became a member of Winchester Commandery by affiliation in 1924, they constitute the quartet of Grand Commanders supplied by Winchester Commandery to the Grand Commandery of Virginia.

But let us return now to 1871. Beginning with that year Winchester Commandery has been active continuously to the present time. It has made returns to the Grand Commandery each year with the exception of four—1872, 1874, 1892, and 1893. When Alexander M. Baker became a Knight Templar (about 1872) he became active almost immediately in Winchester Commandery. In the returns to Grand Commandery for 1874 he is listed as Standard Bearer of the Commandery in Winchester. In 1875 he was made Captain General and, with the exception of only two or three years, held various offices in the Commandery, until 1899, when he became Commander. He relinquished this office only when he became Grand Commander of the Grand Commandery of Virginia in 1912. Throughout the remainder of his life his interest in Templary was outstanding and his special delight was to act as Grand Marshal at the installation of officers of the Grand Commandery from year to year. No one else ever served in this office if Sir Knight Baker was present. He had mastered the Templar ritual early in his Masonic career and the same was true of the ceremonial and military aspects of Templary. Perhaps his greatest boast was the fact, that he had been a student at Washington College under General R. E. Lee. We remember discussing this subject with him on a number of occasions. Another of General Lee's students was William B. McChesney, of Staunton, who, like C. Vernon Eddy, served as head of all of the Grand Bodies of York Rite Masonry in Virginia.

Another stalwart of Winchester Templary in its more recent history was C. W. Hensell, who served as Commander of Winchester Commandery for fourteen years (1885-1899 inclusive). Previously he had also served as Recorder for several years and it was under his leadership, that Alexander M. Baker received most of his training in Templar tactics and ritual. Just as the mantle of Sir Knight Hensell seems to have fallen upon the shoulders of Sir Knight Baker, so did the latter's mantle descend in turn to C. Vernon Eddy. For within two years of his joining Winchester Commandery, Sir Knight Eddy was appointed Warder (1902), then Senior Warden (1904-1908 inclusive), then held no office for several years, and then became Generalissimo of the Commandery until he was made Commander in 1917. He became Grand Commander of Virginia in 1925-1926 and Grand Recorder in 1929, an office which he still holds.

The membership of Winchester Commandery during the period following 1871 has also shown a remarkable growth. From a little more than a dozen members in that year the membership increased to 29 in 1878, then fell back to 16 in 1894 and remained stationary for the four years after that. In 1898 there were 20 members and, by the end of the following year, which was Alexander M. Baker's first year as Commander, there were 33 members. For each of the succeeding years there was a healthy growth and, in 1910, the membership of the Commandery stood at an even 100.

An event of extreme importance in the history of Winchester Commandery took place in 1900. On March 2d of that year, the cornerstone of the old Market House was opened and among its contents were found certain documents and three jewels bearing eloquent testimony to the existence of Templar Masonry in Winchester as early as 1813. Because of their importance, we reproduce the documents here in full.

A List of the Officers and Members of Winchester Grand Encampment of Sir Knight Templars No. 1 Held in the fields of Winchester, state of Virginia.

Founded *Anno Domini* 1813, *Anno Lucis* 5813, and in the Era of Sir Knight Templars 831.

OFFICERS

Most Excellent Sir Knight Daniel Walker Thomas, Esqr., Grand Generalissimo
Reverend Sir Knight George Reed, Excellent Grand Captain General
Excellent Sir Knight Lemuel Bent, Esqr., Grand Captain of the Host
Excellent Sir Knight Peter Lauck, Grand Standard Bearer
Excellent Sir Knight Conrad Kremer, Grand Marshal
Excellent Sir Knight Samuel H. Lauck, Grand Registrar
Excellent Sir Knight James Hill, Grand Treasurer
Excellent Sir Knight James Foster, Grand Sword Bearer

MEMBERS

Sir Robert Maloney
Sir Henry Severs
Sir William P. Helm
Sir Dolphin Drew, Esqr.
Sir William Herrin
Sir Jacob R. Thomas

Sir William Kelley
Sir John A. Haupi
Sir Warner Throckmorton, Esqr.
Revd. Sir Norman Nash
Sir Abraham Lang
Sir Joseph P. Thomas

Sir Presley Marmaduke
Sir Isaac Hershell
Sir Edward Jackson
Sir John Wilson
Sir Cyrus B. Baldwin
Sir James Keller

Sir William W. Blanchard
Sir John Denton
Sir Philip Klipstine
Sir John R. Hayden
Sir John Kern

Deposited (together with a Triangle, Cross, and Star—Jewels of our Order) on the thirtieth day of the seventh month (called July) *Anno Domini* 1821, *Anno Lucis* 5821, and in the Era of Sir Knight Templars 839.

Done by order of our said Encampment at Winchester.
    D. W. THOMAS, M. E. G. G. L.
    GEORGE REED, E. G. C. G.
    LEMUEL BENT, E. G. C. H.
Attest:
SAMUEL H. LAUCK, E. G. R.

The object of this deposit is to shew to some future age, that the Science of Free Masonry is in a flourishing state, not being trameled with Governmental fetters as in ages past. It is also designed to shew that the Religion of Jesus Christ is flourishing and fast gaining ground on Heathenism, which has for so many centuries inveloped the world in gross darkness and idolitry. It is hoped when these lines shall again be exhibited to the human eye, it will be High Meridian of Gospel day, when the glorious sun of righteousness shines forth its refulgent beams to Earth's remotest bounds and all the inhabitants thereof shall be then held captives of the all-glorious Emmanuel. That the Great God of the universe may hasten the time is the prayer of

    DANIEL WALKER THOMAS, Esqr. Most Excellent Grand Generalissimo of the Grand Encampment of Virginia, held in the fields of Winchester, 30th day of the 7th month (called July) *Anno Domini* 1821, *Anno Lucis* 5821, and in the Era of Sir Knight Templars 839.
    AMEN.

Our only comment on this fine expression of sentiment is, that it is one of the most outstanding Templar documents we have seen anywhere. That the hopes of Daniel Walker Thomas have not been realized during the 125 years, which have elapsed since the date of these documents, is indeed a pertinent commentary on the so-called "progress", which we have made during that period.

It is to be much regretted that the extant minute books of Winchester Commandery do not go farther back than September 21, 1916. On that date Grand Commander Joseph T. Houck visited the Commandery for the annual inspection. A total of 37 Sir Knights attended this occasion and the inspection was held, not in the asylum but in the city hall plaza. On November 3d Past Grand Commander A. M. Baker urged that a large representation be sent from Winchester to the Grand Encampment at Philadelphia in 1919 (nearly three years later). A committee was appointed to make plans to this end. The dues at that time were $3.00 per year, the fee for the Orders $25.00, and the cost of the uniform $50.00. The ascension services on May 20, 1917 were held at Front Royal with representatives of Luray, Fairfax, and Piedmont Commanderies as well as from Winchester in attendance. On September 7, 1917 the Commandery made a donation of $5.00 for the relief of Jewish sufferers in the war zone in Europe. Sir Knight C. Vernon Eddy became Commander on September 7, 1917. The Commandery was again inspected that year by Sir Knight Joseph T. Houck, P. G. C., and Sir Knight A. M. Baker is shown as continuing his enthusiastic interest and activity in the affairs of Winchester Commandery throughout this entire period.

On September 16, 1918 the Commandery made a contribution of $119.00 to the emergency war fund then in process of being raised by the Grand Master of the Grand Encampment, U. S. A. In their patriotic fervor at that time, the Sir Knights also voted to purchase an American flag at a cost of $20.00. At the Christmas observance of 1918 five boxes of candy and two $5.00 gold pieces were sent to widows of former members of Winchester Commandery. On September 5, 1919 the Commandery ordered a special Pullman car to be reserved for the Sir Knights desiring to attend the Grand Encampment at Philadelphia. On November 7, 1919 Sir Knight Baker reported, that

Sir Knight C. Vernon Eddy had been appointed to the office of Grand Standard Bearer in the Grand Commandery of Virginia the preceding month.

For the next few years we note that the interest in Commandery affairs continued on a high level among the members of No. 12. Attendance was usually very good, 15 to 30 members being ordinarily present, even at special conclaves. The annual Ascension and Christmas services drew large crowds and there was also plenty of work as was the case also in the other local Masonic bodies. The financial condition of the Commandery was excellent; for example, on October 1, 1920 the balance on hand was reported as $887.65 and a year later this balance had increased to $1140.82. The Commandery acted as an escort at the laying of the cornerstone of the Handley School on June 13, 1923. Among the visitors on that occasion was Grand Senior Warden Perry W. Widener of the Grand Encampment, U. S. A. Past Grand Commander Frank T. McFaden was elected to membership in Winchester Commandery on September 5, 1924 and his name appears in the minutes regularly thereafter until his death in 1933. As the result of the offering taken at the Christmas observance that year ministrations to fourteen widows of former Commandery members were made possible.

In October, 1925 Grand Commandery met in Lynchburg. At that time Sir Knight C. Vernon Eddy was made Grand Commander of Virginia. A report of these proceedings was made to Winchester Commandery on November 6th of that year by Past Grand Commander A. M. Baker. The Commandery was inspected by Sir Knight W. Crews Wooding, of Danville, on May 8, 1926 and, on November 5th, Past Grand Commander Baker reported on the proceedings of Grand Commandery in October, at which Sir Knight Eddy presided. On November 12, 1931 Grand Commander James H. Price paid an official visit to the Commandery. He was accompanied by Grand Recorder C. Vernon Eddy (who had held office since 1929) and other distinguished visitors. In May, 1933 Grand Commandery met in Winchester, the local Commandery appropriating the sum of $500.00 to assist in financing the conclave, and a committee headed by Sir Knight H. B. McCormac made all arrangements for entertaining the visiting Sir Knights. This was the first meeting of the Grand Commandery in Winchester since 1830. In the minutes of Winchester Commandery for November 3, 1933 we note that an appropriate memorial was read on the passing of Past Grand Commander McFaden, a member of that Commandery as previously noted.

Through the years since 1933 Winchester Commandery has continued its special interest in the Christmas observance, at which time the widows of former members, also other needy persons have been remembered from year to year in a very tangible way. It also gave its active support to the various campaigns conducted for the financial support of our country during World War II, likewise to various local community projects of a public or charitable nature. After a drop in membership during the decade starting in 1930, it has again resumed its customary activity in the conferring of the Orders and the interest of its members is now on a high level. The peak membership of nearly 200 in 1926 bids fair to be parallelled once more in the next two or three years, the present roster having a total of 116 Sir Knights listed therein. The Commander for 1948-1949 is Rev. Robert A. Whitten; Treasurer, Charles P. McVicar; and Recorder, Harold C. Jones. Past Commander Roy A. Larrick is now an officer in the Grand Commandery of Virginia.

Winchester Commandery has furnished four Grand Commanders to the Grand Commandery, Knights Templar of Virginia: Daniel Walker Thomas (1823-1830), Alexander M. Baker (1912-1913), Frank T. McFaden (1907-1908), and C. Vernon Eddy (1925-1926). We have been unable to locate any authentic information about Daniel Walker Thomas save that, which has already been set forth in the preceding pages of this book. The Masonic careers of the other Sir Knights, who served as Grand Commanders, have already been treated elsewhere in this volume, Sir Knight Eddy in the dedicatory pages, Sir Knight McFaden in the Lodge section, and Sir Knight Baker in the Commandery section.

COMMANDERS OF WINCHESTER ENCAMPMENT NO. 1 AND WINCHESTER COMMANDERY NO. 12 (1812-1949)

†*Daniel Walker Thomas 1812-1830
*Samuel H. Davis 1830-1831
(Commandery dormant or no information available)..1831-1870
*John B. T. Reed 1870-1871
*Henry M. Brent, Jr. 1871-1875
*John J. Jordan 1875-1879
*H. Clay Krebs 1879-1880
*John J. Jordan 1880-1882
*George E. Bushnell ....1882-1885 (?)
*C. W. Hensell 1885-1899
†*Alexander M. Baker 1899-1913
W. E. Cooper 1913-1917
† C. Vernon Eddy 1917-1918
*A. C. Slonaker 1918-1919
H. C. Sheetz, Sr. 1919-1920
*Claude B. Stickley 1920-1921
*William B. Wagner 1921-1923
J. B. Beverley, Jr. 1923-1924
C. S. Hartman 1924-1925
Lewis N. Barton 1925-1926
Walter M. Shade 1926-1927
Claude R. Cammer 1927-1928
D. R. Slonaker 1928-1929
Allen B. Gray 1929-1930
*Frank H. Dorsey 1930-1931
P. M. Shirey 1931-1932
Dudley C. Lichliter 1932-1933
W. B. Goode 1933-1934
Harold C. Jones 1934-1935
George N. Buck 1935-1936
M. V. B. Snoke 1936-1937
O. C. Cassell 1937-1938
W. E. Hewitt 1938-1939
*Brady W. Largent 1939-1940
Douglas O. Grimm 1940-1941
George S. Taylor 1941-1942

---
*Deceased.
† Also Grand Commander.

Roy A. Larrick 1942-1943
Mifflin B. Clowe, Sr. 1943-1944
*Irvin G. Birer 1944-1945
J. Lee Miller 1945-1946
H. C. Sheetz, Jr. 1946-1947
Victor W. Wheeler 1947-1948
Robert A. Whitten 1948-1949

TREASURERS

*Solomon Heister 1812-1831
(Commandery dormant or no information available) ..1831-1870
*C. W. Reed 1870-1871
*William L. Bent 1871-1874
*Henry Kinzel 1874-1886
*George E. Bushnell 1886-1898
*M. H. G. Willis 1898-1900
*George R. Blake 1900-1904
*G. H. Kinzel 1904-1915
*J. L. Cooper 1915-1918
D. M. Swink 1918-1919
W. E. Cooper 1919-1924
H. C. Sheetz, Sr. 1924-1932
C. S. Hartman 1932-1944
*Brady W. Largent 1944-1945
Charles P. McVicar 1945-

RECORDERS

*Sutton I. Harris 1812-1829
*George Reed 1829-1830
*Nash L. Gordon 1830-1831
(Commandery dormant or no information available) ..1831-1870
*C. A. B. Coffroth 1870-1879
*C. W. Hensell 1879-1882
*H. Clay Krebs 1882-1897
*J. E. Correll 1897-1908
*C. W. Wilson 1908-1909
*I. N. Good 1909-1913
D. M. Swink 1913-1918
W. E. Cooper 1918-1919
*C. W. Trenary 1919-1930
Walter M. Shade 1930-1936
Charles P. McVicar 1936-1940
Harold C. Jones 1940-

*Deceased.

CHARTERS OF THE MASONIC BODIES
OF WINCHESTER

CHARTER OF WINCHESTER HIRAM LODGE NO. 21

DAVID ROBERTSON, G. M.

[SEAL]

To all whom these presents may concern greeting:

Whereas the Lodge of Ancient Free and Accepted Masons held in the town of Winchester in the county of Frederick in the state of Virginia under the designation of the Winchester Lodge No. 12 having been originally established by a warrant bearing date Anno Lucis five thousand seven hundred and sixty-eight, granted by Right Worshipful William Ball Provincial Grand Master acting under the authority of the Grand Lodge of England which warrant the said Lodge No. 12 did on the seventeenth day of March A. L. five thousand seven hundred eighty-seven surrender to the Right Worshipful Grand Lodge of Pennsylvania and in lieu thereof did receive from the said Grand Lodge of Pennsylvania a charter bearing date the day of the said surrender, and in process of time it becoming desirable to the Brethren composing the said Lodge No. 12 to place themselves under the jurisdiction of our Grand Lodge and they having obtained from the said Grand Lodge of Pennsylvania full consent so to do, with a receipt for all fees and dues and the reputation of the tongue of good report, and having by virtue of a Dispensation dated February the fourth A. L. five thousand eight hundred and seven worked under the authority of our Grand Lodge and proved to our satisfaction that they are well skilled in our Ancient Mysteries and zealous in promoting the purposes of charity and universal benevolence, therefore

Know ye that we David Robertson Grand Master of Masons in the State of Virginia, by and with the consent of our Grand Lodge do hereby appoint our trusty and well beloved brethren the Worshipful Peter Lauck, Master; William Silver, Senior Warden; and Lewis Barnett, Junior Warden, together with the other true and faithful brethren composing the said Lodge to continue to work as a regularly constituted Lodge of Ancient Free and Accepted Masons in the town of Winchester aforesaid under the name title and designation of the Winchester Hiram Lodge Number Twenty one hereby requiring and enjoining all regular Lodges to hold, acknowledge and respect them as such. And we do hereby grant and commit to the Master, Wardens and Brethren aforesaid, and their successors full power and authority to receive and enter Apprentices, to pass Fellow Crafts, to raise Master Masons and to perform all other works of the Craft, agreeably to the ancient Customs and Usages of Free Masons and the ordinances and regulations of the Grand Lodge of Virginia and no otherwise; and also to chuse a Master and Wardens and other Officers annually and to exact from their members such fees as they shall judge necessary for the support of their said Lodge, the relief of their Brethren in distress and the regular payment of their annual contribution towards the Grand Charity Fund. And we do hereby require and enjoin the Master, Wardens and Brethren aforesaid and their successors, to record in their Books, along with this present Charter their own regulations and Bye Laws and their whole acts and proceedings from time to time as they occur. And also to correspond with our Grand Lodge whenever occasion may require and to attend the meetings thereof regularly by their proper representatives or deputies, and also to pay due respect and obedience to all such ordinances and instructions as they may from time to time receive from the Grand Lodge or from the Grand Master for the time being. And lastly the Master, Wardens and Brethren aforesaid in behalf of themselves and their successors do by accepting hereof solemnly engage strictly to conform to all and every of the foregoing requisitions and injunctions and at all times to acknowledge and recognize the Grand Lodge and Grand Master of Virginia as their superiors, and as such to obey them or either of them in all things appertaining to the Craft.

Done in the Grand Lodge of Virginia in the City of Richmond, this sixteenth day of December Anno Lucis 5807, Anno Domini 1807.

WM. H. FITZWHYLSONN G. S.

CHARTER OF JOHN DOVE CHAPTER NO. 21, R. A. M.

Most Excellent John P. Little Grand High Priest,

Most Excellent R. E. Withers Grand King,

Most Excellent B. M. Harris Grand Scribe,

OF THE
GRAND ROYAL ARCH CHAPTER OF VIRGINIA,

To all whom these Presents may Concern, Greetings:

WHEREAS it hath been duly represented to us, that in the Town of Winchester, Frederick County, State of Virginia, there reside a number of Companions, Royal Arch Masons, who are desirous of associating together, agreeably to the Constitutions of Ancient Masonry; and it appearing to us to be, for the increase and promotion of the Royal Art, that the said Companions should be encouraged, and properly enabled to proceed and work as heretofore they have been accustomed: Now therefore,

KNOW YE, That WE, the said MOST EXCELLENT John P. Little GRAND HIGH PRIEST, MOST EXCELLENT R. E. Withers GRAND KING, and MOST EXCELLENT B. M. Harris GRAND SCRIBE, of the Most Ancient and Honorable Society of Royal Arch Masons, for the Commonwealth of Virginia, and the Masonic jurisdiction thereunto belonging, by and with the consent and approbation of the Grand Chapter, testified by the rules and regulations of said Grand Chapter, do hereby constitute and appoint our worthy Companions, Henry M. Brent, Jr., M. E. HIGH PRIEST, Joseph M. Ginn, KING, and C. E. Bennet, SCRIBE; together with all such other Companions as are now, or may at any time hereafter become members, a just, true, regular and warranted CHAPTER OF ROYAL ARCH MASONS, according to the old Constitutions, by the name, title, and designation of

JOHN DOVE CHAPTER NO. 21

And further do hereby require and ordain, all regular Chapters to receive, acknowledge, and respect them as such; hereby granting and committing to them and their succesors in office, full power and authority to open and hold a Chapter of Royal Arch Masons, and by virtue of these presents, to confer the MARK MASTER, PAST MASTER, SELECT MASTER, ROYAL MASTER, MOST EXCELLENT MASTER, and ROYAL ARCH Degrees of MASONRY, according to the known and established customs and practices of Ancient Masonry, and not otherwise: and also, to elect and choose High Priests, Kings, Scribes, and other Officers, annually, at such time or times as to them shall seem most proper. And also, to exact from their members, such contributions as they shall judge necessary, for the support of their Chapter, the relief of their Companions in distress, and fees to the Grand Chapter fund, agreeably to the Constitutions of Masonry, and the laws of the Grand Chapter of Virginia; recommending to the Companions aforesaid, to reverence and obey their superiors in all things lawful and honest, as becomes the honour and harmony of Masons; and to record in their Chapterbooks this present Charter, with their own private regulations and by-laws, and their whole acts and proceedings, from time to time, as they occur; and by no means to desert their said Chapter hereby constituted, or form themselves into separate meetings, without the consent and approbation of their High Priest, King and Scribe: all which, by acceptance hereof, they are holden and engaged to observe. And the Companions aforesaid, by accepting hereof, acknowledge and recognize the Grand High Priest, Grand King, Grand Scribe, and Grand Chapter of Virginia as their superiors and shall pay due regard to all such instructions and recommendations as they have or shall hereafter receive from them. And they are hereby also required to correspond with the Grand Chapter of Virginia, and to attend the meetings thereof by their proxies or deputies, authorized under the signature of their Secretary, and the Seal of their Chapter. And for the more effectual preservation of these presents, the same are hereby directed to be recorded in the Books of the Grand Chapter.

IN TESTIMONY WHEREOF, we have herein superscribed our names, and caused our Grand Secretary to subscribe his name and affix the Seal of the Grand Chapter of Virginia.

(SEAL)

Done at City of Richmond, State of Virginia, this 17th day of December Anno Lucis 5869 Anno Domini 1869 Royal Arch Masonry 2399

JOHN DOVE, Grand Secretary.

CHARTER OF RECOGNITION ISSUED TO WINCHESTER ENCAMPMENT NO. 1 AT THE INSTANCE OF JAMES CUSHMAN IN 1824

BY THE MOST EMINENT AND RIGHT WORSHIPFUL HENRY FOWLE, DEPUTY GENERAL GRAND MASTER OF THE GENERAL GRAND ENCAMPMENT OF THE UNITED STATES OF AMERICA

In Hoc Signo Vinces

To all whom it may concern, be it known, that whereas a petition has been presented from DANIEL WALKER THOMAS, GEORGE REED, LEMUEL BENT, PETER LAUCK, SAMUEL H. LAUCK, JAMES FOSTER, JOHN FREDERIC, JOHN KERN, SAMUEL H. DAVIS, SOLOMON HEISTER, CONRAD KREMER, SUTTON I. HARRIS and WILLIAM W. BLANCHARD, all KNIGHTS TEMPLARS, residing in Virginia, in the town of WINCHESTER or its vicinity, praying for a CHARTER of recognition from the GENERAL GRAND ENCAMPMENT, authorizing them to assemble as a regular ENCAMPMENT in the said town of WINCHESTER; and whereas said petition is accompanied with satisfactory vouchers and recommendations,—

NOW THEREFORE, by virtue of the power and authority in me vested by the CONSTITUTION of the GENERAL GRAND ENCAMPMENT, I do hereby authorize and empower the said DANIEL WALKER THOMAS, and his associates above named, to form, open and hold a regular COUNCIL of KNIGHTS OF THE RED CROSS, and an ENCAMPMENT of KNIGHTS TEMPLARS and KNIGHTS OF MALTA of the order of ST. JOHN OF JERUSALEM, in the said town of WINCHESTER by the name, style or title of WINCHESTER ENCAMPMENT; and the said ENCAMPMENT is hereby invested with full power to assemble together on all proper and lawful occasions; to create KNIGHTS of the RED CROSS, KNIGHTS TEMPLARS and KNIGHTS OF MALTA; to make BY-LAWS for their own government, and generally to do and transact all such matters and things as may and ought to be done and transacted consistently with the ancient usages and customs of the INSTITUTION; and of the said ENCAMPMENT I do hereby appoint the said SIR DANIEL WALKER THOMAS to be the first GRAND COMMANDER under our JURISDIC-

Charter of Recognition

TION, the said SIR GEORGE REED to be the first GENERALISSIMO, and SIR LEMUEL BENT to be the first CAPTAIN GENERAL; and I do require the said WINCHESTER ENCAMPMENT to communicate to either of the GENERAL GRAND OFFICERS an ANNUAL RETURN of all the candidates accepted and rejected, and to pay TWO DOLLARS for each candidate accepted, for the benefit of the funds of the GENERAL GRAND ENCAMPMENT, until the said payment shall be remitted by the GENERAL GRAND ENCAMPMENT, or there shall be a GRAND ENCAMPMENT constitutionally established in the State wherein the said WINCHESTER ENCAMPMENT is holden. And furthermore, I do enjoin it upon the said ENCAMPMENT to conform in all their doings to the CONSTITUTION, LAWS and EDICTS of the GENERAL GRAND ENCAMPMENT, and in failure thereof, this CHARTER, with all the powers herein granted, are to cease and be of no further validity.

GIVEN under my hand and the seal of the GENERAL GRAND ENCAMPMENT, at BOSTON, in the State of Massachusetts the Fourth Day of July, Anno Domini One thousand eight hundred & twenty four.

JOHN J. LOVING
General Grand Recorder

[SEAL]
HENRY FOWLE

ACKNOWLEDGMENTS

It is with a sense of deep obligation, as well as of sincere appreciation, that the author acknowledges assistance in the preparation of this work from the following:

To the general committee appointed by the Masonic bodies of Winchester for the planning and supervision of the work and consisting of Brothers Lewis N. Barton, Chairman, Thurman Crosslin, Eugene F. Dearing, C. Vernon Eddy, John H. Fisher, Claude M. Grim, Laurens P. Jones, Roy A. Larrick, and Charles P. McVicar. This committee was most cooperative at all times and rendered invaluable service at all stages of the work. The services rendered by Brother Lewis N. Barton in the work of "digging up" information (we know of no better way to express it than this), checking and double-checking data, reading the manuscript and both galley and page proofs, and attending otherwise to a multiplicity of details connected with the preparation and publication of this work should be accorded special mention. He has been tireless in his devotion to the cause and his painstaking and careful efforts have prevented a number of mistakes and reduced markedly the number of errors, which may have crept into this volume.

To Brother Ralph Y. Grubbs for his excellent and painstaking work in making many of the photographs used for the illustrations; also to Miss Elizabeth Barr, daughter of Brother C. Fred Barr deceased, who made available to the committee a number of negatives and prints for purposes of illustration.

To Brothers John L. Kater and Henry L. Bush for assistance in compiling the lists of officers, also to Brother C. L. Searcy and Miss Doris V. Sartelle for aid in typing certain parts of the manuscript.

To Brother W. B. Goode and Mr. W. W. Glass for their critical reading of the completed manuscript and for many suggestions made by them for changes and corrections.

In a very real sense, therefore, this volume is the product of many minds and the author is glad to give to his able and willing co-workers in this joint enterprise the credit which is so justly their due.

PART FIVE

1949-1979

Winchester Hiram Lodge No. 21
Ancient Free and Accepted Masons
1949 - 1979

In the years since the first printing of this book in 1949, Winchester Hiram Lodge has continued to prosper. A report of the Trustees in January, 1950 showed that the printing of this book cost a total of $3,188.87 for 500 bound copies and 200 unbound copies. These unbound copies were later bound and it is the exhaustion of this supply that necessitated the reprinting and undating at this time. This same report disclosed that the Lodge was in excellent financial condition so it was decided to invest $700.00 in the purchase of new robes for the degree work for which the Brethren had asquired quite a reputation of excellence.

In 1951 it was felt necessary to increase the dues from $6.00 to $9.00 per year because of rising costs. The initiation fees were also increased from $75.00 to $100.00. The Grand Master approved these changes to take effect in January 1952.

Winchester Hiram celebrated the Bicentennial of George Washington's entrance into Masonry in July, 1952 by inviting the author of this chronical, Past Grand Master William Mosley Brown to speak at the July Stated Communication. Brown also wrote the book, *George Washington—Freemason*.

In September, 1953, Brother Forrest Oglesby, a member of this Lodge and Pastor of the Braddock Street Methodist Church, Winchester, Va. conducted commemorative services at the Market Street Methodist Church, Winchester, celebrating the 100th anniversary of the laying of the cornrestone by Hiram No. 21 with Past Grand Master Edwin P. Hunter, a former member of this Lodge officiating. A large delegation from Winchester Hiram attended.

At the close of year 1953, Most. Wor. C. Vernon Eddy requested he not be nominated for another year as Secretary of the Lodge, a position he had held for more than 30 years. The Brethren reluctantly complied with his wishes and elected Past Master Taylor F. Simpson to the office.

254-4   FREEMASONRY IN WINCHESTER, VA.

The beginning of a movement in 1954 to remodel and renovate the Temple building culminated some 32 years later. It was in this year also that the John Dove Chapter No. 21, Royal Arch Masons inquired of the Lodge as to the possibility of the Chapter securing a meeting room in the Temple. A committee was appointed to investigate. It reported back in February of that year that they had concluded the cost of remodeling the space then occupied by Barr Studio in the rear of the second floor, would be prohibitive and requested more time to study the matter. In July the committee reported that they had found no space of sufficient size in the present building that could be converted for the use of the other bodies of Masonry and strongly recommended that no attempt be made to change any of the interior construction or exterior walls of the present building. A further study estimated that it would cost approximately $22,500 to erect a one-story building on the lot at the rear of the Temple which could be rented to the other three bodies. (The Order of the Eastern Star had joined the Chapter and Commandery in the request for space.) It was further estimated that a two-story building with Lodge room on the second floor and a storeroom or warehouse on the first floor would cost approximately $45,000. The committee recommended that the Lodge should carefully consider if it was advisable to spend the amount required to provide quarters for the other three bodies. The suggested project was abandoned.

In March, 1957, the Lodge voted to sponsor a chapter of DeMolay and authorized the expenditure of $300.00 for this purpose and gave permission for the Chapter to use the banquet hall on the third floor of the Temple as a meeting place. In November, 1959, the C. Vernon Eddy Chapter of DeMolay was instituted by a Degree Team from Ft. Belvoir, Virginia.

On Saturday, May 1, 1965 the Lodge celebrated the 100th anniversary of the initiating, passing and raising of William McKinley in this Lodge in 1865. Most Worshipful Walter Albert Porter, Grand Master of Masons in Virginia, presided and Most Wor. Edgar L. Ott, Grand Master of Masons in Ohio, McKinley's native State, was in attendance as well as quite a delegation of officers and members from William McKinley Lodge #431 in Canton, Ohio. The Officers of that Lodge

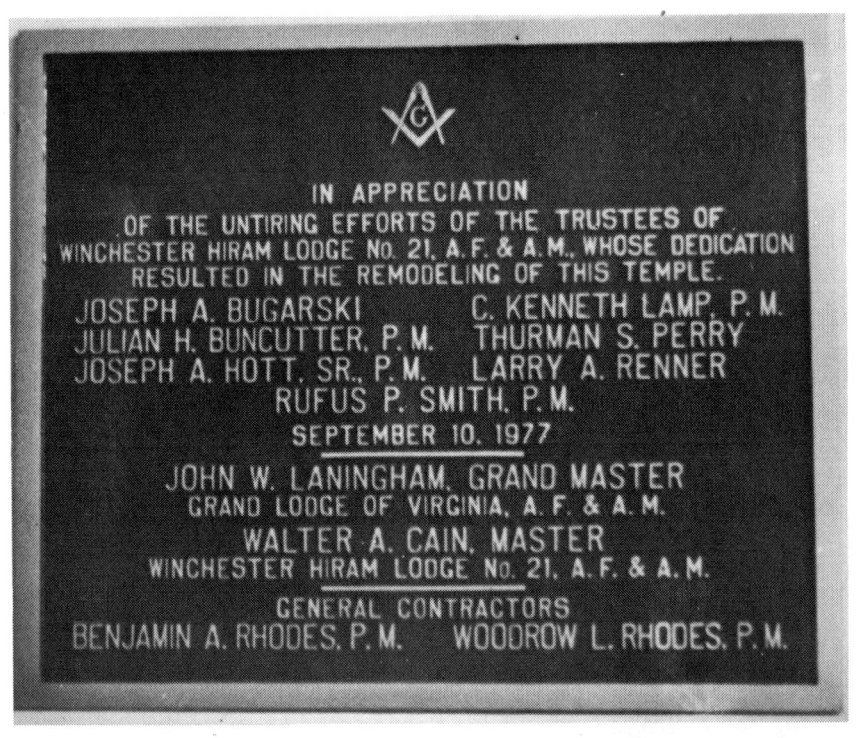

> IN APPRECIATION
> OF THE UNTIRING EFFORTS OF THE TRUSTEES OF
> WINCHESTER HIRAM LODGE NO. 21, A.F. & A.M., WHOSE DEDICATION
> RESULTED IN THE REMODELING OF THIS TEMPLE.
> JOSEPH A. BUGARSKI   C. KENNETH LAMP, P.M.
> JULIAN H. BUNCUTTER, P.M.   THURMAN S. PERRY
> JOSEPH A. HOTT, SR., P.M.   LARRY A. RENNER
> RUFUS P. SMITH, P.M.
> SEPTEMBER 10, 1977
> JOHN W. LANINGHAM, GRAND MASTER
> GRAND LODGE OF VIRGINIA, A.F. & A.M.
> WALTER A. CAIN, MASTER
> WINCHESTER HIRAM LODGE No. 21, A.F. & A.M.
> GENERAL CONTRACTORS
> BENJAMIN A. RHODES, P.M.   WOODROW L. RHODES, P.M.

This plaque, situated on the second floor of Hiram Temple, was dedicated on September 10, 1977 in appreciation of the trustees who participated in the remodeling and renovation of the Temple. Trustees giving their untiring efforts in the above project are shown in the photo below and are, left to right: Joseph A. Hott, Sr., P.M.; Joseph Bugarski, Rufus P. Smith, P.M.; Thurman S. Peery, Julian H. Buncutter, P.M.; C. Kenneth Lamp, P.M., and Larry A. Renner.

assumed all the stations and conferred the Master Mason's Degree on a Fellowcraft of that Lodge who had accompanied them to Winchester for this special occasion. Following the closing of the Lodge, dinner was served in the cafeteria of the James Wood High School followed by the presentation of the play, *William McKinley—Freemason.*

Winchester Hiram celebrated the 200th anniversary of the Lodge at a Special Communication on Saturday, October , 1968. Following the meeting a banquet was served in the George Washington Hotel at which the Hon. Brother John O. Marsh, Jr., then United States Congressman from the Seventh Congressional District of Virginia, was the speaker. The Justin Lawrie Singers from Washington, D. C. provided musical entertainment. Reports at the end of that year show that the Lodge was continuing to prosper with a total membership of 250.

One of the outstanding events to take place in Winchester Hiram happened on Saturday afternoon, May 9, 1970 when at the request of Most Wor. William T. Watkins, Grand Master of Masons in Virginia, the Lodge was convened and the Grand Master exercised one of his prerogatives and made the Hon. Harry F. Byrd, Jr., United States Senator from Virginia, and a resident of Winchester, Virginia, a "Mason on sight." Members of Treadwell Lodge #213, in Berryville, Virginia, initiated Mr. Byrd; Members of Spurmont Lodge #98 Strasburg, Virginia, conferred the Fellowcraft Degree. Following a dinner served by members of McKinley Chapter #19, O.E.S., and members of Bethel #47, I.O.J.D. in the banquet hall, the officers of Winchester Hiram conferred the Master Mason's Degree. The entire Grand Line of Grand Lodge Officers was present as well as five Past Grand Masters of Virginia and one each from the neighboring jurisdictions of Maryland, West Virginia, and the District of Columbia. Brother Byrd subsequently petitioned Winchester Hiram No. 21 for membership and was accepted on June 9, 1970.

Efforts to do something about the Temple building were renewed in 1971. To either remodel the present building, or find a more convenient place to meet on a suitable tract of land elsewhere in the city and build a new Temple, keeping this building as a museum were the options. The new building would house the other bodies of Masonry then meeting

Winchester Hiram Lodge, No. 21
A. F. & A. M.

The Oldest Masonic Lodge West of the Blue Ridge Mountains
CHARTERED OCTOBER 1768

December 15, 1976

W. Elliott Button
P. O. Box 146   Secretary

Meets Second Tuesday in Each Month in Masonic Temple
116-120 N. Loudoun St.
WINCHESTER, VIRGINIA

The Honorable Stewart Bell, Mayor
City of Winchester, Virginia

Dear Sir:

At a Stated meeting of Winchester Hiram Lodge No.21, A.F. & A.M. held in the Masonic Temple, 118 North Loudoun Street, Winchester, Va. on Tuesday evening, December 14, 1976, the following resolution was unanimously approved:

WHEREAS, The Masonic Fraternity of this area which includes John Dove Chapter No.21 Royal Arch Masons, Winchester Commandery No.12 Knights Templar, and McKinley Chapter No.19, Order of the Eastern Star, having had access and the privilege of occupying a room on the third floor of the Rouss City Hall for their meetings since the building was erected in 1900,

AND WHEREAS, These organizations and the City Council have had a very pleasant and harmonious association over a period of 76 years, and these organizations being grateful for the cooperation of the present and past City Council members,

THEREFORE, BE IT RESOLVED, That Winchester Hiram Lodge No.21 A.F. & A.M. representing the above mentioned Masonic groups, hereby relinquish all rights and privileges for the use of said rooms in Rouss City Hall effective December 15, 1976.

Given under the seal of Winchester Hiram Lodge No.21 A.F. & A.M. this 14th day of December 1976.

_____ Trustee
_____ Trustee
_____ Trustee
_____ Trustee
_____ Trustee

Attested:
_____ Secretary

on the third floor of Rouss City Hall as well as Hiram No. 21.

In the meantime, the Loudoun Street Mall was completed, sponsored by the Downtown Retail Merchants Association in order to revitalize the downtown shopping area. The occupants and owners of all buildings on the Mall were asked to remodel their building fronts in keeping with the master plan that had been developed. It was the concensus of opinion of the Mall Committee that the front of the Masonic Temple was one of the most beautiful on the Mall, and recommended that nothing other than a general cleaning of the front be done.

The Real Estate Committee from time to time, brought to the attention of the Lodge, properties that were available and options were taken on several but nothing was ever consumated. Finally, in October 1974 the Trustees received authorization to make any needed repairs and improvements to the Temple building, both inside and out, that they deemed necessary.

Beginning with the third floor of the Temple, the kitchen was enlarged, new equipment was installed, the ceiling was lowered and new draperies hung and carpeting laid. Also, window air conditioner units were added. Members of McKinley Chapter #19, O.E.S. helped select and coordinate the draperies and decor. Next came the remodeling of the hallway and stairs. An electric stair-chair was installed from the first floor to the second, and from the second to the third floor. This proved to be one of the best investments the Lodge ever made since the Building did not lend itself to the installation of an elevator. Members who had been unable to climb the long stairs to the third floor could now attend Lodge. Following the hall improvements, the second floor room used by the DeMolay and Job's Daughters, was remodeled and carpeted.

During this initial renovation period, the Lodge was notified that the owner of Barr's Photography Studio, (located to the rear of the second floor,) was going out of business on June 1, 1975 which made that area available for remodeling. This project was a tremendous task. The entire area was gutted leaving only the outside walls. These had to be remortarized and leveled off and steel beams installed. A steel roof was put on over which a concrete slab was poured so that any future addition of a third floor could be built. The vacant offices in the front of the second floor were converted into coaching rooms and a lounge. The former lounge was converted into an entrance way to the room later designated as the "McKinley Room." Again, the members of the Eastern Star assisted in coordinating the decor of this room and when the Chapter and Commandery furnishings were brought over from City Hall, the Eastern Star had the basic furniture reupholstered to match the carpet and wall panels. On the outside the brick walls were pointed up and a coat of waterproofing applied. The completion of this work took two years and when it was finished, the Lodge invited the Royal Arch Masons, the Commandery and the Order of the Eastern Star to occupy the newly-made quarters. This they did in December, 1976 ending a tradition begun in 1809 when the Lodge assisted the "City Fathers" financially in the construction of a Market House in which a room was reserved for their use.

On January 11, 1977, Wor. Bro. Walter Shade, with a delegation consisting of a representative from John Dove Chapter, Winchester Commandery and McKinley Chapter, Order of the Eastern Star, met with the Council, City of Winchester, and formally returned the meeting room on the third floor of Rouss City Hall to the City.

At a Special open meeting on September 10, 1977, a plaque was unveiled on the second floor and dedicated to the Trustees of Hiram Lodge No. 21, A.F. and A.M. who saw this project through to a successful finish. Most Wor. H. Bruce Green, Past Grand Master of Masons in Virginia was the dedication speaker.

All that remains to be done now is to install a more satisfactory system of lighting in the historical Blue Lodge room so that the beauty of the paintings covering the walls, may be enjoyed more fully. The Lodge continues to grow and prosper as substantiated in the 1978 annual report to the Grand Lodge showing a total membership of 279.

RAISINGS AND AFFILIATIONS
Winchester Hiram Lodge No. 21 — 1949-1979

A

Date of raising or *affiliation

Adams, Henry P.	May 23, 1950
Allen, Joseph O.	*Jan. 13, 1976
Alverez, Allen O.	Jun. 4, 1970
Ambrose, Edward	Mar. 30, 1954
Ambrogi, Lawrence R.	Nov. 20, 1973
Andrews, Charles	Nov. 29, 1966
Anderson, Charles D.	*Apr. 8, 1975
Anderson, Donald D. Jr.	Sep. 23, 1952
Armstrong, Kenneth F.	Nov. 27, 1956
Anderson, Marion H.	June 21, 1955
Arrick, John D.	*Sep. 15, 1968
Atkinson, J. Scott, Jr.	Jul. 15, 1969
Atkinson, J. Scott, Sr	*Oct. 9, 1956

B

Babbitt, James T.	*Dec. 14, 1976
Baker, Jasper T.	Apr. 20, 1971
Barbour, Robert S. III	Jul. 26, 1977
Barnett, Paul K.	Oct. 5, 1968
Barton, Charles W.	Nov. 27, 1956
Basore, Arlie W.	*Apr. 18, 1969
Beach, Robert T.	*Apr. 12, 1977
Beard, Clarence L.	*Jun. 10, 1956
Beaver, James L.	Jun. 15, 1965
Bentzel, Fred D.	May 27, 1958
Black, William H. Jr.	Aug. 31, 1965
Blanchard, Mahon R.	*May 14, 1968
Blankenship, James T.	Jan. 24, 1978
Blosser, Maurice O.	Apr. 2, 1963
Bray, Richard W.	Jun. 18, 1977
Bridgeforth, Wm. E. Jr.	Feb. 11, 1967
Braunlich, Ben H.	*Dec. 13, 1960
Boice, James H.	Feb. 28, 1978
Brodick, Harold J.	*Oct. 13, 1970
Brown, Lambert J.	Sept. 25, 1973
Bucher, Holmes A.	Nov. 1, 1955
Bucher, Thomas L.	Nov. 19, 1963
Bugarski, Joseph	Jul. 16, 1963
Burdette, Layton H. Jr.	Mar. 18, 1954
Bush, Roland D.	May 15, 1951
Button, W. Elliott	*Dec. 11, 1951
Byrd, Harry F. Jr.	May 9, 1970

C

Cain, Walter A.	Oct. 20, 1970
Cammer, Daniel C.	May 25, 1963
Cannon, Forrest K.	Apr. 6, 1977
Carley, William R.	*Sep. 14, 1965
Carr, Clay B.	*Aug. 11, 1970
Carter, Cecil C.	Oct. 1, 1974
Carter, W. Smoot	Mar. 24, 1964
Cather, Charles E. Jr.	Mar. 19, 1968
Clark, J. H. Jr.	Oct. 6, 1970
Clevenger, William F.	Sep. 5, 1950
Clewell, Lewis H.	July 25, 1961
Cline, R. Frederick	Jul. 31, 1951
Coffey, Warren L.	Mar. 27, 1956
Cole, Raymond H.	*Jan. 13, 1976
Cooper, Robert C.	Mar. 29, 1955
Copenhaver, Edward C.	*Jan. 13, 1970
Copenhaver, Wm. E.	Jul. 16, 1968
Courtney, Frank A.	Oct. 21, 1958
Craig, James O.	Jun. 15, 1975
Clark, Sam J.	Apr. 13, 1971
Cramer, Oliver G. Jr.	Sep. 5, 1958

Crim, James M.	Jun. 15, 1965	Glaize, George W.	Oct. 6, 1970
Crisman, Richard Z.	Sep. 5, 1950	Glaize, John L.	Apr. 28, 1953
Crites, Donald L.	Dec. 7, 1965	Goodridge, Carroll C.	Mar. 27, 1956
Culbert, Stephen T. Jr.		Gordon, C. Langdon	Nov. 28, 1961
	Oct. 21, 1970	Grant, David E.	*Jun. 12, 1951

D

		Gray, Robert L.	Aug. 31, 1954
Davis, James V.	*Sept. 13, 1977	Griffith, George T. Jr.	Mar. 3, 1959
DeHaven, P. Gayle	Nov. 21, 1972	Grimes, Jerry L.	Nov. 1, 1977
DeMoya, Peter P. Jr.	*Apr. 9, 1968	Grove, Claude M.	Mar. 22, 1960
Dickson, Wilson C. Jr.		Guard, Edward J.	Jul. 31, 1951
	Mar. 25, 1958		

H

Diehl, James H.	*Jan. 11, 1972	Harden, John A.	Oct. 29, 1963
Doggett, Aubrey W.	*Jan. 11, 1966	Harris, J. Wayne	Apr. 19, 1977
Donica, Fred M.	July 14, 1943	Hash, Warren G.	Nov. 28, 1961
Donnelly, Robert S.	*Oct. 13, 1970	Heishman, Clyde L,	*May 1, 1065
Duvall, John W.	May 26, 1953	Helsabeck, Numa	*Oct. 8, 1974
Duvall, Richard L.	Apr. 22, 1969	Henkel, Carroll H.	*Jan. 11, 1955

E

		Hepfer, John M.	*Nov. 10, 1953
Eastridge, Wm. C.	*Oct. 9, 1956	Hepner, Kirby, L. Jr.	May 18, 1968
Edens, H. Bruce	Mar. 19, 1968	Heppner, Frederick G.	Feb. 6, 1979
Edwards, Clifton P.	May 27, 1958	Herring, Charles E. Jr.	
Edwards, Clinton R.	Apr. 21, 1970		*May 8, 1956
Elliott, LeRoy J. Jr.	Apr. 16, 1977	Herring, Donald S.	Aug. 5, 1969
Elliott, Lester A. Jr.	Aug. 21, 1951	Hershey, J. Andrew	Nov. 15, 1977
Elliott, Sargent C.	*Apr. 30, 1964	Hershey, Roy B.	Mar 29, 1969
Emmart, Wade C.	Jul. 16, 1963	Hill, Arthur O.	*May 10, 1960
Evans, Kenneth W.	Jun. 23, 1970	Hoffman, Dale A.	Aug. 4, 1964
Evans, William R.	*Oct. 10, 1978	Hoffman, Gerald F.	Oct. 14, 1969
Everly, William W.	May 21, 1968	Holliday, Donald D.	June 28, 1977

F

		Holliday, Melford	Aug. 2, 1960
Faulkner, J. Olin	*Sep. 10, 1957	Hoover, George B.	Sep. 22, 1964
Fauver, William E.	Mar. 28, 1967	Hott, Joseph A. Sr.	Jul. 25, 1961
Feagans, Robert R.	Nov. 4, 1976	Hughes, Richard L. Jr.	
Fernandes, Ernest C.	Sep. 4, 1956		Sept. 25, 1956
Forsyth, Robert K.	Oct. 4, 1975	Hutchins, William D.	Mar. 5, 1968
Fragakis, Nicholas G.	*Dec. 8, 1953	Hyde, Frederick A.	Apr. 2, 1946
Funk, Norman L. Jr.	Sep. 15, 1964	Houser, Charles E.	Oct. 6, 1959

G

		Humphries, Harden G.	
Garber, Carroll L.	*Oct. 10, 1967		*Nov. 8, 1977
Garber, George H.	Nov. 7, 1950	Hunter, Robert H. Jr.	
Geraci, Joseph C.	Oct. 13, 1959		*Aug. 14, 1979

Huntsberry, Edward R. Jr.
　　　　　　　　May 1, 1951
Hutchinson, Marvin K.
　　　　　　　　Jun. 31, 1955
Golladay, James W. Jr.
　　　　　　　　Mar. 5, 1968
I
Ireland, Pierce G. *Jan. 14, 1958
J
Jacobs, Raymond L. Jr.
　　　　　　　　Jun. 2, 1959
Jenkins, G. Nathan　Nov. 19, 1974
Jenkins, Jack K. Jr.　Apr. 24, 1956
Jenkins, Joseph T.　Nov. 23, 1971
Jenkins, LeRoy R.　*Jan. 9, 1973
Johns, Aubrey W.　May 15, 1951
Johnson, Arthur E.　Oct. 18, 1977
Johnson, Robert B.　May 16, 1961
Johnson, Walter B. *Aug. 13, 1957
Jones, Donald K.　Oct. 16, 1979
Joppa, Martin A.　Jan. 23, 1979
K
Kave, Albert J.　Apr. 25, 1972
Keiter, Ronald L.
Keller, James R.　Sep. 4, 1956
Kelly, James F.　*Feb. 5, 1964
Kerlin, Raymond H. Jr.
　　　　　　　　Jun. 2, 1970
Kerr, Jack R.　Dec. 3, 1963
Kitchen, David J. II Aug. 9, 1954
Kyle, Edward H.　Nov. 6, 1951
L
Lamp, C. Kenneth　Aug. 31, 1965
Lamp, William K.　Aug. 28, 1976
Lauck, Charles E.　Mar. 24, 1970
Leonard, Rufus H. Jr. Dec. 1, 1953
　　　　　　　　*Dec. 17, 1962
Legge, Theadore R.　Jul. 27, 1971
Loar, Harold W.　May 23, 1967
Luttrell, W. Chester Apr. 18, 1961
Mc
McClain, D. Kenneth Jun. 3, 1974

McGee, Donald J.　*Jun. 8, 1974
McIlwee, Charles R, May 25, 1976
McInturff, Wayne E. Nov. 22, 1977
McKay, Julian B.　May 23, 1950
McRoberts, James V. *Jan. 9, 1962
M
Madagan, Harold F. Jr.
　　　　　　　　Jun. 27, 1967
Manuel, H. Clay　Jun. 16, 1957
Marshall, Edward J. Mar. 16, 1976
Marshall, Kenneth F. May 23, 1972
Martin, Carl E.　Aug. 18, 1959
Mason, Carroll D.　Nov. 24, 1959
Massie, James M.　May 27, 1959
Masters, George B.　Nov. 7, 1950
Mellon, Donald H.　Mar. 24, 1964
Melvin, Donald F.　*Feb. 2, 1971
Mercer, Burton B.　Jun. 15, 1954
Milam, John H.　Oct. 19, 1965
Miller, George W.　May 17, 1952
Miller, Russell D.　*Jan. 9, 1969
Moore, Thomas W. Dec. 29, 1964
Moser, John C.　Sep. 10, 1966
Mowery, Glenn M. Sr. Aug. 4, 1970
Mumpower, Arthur W.
　　　　　　　　Apr. 22, 1952
Munson, R. A. B.　*Mar. 2, 1968
Myers, Riley E., Jr.　Dec. 1, 1953
N
Nash, William D.　Mar. 30, 1954
Newlin, C. Raymond *Feb. 20, 1979
Newlin, Joseph B.　Mar. 28, 1967
O
Oglesby, Forrest B. Sept. 15, 1953
P
Palmer, Robert E.　Apr. 18, 1961
Payson, Harold A.　*Oct. 13, 1970
Perry, Thurman S.　Nov. 30, 1965
Pinner, Roy F.　*Apr. 10, 1951
Poston, George F.　Jul. 2, 1957
Prosser, Courtland R.
　　　　　　　　*Dec 17, 1962

Pulley, George E. II Oct. 6, 1959
R
Rader, Laurence F. Jun. 23, 1970
Ramsbottom, Russell L.
    *Dec. 8, 1953
Ramsden, Henry T. Aug. 11, 1970
Reed, Proctor, Jr. Apr. 15, 1975
Renner, Connie I. May 20, 1952
Renner, Larry A. May 27, 1967
Rhodes, Benjamin A. Apr. 22, 1952
Rhodes, Woodrow L. Sep. 23, 1952
Ritter, George H. Nov. 29, 1960
Ritter, Clinton R. Nov. 20, 1970
Ritter, Frederick M. Apr. 28, 1953
Robinson, F. Albert, Jr.
    Apr. 21, 1970
Rogers, Ben E. Jr. Jun. 2, 1959
Rogers, Raymond P. Jr.
    May 24, 1955
Rosenberger, Richard J.
    May 26, 1953
Routten, Carl E. *Oct. 9, 1956
S
Salomon, Enzio B. Aug. 31, 1954
Sandy, Robert L. Nov. 25, 1969
Sartelle, Donald W. May 21, 1951
Scorgie, Robert D. F. Apr. 1, 1975
Sempeles, Manuel G. Jun. 5, 1979
Semples, James G. Apr. 2, 1963
Shanholtz, Floyd L. Mar. 2, 1965
Sheetz, Richard E. May 24, 1970
Shendow, William Dec. 7, 1976
Shiflett, Cecil E. *Apr. 13, 1976
Simms, James D. *Sep. 9, 1952
Sims, Chaille P. Sr. *Nov. 9, 1965
Skelton, Richard K. Aug. 2, 1977
Slawson, Donald E. May 2, 1972
Smallwood, Robert G. Jul. 27, 1971
Smith, James E. Mar. 3, 1958
Smith, Lowell A. *May 28, 1963
Smith, Rufus P. Apr. 6, 1954

Speake, T. Stanley *May 8, 1951
Snellings, Sidney L.
    *Apr. 13, 1954
Stephenson, Robert C.
    Mar. 5, 1966
Stern, William C. Sep. 17, 1974
Steryous, Kenneth E. Aug. 4, 1964
Stretchberry, Joseph A.
    Sep. 23, 1952
Strickler, John T. *Jul. 9, 1963
Stone, Hubert M. Oct. 16, 1951
Stotler, J. Bryan Oct. 21, 1958
Stowe, Joel O. *Nov. 13, 1973
Straw, Harry G. *Jul. 27, 1963
Stuart, George C. *Jun 14, 1977
Swanson, Laurence C.
    *May 11, 1971
T
Taylor, Curtis D. Oct. 7, 1975
Thompson, Bigelow C.
    May, 1, 1951
Thompson, Billy R.
    *Sept. 12, 1978
Trenary, Richard D. Apr. 28, 1953
Trenary, Robert B. Nov. 1, 1955
Triplitt, Charles W. Sept. 5, 1972
Truslow, Elmer W. Apr. 3, 1978
Turner, Edward P. *Apr. 11, 1950
Tyler, Homer W. Jr. Nov. 29, 1960
V
Valentine, Duane E. *Oct. 10, 1967
VanHorn, William J. Mar. 3, 1959
Veller, Robert H. Sep. 15, 1964
Voight, Edward F. Nov. 20, 1975
Voight, Lokie L. May 31, 1960
W
Wallace, Charles O. Nov. 23, 1965
Wallace, L. Winston, Jr.
    May 23, 1950
Webster, Zane K. Jul. 15, 1969
Wheeler, Albert O. *Apr. 8, 1969

Whitacre, Floyd A.   Jun. 4, 1968
White, W. Allan   Nov. 4, 1975
Whitesell, Harry S. *Jun. 29, 1965
Whitmore, Woodrow W.
                     Apr. 6, 1954
Wilkins, James R.   *Jul. 12, 1960
Williams, John S.   Jul. 24, 1962
Williams, Irvin L.   May 29, 1962
Williams, Marvin E. Jr.
                     *Jun. 11, 1957
Williams, Ralph   *July 8, 1975

Williamson, Lamont W.
                     Nov. 24, 1959
Willis, Wm. D. Sr.   Apr. 23, 1968
Wilson, Louis S. Sr. Oct. 16, 1973
Wilson, S. Blaine   Jul. 7, 1969
Windle, Norman E.   Apr. 23, 1968
Woodside, Gilbert V. *Jun. 14, 1977

Z

Zickefoose, Mendle S. Jul. 27, 1965
Zickefoose, Moneth W.
                     Sep. 10, 1966

Past Masters of Winchester Hiram No. 21
1949-1979

*Thurman Croslin ____ 1949-1950
Eugene F. Dearing ___ 1950-1951
*Taylor F. Simpson (PDDGM)
_____ 1951-1952
*Gilbert R. Whitmire __ 1952-1953
R. Ray Sartelle _____ 1953-1954
*John L. Kater _____ 1954-1955
*Clyde Logan _____ 1955-1956
William F. Clevenger _ 1956-1957
R. Samuel Wine (PDDGM)
_____ 1957-1958
*Julian H. Buncutter __ 1958-1959
*Benjamin A. Rhodes (PDDGM)
_____ 1959-1960
*Woodrow L. Rhodes __ 1960-1961
*Rufus P. Smith (DDGM) 1961-1962
*Robert C. Cooper (PDDGM)
_____ 1962-1964
*Frank A. Courtney ___ 1964-1965
*George T. Griffith, Jr. 1965-1966
*Lokie L. Voight (PDDGM)
_____ 1966-1967

*James M. Massie _____ 1967-1968
*Joseph A. Hott, Sr. __ 1968-1969
*Maurice O. Blosser __ 1969-1970
*Dale A. Hoffman ____ 1970-1971
*C. Kenneth Lamp ____ 1971-1972
*Donald D. Anderson, Jr.
_____ 1972-1973
*W. Chester Luttrell __ 1973-1974
*Harold W. Loar _____ 1973-1975
*James W. Golladay, Jr. 1975-1976
*Walter A. Cain _____ 1976-1977
*Glenn M. Mowery ___ 1977-1978
*Theodore R. Legge ___ 1978-1979
  (Affiliated)
Harry G. Straw
Donald E. Melvin
Cecil E. Shiflett
Robert T. Beach
George C. Stuart
Gilbert V. Woodside

* Indicates Living

Secretaries of Winchester Hiram Lodge No. 21
1949 - 1979

C. Vernon Eddy 1937-53
*Taylor F. Simpson 1953-64
*Robert C. Cooper 1964-74
*W. Elliott Button 1974-

* Indicates Living

Treasurers of Winchester Hiram Lodge No. 21
A.F. & A.M. — 1949 - 1979

Claude M. Grim 1940-52
*Lewis N. Barton 1952-54
Wilbur E. Hewitt 1954-56
*John L. Kater 1956-75
*Julian H. Buncutter 1975-

* Indicates Living

Trustees of Winchester Hiram Lodge No. 21
1949 - 1979

Claude M. Grim 1937-1952
*Wendell B. Goode 1938-1960
Claude R. Cammer 1944-1960
Mifflin B. Clowe 1953-1956
*Sebert J. Smith 1956-1962
Laurens P. Jones 1957-1963
John L. Glaize 1960-1963
Hoye L. Riley 1960-1963
Herbert W. Harmer 1961-1966
*Benjamin A. Rhodes ... 1962-1967
*Rufus P. Smith 1963-1968
*Richard J. Rosenberger 1963-1968
*Julian H. Buncutter ... 1963-1968
*Taylor F. Simpson 1966-1971
*Frank A. Courtney 1967-1972
*Lokie L. Voight 1968-1973
*Larry A. Renner 1968-73
*Walter B. Hamrick 1969-74
*Thurman S. Perry 1970-75
*Julian H. Buncutter ... 1971-76
*Joseph A. Hott, Sr. ... 1972-77
*Rufus P. Smith 1973-78
*Joseph Bugarski 1974-79
*Larry A. Renner 1975-80
*C. Kenneth Lamp 1976-81
*Harold W. Loar 1977-82
*Glenn M. Mowery 1978-83

* Indicates Living.

Winchester Commandery No. 12
Knights Templar
1949 - 1979

Through the years from February 1949 to the present writing we have found Winchester Commandery No. 12 to be active and on the incline due greatly to the increase in membership, eventho a big loss has been felt through death, demits and non-payment of dues. Our membership has increased from 112 in 1949 to 158. This increase has been caused by active Commanders over the years just past, another reason, most of the Orders were conferred by the local Commandery. We were favored on several occasions by Columbia Commandery No. 2, of the District of Columbia, Old Dominion Commandery No. 11 of Alexandria, Virginia and Arlington Commandery No. 29 of Arlington, Va. who assisted in the Order of the Temple.

Some of the highlights of outstanding interest that is found of record in our minutes are as follows:

In October 1949 P. C. Lewis N. Barton advised the Commandery that he had located an old gavel bearing a name plate stating that it was made from wood taken from the Confederate Ram Merrimac and had been presented to Winchester Commandery in the year 1875 by V. E. James G. Bain. Sir Knight Laurens P. Jones was made a committee to request permission of the Master of Hiram Lodge to have the gavel placed in the trophy room of Hiram Lodge. Sir Knight Jones reported later the request had been granted.

A letter was read from the Grand Commandery stating that as of May 11, 1951 the fee for the Order would be $75.00, this amount being the minimum set by the Grand Commandery and upon a motion duly seconded Winchester Commandery voted that a fee not less than $25.00 accompany all petitions and the balance of $50.00 be paid before the Order of the Temple would be conferred.

In December 1951, a Knight Templar sword belonging to J. J. Jordon, a merchant in the 1890's, was given to Em.

C. Vernon Eddy by Thomas B. Spillman, as a donation to Winchester Commandery.

In October 1952, Em. Commander J. Scott Atkinson stated that Rt. Em. C. Vernon Eddy had been elevated to the office of Grand Junior Warden of the Grand Encampment of Knights Templar of the U. S. at the 45th Triennal Conclave in New Orleans, La. on September 20 thru 26, 1952.

On December 2, 1955 at the State Conclave of Winchester Commandery, a letter was read from the Grand Encampments 46th Triennal Conclave adopting a resolution to establish a Knights Templar Charity for the treatment of needy suffers of eye diseases. An annual assessment of $1.00 per member each year was levied on the Grand and Subordinate Commanderies, the assessment to begin for the year 1956. Grand Recorder C. Vernon Eddy and Recorder H. C. Jones were appointed a committee to draw up an amendment to the by-laws to include the $1.00 assessment for the Knights Templar Eye Foundation, Inc. A resolution was presented an dadopted to furnish the 8th floor of the George Washington National Masonic Memorial Building in Alexandria as a Chapel to be known as the Knights Templar Room by assessing 15¢ per member for the year 1956 only. A motion was made that Winchester Commandery absorb this 15¢ assessment, the motion passed.

On September 23, 1957 a special conclave was called for the purpose of entering into a proposition jointly with John Dove Royal Arch Chapter and McKinley Chapter Order of the Eastern Star to purchase a certain property located near Kernstown, Va. on U. S. Route 11 to be used as a Masonic Temple. After considerable discussion a motion was made by Sir Knight John H. Fisher, seconded by P. C. Taylor L. Barr, that the Commandery reject this proposal, the motion was carried by a large majority. Sir Knight John H. Fisher made a motion and was seconded by Sir Knight James R. Alexandria, that the three bodies appoint a committee to meet with Winchester Hiram Lodge No. 21 for the purpose of arranging for a room in the Masonic Temple Building as a meeting place.

At the stated conclave held March 3, 1961 Past Commander C. Vernon Eddy was made an honorary member of Winchester Commandery No. 12.

On June 4, 1976 a motion was made by Sir Knight

View of McKinley Room set up for Commandery.

Proctor Reed, Jr. that Winchester Commandery move to the room which is being remodeled in the Hiram Lodge Building. The membership had been notified of this action and a vote was taken upon the motion, the results was 15 favored the move and 3 against moving when the room was complete.

On September 23, 1976 a letter was received from the Trustees of Winchester Hiram Lodge No. 21, informing the Commandery and other bodies using the new remodeled room the privileges extended and the rental cost of same.

The stated conclave held November 5, 1976 was the last meeting in the Asylum in the City Hall by Winchester Commandery No. 12, which had been meeting there for more than 75 years.

The stated conclave of December 3, 1976 was the first meeting held in the new Asylum in the Masonic Temple on the Loudoun Street Mall.

The stated conclave held June 2, 1978 it was announced that at the 156th Grand Conclave held May 11, 12 & 13, 1978 in Alexandria, Virginia our own P. C. James W. Golladay, Jr. was elected to the High Office of Grand Captain General of the Grand Encampment of Virginia. He was then introduced to the Winchester Commandery No. 12.

Membership as of November 30, 1979

Ackenbom, Hugo G. Jan. 7, 1972
Allen, D. Blanton x 1964
Ames, Lewis B. d 1979
Anderson, Marion H. d 1961
Andrews, Charles D. s 1969
Arrick, John D. March 30, 1946
Atkinson, Scott J. Sr. d 1971
Bacon, Benjamin B. d 1965
Ballard, Ralph K. d
Barnett, Paul Keyton April 7, 1978
Barr, Taylor L., P. C. Nov. 7, 1952
Barrett, Richard J. x 1977
Barton, Lewis N., P. C. Feb. 3, 1922
Bayles, Harry A. Sr. d 1974
Bean, Roland F. Nov. 15, 1975
Beaver, James L. June 11, 1966
Bird, James W. d 1976
Black, William H., Jr. June 11, 1966
Blosser, Maurice O. Oct. 10, 1964
Board, Charles B. d 1964
Boger, Linal H. October 20, 1969
Bosserman, W. H. d 1967
Bowers, Harry H. d 1964
Braunlich, Ben H. d 1963
Bridgeforth, Wm. E., Sr. d 1979
Bridgeforth, Wm., Jr. Oct. 21, 1967
Brondstater, Leland W. Nov. 7, 1975
Brown, Douglas C. d 1965
Brown, Lambert, J. Nov. 15, 1975
Brown, Richard B. d 1965
Brown, Wiliam H. d 1979
Bugarski, Joseph, P. C. Apr. 5, 1964
Buncutter, Julian, P. C. Nov. 4, 1960
Burford, James D. d 1967
Burke, B. Bryan June 17, 1949
Burn, James W. February 28, 1970
Bush, Roland Dovel Dec. 10, 1977
Button, Elliott W. October 19, 1974
Byrd, Harry Flood, Jr. Dec. 10, 1977
Cain, Walter A. April 2, 1971
Cammer, Claude R. d 1972
Carlson, Earl E. October 3, 1970
CarsKaden, William A. x 1964
Carr, Clay B., P. C. August 1, 1966
Carroll, Arthur N. d 1966
Carter, Cecil C. November 15, 1975
Carter, Smoot W. d 1969
Choucleris, James d 1964
Clark, J. H., Jr. April 2, 1971
Clark, Sam J. d 1973
Clewell, Lewis H. d 1967
Clowe, James S. October 22, 1948
Clowe, Mifflin B. Jr. s 1967
Coffey, Warren L. Nov. 30, 1956
Cook, Dwight H. Nov. 15, 1975
Copenhaver, Edward C. 2/28/70
Copenhaver, Wm. E., P. C. 2/28/70
Courson, William L. d 1966
Currence, Ford x 1969
Daugherty, Delisle C. Dec. 6, 1957
Dearing, Eugene F. Sr. d 1977
Dehaven, Gayle P. Oct. 19, 1974
Dellinger, Aubey A., Jr. 11/13/76
Donica, Frederick M. May 27, 1967
Downing, Thomas W. x 1966
Duncan, Richard E. June 2, 1979
Eddy, Vernon C. d 1963
Edwards, Clifton P., P. C. 6/11/66
Edwards, Clinton R. Nov. 5, 1971
Fauver, William E. April 4, 1969
Fisher, John H. June 15, 1950
Fravel, Cecil H. October 29, 1966
Frazier, Gilbert R. Jan. 19, 1950
Frye, Lucius C. June 2, 1979
Funk, Norman L. May 2, 1969
Garber, James T. Nov. 15, 1975
Georges, Peter N. d 1978
Golladay, J. W., Jr., P. C. 10/3/70
Good, George W. October 5, 1923
Goode, Wendell B., P. C. 4/6/28

Grant, David E.	d 1977
Grant, James W.	June 2, 1979
Gray, Robert L.	August 26, 1955
Green, Edwin C.	d 1978
Gregory, Harry E.	x 1962
Griffith, Geo. T., Jr.	June 17, 1960
Griffith, Haywood S.	Feb. 28, 1970
Grimm, Douglas O., P. C.	5/12/33
Grimm, Randolph M.	d 1962
Grubbs, Kinzel B.	January 29, 1974
Haines, Floyd W.	February 6, 1976
Halterman, Tom D.	d 1978
Hancock, Wm. J. M.D.	2/29/68
Harden, John A.	April 24, 1965
Hartsock, Granville, Jr.	6/2/44
Hash, Warren G.	d 1975
Haymaker, Howard C. Jr.	d 1969
Hepfer, John M.	d 1970
Holliday, Donald Dwain	12/10/77
Holliday, Herbert C.	Nov. 3, 1950
Holliday, Melford	June 1, 1973
Hollingsworth, John W.	11/13/76
Hott, Joseph A.	October 10, 1964
Hottle, Joseph A.	October 19, 1974
Hottle, Joseph D.	d 1979
Hunter, Philip N.	d 1978
Huntsberry, E. Rhodes, Jr.	11/5/71
Hutchings, Edwin G.	d 1979
Irvin, John G.	September 27, 1969
Irvin, George R., Jr.	July 1, 1966
Jenkins, Jack Sr.	d 1976
Jenkins, Jack, Jr.	Nov. 23, 1956
Johnson, Arthur Edwin	Apr. 8, 1978
Jones, David M. Honorary	d 1972
Jones, Laurens P.	d 1977
Judy, James W.	February 28, 1970
Kaknis, Gus J.	d 1967
Keller, Paul M.	February 6, 1976
Kerlin, Raymond H.	x 1970
Kerr, Jack R.	October 10, 1964
Kibler, Aubrey H.	Sept. 27, 1969
Kines, Shirley J.	d 1969
Kinzie, John, Rev.	October 21, 1967
Knode, John H., Jr.	Sept. 25, 1953
Laing, Robert Edward	April 8, 1978
Laing, Silas Moody	April 14, 1973
Lamp, Kenneth C.	June 11, 1966
Larson, Ralph H.	d 1970
Leonard, Rufus H. Jr.	d 1976
Lichliter, Dudley C., P. C.	11/16/22
Loar, Harold William	Dec. 10, 1977
Logan, Clyde, P. C.	Sept. 26, 1946
Luttrell W. Chester, P. C.	4/6/62
Lutz, Alvin A.	d 1974
Madagan, Harold F., Jr.	7/5/68
Manuel, Clay H.	d 1974
Manuel, Robert F.	d 1970
Marks, William E.	Sept. 27, 1969
Marshall, Aubrey C.	d 1972
Massie, James M.	April 5, 1964
MacNally, Wm. J., Jr.	May 15, 1965
McCarty, Dennis P.	April 5, 1964
McCormick, Hugh D.	Aug. 2, 1957
McInturff, Gilbert S.	Feb. 28, 1970
Mellon, Donald H.	x 1971
Mercer, Burton B.	d 1964
Messenger, Phillip T.	Sept. 30, 1978
Milam, John H.	May 27, 1967
Miller, James L., P. C.	May 27, 1938
Miller, Robert K.	Oct. 19, 1974
Moore, Charles Franklin	6/1/74
Morris, Theodore J.	d 1969
Morrison, George E., III	6/2/79
Morrison, R. G.	October 21, 1967
Mowery, Glenn Marshall	12/10/77
Mumaw, Sherley L.	April 4, 1967
Myers, Riley E.	d 1973
Myers, Ward E., Jr.	Oct. 19, 1974
Newlin, Joseph B.	d 1969
Omps, Voyne B.	November 5, 1954
Palmer, Robert E.	d 1968
Parker, Alvin A.	June 2, 1979
Partlow, Jack D.	Feb. 28, 1970
Penner, Ray F.	x 1970

Peo, Ralph W. May 2, 1969
Perry, Thurman S. March 26, 1966
Priode, Bob October 3, 1968
Prosser, Cortland R. d 1978
Pruett, Frank R. June 15, 1950
Pully, George II d 1962
Radford, German E. x 1975
Rautton, Carl E. d 1975
Reed, Proctor Jr. x 1977
Reiley, John F. October 19, 1974
Renalds, Marvin W. d 1972
Rhodes, Benjamin A., P. C. 12/4/59
Rhodes, Woodrow L. Dec. 4, 1959
Richards, David M. Oct. 19, 1974
Rinehart, Carl R. Sept. 27, 1969
Ritter, W. H. October 21, 1967
Robinson, Charles A. d 1976
Robinson, Fred A., Jr. Oct. 3, 1970
Rogers, W. E. d 1964
Rosenberger, Richard J. 6/4/54
Rosenberger, Thomas B. 6/4/54
Rupprech, William G., Jr. 11/13/76
Sager, Clayton D. d 1972
Sheetz, Harold C. Jr. d 1974
Shiley, Wesley L. x 1976
Shipe, Herbert H. June 2, 1979
Simpson, Taylor F. x 1970
Slonaker, Dailey R. x 1969
Schumacher, Franklin E. 10/22/48
Semples, James G. Sept. 1, 1967
Shade, Walter M., P. C. 12/6/20
Shaffer, John D. Nov. 26, 1948
Shannon, James April 1, 1935
Shendow, William April 8, 1978
Showman, Raymond N. Feb. 3, 1978
Simoniz, John P., Jr. Oct. 8, 1955
Sirbaugh, Carl W. d 1964
Skelton, Richard Edward 4/8/78
Smallwood, Robert G. June 2, 1979
Smith, Donald E. d 1962
Smith, R. P., P. C. October 8, 1955
Smith, Sebert J. Sept. 29, 1945
Snellings, Sidney L. Oct. 29, 1966

Snyder, George H. d 1962
Stewart, S. C., Jr., P. C. 10/19/74
Stickley, Mm. M., III June 25, 1948
Stollings, Clyde Vernon 11/19/77
Stone, Hubert M., P. C. 6/2/53
Stoneburner, Oliver H. 10/3/70
Straw, Harry G. Sept. 18, 1929
Stotler, J. Bryan Nov. 20, 1959
Stuart, George C. June 6, 1978
Swanson, Laurence C. Jan. 7, 1972
Taylar, George S. d 1973
Tisinger, Buddy N. Sept. 4, 1970
Trenary, Richard D. x 1967
Trenary, Robert B. Nov. 23, 1956
Trotter, Hubert d 1961
Turner, Warren C. April 12, 1975
Vance, Donald H. Nov. 15, 1975
Voight, Lokie L. April 24, 1965
Wallace, Charles O. x 1975
Wallace, Lawrence W., Jr. 11/15/75
Warner, Russell S. d 1973
Watson Leon V. d 1979
Wheeler, Victor W. d 1964
Whitacre, Floyd A. June 2, 1979
Whitaker, Herman B. d 1969
White, Warren Allan Dec. 10, 1977
Whitesell, Harry S. Oct. 21, 1967
Wicks, Benton M. d 1971
Wilkins, John R. June 1, 1974
Willard, Charles s 1976
Williams, Irvin I. April 2, 1971
Williams, Joseph A., C. 3/5/71
Wilkins, Marvin A. x 1973
Williams, Marvin E., Jr. 8/4/63
Willis, William D., Sr. Feb. 28, 1970
Wilson, Douglas x 1969
Wilson, Louis S., Sr. Oct. 19, 1974
Wilson, Russell F. August 24, 1963
Windle, Norman E. x 1976
Wine, Richard S. d 1975
Wright, Marvin W., Jr. 11/13/76
Wright, Richard E. Nov. 13, 1976
Wyndham, Darryl E., Jr. 6/2/79

d — deceased.   s — suspended.   x — demitted.

COMMANDERS OF
WINCHESTER COMMANDERY NO. 12
(1949 - 1979)

* Jack K. Jenkins	1949-1950
* Milton D. Bauserman	1950-1951
* J. Scott Atkinson	1951-1954
† Eugene F. Dearing	1954-1955
* Arthur N. Carroll	1955-1956
Taylor L. Barr	1956-1957
Hubert M. Stone	1957-1959
Clyde Logan	1959-1960
Roy F. Pinner	1960-1961
Benjamin A. Rhodes	1961-1962
* Burton B. Mercer	1962-1964
Rufus P. Smith	1964-1965
Julian H. Buncutter	1965-1966
* Philip N. Hunter	1966-1968
* Richard S. Wine	1968-1969
Joseph Bugarski	1969-1970
Clifton P. Edwards	1970-1971
Frederick M. Donica	1971-1972
W. Chester Luttrell	1972-1973
James W. Golladay, Jr.	1973-1974
Clay B. Carr	1974-1975
William E. Copenhaver	1975-1976
* David E. Grant	1976-1977
Shadric C. Stewart, Jr.	1977-1978
Joseph A. Williams	1978-1979
William E. Marks	1979-1980

TREASURERS

* Charles P. McVicar	1949-1956
Rufus P. Smith	1956-1957
Taylor L. Barr	1957-

RECORDERS

* Harold C. Jones	1949-1959
* Henry Clay Manuel	1959-1963
* J. Scott Atkinson	1963-1965
Rufus P. Smith	1965-

* Deceased
† Demit

John Dove Chapter No. 21
Royal Arch Masons
1949 - 1979

The following is a supplement to the Royal Arch Chapter section of the history, *Freemasonry in Winchester, Virginia*, by Past Grand High Priest William Moseley Brown publisher in 1949.

Very little has been written regarding the meeting places of the Royal Arch Chapter since it was organized in Winchester in 1799. We believe it is fitting that a concise report be written from all available records.

The first Chapter meeting was held in the "room of Lodge No. 21", but neither the Blue Lodge or Chapter minutes indicate where the "Lodge Room" was at that time. The first Lodge room owned by the Masons of Winchester was the "Mason's Hall" erected by the Blue Lodge in 1809 as a second story above a 20-foot addition to the public Market House being built by the City. The entire building was demolished in 1821 and a larger Market House erected. The Masons added a 47-foot long room as a second story of the new building. The second "Mason's Hall" was demolished in 1899 at the same time the public Market House was demolished to make space for the Rouss City Hall.

The "Mason's Hall" was occupied by various Masonic groups from 1809 to 1899 but there isn't any written evidence that the Royal Arch Chapter held its meetings there until 1867 when Hiram Lodge gave the Chapter free use of the room with the stipulation that the Chapter pay for all repairs needed. The Chapter made the repairs and held its meetings there until the building was demolished in 1899.

At the time the City was considering the construction of a City Hall, Charles Broadway Rouss wrote the following letter to the City: "This is my proposition: I will give $30,000 toward the erection of a city hall if you will raise a like amount, and Mr. Rouss added: The hall will not be large enough for all the city offices and provide for the Masons' meeting in the north end of the public market. A separate building must be provided."

The Rouss City Hall was erected in 1900 and the City designated a room on the third floor for the use of the Masons, thereby complying with the wish of Mr. Rouss. John Dove Chapter moved to the Rouss City Hall when it was completed and held its meetings there until moving to the lovely "McKinley Room" in the Masonic Temple on the Mall. The first meeting held in the new room was December 9, 1976.

At the Stated meeting held February 11, 1949, $150.00 was approved as part payment for the history being written, and on January 13, 1950, the balance of $150.00 was ordered paid. The dues in 1949 were $3.00 per year and the Annual Report showed 143 members on the roll. On May 13, 1949, the Chapter ordered the altar Bible to be rebound.

The sesqui-centennial celebration of the organization of Capitular Masonry in Winchester was held in the Masonic Temple September 9, 1949. Past Grand High Priest C. Vernon Eddy presided and Past Grand High Priest William Moseley Brown made a most informative and interesting address. Dinner was served to 80 in attendance prior to the meeting.

At the Stated Conclave on November 11, 1949, a bill of $6.40 was approved for restoring the Chapter Charter. An offer was received to purchase two benches and three old chairs from the Chapter. After discussion, it was decided not to sell them.

The Jewels of the Principal Sojourner and King having been lost, new ones were ordered December 9, 1949 at a cost of $17.41.

January 13, 1950 the Chapter approved having a pedestal made for the bust of John Dove.

At a Special Convocation on January 27, 1950, District Deputy Grand High Priest Thomas W. Downing, in his official visit remarks, called attention to the ratio of membership in Blue Lodges and Chapters, i.e.: "Virginia being fourth in the several states, however, there are but 30% of Blue Lodge Masons in Virginia in its Chapters."

The Chapter voted May 11, 1951 to renew the subscription to the "Royal Arch Mason," published quarterly at a cost of $150.00, and to be mailed to each member.

View of McKinley Room set up for Chapter.

A Special Convocation was held November 6, 1954 at the request of Mizpah Chapter No. 288 of Pittsburgh, Pennsylvania, and the Royal Arch degree was conferred. The meeting was held in Hiram Lodge, Winchester, Virginia. Grand Chapter officers were present from Pennsylvania, Ohio, District of Columbia, Maryland and Virginia. Dinner was served to 135 persons prior to the meeting.

Past Grand High Priest C. Vernon Eddy and Past High Priest William E. Cooper were made Honorary Members on December 9, 1955.

The By-Laws dated August 6, 1956 raised the dues from $3.00 to $5.00 per annum. October 9, 1959, the Chapter voted to join Hiram Lodge and Winchester Commandery in having cards printed showing the time and place of meetings of each group. These were distributed to hotels, motels, and other public places to be available to visitors to this city.

A letter was received October 9, 1959 from the Order of the Eastern Star asking permission to install a piano in the Chapter room. Permission was given to either install a piano or repair the organ. The Order of the Eastern Star had held its meetings in the Chapter room since 1944.

A letter was read January 11, 1963 from Hiram Lodge

stating that the Lodge was starting a museum and asked for the deposit, as a loan, of any Masonic items of interest or historic value. The first time a proficiency certificate qualifying a member to be installed as High Priest, was read on September 13, 1963. Companion Rufus Smith was the qualified member. He was elected and installed on the same night.

A committee on property reported on February 12, 1965 that the planned improvements to the Chapter room would cost as follows: Air-conditioning- $1,300.00; painting- $700.00; and an estimated $3,000.00 was quoted by the City for extending the proposed elevator from the second floor to the third floor of City Hall. The total improvements came to $5,000.00. The Chapter approved $2500.00 provided the Commandery and Eastern Star paid the balance. Both groups had previously expressed an interest in the project. The City later decided not to install the elevator.

July 9, 1965 the Chapter was informed that the O.E.S. had volunteered to purchase a new room-size rug. At this same meeting, the Chapter decided to prohibit smoking in the Chapter room. It may be assumed that chewing tobacco was also prohibited, for while the above repairs were being made, six solid brass antique cuspidors were removed from the room.

Arrangements were made on October 10, 1969 to celebrate the 100th Anniversary of John Dove Chapter No. 21. A dinner including the ladies, was served. No further information is available except a letter was received from the Secretary of Shenandoah Chapter No. 17 expressing thanks for the wonderful meal and entertainment served their members and their ladies on October 17, 1969.

High Priest Chester Luttrell announced on March 13, 1970 that he was having as his guests, the members, their ladies and Chapter Widows at his home Saturday evening to a Covered Dish Supper. He expressed the hope that other members would do the same on a Saturday night of each month after the Stated Conclave. Any money raised at the suppers was to be sent to the Masonic Home for the Endowment Fund. The members were enthusiastic and started immediately to have these dinners each month. Excellent food and very pleasant associations were enjoyed each month for several years and it is regretted they have been discontinued.

A dinner was held in the Masonic Temple April 17, 1970

for members and their wives. The Royal Arch Widows' Degree was conferred on a number of ladies.

On June 10, 1971, the Secretary was instructed to write a letter to Mrs. Martha Donley thanking her for the gift of a Square and Compass given to the Chapter in honor of her father, Excellent Sam J. Clark. Companion Clark was High Priest of this Chapter at that time. It was ordered that the Jewels be appropriately engraved.

As of November 11, 1971 the dues were raised from $8.00 to $10.00 per year. On January 13, 1972, arrangements were made for members and their wives to attend a dinner at the Lee-Jackson Restaurant on January 27, 1972 to pay homage to the Past High Priests. February 10, 1972 minutes show that a letter of thanks was ordered to be sent to Mrs. Dorothy Arrick for the lovely Bible given to the Chapter.

On September 14, 1972, the Rt. Ex. James B. Williams, Jr. presented 21 Officers' aprons as a gift from Mt. Vernon Chapter No. 14 to John Dove No. 21. This presentation was made on behalf of Rt. Ex. Sam J. Clark, a Past High Priest of Mt. Vernon Chapter No. 14 and as a goodwill gesture through him for serving John Dove Chapter faithfully until his failing health caused him to relax the activities he enjoyed.

On September 12, 1974 the Secretary was instructed to write a letter of thanks to a Past Matron of McKinley Chapter for a new vacuum cleaner she donated for the use of the three groups meeting in the same room.

Discussions were held on April 17, 1976 regarding the publishing of a monthly Trestleboard by the Blue Lodge, John Dove Chapter and Winchester Commandery, giving details of the activities of each group for the month. This has developed into a six-page bulletin mailed to each member. The Order of the Eastern Star, the C. Vernon Eddy Chapter of DeMolay, Bethel No. 47, International Order of Job's Daughters, and the Winchester Shrine Club joined in the project, making a complete coverage of all Masonic-related activities in the area.

An invitation having been received from Hiram Lodge for the Chapter to move from the Rouss City Hall to a new room in the Masonic Temple was accepted on June 10, 1976 and the Chapter agreed to comply with the conditions stipulated in the letter. The Chapter made preparations to move, and on November 11, 1976 voted to pay one-half of the expense to refinish two deacons chairs found in the attic of City Hall, and asked the Commandery to pay the balance. These chairs and two old benches are valuable, and are now in use at the entrance to the McKinley Room.

The first meeting in the new room in the Masonic Temple on the Mall was held on December 11, 1976.

On November 19, 1977, a joint meeting of Royal Arch Chapters in this District was held in the McKinley Room. Recently elected Grand High Priest Robert M. Priode made his official visit. Among the many members and ladies present were a number of grand Chapter Officers. Prior to the meeting, a delicious dinner was served by the members of the Eastern Star. During the meeting the ladies were entertained in the Banquet Room and after the meeting a tour of the Temple was given and many compliments were received on the beautiful "McKinley Room."

At the July 13, 1978 meeting the Chapter voted to send Hiram Lodge No. 21 $150.00, the amount due for the publishing of this supplement.

John Dove Chapter No. 21 R.A.M.
1949 - 1979

	Exalted or *Affiliated
Hugo Gerhard Ackenbom	6/10/71
Henry Pennington Adams	5/22/52
D. Blanton Allen	Feb. 13, 1959
Allen Ogden Alvarez	8/13/70
Edward Ambrose	April 20, 1956
Lawrence R. Ambrogi	4/8/76
Lewis Bingham Ames	12/20/69
Donald D. Anderson, Jr.	12/2/52
Marion H. Anderson	Jan. 13, 1956
John D. Arrick	*Feb. 10, 1967
K. Frazier Armstrong	2/13/59
Charles Dwain Andrews	7/28/67
J. Scott Atkinson (By Dimit from Salem R.A.C. #18, Cumberland, Md.	
John Scott Atkinson, Jr.	8/22/69
Jasper Thurman Baker	8/19/71
Paul Kayton Barnett	Nov. 10, 1977
Nathan Malcolm Barry	12/20/69
James Lee Beaver	March 26, 1966
Fred Dill Bentzel	May 12, 1961
William Black, Jr.	March 26, 1966
Maurice Otis Blosser	1/31/64
Charles E. Bowerman	12/20/69
Ben H. Braunlick	May 22, 1952
Wm. E. Bridgeforth, Jr.	8/25/67
Norman Lee Brigance	3/23/78
Leland Brondstater	Nov. 13, 1975
Leland W. Brondstater	6/28/51
Lambert Joseph Brown	4/25/74
Roland D. Bush	April 24, 1952
Julian Henry Buncutter	1/27/52
Joseph Bugarski	Jan. 31, 1964
Walter Elliott Button	Feb. 8, 1952
Harry F. Byrd, Jr.	Feb. 2, 1974
Wm. Franklin Clevenger	2/23/51
Richard Zirkle Crisman	2/23/51
Walter A. Cain	Feb. 26, 1971
Clay B. Carr	June 12, 1969
Cecil Carl Carter	Sept. 4, 1975
Warren Smoot Carter	8/28/64
J. H. Clark	Feb. 26, 1971
Sam Clark	*July 12, 1968
Lewis H. Clewell	April 13, 1962
Warren Lee Coffey	Aug. 24, 1956
Edward C. Copenhaver	12/20/69
William E. Copenhaver	12/20/69
Frank Anderson Courtney	3/17/60
James Ogden Craig	Feb. 10, 1977
Stephen T. Culbert	Jan. 18, 1973
P. Gayle DeHaven	April 24, 1973
Frederick M. Donica, Sr.	1/21/66
Frederick M. Donica, Sr.	2/10/77
William Claude Eastridge	5/29/59
Clifton P. Edwards	Feb. 13, 1959
Clinton R. Edwards	Aug. 13, 1970
J. Olin Faulkner	Nov. 8, 1957
William Edward Fauver	3/31/69
Robert Ralph Feagans	2/10/77
Ernest C. Fernandes	4/13/62
Joseph B. Funk	*Jan. 12, 1956
Norman Lee Funk, Jr.	1/15/65
Carroll Lee Garber	
James Trenton Garber	12/2/53
Willard Craven Gleason	5/12/61
Robert Lee Gray	Feb. 18, 1955
Harry E. Gregory	*Aug. 9, 1957
James W. Golladay, Jr.	6/12/69
David Emery Grant	June 9, 1950
George T. Griffith, Jr.	3/17/60
Kinzel B. Grubbs, Jr.	8/14/52
Edward Jackson Guard	4/24/52
Floyd Haines	Sept. 12, 1974
William J. Hancock	9/12/66
Warren Gamaliel Hash	5/1/63
C. Howard Haymaker, Jr.	2/18/55
John M. Hepfer	May 9, 1952
Heppner, Fred G.	5/30/79
Charles E. Herring, Jr.	5/11/56
Donald Stuart Herring	
Donald D. Holliday	Nov. 10, 1977
Melford Holliday	April 14, 1961
Mt. Ex. A. B. Honts	4/10/59
Joseph A. Hott, Sr.	May 11, 1962
Edward R. Huntsberry, Jr.	4/24/52
Raymond L. Jacobs, Jr.	4/14/61
Jackson K. Jenkins, Jr.	8/24/56
Aubrey William Johns	12/2/53

Arthur Edwin Johnson 3/23/78
John Luther Kater Jan. 27, 1950
Raymond Howard Kerlin 3/10/50
Jack Rodney Kerr May 22, 1964
John Kingie July 28, 1967
John Henry Knode, Jr. 9/4/52
Clarence Kenneth Lamp 3/26/66
Ralph H. Larson March 10, 1950
Rufus H. Leoonard, Jr. 3/17/60
Harold William Loar Jan. 18, 1973
Harry L. Lovett *Dec. 11, 1953
W. Chester Luttrell Dec. 8, 1961
Harold F. Madagan, Jr. 3/8/68
H. Clay Manuel June 20, 1958
Robert Frederick Manuel 8/14/52
James Milton Massie 4/13/61
George Baxton Masters 6/28/51
Daniel K. McClain Feb. 10, 1977
Julian Brownley McKay 2/23/51
Donald Mellon March 31, 1969
Donald Homer Mellon 8/28/64
Burton Briggs Mercer 2/18/55
John Milam March 26, 1966
Reginald G. Morrison June 9, 1967
John Calvin Moser June 9, 1967
Glen M. Mowery, Sr. 5/25/72
Shirley Lewis Mumaw 3/26/66
Riley E. Myers Jan. 13, 1956
Joseph B. Newlin July 28, 1967
Voyne B. Omps June 9, 1950
Robert Earl Palmer Dec. 8, 1961
Arthur N. Patterson July 18, 1958
Thurman Stuart Perry 3/26/66
Richard Petrie May 12, 1967
Roy Franklin Pinner June 28, 1951
Mt. Ex. Bob Priode Nov. 11, 1976
Cortland Prosser Nov. 13, 1975
George E. Pully, II April 14, 1961
Carl E. Rautten *Feb. 13, 1959
Proctor Reed Sept. 4, 1975
Connie I. Renner Dec. 19, 1952
Larry Allen Renner Jan. 18, 1973
Benjamin Alvin Rhodes 12/19/52
Woodrow Lee Rhodes Dec. 2 1953

William E. Richards July 27, 1972
Clinton Ritter Nov. 13, 1975
F. Albert Robinson, Jr. 8/13/70
William G. Rupprecht 9/4/75
Richard J. Rosenberger 12/2/53
Robert D. F. Scorgie Nov. 11, 1976
James G. Sempeles Aug. 25, 1967
Lloyd Shanholtz
Manuel G. Sempeles 11/8/79
William Shendow Nov. 10, 1977
Richard Edward Skelton 3/23/78
Robert G. Smallwood 5/30/79
Rufus P. Smith Nov. 6, 1954
Sidney Lockhart Snellings 9/12/66
William C. Stern July 28, 1977
Shadric C. Stewart, Jr. 8/22/69
Hubert M. Stone Sept. 4, 1952
Joseph Allen Stretchberry 6/19/53
George Calvert Stuart 7/13/78
Lawrence C. Swanson 6/10/71
Curtis D. Taylor July 28, 1977
George E. Teel *Jan. 13, 1961
Buddy Nyle Tisinger 12/20/69
Robert Benjamin Trenary 8/24/56
Richard Daniel Trenary 12/2/53
Homer W. Tyler, Jr.
William J. Van Horn 1/24/62
Lokie D. Voight Jan. 24, 1964
Charles Oscar Wallace 3/26/66
Lawrence W. Wallace, Jr. 2/23/51
Russell Stevens Warner 3/10/50
Floyd A. Whitacre 5/30/79
Howard T. White Sept. 4, 1952
Warren A. White July 28, 1977
Harry Sellers Whitesell 8/25/67
Irvin Isaac Williams Jan. 15, 1965
Marvin E. Williams, Jr. 6/20/58
Wm. David Willis, Sr. 8/22/69
Louis Smith Wilson, Sr. 4/25/74
Norman Edward Windle 3/31/69
Richard Samuel Wine 1/27/50
R. Wilson Wright May 22, 1952
Mendel Zickefoose March 26, 1966

High Priests of John Dove Chapter No. 21, R.A.M.
1949 - 1979

Jack K. Jenkins	1948-49	*Rufus P. Smith	1962-66
M. D. Bauserman	1949-51	W. Smoot Carter	1966-67
R. Ray Sartelle	1951-52	*Joseph Bugarski	1967-68
Eugene F. Dearing	1952-53	*W. Chester Luttrell	1968-70
Laurens P. Jones	1953-54	Sam J. Clark	1970-71
Victor W. Wheeler	1954-55	*John D. Arrick	1971-72
*Gilbert R. Whitmire	1955-56	*Clay B. Carr	1972-73
J. Scott Atkinson	1956-57	*Shadric C. Stewart	1973-74
*Taylor L. Barr	1957-58	*William E. Copenhaver	1974-76
R. Samuel Wine	1958-59	*Walter A. Cain	1976-77
*Julian H. Buncutter	1959-60	*Clinton R. Edwards	1977-78
*Roy F. Pinner	1960-61	*James W. Golladay, Jr.	1978-79
*Hubert M. Stone	1961-62	*W. Elliott Button	1979-

* Indiciates Living.

Secretaries John Dove Chapter No. 21, R.A.M.
1949 - 1979

C. Vernon Eddy	1948-54	*Frederick M. Donica	1967-70
*Taylor F. Simpson	1954-64	*W. Chester Luttrell	1970-79
*Donald H. Mellon	1964-66	*Clay B. Carr	1979-
*Charles O. Wallace	1966-67		

*Indicates Living

Treasurers, John Dove Chapter No. 21, R.A.M.
1949 - 1979

Roy A. Larrick	1948-54	*Harry Whitesell	1971-
*Clyde A. Logan	1954-71		

*Indicates Living

McKinley Chapter No. 19
Order of the Eastern Star
Winchester, Virginia

Organized April 6, 1929

1929 – 1979

Published by authority of
McKinley Chapter No. 19
Order of the Eastern Star

The McKinley Room
Home of McKinley Chapter No. 19, O. E. S.
116 North Loudoun Mall — Winchester, Virginia

A view of the OES East in McKinley Room

Another view - Facing the West

254-C

Ella L. Hodges

Worthy Matron 1931-1932
Worthy Grand Matron 1950-1951

Daisy B. Shade

Worthy Matron 1929-1930

Fifty Years in Winchester, Va.

McKinley Chapter No. 19, O.E.S.

1929 - 1979

By Walter M. Shade, P.P.

McKinley Chapter No. 19, O.E.S.

Prior to 1929, Winchester, Virginia did not have a Chapter of the Order of the Eastern Star. A number of local men and women joined the Order in Berryville, Virginia.

In early 1929 these local member began a plan to organize a Chapter in Winchester. A group consisting of 17 of the Berryville members from the Winchester area plus 18 local men and women met to consider the requirements and responsibilities of the task, including money required, a suitable meeting place, and most important, the selection of a name for the proposed Chapter. These tasks were quickly solved and application was made to the Grand Chapter of Virginia, Order of the Eastern Star, for a dispensation to form a Chapter in Winchester, and to hold meetings.

During the planning period it was decided right and proper that credit be given the man who spent much of his life in promulgating the rituals, codes, principles and tenets of the Order that has grown and now has more than 14,000 chapters that encircle the earth with more than 3,000,000 members. Dr. Rob Morris, "Master Builder of the Order of the Eastern Star," was born near Boston Massachusetts on August 31, 1818. He received many educational advantages in New York which qualified him as a successful lawyer, lecturer, educator, and instructor in Free Masonry. He devoted many years in research and creative writing. He became a Master Mason on March 5, 1849. He soon became interested in an idea that the female relatives of Master Masons should share the benefits from this fraternal order. With this desire, and his fertile mind, he set forth to evolve an Order which would benefit both men and women.

Dr. and Mrs. Morris worked on the idea and invited brother Masons and their wives to their home to discuss the plans. Dr. Morris demonstrated the theories he had fomulated. This may rightfully be termed the origin of the Order although it was many years before it was recognized as such.

In 1850, Dr. Morris systematized the degrees. He incorporated the names of the heroines upon which the beautiful work was built, established the signs and passes, colors and emblems of the Order. The fundamental principles have remained unchanged through the years.

In 1866, Dr. Morris transferred his material and plans to Robert McCoy, and under his guiding hand the Supreme Grand Chapter was organized. The General Grand Chapter as we know it today was organized in Indianapolis, Indiana, November 16, 1876. The first ritual was compiled and published in 1868. This was the beginning of organized Chapters of the Order of the Eastern Star.

In 1880, the General Grand Chapter conferred on Dr. Morris the title of "Master Builder of the Order of the Eastern Star." Dr. Morris died on July 31, 1880 and was buried in La Grange, Kentucky. A marble monument has been erected to his memory by Master Masons and Eastern Star members from all over the world. On one side of the shaft is the Square and Compass and on the other side is the Five-Pointed Star. May the beautiful "Star in the East" ever remain the glory of the Order of the Eastern Star and light the pathway of the members in the fulfillment of their vows.

The name unanimously selected for the new Chapter was "McKinley" in honor of William McKinley who had been raised a Master Mason by Winchester Hiram Lodge No. 21, A.F. & A.M. on May 3, 1865. He was later elected the 25th President of the United States of America.

President McKinley wore a Masonic apron and made his last formal address at Alexandria, Virginia, on the 100th anniversary of George Washington's funeral, thereby, ending as well as beginning his Masonic association in Virginia.

May 20, 1899, President McKinley was a visitor in the Masonic Temple in Winchester where McKinley Chapter has its beautiful permanent meeting place.

The Chapter is grateful to the McKinley family for granting permission for the Chapter to use his name.

After selecting the name "McKinley" for the proposed

Chapter, the group of 30 women and 5 men asked the Grand Chapter of Virginia in Richmond, Virginia for a dispensation to organize a Chapter in Winchester. This request was approved and the Dispensation was presented at an organizational meeting on April 6, 1929 in a room on the third floor of the Farmers and Merchants National Bank building, located at the corner of North Loudoun Street and Rouss Avenue, Winchester, Virginia. This room was used by the Rotary Club of Winchester, and as the proposed Chapter had no treasury, it was fortunate that the Bank charged no rent. Also, the Chapter had free use of china, silver, and other equipment belonging to the Rotary Club. The new group purchased new furniture to the extent of their finances, but facilities remained inadequate until the Chapter moved to the Rouss City Hall 15 years later. One charter member commented recently (1978), "when visitors were expected at a meeting, chairs were borrowed from the Jones Funeral Home, carried to the third floor meeting room, and returned down the long flight of stairs following the meeting and delivered to the funeral home that same night." These laborious tasks were cheerfully performed by all members, both men and women, always hoping for a better situation. The indomitable spirit of these early members could not be subdued or overcome as their pride and courage served them well through the "great depression'," Not a sign of dismay or a word of discord was heard during these times and no suggestion was ever made to surrender the "Charter". This has been the spirit of McKinley Chapter members for 49 years which has brought it to the present flourishing condition with 155 members.

At the organizational meeting on Saturday, April 6, 1929, the following officers of the Grand Chapter of Virginia were present: Anna Bierer, Worthy Grand Matron, B. G. Porter, Worthy Grand Patron, Agnes Shiery, Grand Chaplain, Gladys Deming, Grand Marshal, and Past Worthy Grand Matron, Florence Clift.

The Worthy Grand Patron ordered the dispensation to be read. It included the following persons who were declared Charter Members:

Daisy B. Shade	Lena Lichliter	Thelma Brown
Nellie Austin	Bessie Brown	Grace E. Hewitt
Grace Shade	Maggie Woods	Elmer V. Hodges
Bessie Jones	Vernne Kremer	Arthur H. Austin

Ella L. Hodges   Pearle Largent   Lily McVicar
Lucia Shade   Lela Woods   Emma Beck
Gladys B. Wright   Walter Shade   Irene Hodgson
Edith Lichliter   Harold Jones   Edith Davis
Anna Mae Snoke   Marie B. Shade   Gabrella Ebert
Dora Hartman   Mary Cassell   Ida F. Dawson
Elizabeth Grim   Corrine Carskaden   William Brown
Bertie Snyder   Pearl Brown

The Worthy Grand Patron declared McKinley Chapter, Order of the Eastern Star duly constituted. The first and fourth Monday evenings of each month were designated as meeting nights.

The following officers were elected:

    Daisy B. Shade   Worthy Matron
    Harold Jones   Worthy Patron
    Bessie Jones   Associate Matron
    Walter Shade   Associate Patron
    Ella L. Hodges   Conductress
    Marie Shade   Associate Conductress

The following officers were appointed by the Worthy Matron:

    Thelma Brown   Secretary
    Irene Hodgson   Treasurer
    Dora Hartman   Chaplain
    Mary Cassell   Marshall
    Elmer V. Hodges   Organist
    Grace Shade   Ada
    Pearl Brown   Ruth
    Nellie Austin   Esther
    Corrine Carskaden   Martha
    Lucia Shade   Electa
    Emma Beck   Warder
    William Brown   Sentinel

The officers were installed by the Worthy Grand Matron, Anna Bierer, a member of Front Royal Chapter No. 6, as the Installing Matron, and Gladys Deming, Grand Marshal as Installing Marshal. The newly installed Worthy Matron made the following committee appointments:

    Finance: Irene Hodgson, Harold Jones and Elmer Hodges
    Gifts: Bessie Brown, Mary E. Grim and Lily B. McVicar

Flowers:	Bessie Jones, Gabrella Ebert and Grace Shade
Ways and Means:	Thelma Brown, Corrinne Carskaden, Mary Cassell and Emma A. Beck
Refreshments:	Marie Shade, Nellie Austin and Lucia Shade
Room:	Walter Shade, Elmer Hodges and Harold Jones
Music:	Elmer Hodges, Anna May Snoke and Pearl Brown
Publicity:	Ella Hodges and William Brown

The Worthy Matron, Sister Daisy Shade, expressed appreciation for the honor of having been elected the first Worthy Matron of McKinley Chapter and pledged her utmost ability to work for the good of the Chapter at all times in the future.

Thus we learn that from the humble beginning of this Chapter in 1929, 30 women and 5 men, dedicated to their vows, worked many long hours and with meticulous planning produced a program that provided minute details needed for a successful launching of McKinley Chapter, O.E.S. Without money, or a permanent meeting place, but bubbling over with enthusiasm and with a vision for the future, they built a Chapter which was to grow unceasingly for the next 49 years and beyond. The Chapter continued to work under the authority of the U.D. (under dispensation without a number) until the Charter was received on October 22, 1929, with the number "19" assigned.

The first regular meeting after the Dispensation was held on April 22, 1929. Seventeen officers were present. Bills amounting to $397.38 were read. A motion was passed to borrow $400.00 from the Farmers and Merchants National Bank of Winchester. This motion stipulated that the note be made for 60 days and renewable every 60 days until paid in full. This indicated the Chapter would owe $400.00 with a balance in the treasury of $2.62. Another report was made showing a member had collected $95.00 in fees. This increased the balance on hand to $97.62. After paying $101.57 for the Dispensation and miscellaneous expenses, the Chapter carried a net debt of $403.95. By hard work this debt was paid in full on April 22, 1930.

The first petitions to the new Chapter were from Mrs. Mayme C. Bott, Mr. Joseph L. Wright and Mr. George F. Norton.

According to the minutes, plans were made to serve dinner to the Winchester Shrine Club on May 20, 1929 in the Chapter room. At the meeting of May 27, 1929 it was reported that a profit of $23.00 was made on this dinner. From the foregoing, we lern how the members started immediately to make the Chapter a success.

The by-laws were approved at the May 6, 1929 meeting. At the May 27, 1929 meeting the minutes show 25 members and 8 visitors present. A yard party was held on the lawn of the Fairfax Hotel and a net amount of $28.29 was received. One member donated the "Star" which hangs in the East. Dishes with O.E.S. initials were purchased at a cost of $62.42.

At the October 22, 1929 meeting there were 53 persons present. Marvin D. Switzer, Worthy Grand Patron, presented the Charter, saying, "You will now be known as McKinley Chapter No. 19 instead of McKinley Chapter under dispensation."

At that time, the express on a barrel of apples sent to the O.E.S. Home in Richmond cost $2.14. On February 3, 1930, the budget for the year 1930 was $352.00 and was approved. The balance of $75.00 on the $400 note borrowed from the Farmers & Merchants National Bank on April 22, 1929, was ordered paid.

On March 3, 1930, the following officers were elected and installed on March 24, 1930:

Bessie Jones	Worthy Matron
Walter Shade	Worthy Patron
Ella Hodges	Associate Matron
Charles Lowery	Associate Patron
Marie Shade	Conductress
Thelma Brown	Associate Conductress

The Treasurer reported a solvency at the end of the first year and the Ways & Means projects continued to add revenue to the Chapter treasury. Applications had been received at every meeting until February 4, 1930. The annual banquet of the Rouss Fire Company had been served, a luncheon for Hiram Lodge, a dinner for the Scottish Rite

Masons and monthly dinners continued to be served to the Winchester Shrine Club.

May 5, 1930: The following were purchased at a total cost of $80.50: 8 doz. forks, 8 doz. teaspoons, 5 doz. knives, 1-1/2 doz. tablespoons, 6 butter knives and 6 sugar shells, a total of 282 pieces. Also purchased were 6 dozen glass sherbets costing $6.42.

October 22, 1930: A joint meeting was held in Front Royal for a visit by the Worthy Grand Matron. McKinley Chapter No. 19 voted to give her $5.00 in "gold."

November 24, 1930: At a cost of $4.50 each, 12 white chairs were purchased.

Election of officers for the third year was held on March 2, 1931 with the following results:

Ella L. Hodges	Worty Matron
Charles Lowery	Worthy Patron
Marie Shade	Associate Matron
William Brown	Associate Patron
Thelma Brown	Conductress
Mary Cassell	Associate Conductress

All officers were installed on March 23, 1931.

At a meeting on April 6, 1931, two new members were received. A social hour was held following the meeting and various games were played. The new members were given an extra initiation by proving they were experts at laughing in one corner of the room, singing in the second corner, crying in the third corner, and dancing in the fourth corner.

On April 27, 1931, a motion was made to change the meeting night from the first and fourth Monday to the second and fourth Monday nights. This was approved at a meeting held on May 4, 1931. The 1931 calendar year was a busy one. New members were initiated frequently. Dinners were served during the year but with a declining income from them. This period was in the middle of the "great depression," but these brave people never relaxed. An invitation was extended to the members of Hiram Lodge No. 21 to be guests of McKinley Chapter on October 26, 1931. At the November 23 meeting, the following receipts were reported: October Shrine dinner: $9.15; Knights Templar dinner: $17.50; November Shrine dinner: $10.19; Card Party: $16.91. The Chapter was asked by a local group to serve its members their annual dinner at 50¢ per plate on March 14, 1932, but the request was turned down.

The first public installation of officers was held on March 22, 1932. Those elected officers installed were:

Marie B. Shade	Worthy Matron
William Brown	Worthy Patron
Thelma Brown	Associate Matron
Mary Cassell	Conductress
Bertha Carter	Associate Conductress

After the Installation, the Secretary wrote, "The entertainment made the Chapter room rock with laughter."

It is interesting to note the effects of inflation from 1932 to the present time (1978). The expenses of a delegate to the 1932 Grand Chapter session was $1.53 for meals and $20.72 for all other expenses.

On September 12, 1932, 30 chairs were purchased costing $1.70 each, but on October 10, 1932 the Chapter learned the Company making the chairs had declared bankruptcy and the chairs would not be delivered. On November 14, 1932 three baskets of apples were sent to the O.E.S. Home in Richmond, Virginia. Members of McKinley Chapter were elated that year to learn that the interest on their savings had increased from 3% to 4%.

The first memorial service in McKinley Chapter was held on August 28, 1933 to honor Junior Past Worthy Matron Marie Shade who died on July 25, 1933. It was a "beautiful and impressive memorial." Later, on November 27, 1933, the Ways and Means Committee presented the Chapter a beautiful Eastern Star Flag in her memory.

The 1933-34 Chapter year proved to be as successful as the preceding year. The Chapter had been busy with initiations, the serving of dinners to many organizations (9 Shrine dinners were served for a net income of $51.90). A Yard Party netted a profit of $20.50; a Moving Picture at the Capitol Theatre sponsored by the Chapter for two nights, netted $17.00. The audit report showed receipts of $548.78 and disbursements of $548.07, a gain for the year of only 71¢.

On April 9, 1934, the Worthy Grand Matron visiting her home Chapter, stated, "McKinley Chapter No. 19 did the best ritual work of any Chapter in the State."

In this same year, a Building Committee was appointed with instructions to find a suitable meeting place. This was not accomplished until 42 years later when the Chapter moved to the beautiful room in the Masonic Temple on the Mall in December, 1976. The 5th anniversary of the Chapter was celebrated with appropriate festivities.

On October 8, 1934 a report was made to the Chapter that a hand-crocheted bedspread had been chanced off at the Capitol Theatre and the winning ticket was held by Herbert Harmer. The handwork was done by Mary Cassell, Daisy Shade, Ella Hodges, and Elsie Louderback. Net amount received was $189.45.

July 8, 1935: Members were invited to a picnic at Jordan Springs to be held on July 17 by the Shrine Clubs of Winchester, Virginia, Martinsburg, West Virginia, and Hagerstown, Maryland. The only requirement was "come early, look pretty, eat plenty and smile." Invitation accepted.

June 12, 1939 — Three dozen white chairs with "Eastern Star" stenciled on the back of each were purchased. The cost was $18.00 per dozen.

During the period 1939 to 1945 an all-out effort was made to raise money or do volunteer work for the Red Cross, the Hospital, and other war-related projects, overseas and in the local community. One member reported 900 hours of volunteer work performed. The Chapter contributed money to the Grand Chapter of Virginia to aid in purchasing two ambulances to be given to the U. S. Army for service overseas. In 1942 transportation for local volunteer work was curtailed by the rationing of gasoline and tires.

The annual report of 1943 to the Grand Chapter listed 86 members.

On May 10, 1945, a member returned to the Chapter treasury the full $25.00 advanced to her for expenses as a delegate to the Grand Chapter session saying, "I wish to assume that expense, and the money (advanced) be used for worthy causes."

November 22, 1943 — A petition was sent to Hiram Lodge asking permission to use a room in the Masonic Temple to hold meetings. As space in the Temple was not available, permission was granted by John Dove Chapter, Royal Arch Masons, and the Winchester Commandery to the Chapter to share their rooms in Rouss City Hall.

The moving date to Rouss City Hall is not recorded. The Dispensation from the Grand Chapter giving permission to move was read on May 22, 1944, and on June 12, 1944 it was reported that "the fire insurance on our furniture has been transferred to the Rouss City Hall."

At the request of the Federal Government, and because of war conditions, the Grand Chapter Session to be held on May 8 and 9, 1945, was cancelled.

The November 24, 1947 meeting was held in the banquet room of the Masonic Temple because heat was no longer available in the City Hall meeting room.

In July, 1949 the John Dove Royal Arch Chapter celebrated its 150th birthday and asked McKinley Chapter No. 19 to serve 100 to 150 dinners in the Masonic banquet room.

At the 1950 election of officers, Kathleen Atkinson and husband Scott, were elected as Worthy Matron and Worthy Patron. This was the first time that a man and wife served McKinley Chapter in the East together.

During the first 21 years of existence, McKinley Chapter members became well known throughout the state for their industry, dedication to the Eastern Star tenets and total dedication of helping win the Second World War. The Chapter had been honored by the appointment of its members to many Grand Chapter offices.

An important date for McKinley Chapter was June 23, 1947. At the Grand Chapter session in Richmond, Virginia, Sister Ella L. Hodges, Past Matron of McKinley Chapter 19, was nominated from the floor by Worthy Matron Mary C. Omps, McKinley Chapter No. 19, Winchester, for the office of Associate Grand Conductress. Three others were nominated, but "Sister Ella" was elected by a majority vote of 478 to 390. This was a distinct honor to be the first one in 43 years to be elected by this method of nomination.

Sister Ella Hodges advanced annually through the several Grand Chapter stations until May 11, 1950 when she was elected Worthy Grand Matron. In her acceptance speech, she stated her motto would be, "A Prayer, A Smile, A Deed."

After the election a reception was held in the John Marshall Hotel for the newly elected Worthy Grand Matron, Worthy Grand Patron and Worthy Matrons and Patrons who were in attendance. A total of 180 persons attended the reception.

On May 22, 1950 at the First Baptist Church, Winchester, Virginia, a homecoming reception was held for the

Worthy Grand Matron. A large number of persons from all sections of the state were in attendance.

The Worthy Grand Matron, Ella L. Hodges, made her official visit to her home Chapter on October 7, 1950. The Visitation was held in the Winchester Armory with more than 200 in attendance. Included in this number were 10 Past Grand Matrons, 8 Past Grand Patrons, 14 Grand Officers, 23 Grand Committee members, 20 Worthy Matrons, 9 Worthy Patrons, 95 Past Matrons and Patrons. It was truly a gala affair and established McKinley Chapter No. 19 as one of the most progressive chapters in the state.

During Sister Ella's term, there were 26 guests in the O.E.S. Home in Richmond, Virginia, and an addition was being erected to accommodate an additional 18.

July 24, 1950: A motion was made to raise the Chapter dues for the first time. The motion to increase the dues from $4.00 to $6.00 per year was approved August 24, 1950.

Beginning in 1930 and continuing to 1975, the Chapter sent from one to six bushels of apples to the O.E.S. Home in Richmond at Thanksgiving time. Gifts were also sent to each guest in the Home at various times. One year a friend of the Chapter offered to donate 50 bushels of apples if needed.

During the years 1950 to 1960, 67 dinners and/or lunches were served to the three local Masonic bodies and other organizations. Some of them were: May 22, 1950 dinners for 159 persons were served for Hiram Lodge No. 21; June 15, 1950, dinners were served to 40 Knights Templar, and again on February 16, 1951, the Knights Templar had 95 in attendance for a dinner.

It is refreshing to learn that after funds had been solicited for indigent school children and monthly checks sent, one check was returned with the notation, "not needed."

The 1954 annual report to the Grand Chapter showed the membership of McKinley Chapter to be 120.

There were 54 visitors at the October 25, 1954 Friendship Night.

At the January 1955 meeting it was announced that the Chapter had taken 12 orphans to the Eastern Star picnic the preceding summer; furnished them a full Christmas dinner including a 22-lb. turkey, purchased shoes and other clothing, and gave a box of candy to each boy and girl. These children were a special project of the Chapter. These same children were invited to a Chapter Christmas party in December 1958 at which time the children entertained the Chapter by singing carols.

The 1956 Friendship Night was held on September 24. Hiram Lodge members were invited. Twelve accepted the invitation. We now quote the minutes, "Several of them gave their version of how an Eastern Star meeting was conducted. It was hilarious, good fun and enjoyed by all." At the same meeting an announcement was made that a new Chapter of the Eastern Star would be organized in Berryville, Virginia, on October 27, 1956. The Berryville Chapter in which 17 Charter member of McKinley Chapter formerly belonged, had surrendered its Charter and a new one was being organized.

During 1959 the Chapter continued to send checks to a group of indigent boys and girls. At high school graduation a yearbook and her picture was given to one of the girls. Again, a full Christmas dinner, clothing and gifts were given to each boy and girl.

September 15, 1959 the Chapter, Hiram Lodge, Royal Arch Chapter and the Winchester Commandery had cards printed with time and place of their meetings which were placed in public places to be available to visitors to our city.

The Past Matron's Club purchased a 50-star U. S. Flag for the Chapter room. It was presented on September 15, 1959.

The Chapter was invited to attend the organizational meeting of a DeMolay Chapter on November 27, 1959 at the George Washington Hotel.

Worthy Matron Goldie Warner, presiding over the Chapter in 1959-60, requested that the receipts from the Ways and Means Committee during her year in the East be used to purchase an Eastern Star labrynth rug. This was done at a cost of $297.00.

The current Worthy Matron's photograph was published in the Apple Blossom Program each year for a number of years. A ruling by the Worthy Grand Matron caused this to be discontinued.

During the early part of 1960 discussions were held regarding the organization of a Bethel of Job's Daughters in Winchester. Moral support was needed. Thirty girls were required to form a Bethel.

A memorial service was held on September 12, 1960 for Charter member Elmer Hodges and a more recent initiate, Dorothy Pinner.

The Chapter received a temporary boost in morale when a member reported at a meeting on November 14, 1960 that Hiram Lodge had hired an architect to draw plans for the remodeling of the Masonic Temple. It was believed that the Eastern Star, Royal Arch Chapter and the Winchester Commandery would be invited to use a room in the remodeled Temple, but this did not happen until 1976 or 16 years later.

April 10, 1961 — the Chapter purchased a piano at a cost of $150.00. The piano purchased was dedicated to Sister Mae McIlwee in recognition of her long years of service. Mrs. McIlwee served as Organist for a total of 23 years. Pearle Largent, Treasurer, served 24 years, the longest time any member served as an officer from 1929 to 1978.

One brother, after being initiated on October 23, 1961, stated, "The Conductress was lovely, other officers were charming and members gracious."

December 11, 1961 — The Worthy Matron donated a new Bible for the altar and four smaller ones to be used during appropriate rituals.

November 11, 1963 — The Chapter purchased ten tickets to the Virginia Historical Society display and gave them to indigent boys and girls. Christmas dinner was planned for a family with eight children.

At the May 10, 1965 meeting it was reported that the Chapter had served 319 persons for Hiram Lodge No. 21 during the 100th year celebration of the raising of William McKinley in Hiram Lodge on May 3, 1865.

June 28, 1965: The Chapter purchased carpeting for the meeting room on the third floor of City Hall at a cost of $1,455.00.

On January 8, 1968, the initation fee was raised from $10.00 to $20.00; the annual dues were increased from $6.00 to $8.00 and the affiliation fee from zero to $5.00.

A Memorial Service was held on July 26, 1971 for Scott Atkinson who served eight terms as Worthy Patron. Scott and Kathleen Atkinson were the first husband/wife team to serve McKinley Chapter as Worthy Matron and Worthy Patron.

Exciting news came to the Chapter on June 12, 1972: TheTrustees of Winchester Hiram Lodge planned to remodel the Masonic Temple building on Loudoun Street, and one of the projects under consideration was the remodeling of the second floor where Barr's Photography Studio had been located and leased from the Masonic Lodge for many years. The three allied Masonic Bodies, John Dove Chapter No. 21, Royal Arch, Knights Templar (Winchester Commandery), and the Order of the Eastern Star, were to be invited to meet regularly in an all-purpose room in the remodeled part. It was not until April 28, 1975, however, that the Chapter received definite knowledge that their 46-year search for a permanent meeting place was ended. On this date at a regular meeting, a letter was received from Hiram Lodge thanking the "Star" for the gift of a new coffee urn for the recently remodeled kitchen in the Temple, the first project undertaken by the Trustees. They informed the Chapter in that letter that the room was being prepared. They also asked that a committee be appointed from the Eastern Star to work with the committees from the two other Masonic bodies designated to use the room and the lodge Trustees to plan for the needs of each organization and to suggest proper decor. At this meeting, the Worthy Matron thanked a Past Matron for her generous gift of a new Hoover vacuum cleaner.

On June 4, 1975 at a Grand Visitation in Berryville, Past Grand Matron, Ella L. Hodges, a charter member of McKinley Chapter No. 19, was presented a 50 year service pin by the Worthy Grand Matron. On September 22, 1975 a 50 year service pin was also presented to Past Matron, Emma Duncan.

From April 1976 to December 13, 1976 when the first Chapter meeting was held in the beautiful new and permanent home on the second floor of the Masonic Temple, General Order No. 1 was: "Full speed ahead" and the order was obeyed.

Decisions were made regarding the furniture that could be utilized in the new room, the furniture that could be refinished or upholstered, the furnishings or equipment to be disposed of and the cleaning of things to be moved.

The committee working with the Trustees of Hiram

Lodge and other committees were very busy deciding on the color scheme, including floor covering and wall panels.

The ingenuity of installing a light over each star point station of the same color of that station and a clear one over the altar was solved by a control panel located at the Secretary's desk. The indirect lighting system may be dimmed as desired during meetings. The effect of the lighting system during ceremonials is very impressive. The accent of red in the rug, upholstery and wall panels blend to make it "the most beautiful Eastern Star meeting place ever seen" as expressed by many visitors.

The members of McKinley Chapter worked and saved through the years looking to the future for a permanent meeting place. They have had the pleasure of using some of their savings on upholstering and various other means of beautifying the Chapter room.

During the latter part of 1977 and early 1978, many compliments were paid the Chapter on the beautiful room as it appeared when set up for meetings, except the out-dated chairs and pedestals at the Star point stations. On March 13, 1978 the Chapter voted to purchase nine white arm-chairs upholstered in white vinyl, each carrying the symbol of the officer's station where used. Also, five white pedestals with lighted symbols the color of the star point represented were bought.

On December 13, 1976 the first meeting in the new room, the Worthy Matron thanked two Past Matrons for their gift to the chapter of a large and beautiful ceremonial rug. Another Past Matron was thanked for the gift of the speaker system in the room. On the same night, a resolution was adopted to petition Hiram Lodge to name the new room the "McKinley Room".

Past Matrons Club

In June 1947, Past Matron Pearle Largent, invited the Past Matrons of McKinley Chapter No. 19 to meet with her to consider forming a Past Matrons Club. A number attended, and after discussion, it was unanimously decided that a club be formed.

The club was formed and the name selected was: Past Matrons Club of McKinley Chapter No. 19.

The following officers were elected: Pearle Largent, President; Nancy Jones, Vice President; and Hilda Mason, Secretary. The officers are elected each year.

The primary objectives of the club are: to be of service to the officers of the Chapter, to promote fellowship among all the members and act as substitute officers when needed.

The club is proud of the assistance it has given. Some of the projects sponsored are: the purchase of a 50 Star United States flag, kneeling cushions and altar cloth for the new McKinley Room and draperies for the previous meeting room in Rouss City Hall.

Each year a Christmas party and dinner is given to honor the current Chapter officers and all Past Patrons. The club continues to grow as the Chapter has more Past Matrons on its membership roll.

Worthy Matrons look forward to the time when they will be eligible to join the club, and club members are glad to have a new member each year.

The 1978-1979 officers of the club are: Donna McIlwee, President; Nancy Jones, Vice President; and Lola Petrie, Secretary-Treasurer.

There have been 25 Worthy Patrons. Of that number, 11 served more than one year for a total of 35 years, and 14 served one year only. It is also interesting to note that no Worthy Matron has either succeeded herself, or been elected to serve a second year in the "East."

McKinley Officers 1978-79

At this printing, the Officers of McKinley Chapter No. 19, O. E. S., Winchester, Virginia, are:

Worthy Matron	Beulah Shanholtz
Worthy Patron	Clay Carr, P.P.
Associate Matron	Nancy Stern
Associate Patron	William Stern
Secretary	Bernice Lundmark, P.M.
Treasurer	Virginia Gregory, P.M.
Conductress	Carolyn Riggleman
Associate Conductress	Teresa Jenkins
Chaplain	Barbara Wood
Marshal	Nancy Norman
Organist	Emma Duncan, P.M.
Adah	June Loar, P.M.
Ruth	Gladys Hamilton
Esther	Ilean Miller
Martha	Sarah Alice Jeffrey
Electa	Donna McIlwee, P.M.
Warder	Ola Martin

Sentinel _____ Russell Miller
Prompter _____ Alice Carr

The Trustees of Hiram Lodge deserve much credit for seeing that storage spaces were built to protect paraphenalia and furnishings for each of the three organizations using the new room. McKinley Chapter will always be indebted to Hiram Lodge No. 21, A. F. & A. M. for providing the meeting room, the use of the kitchen and banquet room, and particularly for the use of the electric chair-lifts which enable handicapped members to attend meetings. As a token of their appreciation for the above which was provided them at great expense, McKinley Chapter invited the members of Hiram Lodge to a dinner in the banqet room of the Temple on March 8, 1977, and again October 10, 1978.

McKinley Chapter will complete 50 years of Service on April 6, 1979, and an appropriate Golden Anniversary meeting is being planned for April 8, 1979.

Past Matrons

Daisy B. Shade	1929-30	Virginia Gregory	1954-55
Bessie Jones	1930-31	Lola Petrie	1955-56
Ella B. Hodges	1931-32	Margaret Bridgeforth	1956-57
Marie B. Shade	1932-33	Genevieve Fox	1957-58
Thelma C. Brown	1933-34	Jeanne Milton	1958-59
Mary L. Cassell	1934-35	Goldie Warner	1959-60
Pearle R. Largent	1935-36	Pauline Haymaker	1960-61
Emily Hiner	1936-37	Emma Duncan	1961-62
Justa Quick	1937-38	Margaret Duvall	1962-63
Hilda H. Mason	1938-39	Louise Bush	1963-64
Ethel Morrow	1939-40	Margaret Button	1964-65
Elsie Louderback	1940-41	Evelyn Jackson	1965-66
Clara Colbert	1941-42	Alice Trenary	1966-67
Grace E. Hewitt	1942-43	Mabel Heishman	1967-68
Nan Choucleris	1943-44	Isabelle Donica	1968-69
Margaret Pine	1944-45	Bernice Lundmark	1969-70
Nancy Jones	1945-46	Rosie Hott	1970-71
Helen B. Grimm	1946-47	Edna Basore	1971-72
Mary Omps	1947-48	Evelyn Masters	1972-73
Kathryn Whetzel	1948-49	Mildred Eyler	1973-74
Thelma Barr	1949-50	Freeda Fuller	1974-75
Kathleen Atkinson	1950-51	Marie Everly	1975-76
Pauline Spring	1951-52	Donna McIlwee	1976-77
Ruth Wheeler	1952-53	June Loar	1977-78
Emily Crisman	1953-54		

Caldwell, Marjorie A.   Served as Matron in Berryville, Virginia

Georges, Louise   Served as Matron in Bristol, Virginia

Past Patrons

Harold C. Jones	1929-30	Howard Haymaker	1956-58
Walter Shade	1930-31	Woodrow Whitmore	1958-59
Charles Lowery	1931-32	Laurens Jones	1959-60
William Brown	1932-33	Elliott Button	1960-61
O. C. Cassell	1933-34	Scott Atkinson	1961-62
Charles P. McVicar	1934-35	Woodrow Whitmore	1962-63
Harold C. Jones	1935-36	Henry Bush	1963-64
Walter Shade	1936-37	Elliott Button	1964-65
John Chapman	1937-38	Scott Atkinson	1965-66
O. C. Cassell	1938-39	Frederick Donica	1966-67
Walter Shade	1939-40	Elliott Button	1967-68
Douglas Grimm	1940-41	Frederick Donica	1968-69
Walter Shade	1941-44	Harry Whitesell	1969-70
Laurens Jones	1944-45	Joseph Hott	1970-71
Scott Atkinson	1945-48	Henry Bush	1971-72
R. Ray Sartelle	1948-49	(pro-tem)	
Scott Atkinson	1949-51	George Masters	1972-73
Robert A. Whitten	1951-52	Elliott Button	1973-74
Victor Wheeler	1952-53	Clay B. Carr	1974-75
Laurens Jones	1953-54	Joseph Hott	1975-76
Scott Atkinson	1954-55	Glenn Mowery, Sr.	1976-77
Carl Fischer	1955-56	Harold Loar	1977-78

Brodrick, Harold   Served as Patron in Holbrook, Arizona

Caldwell, Robert D.   Served as Patron in Berryville, Virginia

SECRETARY

Thelma Brown	1929-30
Daisy Shade	1930-40
Ella L. Hodges	1940-50
Hilda H. Mason	1950-64
Kathleen Atkinson	1964-65
Margaret Duvall	1965-70
Bernice Lundmark	1970-Present

TREASURER

Irene Hodgson	1929-31
Grace E. Hewitt	1931-41
Kathryn Whetzel	1941-43
Pearle Largent	1943-67
Louise Bush	1967-68
Virginia Gregory	1968-Present

1978 Membership List

	Initiated or *Affiliated
*Ackenbom, Dora Lucille	September 25, 1961
Anderson, Selma	June 22, 1953
Barr, Thelma	January 27, 1941
Barnes, Thelma	April 25, 1949
Basore, Arlie W.	October 10, 1977
Basore, Edna	October 9, 1961
Beach, Eva Rozella	August 14, 1978
Beach, Eva Marie	August 14, 1978
Beach, Robert D.	August 14, 1978
Boxley, Genevieve	June 28, 1948
*Boyce, Bertha	March 25, 1946
Braunlich, Ethel	October 22, 1951
Bray, Richard W.	September 19, 1977
Bray, Tommi Anne	September 19, 1977
Bridgeforth, Margaret	November 13, 1944
*Brodrick, Harold J.	March 9, 1957
Brown, Lambert	February 11, 1974
Brown, Lillian	February 11, 1974
Bugarski, Thelma	November 13, 1967
Bush, Henry	October 23, 1961
Bush, Louise	May 23, 1949
Button, Margaret	May 28, 1956
Button, W. Elliott	May 28, 1956
*Caldwell, Marjorie	January 26, 1976
*Caldwell, Robert D.	January 26, 1976
Cammer, Eleanor	March 12, 1962
Carper, May	June 24, 1929
Carr, Alice	February 24, 1941
Carr, Clay B.	February 14, 1972
Carter, Cecil C.	November 24, 1975
Carter, Wilma	November 24, 1975
Castleman, Gertrude	December 2, 1929
Choucleris, Nan	March 9, 1936
Coffey, Elvena	March 11, 1957
*Cooper, June M.	July 24, 1978
*Copenhaver, Ethel	May 27, 1974
*Copenahver, Marjorie	April 8, 1974
Copenhaver, William E.	April 22, 1974
*Coryell, Edna	May 22, 1978
Crisman, Emily H.	December 10, 1945
Dearing, Lillian	April 28, 1947
*Duncan, Emma	March 25, 1955
Dunlap, Donna	January 11, 1965
Edwards, Linda Jean	December 9, 1968
Evans, Kenneth Wayne	February 8, 1971
Evans, Rosita	February 8, 1971
Everly, Marie	November 11, 1968

Eyler, Mildred	October 9, 1967
Fanning, Virginia	November 11, 1963
Fisher, Frances	November 25, 1946
Fuller, Freeda	June 27, 1961
Funk, Norman	June 23, 1969
*Georges, Louise	April 8, 1946
*Glasscock, Billy D.	March 9, 1970
Golliday, James W., Jr.	February 10, 1975
Grant, Katherine	April 24, 1939
Gray, Mary	May 28, 1956
Gregory, Ellen	December 9, 1946
*Gregory, Virginia	February 5, 1946
Grimm, Douglas	February 27, 1939
Grove, Helen L.	May 22, 1972
Haines, Ruth	October 31, 1931
Hamilton, Elison	January 28, 1974
Hamilton, Gladys	January 28, 1974
Harden, Mary Jane	February 10, 1964
Harper, Doris	February 23, 1942
Haymaker, Pauline	December 11, 1950
Heishman, Mabel	July 9, 1956
Hess, June L.	July 22, 1974
Hodges, Ella L.	April 6, 1929
*Hoffman, Ruth	January 13, 1969
Holliday, Dorothy	September 19, 1977
Holliday, Margaret	December 9, 1946
Holliday, Melford	July 8, 1963
Hott, Joseph, Sr.	January 13, 1969
Hott, Rosie	November 27, 1961
*Hottel, Virginia	November 27, 1939
Hughes, Mary	February 14, 1972
Hughes, R. Harold	May 9, 1977
Jackson, Evelyn	February 24, 1941
Jeffrey, Sara Alice	March 9, 1977
*Jenkins, Harland	October 13, 1975
*Jenkins, Marjorie	October 13, 1975
Jenkins, Teresa Marie	July 23, 1973
Jolley, Mary Jo	June 28, 1976
Jones, Nancy	September 19, 1938
Laise, Virginia	December 28, 1931
Largent, Pearle	April 6, 1929
Lefavor, Bobbi B.	April 22, 1974
Loar, Harold W.	February 25, 1974
Loar, June C.	October 22, 1973
*Lundmark, Bernice	April 24, 1961
Martin, Erma	April 26, 1954
Martin, Ola K.	October 10, 1977
Masters, Evelyn	February 26, 1951
Masters, George B.	February 8, 1971
*Maynard, Beatrice	September 28, 1959
McCormick, Catherine	January 22, 1945

Boyles, Harry	Initiated September 23, 1929
Braunlich, Ethel	Initiated October 22, 1951
Bray, Richard	Initiated September 19, 1977
Bray, Tammi Anne	Initiated September 19, 1977
Bridgeforth, Margaret	Initiated November 13, 1944
Brodie, Cora	Affiliated July 7, 1930
Brodrick, Harold	Affiliated March 9, 1970
Brodrick, Vivian	Affiliated March 9, 1970
Brown, Bessie	Initiated April 6, 1929
Brown, Eleanor	Initiated August 18, 1931
Brown, Ella	Affiliated April 7, 1930
Brown, Ella	Affiliated January 10, 1949
Brown, June Spring	Initiated June 27, 1955
Brown, Lambert	Initiated February 11, 1974
Brown, Lillian	Initiated February 11, 1974
Brown, Pearl	Initiated April 6, 1929
Brown, Thelma	Initiated April 6, 1929
Brown, William	Initiated April 6, 1929
Bugarski, Thelma	Initiated November 13, 1967
Bush, Henry	Initiated October 23, 1961
Bush, Louise	Initiated May 23, 1949
Bushnell, George	Initiated August 18, 1931
Button, Margaret Day	Initiated May 28, 1956
Button, Walter Elliott	Initiated May 28, 1956
Cahill, Howard	Initiated December 12, 1932
Cahill, Margaret	Initiated March 25, 1935
Caldwell, Marjorie	Affiliated January 26, 1976
Caldwell, Robert	Affiliated January 26, 1976
Cammer, Eleanor Bush	Initiated March 12, 1962
Capper, Henrietta	Initiated June 24, 1929
Capper, Mary	Affiliated July 22, 1929
Carpenter, Betty	Initiated February 26, 1951
Carpenter, Louise	Initiated June 25, 1945
Carper, Mary	Initiated June 24, 1929
Carr, Alice Jackson	Initiated February 24, 1941
Carr, Clay B.	Initiated February 14, 1972
Carskaden, Corrine	Initiated April 6, 1929
Carter, Bertha	Initiated June 24, 1929
Carter, Cecil	Initiated November 24, 1975
Carter, Edna	Initiated June 24, 1929
Carter, Wilma	Initiated November 24, 1975
Cassell, Mary	Initiated April 6, 1929
Cassell, O. C.	Affiliated March 2, 1931
Castleman, Gertrude	Initiated December 2, 1929
Chambers, Armorel	Initiated November 28, 1932
Chambers, Charles	Affiliated April 27, 1970
Chambers, Rachel	Affiliated April 27, 1970
Chapman, Frances	Initiated September 20, 1935
Chapman, John	Affiliated September 20, 1935
Choucleris, Nan	Initiated March 9, 1936

Clark, Stella	Affiliated April 7, 1930
Coffey, Elvena	Initiated March 11, 1957
Coffman, Maurye	Affiliated July 27, 1931
Colbert, Clara	Affiliated May 4, 1931
Colston, Virginia	Affiliated June 22, 1931
Cooley, Davis	Affiliated October 26, 1931
Cooley, Olive	Affiliated October 26, 1931
Cooper, June M.	Affiliated July 24, 1978
Copenhaver, Ethel	Affiliated May 27, 1974
Copenhaver, Marjorie	Affiliated April 8, 1974
Copenhaver, William	Initiated May 27, 1974
Coryell, Edna	Affiliated May 22, 1978
Crabill, Betty Jean	Initiated November 25, 1946
Crabill, Edna Showman	Initiated May 25, 1953
Crisman, Emily	Initiated December 10, 1945
Crosslin, Jewell Irene	Initiated January 13, 1947
Cuthbert, Elizabeth	Initiated July 8, 1940
Davis, Edith	Initiated April 6, 1929
Davis, Julia	Initiated December 2, 1929
Dawson, Ida	Initiated April 6, 1929
Dearing, Lillian	Initiated April 28, 1947
Denton, Emily	Initiated February 23, 1942
Dettra, Lula	Initiated March 13, 1944
Donica, Frederick	Initiated May 26, 1958
Donica, Isabelle	Initiated May 26, 1958
Duncan, Elizabeth	Affiliated March 13, 1944
Duncan, Emma	Affiliated March 28, 1955
Dunlap, Anna	Initiated December 12, 1949
Dunlap, Charles	Initiated April 24, 1950
Dunlap, Donna Ploss	Initiated January 11, 1965
DuPay, Katherine	Affiliated March 10, 1952
DuPay, Marion	Initiated April 26, 1954
Duvall, Margaret	Initiated February 27, 1956
Ebert, Gabrella	Initiated February 27, 1939
Ebersole, Ruth	Initiated February 27, 1939
Edwards, Linda Mason	Initiated December 9, 1968
Emmons, Phoebe Franklin	Initiated February 9, 1945
Evans, Kenneth	Initiated February 8, 1971
Evans, Rosita	Initiated February 8, 1971
Everly, Marie	Initiated November 11, 1968
Eyler, Mildred	Initiated October 9, 1967
Fanning, Virginia	Initiated November 11, 1963
Feagans, Sallie	Initiated July 22, 1946
Fischer, Carl	Affiliated January 11, 1954
Fischer, Katherine	Affiliated January 11, 1954
Fisher, Frances	Initiated November 25, 1946
Fling, Nora	Affiliated February 24, 1947
Fosbrink, Lydia	Affiliated September 23, 1940

Fuller, Freeda	Initiated June 27, 1961
Funk, Norman L., Jr.	Initiated June 23, 1969
Gant, Hazel	Affiliated April 14, 1958
Georges, Louise	Affiliated April 8, 1946
Geraci, Barbara Ann	Initiated October 26, 1960
Glasscock, Billy D.	Affiliated March 9, 1970
Golladay, James W., Jr.	Initiated February 10, 1975
Goode, Velma	Affiliated January 23, 1950
Grant, Katherine	Initiated April 24, 1939
Gray, Cornelia	Initiated July 22, 1929
Gray, Louise	Initiated July 22, 1929
Gray, Mary	Affiliated September 28, 1931
Gray, Mary	Initiated May 28, 1956
Gregory, Ellen	Initiated December 9, 1946
Gregory, Virginia	Affiliated February 25, 1946
Grim, Elizabeth	Initiated April 6, 1929
Grim, Mary	Initiated September 23, 1929
Grimm, Douglas	Initiated February 27, 1939
Grimm, Helen	Initiated February 27, 1939
Grimm, Olive	Initiated February 26, 1951
Grove, Helen	Initiated May 22, 1972
Grubbs, Anne	Initiated March 14, 1949
Grubbs, Kinzel B.	Initiated February 5, 1952
Haines, Iona Marie	Initiated May 25, 1931
Haines, Ruth	Initiated October 25, 1937
Hamilton, Edison	Initiated January 28, 1974
Hamilton, Gladys	Initiated January 28, 1974
Harden, Mary Jane	Initiated February 10, 1964
Harmer, Pearl	Initiated October 22, 1929
Harper, Doris	Initiated February 23, 1942
Harper, Nancy Jean	Affiliated February 23, 1970
Hartman, Dora	Initiated April 6, 1929
Haymaker, Howard	Initiated May 25, 1953
Haymaker, Pauline	Initiated December 11, 1950
Heeps, Helen	Initiated January 27, 1941
Heishman, Mabel	Initiated July 9, 1951
Hepfer, Gertrude	Affiliated January 11, 1954
Hepner, Louise	Initiated November 11, 1974
Hess, June	Initiated July 22, 1974
Hewitt, Grace	Initiated April 6, 1929
Hodges, Ella L.	Initiated April 6, 1929
Hodges, Elmer	Initiated April 6, 1939
Hodgson, Irene	Initiated April 6, 1929
Hodgson, Joseph	Affiliated April 7, 1930
Hoffman, Ruth	Affiliated January 13, 1964
Holliday, Dorothy	Initiated September 19, 1977
Holliday, Margaret	Initiated December 9, 1946
Holliday, Melford	Initiated July 8, 1963
Horton, Alma	Affiliated April 6, 1931

Hott, Joseph A., Sr.	Initiated January 13, 1969
Hott, Rosie	Initiated November 27, 1961
Hottel, Virginia	Affiliated November 27, 1929
House, May	Affiliated July 22, 1929
House, S. Porter	Affiliated July 22, 1929
Hughes, Mary	Initiated February 14, 1972
Hughes, R. Harold	Initiated May 9, 1977
Huntsberry, Virginia	Initiated April 22, 1932
Hutchinson, Margaret Haymaker	Initiated June 10, 1957
Huyett, Linda	Affiliated May 4, 1931
Ireland, Marjorie	Affiliated April 9, 1934
Jackson, Evelyn	Initiated February 24, 1941
Jackson, Hilda	Initiated December 2, 1929
Jeffrey, Sarah Alice	Initiated March 9, 1977
Jenkins, Harland	Affiliated October 13, 1975
Jenkins, Marjorie	Affiliated October 13, 1975
Jenkins, Teresa Marie	Initiated July 23, 1973
Johnson, Violet	Initiated July 2, 1965
Jolley, Mary Jo	Initiated June 28, 1976
Jones, Bessie	Initiated April 6, 1929
Jones, Harold	Initiated April 6, 1929
Jones, Laurens	Initiated March 13, 1944
Jones, Nancy	Initiated September 19, 1938
Kercheval, Dell	Affiliated November 9, 1931
Kerfoot, Estelle	Affiliated May 4, 1931
Kohler, Gelsomina	Affiliated March 11, 1957
Kremer, Vernie	Initiated April 6, 1929
Lacy, Roy	Initiated December 12, 1955
Laise, Katherine	Initiated November 3, 1930
Laise, Sarah Virginia	Initiated December 28, 1931
Largent, B. W.	Initiated December 12, 1932
Largent, Ellen B.	Initiated July 12, 1951
Largent, Pearle	Initiated April 6, 1929
Larrick, Viola	Affiliated March 9, 1970
Larson, Bernice	Initiated March 23, 1949
Lefavor, Bobbi W.	Initiated May 27, 1974
Leighton, Dolores	Initiated June 8, 1959
Lichliter, Edith	Initiated April 6, 1929
Lichliter, Lena	Initiated April 6, 1929
Lloyd, John W., Jr.	Initiated March 8, 1948
Lloyd, Pauline	Initiated March 8, 1948
Loar, Harold	Initiated February 25, 1974
Loar, June	Initiated October 22, 1973
Logan, Alfretta	Initiated March 11, 1957
Louderback, Elsie	Affiliated April 27, 1931
Lowery, Bertha	Affiliated October 22, 1929
Lowery, Charles	Affiliated October 22, 1929
Lundmark, Bernice	Affiliated November 23, 1945

Manuel, Gretna	Initiated January 12, 1959
Martin, Erma	Initiated April 26, 1954
Martin, Hobart	Initiated November 10, 1958
Martin, Ola	Initiated October 10, 1977
Mason, Hilda	Initiated January 5, 1931
Massie, Dorothy	Initiated November 9, 1959
Masters, Evelyn	Initiated February 26, 1951
Masters, George	Initiated February 8, 1971
Maynard, Beatrice	Affiliated September 28, 1959
McCanns, Elaine J.	Initiated June 23, 1947
McCormick, Catherine	Initiated January 22, 1945
McFaden, The Rev. Frank T.	Initiated October 26, 1931
McIlwee, Charles	Initiated July 12, 1976
McIlwee, Donna	Initiated May 12, 1969
McIlwee, Gladys	Initiated March 13, 1961
McIlwee, May	Initiated October 10, 1936
McIlwee, Sara Lee	Initiated January 12, 1948
McVicar, Charles P.	Initiated October 26, 1931
McVicar, Lily	Initiated April 6, 1929
Miller, Gladys C.	Initiated February 27, 1939
Miller, Ilean	Affiliated September 28, 1964
Miller, Jennie	Initiated September 24, 1962
Miller, Russell	Initiated February 8, 1971
Milleson, Lillian	Affiliated August 8, 1931
Milton, Jeanne	Initiated November 8, 1948
Morgan, Julia	Affiliated May 4, 1931
Morgan, Lester H.	Affiliated May 4, 1931
Morrow, Ethel	Initiated February 23, 1931
Mowery, Glenn M., Sr.	Initiated May 22, 1972
Mowery, Helen	Initiated May 22, 1972
Mowery, Theresa Ann	Initiated February 14, 1977
Mumaw, Patsy	Initiated June 9, 1969
Newlin, Joseph	Initiated November 27, 1967
Newlin, Nancy	Initiated November 27, 1967
Noble, Margaret C.	Initiated May 9, 1977
Norman, Nancy	Initiated September 13, 1976
Norris, Mary	Initiated June 25, 1945
Norton, George F.	Initiated May 27, 1929
Novick, Jessie	Initiated December 12, 1932
Oliver, Mary Carr	Initiated September 23, 1929
Omps, Mary	Initiated April 24, 1939
Orndorff, Sarah	Initiated February 9, 1959
Orndorff, Susie	Initiated May 28, 1956
Palavid, Harriett Isobelle	Initiated September 26, 1932
Palavid, M. J.	Initiated September 26, 1932
Palmer, Martha	Initiated December 12, 1949
Palmer, Ollie	Initiated November 27, 1961
Palmer, Robert	Initiated November 27, 1961

Parke, Emily	Initiated July 22, 1929
Parker, Betty Jo	Initiated April 24, 1950
Parks, Ruth	Initiated May 25, 1931
Pence, Helen	Initiated July 12, 1951
Pendleton, Doris	Initiated July 22, 1974
Perry, Inez	Initiated May 23, 1966
Petrie, Lola	Initiated September 24, 1945
Pierce, Gail Ploss	Initiated January 11, 1965
Pine, Margaret	Initiated September 20, 1935
Pinner, Dorothy	Initiated May 27, 1956
Place, Christine Ploss	Initiated June 26, 1961
Ploss, Marian	Affiliated September 25, 1961
Polhemus, Lelah	Affiliated July 14, 1946
Poling, Evelyn	Affiliated March 13, 1978
Porter, Colleen Grimm	Initiated July 12, 1951
Pridgen, Kathleen	Initiated May 26, 1958
Pully, Thelma	Initiated November 10, 1958
Quick, Justa	Initiated July 22, 1929
Reed, Dorothy	Initiated September 8, 1975
Reed, Proctor, Jr.	Initiated September 8, 1975
Renner, Larry	Initiated July 10, 1972
Renner, Sharon	Initiated September 11, 1972
Renner, Virginia	Initiated July 10, 1972
Rhine, Sylvia	Initiated November 14, 1960
Rhoden, Katie	Affiliated June 22, 1931
Richard, Jeanne	Initiated June 9, 1969
Riggleman, Carolyn	Initiated July 23, 1973
Rose, Margaret	Initiated December 10, 1934
Rossbach, Thea	Initiated May 9, 1977
Salomon, Pauline	Initiated September 28, 1942
Sampsell, Willie M.	Affiliated August 18, 1931
Sandy, Darlene	Initiated September 28, 1970
Sandy, Janie S.	Initiated February 12, 1973
Sandy, Robert L., Jr.	Initiated September 28, 1970
Sartelle, Doris	Initiated January 27, 1947
Sartelle, Dr. Ray	Initiated January 27, 1947
Saunders, Eva	Initiated May 27, 1940
Schumacher, Eugene	Initiated November 22, 1948
Schumacher, Nancy	Initiated November 22, 1948
Schwalb, Helen	Initiated October 25, 1943
Seabright, Geneva	Initiated August 26, 1929
Sencindiver, Mary	Initiated August 26, 1929
Shade, Daisy B.	Initiated April 6, 1929
Shade, Grace	Initiated April 6, 1929
Shade, Lucia	Initiated April 6, 1929
Shade, Marie	Initiated April 6, 1929
Shade, Walter	Initiated April 6, 1929
Shaffer, Julia	Affiliated September 11, 1961

Shanholtz, Beulah	Initiated June 27, 1966
Simpson, Georgie	Initiated March 13, 1950
Smith, Janet Largent	Initiated June 25, 1945
Smith, Margaret	Initiated April 24, 1939
Smith, Rufus	Initiated April 25, 1977
Snapp, Ann Bell	Initiated January 5, 1931
Snellings, Dorothy	Affiliated March 8, 1954
Snoke, Anna Mae	Initiated April 6, 1929
Snyder, Bertha	Initiated April 6, 1929
Snyder, Zaida	Initiated August 26, 1929
Spates, Carrie	Initiated February 28, 1938
Spicer, Alma B.	Initiated January 23, 1978
Spring, Pauline	Initiated May 27, 1935
Stern, Nancy	Affiliated April 12, 1971
Stern, William	Initiated November 24, 1975
Stone, Doris	Initiated May 27, 1956
Stone, Jo An	Initiated June 22, 1953
Stowes, Marjorie	Initiated May 26, 1947
Straw, Anna	Affiliated June 27, 1955
Stretchberry, Eva	Initiated July 22, 1929
Sybert, Virginia	Initiated November 24, 1941
Taylor, Hattie	Initiated November 27, 1937
Theis, Anna	Affiliated January 6, 1930
Trenary, Alice	Initiated January 28, 1957
Van Horn, Betty	Initiated October 26, 1959
Van Stronder, Byron	Affiliated May 22, 1961
Van Stronder, Geraldine	Initiated June 26, 1961
Vest, Allie	Affiliated April 22, 1940
Ware, Ida	Initiated September 23, 1929
Walker, Maxine	Affiliated March 13, 1978
Wallace, Ellen	Initiated March 21, 1966
Warner, Goldie	Initiated November 14, 1949
Warner, Russell	Initiated June 8, 1959
Webber, Marjorie Van Horn	Initiated July 9, 1962
Wheeler, Ruth	Initiated February 12, 1964
Wheeler, Victor	Initiated February 25, 1952
Whetzel, Kathryn Myers	Initiated May 27, 1940
Whitacre, Floyd	Initiated September 28, 1970
Whitacre, Imogene	Initiated September 28, 1970
White, Candice	Initiated June 26, 1978
White, Deliaetta	Initiated February 8, 1960
White, Louise	Initiated April 24, 1950
White, Lucy	Initiated January 13, 1947
White, Warren	Initiated June 26, 1978
Whitesell, Harry S.	Affiliated February 8, 1965
Whitesell, Mary Nancy	Affiliated February 8, 1965
Whitmore, Celia	Initiated July 9, 1956
Whitmore, Woodrow	Initiated August 16, 1956

Whittier, Robert	Initiated December 12, 1949
Whittier, Ruth	Initiated October 23, 1944
Williams, Ernie	Initiated June 10, 1957
Winkfield, Billie Ann	Initiated October 9, 1961
Wilson, Eileen	Initiated March 11, 1957
Wilson, Louis	Initiated April 25, 1977
Wilson, Margel	Initiated April 25, 1977
Wilson, Marilyn	Initiated September 13, 1976
Wilson, William	Initiated September 13, 1976
Wood, Barbara	Initiated July 22, 1974
Woods, Lela	Initiated April 6, 1929
Woods, Maggie	Initiated April 6, 1929
Wratchford, Helen	Initiated March 21, 1966
Wright, Gladys	Initiated April 6, 1929
Wright, Joseph	Initiated May 27, 1929
Yeakley, Lois	Initiated May 27, 1940
Yenter, Minnie	Affiliated October 22, 1951
Young, Edna	Affiliated May 4, 1931

ROSTERS
OF THE MASONIC BODIES,
WINCHESTER, VIRGINIA
1949

ROSTER OF MEMBERS
WINCHESTER HIRAM LODGE NO. 21
A. F. & A. M.

February 1, 1949

Name	Date of Raising (or Affiliation)
Alexander, James R., Jr.	May 28, 1940
†Allen, Frank L.	March 9, 1897
Anderson, Dr. C. R.	December 12, 1916
†Arnold, Lester D.	March 11, 1924
Bageant, Roy L.	November 2, 1937
†Baker, Earl Edwin	March 9, 1937
Baker, Leary Green	September 10, 1946
Baker, W. Woodhull	October 28, 1920
Barr, Curtis R.	September 29, 1942
Barr, Taylor Lee	June 3, 1947
Barton, Lewis N.	July 29, 1921
Battaile, William M.	May 6, 1947
Bauserman, Milton D.	Aug. 29, 1944
†Beardsworth, Richard	Apr. 10, 1906
Beverley, J. B., Jr.	December 13, 1916
†Booze, J. W.	August 11, 1942
†Bosserman, W. H.	Nov. 12, 1918
†Bowen, Forest H.	October 8, 1946
Bowers, G. Richard	August 2, 1938
Bowers, H. H.	September 15, 1922
Bowers, Maurice E.	March 19, 1935
Boyd, J. Thomas	December 20, 1927
Boyles, H. A.	May 31, 1921
†Bridgeforth, W. E.	Oct. 8, 1935
Brown, C. Douglas	August 8, 1933
Brown, John I.	August 23, 1923
Brown, Leslie M.	July 6, 1926
Brown, Richard B.	March 15, 1921
Brown, William H.	August 23, 1923
Buncutter, Julian H.	Sept. 28, 1948
†Burgess, C. S.	November 12, 1935
Bush, Henry Lee	June 24, 1947
Bushnell, George B.	March 13, 1900
Byrd, Harry F.	August 13, 1929
Cahill, Augustus H.	April 2, 1946
Cahill, Howard J.	September 22, 1931
Cahill, LeRoy F.	November 26, 1937
†Cameron, Dr. W. D.	Jan. 13, 1948
Cammer, C. R.	January 16, 1917
Carper, Ernest A.	October 19, 1926
Carper, Harvey F.	October 19, 1926
Carskaden, W. A.	March 22, 1927
Carson, Nicholas	November 4, 1930
Cassell, O. C.	May 22, 1928
†Cawthorne, Ted H.	July 10, 1945
Chambers, Gus	June 3, 1930
Choucleris, James	December 4, 1930
Clark, Dr. H. E.	December 29, 1916
Clowe, M. B.	May 20, 1919
Clowe, M. B., Jr.	April 2, 1946
Cochran, Dr. F. A.	February 13, 1900
Cock, J. Lee	June 29, 1921
†Cooper, Charles A.	March 11, 1924
Cooper, W. E.	May 31, 1898
Courson, W. L.	December 16, 1921
†Courtney, J. L.	April 10, 1945
†Crosslin, Thurman	March 14, 1944
Cuthbert, E. Earl	December 7, 1937
Dearing, Eugene F.	July 31, 1945
Dechert, Robert B.	March 20, 1945
DeHaven, G. M.	June 18, 1929
Denton, Harry T.	April 8, 1941

†Affiliated.

Name	Date of Raising (or Affiliation)	Name	Date of Raising (or Affiliation)
Dovell, Carroll F.	May 9, 1944	Hall, Clyde E.	November 28, 1944
Dubin, B. James	August 8, 1933	Halterman, Tom D.	October 15, 1935
Duffey, Hugh S.	May 26, 1922	Hamburger, Myer	June 3, 1930
Dunlap, Charles W.	August 19, 1947	†Hamrick, Walter B.	Feb. 12, 1946
Ebersole, Matthew H.	December 6, 1938	Harmer, Herbert W.	Sept. 17, 1929
Eddy, C. Vernon	April 11, 1899	Harper, Roy	March 28, 1944
Eddy, John V.	June 18, 1929	Harry, C. Burton	March 10, 1931
Fansler, Forest H.	May 1, 1924	Hartman, Clayton S.	Nov. 15, 1918
Fansler, George E.	June 2, 1914	Hatcher, Richard F.	June 19, 1928
Fansler, Ralph S.	September 21, 1920	Heeps, William H.	June 18, 1940
†Fant, Julian S.	July 8, 1947	Hewitt, Wilbur E.	October 26, 1923
Ferguson, Abner H.	June 21, 1907	Hodges, Elmer V.	October 18, 1920
Finklestein, Morris	October 15, 1912	Hodgson, Joseph	October 18, 1921
Fisher, John H.	June 9, 1942	†Hofer, Charles E.	Feb. 17, 1948
†Flood, Bolling B.	December 8, 1942	Holliday, Herbert C.	August 6, 1946
Fox, Harry S., Jr.	October 22, 1946	Hook, Edwin R.	February 19, 1924
†Funk, Joseph B.	February 18, 1936	Hoover, John	May 25, 1899
Garber, James T.	February 1, 1944	†Hotinger, J. A.	August 10, 1943
Garton, Vernon B.	May 16, 1902	Hottel, W. J.	April 17, 1930
†Glover, John D.	February 18, 1936	†Humston, Dr. E. A.,	June 11, 1907
Golden, John	November 17, 1931	Hunter, Philip N.	January 25, 1944
Good, George W.	April 2, 1923	Huntsberry, E. R.	September 17, 1929
†Goode, Wendell B.	Sept. 9, 1924	Hyde, Marshall W.	March 23, 1948
Goodyear, Jacob M.	October 26, 1926	Illi, Oscar A.	June 3, 1947
†Gray, Allen B.	May 12, 1914	Jackson, A. H.	March 16, 1920
Gray, R. L., Jr.	December 7, 1920	Jakimier, Theodore F.	January 20, 1921
†Gregory, Harry E.	October 8, 1946	James, Dr. Howard L.	Dec. 3, 1935
Griffith, A. Newton	October 25, 1892	Jenkins, Brown E.	May 27, 1947
Grim, Cecil C.	June 1, 1926	Jenkins, J. K.	July 5, 1932
Grim, Claude M.	June 20, 1916	Johnston, Samuel N.	June 29, 1926
Grimm, Douglas O.	July 5, 1932	Jones, Harold C.	June 12, 1923
Grimm, Dr. R. M.	April 11, 1911	Jones, Harold Courtney	March 15, 1947
Grubbs, Kinzel B., Jr.	April 6, 1948	†Jones, J. Luther	August 12, 1919
Grubbs, Ralph Y.	May 31, 1949	Jones, Laurens P.	May 24, 1938
Haines, Floyd W.	September 26, 1924	Kaknis, G. J.	March 15, 1932
Haines, J. A.	March 15, 1932	Kater, John L.	September 28, 1948
Haldeman, Paul M.	October 3, 1922	Kerlin, Dr. Raymond H.	April 5, 1949

†Affiliated.

Name	Date of Raising (or Affiliation)	Name	Date of Raising (or Affiliation)
Kern, Harry R.	February 20, 1900	Petrie, Richard	August 3, 1943
Kiger, J. A.	May 20, 1913	Pifer, Dr. H. I.	October 8, 1929
Knight, Dr. B. M., Jr.	Nov. 20, 1928	Pine, Charles A.	December 1, 1936
Kohlhausen, B. F.	June 4, 1918	Pingley, H. R.	March 10, 1931
†Larrick, F. J.	September 14, 1920	Plundeke, W. C.	October 7, 1919
Larrick, Hugh S.	June 21, 1906	†Preston, Sam D.	January 9, 1934
Larrick, Roy A.	May 22, 1928	Radford, German E.	Nov. 14, 1944
Larson, Ralph H.	November 23, 1948	Rhame, C. C.	October 25, 1906
Lemley, Gervis E.	August 16, 1917	Rice, Beverly N.	May 27, 1947
Lichliter, Dudley C.	July 14, 1921	Richard, J. W.	July 5, 1917
Lineburg, P. E.	June 18, 1907	Richard, Wyatt H.	January 2, 1925
Lloyd, John Willie, Jr.	Oct. 22, 1946	†Richards, W. M.	January 14, 1930
Logan, Clyde	March 20, 1945	Riley, Hoye L.	July 22, 1930
Louderback, Page G.	August 6, 1946	Robinson, C. Arthur	October 18, 1921
Lutz, Wallace J.	November 23, 1948	Robinson, Fred A.	March 22, 1912
†McCann, C. R.	November 10, 1903	Robinson, H. Delmer	February 5, 1918
McCann, Harry L.	August 30, 1921	Rosenberger, Thomas B.	Aug. 6, 1946
†McCormick, F. N.	Jan. 14, 1930	Russell, B. E.	March 10, 1925
McIlwee, Delmar P.	June 24, 1947	†Salomon, Ralph	Dec. 10, 1935
McVicar, C. P.	December 9, 1912	Sampsell, S. E.	January 31, 1922
McVicar, Charles P., Jr.	May 19, 1942	Sartelle, Dr. R. Ray	November 20, 1945
Manuel, Robert F.	March 23, 1948	Schumacher, F. Eugene	Nov. 4, 1947
Maphis, J. Alan	April 23, 1917	Schwalb, Alfred L.	May 6, 1947
†Martin, H. A.	Feb. 18, 1947	Seabright, Harry M.	June 1, 1926
Miller, J. Lee	November 28, 1933	†Searcy, C. L.	October 13, 1948
Miller, J. P.	October 26, 1914	Sempeles, John P.	July 22, 1930
†Miller, Paul L.	April 10, 1945	Shade, E. Earl	March 15, 1921
Minton, Allen C.	November 28, 1944	†Shade, Walter M.	March 14, 1922
†Morgan, Lester H.	Dec. 11, 1923	Sheetz, H. C.	April 9, 1902
Morris, Theodore	November 4, 1930	Sheetz, H. C., Jr.	November 24, 1925
Noonan, Vincent M.	June 9, 1942	Shiley, W. L.	March 21, 1933
Novick, A. J.	August 23, 1918	Simpson, Taylor F.	March 21, 1933
Omps, Voyne B.	February 28, 1939	Sirbaugh, Carl W.	March 2, 1943
†O'Neal, S. D.	July 9, 1912	Slifer, Edgar P.	February 21, 1928
Palavid, M. J.	February 2, 1932	Slonaker, D. R.	June 22, 1920
Palmer, Richard	November 4, 1947	Slonaker, R. Bruce	April 12, 1906
Pease, M. J.	September 17, 1935	Smith, John G.	June 21, 1904

†Affiliated.

Name	Date of Raising (or Affiliation)	Name	Date of Raising (or Affiliation)
Smith, Paul Asa	June 24, 1947	Whitacre, John W.	September 28, 1948
Smith, Sebert J.	December 7, 1937	White, Roland S.	April 6, 1948
†Snapp, Dr. R. B.	April 8, 1930	Whitmire, Gilbert R.	Nov. 20, 1945
Snoke, M. V. B.	July 14, 1921	†Whitten, Rev. Robert A.	May 10, 1949
†Snyder, Frank W.	April 10, 1928	Williams, R. C.	April 23, 1917
Snyder, George H.	May 25, 1926	Wine, R. Samuel	September 28, 1948
Solenberger, Ansel	September 17, 1935	Wingert, Harold E.	September 7, 1948
Spring, Denver P.	November 27, 1934	Winn, William H.	September 1, 1942
Sybert, Paul W.	June 3, 1941	†Woolfolk, John C.	March 9, 1937
Taylor, George S.	April 26, 1932	Wright, D. E.	October 6, 1910
Taylor, J. Howard	November 16, 1937	Wright, Reubin W.	May 31, 1949
Wallace, L. W.	September 26, 1924	Yeakley, H. E.	May 17, 1921
Walter, Garvin J.	July 6, 1926	Yeatras, Stephen	December 4, 1930
Warner, Russell S.	April 5, 1949	Yost, Dr. E. C.	June 21, 1917
Watson, Leon V.	October 15, 1935	Yost, Jacob H.	August 9, 1917
Wender, L. S.	December 4, 1930	Zeigler, John J.	June 3, 1947
Wheeler, Victor W.	November 14, 1944		

ROSTER OF MEMBERS
JOHN DOVE CHAPTER NO. 21
ROYAL ARCH MASONS
February 1, 1949

Name	Date of Exaltation (or Affiliation)	Name	Date of Exaltation (or Affiliation)
Alexander, J. R., Jr.	March 1941	Bennett, C. D.	March 1941
Anderson, Dr. C. R.	December 1918	Beverley, J. B., Jr.	September 1918
Bageant, Roy L.	November 1938	Bosserman, W. H.	July 1913
Baker, Earl E.	June 1938	Bowers, H. H.	January 1923
Baker, W. W.	December 1921	Boyles, H. A.	February 1923
Barr, Taylor L.	March 1949	Bridgeforth, W. E.	February 1937
Barton, L. N.	December 1921	Brown, C. D.	December 1933
Bauserman, Milton D.	April 1945	Brown, R. B.	December 1921
Bean, E. P.	April 1919	Brown, W. H.	March 1924

†Affiliated.

Name	Date of Exaltation (or Affiliation)	Name	Date of Exaltation (or Affiliation)
Brumback, E. C.	October 1916	Good, G. W.	July 1923
Bushnell, G. B.	April 1900	Goode, W. B.	June 1925
Cahill, Augustus H.	May 1946	Gray, A. B.	April 1912
Cahill, H. J.	February 1932	Gray, R. L., Jr.	January 1921
Cammer, C. R.	October 1922	Grim, C. M.	May 1917
Campbell, C. S. H.	September 1916	Grimm, D. O.	April 1933
Campbell, W. R.	October 1919	Grimm, Dr. R. M.	May 1914
Carper, Ernest A.	July 1928	Haines, F. W.	March 1927
Carper, H. F.	July 1928	Haldeman, P. M.	February 1923
Carskaden, W. A.	June 1927	Halterman, Tom D.	July 1945
Carson, Nicholas	March 1931	Hamburger, Myer	February 1931
Cassell, O. C.	February 1929	Harmer, Herbert W.	April 1945
Chambers, Gus	February 1931	Harper, Roy	July 1945
Choucleris, James	February 1932	Hartman, C. S.	April 1919
Clowe, M. B.	November 1919	Hatcher, R. F.	February 1930
Clowe, Mifflin B., Jr.	May 1946	Hewitt, W. E.	May 1925
Cochran, Dr. F. A.	February 1900	Hodges, E. V.	April, 1921
Cooper, W. E.	March 1899	Hodgson, Joseph	December 1921
Courson, W. L.	April 1922	Holliday, Herbert	May 1948
Crampton, Benjamin	May 1935	Hook, E. R.	February 1925
Crosslin, Thurman	April 1945	Hunter, Philip N.	August 1944
Cuthbert, E. E.	July 1938	Hyde, Marshall W.	March 1949
Dearing, Eugene F.	May 1946	Illi, Oscar	May 1948
Dechert, Robert B.	July 1945	Jackson, A. H.	June 1920
Dovell, Carroll F.	October 1944	Jenkins, J. K.	March 1935
Dunlap, Charles W.	September 1948	Johnston, S. N.	March 1927
Ebersole, M. H.	June 1939	Jones, H. C.	December 1923
Eddy, C. Vernon	January 1900	Jones, J. L.	April 1922
Eidson, S. H., Jr.	January 1921	Jones, Laurens P.	June 1939
Fansler, R. S.	February 1921	Kaknis, G. J.	June 1932
Finklestein, M.	April 1916	Keith, G. G.	May 1918
Fisher, John H.	April 1945	Larrick, R. A.	March 1929
Fosbrink, John G.	March 1937	Lichliter, D. C.	October, 1922
Frazier, L. J.	July 1924	Lineburg, P. E.	October, 1914
Gearing, G. F.	March 1924	Logan, Clyde	July 1945
Georges, Peter	June 1948	McVicar, C. P.	May 1914
Golden, John	December, 1933	Maphis, J. A.	June 1921

Name	Date of Exaltation (or Affiliation)	Name	Date of Exaltation (or Affiliation)
Miller, J. Lee	June 1937	Sheetz, H. C.	May 1903
Miller, Paul L.	February 1928	Sheetz, H. C., Jr.	April 1928
Minton, Allen C.	July 1945	Shiley, Wesley L.	May 1947
Morgan, L. H.	March 1920	Shumacher, F. Eugene	August 1948
Morris, Theodore	March 1931	Simpson, Taylor F.	July 1938
Novick, A. J.	February 1921	Sirbaugh, Carl W.	August 1944
O'Neal, Sam D.	October 1914	Slonaker, D. R.	December 1920
Ott, C. J.	August 1948	Slonaker, R. B.	February 1907
Petrie, Richard	March 1944	Smith, J. G.	June 1905
Pine, Charles A.	November 1938	Smith, Sebert J.	October 1944
Pingley, H. R.	July 1931	Snoke, M. V. B.	November 1921
Plundeke, W. C.	November 1920	Snyder, G. H.	February 1927
Radford, German E.	April 1945	Solenberger, Ansel B.	July 1938
Rhame, C. C.	January 1907	Spring, Denver P.	August 1944
Richard, J. W.	May 1919	Stickley, William M., III	May 1947
Richards, W. M.	November 1929	Taylor, G. S.	January 1933
Robinson, C. A.	December 1921	Taylor, J. Howard	November 1938
Robinson, H. D.	April 1918	Trotter, Herbert	March 1940
Rogers, W. E.	November 1920	Walter, G. J.	May 1927
Rosenberger, T. B.	May 1948	Watson, Leon V.	January 1936
Russell, B. E.	February 1928	Wender, L. S.	March 1931
Salomon, Ralph	March 1941	Wheeler, Victor W.	April 1945
Sartelle, Dr. R. Ray	May 1946	Whitmire, Gilbert R.	May 1947
Schwalb, Albert L.	August 1948	Whitten, Rev. Robert A.	March 1949
Shade, E. E.	November 1921	Wingert, Asa K.	March 1949
Shade, W. M.	July 1922	Yeatras, Steven	July 1931

ROSTER OF MEMBERS
WINCHESTER COMMANDERY NO. 12
KNIGHTS TEMPLAR
February 1, 1949

Name	Date of Knighting (or Affiliation)
Alexander, James R., Jr.	Sept. 29, 1945
Anderson, Dr. C. R.	January 16, 1919
†Atkinson, J. Scott	January 2, 1948
Austin, Rufus F.	November 6, 1942
†Bacon, Benjamin B.	January 3, 1947
Barton, Lewis N.	February 3, 1922
Bauserman, Milton D.	Jan. 26, 1946
Bean, Esten P.	May 29, 1919
Beverley, James B., Jr.	June 18, 1918
Board, Charles B.	March 17, 1915
Borden, Harry L.	August 5, 1921
Bosserman, W. H.	December 12, 1913
Bowers, Harry L.	April 20, 1923
Boyles, Harry A.	June 24, 1927
Brown, C. Douglas	May 30, 1935
Brown, Richard B.	February 3, 1922
Brown, William H.	May 15, 1925
Buck, George N.	May 17, 1918
Burke, B. Bryan	June 17, 1949
Bushnell, George B.	Prior to 1912
Cahill, Augustus H.	May 16, 1947
Cahill, Howard J.	May 9, 1932
Cammer, Claude R.	November 16, 1922
Carroll, Arthur N.	June 2, 1944
Carskaden, William A.	Oct. 16, 1928
Cassell, Osborn C.	June 29, 1929
Choucleris, James	January 6, 1933
Clowe, Mifflin B.	April 19, 1920
Clower, James S.	October 22, 1948
Cochran, Dr. Fred A.	Prior to 1912
Compton, Z. J.	June 22, 1921
†Cone, A. D.	September 1, 1944
Cooper, William E.	Prior to 1912
Courson, William L.	May 19, 1922
†Crampton, Benjamin	October 4, 1935
Dearing, Eugene F.	May 16, 1947
Donahoe, James E.	June 17, 1949
Drake, Bethel H.	June 17, 1949
Duncan, T. Samuel	Prior to 1912
Dunlap, Charles	October 22, 1948
Eddy, C. Vernon	April, 1900
Edwards, Rev. Jonathan	Jan. 27, 1944
†Georges, Peter N.	June 4, 1948
Good, George W.	October 5, 1923
Goode, Wendell B.	April 6, 1928
Gray, Allen B.	March, 1914
Grimm, Douglas O.	May 12, 1933
Grimm, Dr. R. M.	January 1, 1915
Haines, Floyd W.	April 6, 1928
Halterman, Tom D.	January 26, 1946
Hartman, C. S.	May 29, 1919
Hartsook, Granville, Jr.	June 2, 1944
Hewitt, Wilbur E.	March 15, 1927
Hodges, Elmer V.	May 24, 1921
Hodgson, Joseph	January 26, 1922
Honts, Anderson B., Jr.	May 13, 1947
Hook, E. Russel	November 6, 1925
Hunter, Philip N.	September 29, 1945
†Irwin, G. Robert	April 1, 1935
Jackson, A. H.	July 2, 1920
Jenkins, Jack K.	March 24, 1945
Jones, Harold C.	November 7, 1924

†Affiliated.

Name	Date of Knighting (or Affiliation)	Name	Date of Knighting (or Affiliation)
Jones, Laurens P.	September 29, 1945	Schumacher, Franklin	October 22, 1948
Kaknis, Gus. J.	January 6, 1933	Shade, E. Earl	January 26, 1922
†Kines, J. Shirley	April 6, 1917	Shade, Walter M.	December 6, 1920
Larrick, Roy A.	May 30, 1935	Shaffer, John D.	November 26, 1948
Lichliter, Dudley C.	November 16, 1922	†Shannon, James	April 1, 1935
Lineburg, P. E.	March 17, 1915	Sheetz, Harold C., Sr.	Prior to 1912
Logan, Clyde	September 26, 1946	Sheetz, Harold C., Jr.	June 5, 1928
MacNamara, Thomas	May 15, 1923	Shirey, Peter M.	May 17, 1918
McVicar, Charles P.	July 20, 1917	Simpson, Taylor F.	September 29, 1945
†Mathews, J. Leonard	April 1, 1935	Sirbaugh, Carl W.	March 24, 1945
Miller, J. Lee	May 27, 1938	Slonaker, Dailey R.	December 6, 1920
Minton, Allen C.	January 26, 1946	Slonaker, R. Bruce	Prior to 1912
Morgan, Lester H.	July 2, 1920	Smith, Sebert J.	September 29, 1945
Morris, Theodore	June 16, 1931	Snoke, Martin V. B.	February 3, 1922
O'Neal, Samuel D.	May 1915	Snyder, George H.	March 15, 1927
Ott, Cloice J.	October 22, 1948	Solenberger, Ansel B.	April 19, 1940
Paydon, Thomas E.	September 20, 1946	†Stickley, Omar P.	April 1, 1935
Plundeke, W. C.	December 6, 1920	Stickley, William M., III	June 25, 1948
Radford, German E.	January 26, 1946	Taylor, George S.	March 3, 1933
†Renalds, Marvin W.	December 5, 1941	Thompson, Joseph C.	Nov. 3, 1944
Rhame, Charles C.	Prior to 1912	†Trotter, Herbert	April 1, 1935
†Richards, William M.	Feb. 7, 1930	†Turner, R. J.	January 2, 1931
Robinson, C. Arthur	February 27, 1922	Watson, Leon V.	April 3, 1936
Robinson, H. Delmar	May 17, 1918	Wheeler, Victor W.	January 26, 1946
Rogers, W. E.	March 26, 1921	Whitaker, Herman B.	January 26, 1946
†Ross, H. G.	April 1, 1935	Whitten, Rev. Robert A.	June 2, 1944
Samsell, E. Barr	July 18, 1922	Yeatras, Stephen	November 12, 1931

†Affiliated.

INDEX OF NAMES

Abbott, LeGrand 111b
Abbott, Liberty C. 11b
Adair, James 111
Adcock, Will 51
Alexander, James R., Jr. 201, 257, 260, 263
Alexander, J. E. 193
Alexander, Morgan 21, 33, 35, 45
Allen, C. H. 101, 102
Allen, Frank L. 257
Anders, William 84, 90, 92, 93, 123, 155, 183, 199, 202
Anderson, C. R. (Dr.) 137, 257, 260, 263
Andrews, Simon S. 111b
Andrews, W. 83
Andrews, William L. 135
Ango, ―― 109
Anker, Moses 111b
Armentrout, L. W. 137
Armstrong, D. H. 111b
Armstrong, O. W. 111b
Arnold, Benedict 13
Arnold, Lester D. 257
Ashby, Benjamin 21, 37, 48, 156
Atkinson, J. Scott 263
Atkinson, S. C. 111b
Atkinson, William Mayo 134, 193, 201
Austin, Rufus F. 263
Averitt, James B. (Rev.) 111b

Bacon, Benjamin B. 263
Baetjer, Henry 134, 157
Bageant, Roy L. 257, 260
Baily, ―― 58
Baker, Abraham 66
Baker, Alexander Mantz 15, 122, 123, 128, 153, 157, 193, 202, 234, 235, 236, 237, 239, 240, 241, 242
Baker, Earl Edwin 257, 260
Baker, H. L. 111
Baker, Henry M. 131, 150, 153, 191, 201
Baker, Leary Green 257

Baker, Robert L. 111b
Baker, S. B. 153
Baker, W. Woodhull 257, 260
Baldwin, Cyrus B. 76, 238
Baldwin, W. A. 112
Ball, Samuel H. 156
(1) Ball, William 21, 25, 247
(2) Ball, William 67, 170, 173, 175, 200, 202
Ballard, F. L. 111
Banks, N. P. (General) 14, 97
Bantz, Julius 191
Barclay, John 57
Barnett, D. 156
Barnett, Lewis 64, 66, 67, 69, 155, 247
Barr, C. F. 134
Barr, Curtis R. 140, 257
Barr, Robert 155
Barr, Taylor Lee 257, 260
Barrett, Albert L. 112
Barrett, David 128
Barrett, Joseph E. 111b
Barton, Lewis N. 142, 154, 201, 242, 257, 260, 263
Barton, R. T., Jr. 137
Barton, R. W. 81
Battaile, William M. 257
Bauserman, Milton D. 257, 260, 263
Baxter, Sidney S. 88, 89, 149
Bealy, Robert L. 228
Bean, Edwin A. 111b
Bean, Esten P. 260, 263
Bean, Theodore W. 111b
Beard, Robert 228
Beardsworth, Richard 257
Beaty, Robert L. 71, 74
Beckham, Fountain 222
Beckwith, Francis M. 78, 79, 156, 180
Beeler, Joseph 21, 23, 26, 47
Belcher, W. A. 112
Bendell, Herman 111b
Bennet, C. E. 249

265

Bennett, C. D. 260
Bent, Lemuel 75, 77, 78, 79, 81, 152, 176, 178, 179, 180, 181, 200, 227, 228, 229, 237, 238, 252, 253
Bent, William L. 122, 124, 153, 155, 157, 234, 243
Beverley, James B., Jr. 154, 201, 242, 257, 260, 263
Binney, Horace 112
Birer, Irvin G. 243
Blackmer, William W. 112
Blair, John 45
Blair, Montgomery 101
Blair, Samuel 228
Blake, George R. 132, 243
Blanchard, Robert 221
Blanchard, William W. 228, 238, 252
Board, Charles B. 263
Bonney, Seth 111b
Booze, J. W. 257
Borden, Harry L. 263
Bosserman, W. H. 257, 260, 263
Bowen, Forest H. 257
Bowen, Richard 152, 162, 163, 165, 166, 167, 200, 202
Bowers, G. Richard 257
Bowers, Harry H. 257, 260, 263
Bowers, Maurice E. 257
Bowman, S. M. 187, 188, 190
Boyd, J. Thomas 257
Boyles, Harry A. 257, 260, 263
Bradberry, A. W. 111b
Braddock, ——— (General) 13, 52
Bragg, John 211
Branch, Henry (Rev.) 128
Branson, N. A. 111b
Breckenridge, A. R. 138, 150, 154
Breedin, E. C. 200
Brent, Edwin S. 96, 97, 101, 138, 153, 186, 196, 204
Brent, Henry M., Jr. 186, 187, 188, 200, 204, 234, 242, 249
Bridgeforth, W. E. 257, 260
Brigham, John S. 111b
Broach, I. N. 111b
Brock, J. H. 112
Brooke, ——— (Rev.) 188

Brooks, Thomas 56
Brown, Adam 76, 77, 155, 202
Brown, C. Douglas 257, 260, 263
Brown, James W. 112
Brown, Jesse 68
Brown, John 9, 144
Brown, John I. 257
Brown, Leslie M. 257
Brown, Oliver M. 111b
Brown, Richard B. 257, 260, 263
Brown, William (Rev.) 111b
Brown, William H. 257, 260, 263
Brown, William P. 112
Brownell, W. R. 111b
Brumback, E. C. 261
Brundage, Daniel 111b
Bryant, Lampson P. 111
Buck, Eugene T. 118
Buck, George N. 242, 263
Buncutter, Julian H. 257
Burdett, George M. (Dr.) 111b
Burgess, C. S. 257
Burgess, James W. 202
Burke, B. Bryan 263
Burnett, Henry 112
Burnham, A. S. 197
Burtis, George A. 112
Bush, Henry Lee 257
Bushnell, Benjamin 80, 152, 155, 156, 181, 202, 203
Bushnell, George B. 257, 260, 263
Bushnell, George E. 122, 126, 153, 157, 242, 243
Butt, Robert B. 211
Buzzard, Jacob 76
Byrd, Harry Flood 257

Cabell, James Alston 135
Cahill, Augustus H. 257, 261
Cahill, Howard J. 257, 261, 263
Cahill, James 112
Cahill, Leroy F. 140. 257
Callahan, Charles H. 139
Calvert, E. D. 154
Cameron, C. C. 199
Cameron, W. D. (Dr.) 257

Index of Names

Cammer, Claude R. 137, 141, 154, 157, 158, 242, 257, 261, 263
Campbell, C. S. H. 195, 261
Campbell, L. 187
Campbell, William 21, 40, 48
Campbell, W. R. 261
Canfield, John 112
Capper, Meredith 112
Capron, J. R. 112
Carper, Ernest A. 257, 261
Carper, Harvey F. 154, 157, 201, 257, 261
Carr, ——— (Judge) 77, 80
Carrington, Timothy 82
Carroll, Arthur N. 263
Carskaden, William A. 257, 261, 263
Carson, James H. 90, 95, 96, 153
Carson, Joseph S. 153, 183, 200
Carson, Nicholas 257, 261
Cassell, Osborn C. 154, 201, 231, 242, 257, 261, 263
Cather, David C. 137, 140
Cather, H. L. 204
Cather, T. Russell 137, 153, 157
Cawthorne, Ted H. 257
Cebring, ——— 109
Chambers, Gus 257, 261
Chambers, William 174
Chapman, Warren, Jr. 112
Chapman, William 196
Chinn, John J. 202, 203
Chipley, James 148, 200, 202, 203
Choucleris, James 257, 261, 263
Christian, Edward 167
Clare, ———175
Clark, Arthur 168
Clark, Charles H. 155, 181, 202, 203
Clark, H. E. (Dr.) 137, 257
Clark, P. H. 112
Clark, Samuel 211
Clarke, E. R. 112
Clark(e), L. W. 112, 118
Clinton, Dewitt 218, 220, 223, 224, 225
Clinton, W. H. 112
Clowe, Mifflin B. 154, 201, 243, 257, 261, 263

Clowe, Mifflin B., Jr. 257, 261
Clower, James S. 263
Coburne, P. 98
Cochran, C. W. 137
Cochran, Fred A. (Dr.) 137, 257, 261, 263
Cochran, John T. 195, 196, 197
Cock, J. Lee 257
Coffman, W. E. 201
Coffroth, C. A. B. 83, 95, 107, 122, 125, 126, 156, 157, 182, 183, 185, 199, 203, 204, 234, 243
Cole, Jesse 211
Coles, Peyton S. 125
Colt, T. G. 112
Compton, Z. J. 263
Cone, A. D. 263
Conrad, Daniel (Dr.) 112
Conrad, Ed. S. 193
Conrad, Frank E. 127
Conrad, John 152
Conway, H. H. 155
Conway, W. G. 134, 157
Cooley, James C. 112
Coope, A. I. 112
Cooper, Charles A. 257
Cooper, J. L. 243
Cooper, William E. 134, 140, 141, 142, 153, 155, 157, 158, 201, 242, 243, 257, 261, 263
Cornwallis, Lord 46
Correll, J. E. 134, 135, 157, 191, 193, 194, 204, 243
Cortelyou, George B. 132
Courson, Willliam L. 257, 261, 263
Courtney, J. L. 257
Cox, Nicholas 73
Cox, P. D. 112
Craig, John R. 112
Craig, Thomas 21, 39, 42, 43, 44, 45, 47, 156
Crampton, Benjamin 261, 263
Crockwell, John G. 52, 163, 168
Cross, Jeremy 207, 208, 209, 212
Cross, Jerome E. 112

Crosslin, Thurman 8, 141, 142, 154, 257, 261
Cruickshank, David Petrie 133
Crum, Charles L. 112
Cummings, L. F. 112
Cunningham, Earnest L. 136
Currie, L. D. H. 112
Cushman, James 80, 82, 163, 179, 180, 198, 207, 208, 209, 210, 212, 213, 219, 220, 223, 224, 225, 226, 252
Cuthbert, E. Earl 257, 261

Danner, Michael 153, 155
Darling, D. H. 113
Davis, Charles G. 135
Davis, Samuel H. 81, 82, 152, 156, 221, 222, 227, 229, 230, 232, 242, 252
Davis, Thomas N. 133
Davis, William L. 196
Dawe, Phillip D. 211
Dearing, Eugene F. 257, 261, 263
Dechert, Robert B. 257, 261
DeHaven, G. M. 257
Denning, Jabis T. 113
Denny, James H. 113
Denny, Joseph S. 113
Denny, William R. 104, 105, 108, 109, 119, 121, 123, 125, 126, 128, 153, 157
Denton, Harry T. 140, 257
Denton, John 238
Dickinson, D. H. 113
Dike, Edward G. 112
Divinger, George W. 112
Dobie, Samuel 21, 22, 23, 24, 47
Dodds, Solomon 202
Donahoe, James E. 263
Dorsey, Frank H. 154, 201, 242
Doster, William 67, 68
Dove, John (Dr.) 148, 164, 178, 182, 187, 188, 189, 190, 208, 211, 212, 225, 251
Dovell, Carroll F. 258, 261
Dowdall, James Gamul 20, 21, 22, 23, 24, 26, 27, 28, 29, 30, 32, 33, 34, 35, 36, 37, 38, 39, 40, 44, 46,
47, 48, 49, 50, 51, 52, 65, 152, 155, 156, 162, 163, 164, 166, 200
Drake, Bethel H. 263
Drew, Dolphin 152, 237
Drummond, Josiah H. 212, 213
Dubin, B. James 258
Duffey, Hugh S. 258
Duke, R. T. W. 132, 136
Duland, Coe 112
Dunbar, John R. W. 152
Duncan, T. Samuel 263
Dunlap, Charles W. 258, 261, 263

Earles, James D. 113
Early, Jubal A. (General) 100
Ebersole, Matthew H. 201, 258, 261
Eckel, Joseph 208
Eddy, Charles Vernon 7, 8, 133, 137, 138, 140, 141, 142, 143, 153, 157, 158, 192, 193, 194, 195, 197, 201, 204. 230, 235, 236, 239, 240, 241, 242, 258, 261, 263
Eddy, John V. 140, 258
Edwards, Jonathan (Rev.) 263
Edwards, Owen 113
Edwards, Thomas W. 156
Egan, William 113
Eggleston, Joseph W. (Dr.) 139, 150
Eichelberger, C. F. 111
Eidson, S. H., Jr. 261
Ellis, Milton A. 111
Elliott, Peter 202, 203
Emmitt, Owen 113
Ergenbright, Charles H. 197
Evans, French Strother (Rev.) 227, 228
Ewell, R. S. (General) 100, 111a

Fairfax, Lord 12, 13
Fansler, E. W. 137
Fansler, Forest H. 258
Fansler, George E. 137, 258
Fansler, Ralph S. 258, 261
Fant, Julian S. 258
Faulkner, W. W. 153
Fearn, Herbert 113
Ferguson, Abner H. 258

Index of Names 269

Ferrell, Charles H. 113
Ferris, Eugene W. 113
Fessenden, James D. 113
Finklestein, Morris 258, 261
Fisher, Charles E. 113
Fisher, John H. 154, 258, 261
Fitch, G. K. 193, 196
Fitz, James F. 113
Fitzwhylsonn, William H. 248
Flintoff, Charles M. 141
Flood, Bolling B. 258
Flowers, Enoch D. 141
Fordyce, F. M. 113
Fosbrink, John G. 261
Foster, James 71, 74, 77, 83, 84, 155, 179, 222, 223, 227, 237, 252
Foster, Jonathan 71
Fowle, Henry 219, 220, 223, 252, 253
Fox, Harry S., Jr. 258
Fraleigh, D. M. 113
Frame, F. M. 113
Frazier, L. J. 261
Frederick, John 71, 227, 252
Freeman, Clarence D. 141
Fuller, William McP. 157
Funk, J. H. 96
Funk, Joseph B. 258

Galt, William W. 137
Garber, James T. 258
Garton, Vernon B. 258
Gasser, Joseph H. 141
Gearing, G. F. 261
Georges, Peter 261, 263
Gibbens, C. M. 128, 136, 137
Gibbs, James 156
Ginn, Charles L. 113
Ginn, George W. 126, 153, 157, 200, 202, 203
Ginn, Joseph M. 96, 107, 113, 153, 186, 249
Glaize, George F. 157, 202
Glass, W. W. 119
Gleason, Reed 113
Glover, John D. 258
Goertz, Henry H. 85
Goetchius, David R. 113

Golden, John 258, 261
Good, George W. 140, 258, 261, 263
Good, Isaac N. 150, 157, 201, 202, 204, 243
Goodall, Richard H. 113
Goode, Wendell B. 141, 154, 157, 158, 201, 242, 258, 261, 263
Goodyear, Jacob M. 258
Goodyear, Samuel M. 139
Gordon, Nash L. 243
Gould, Adelbert E. 113
Graham, J. R. (Rev.) 143
Grainger, Reed B. 113
Graves, Charles C. 118
Graves, Charles H. 75
Gray, Allen B. 137, 201, 242, 258, 261, 263
Gray, John C. 113
Gray, Richard L. 157
Gray, Richard L., Jr. 258, 261
Green, Charles 111
Green, Gilbert G. 113
Green, Harry K. 141
Gregory, Harry E. 258
Grice, Charles A. 226
Griffith, A. Newton 258
Grim, Cecil C. 258
Grim, Claude M. 137, 140, 141, 154, 155, 157, 158, 201, 258, 261
Grim, G. W. 152
Grimm, Douglas O. 154, 201, 242, 258, 261, 263
Grimm, R. M. (Dr.) 140, 258, 261, 263
Grist, Elwood 113
Grubbs, Kinzel B., Jr. 258
Grubbs, Ralph Y. 258
Gustine, Joel T. 152, 165

Hable, Solomon H. 134, 157
Hackett, C. I. 113
Haines, Floyd W. 258, 261, 263
Haines, J. A. 258
Haldeman, Paul M. 258, 261
Hall, Clyde H. 258
Hall, David (Sr.) 21, 27, 28, 29, 36
Halterman, Tom D. 258, 261, 263

Hamburger, Myer 258, 261
Hamilton, E. L. 113
Hamilton, Gavin (or George) 53, 54,
Hammel, Roger 77
Hamrick, Walter B. 258
Harbison, Edward 114
Harmer, William H. 93, 96
Harmer, Herbert W. 154, 258, 261
Harmer, Jacob 155
Harmer, Stanley E. 138
Harper, Roy 258, 261
Harris, B. M. 249
Harris, Sutton I. 203, 221, 222, 227, 230, 243, 252
Harry, C. Burton 258
Hartman, Clayton S. 154, 201, 242, 243, 258, 261, 263
Hartsook, Granville, Jr. 263
Hatcher, Richard F. 258, 261
Haupi, John A. 237
Havener, J. W. 113
Hay, Edward S. 114
Hay, John 23, 24
Hayden, A. F. 113
Hayden, John R. 221, 238
Hayden, Joseph W. 114
Hayden, T. V. (Dr.) 113
Heeps, William H. 140, 258
Hester, Solomon 81, 82, 152, 227, 230 243, 252
Helm, William P. 237
Helphinstine, Peter 21, 22, 23, 24, 28, 33, 36, 47
Hensell, Charles W. 128, 191, 236, 242, 243
Herrin, William 237
Herrington, Timothy 221
Hershell, Isaac 238
Hester, K. 114
Hewitt, Wilbur E. 154, 201, 242, 258, 261, 263
Hickman, John 59
Hill, James 176, 237
Hill, William B. 231
Hillman, James N. 141, 197
Hines, William 65
Hite, Joist (or Jost) 12

Hodges, Elmer V. 258, 261, 263
Hodgson, Joseph 258, 261, 263
Hofer, Charles E. 258
Hoff, Philip 69, 86, 155, 170, 202
Hoffman, E. D. 113
Holliday, Herbert C. 258, 261
Holliday, William M. 203
Hollingsworth, Solomon 155
Hollis, John W. 156, 181, 199
Hollis, Thomas 156
Holmes, Hugh 148
Homer, H. R. 153, 194, 201
Honts, Anderson B., Jr. 263
Hook, Edwin Russell 258, 261, 263
Hoover, C. E. 125, 126, 157
Hoover, John 258
Hotinger, J. A. 258
Hottel, W. J. 258
Houck, Joseph T. 239
Houghton, Russell 114
Howard, John 21
Howard, William 114
Howell, John 26, 47
Hubard, William J. 193, 195
Hudson, William H. 114
Hull, ———189
Humphreys, John 21, 32, 33, 35, 36, 47
Humston, E. A. (Dr.) 258
Hunt, F. S. 202
Hunter, Edmund Pendleton 83, 84, 92, 143
Hunter, Moses T. 80
Hunter, Philip N. 154, 258, 261, 263
Hunter, R. M. 153
Huntsberry, E. R. 258
Hurst, Frederick 58, 59, 156, 202
Hyde, John P. 191, 201
Hyde, Marshall W. 258, 261

Idé, E. Louis 191
Illi, Oscar A. 258, 261
Irwin, G. Robert 263
Irwin, John A. 114

Jackson, A. H. 258, 261, 263

Index of Names

Jackson, Andrew (General) 87
Jackson, Bernard 71
Jackson, Edward 238
Jackson, Thomas J. (General) 14
Jakimier, T. F. 201, 258
Jamerson, Thomas 57
James, Howard L. (Dr.) 258
Jeffery, Richard 211
Jenkins, Brown E. 258
Jenkins, Charles S. 114
Jenkins, George E. 114
Jenkins, Jack K. 8, 197, 201, 258, 261, 263
Jenkins, William 83, 90, 152, 155, 156, 199
Jesus Christ 238
Jewett, John E. 114
Joachim, Edward A. 197
Johnson, William 56
Johnston, Samuel N. 258, 261
Johnston, Thomas B. 114
Jones, Amos G. 114
Jones, Blackwaite 21
Jones, Daniel W. 114
Jones, Harold C. 201, 241, 242, 243, 258, 261, 263
Jones, Harold Courtney 258
Jones, J. Luther 258, 261
Jones, Laurens P. 154, 258, 261, 264
Jonston, Robert (Dr.) 16
Jordan, John J. 242

Kaknis, Gus J. 201, 258, 261, 264
Karr (or Kaar), David 33
Karr, Hamilton L. 111
Kater, John L. 258
Kay, Robert 114
Kean, John 49, 152, 155, 156, 175, 238
Kean, Nathaniel 202, 203
Keats, John 137
Keith, G. G. 261
Kelly, Robert 114
Kelley, William 237
Kemp, James 42
Kennedy, David 21, 31, 47, 48
Kerlin, Raymond H. (Dr.) 258

Kern, ———— 111a
Kern, Harry R. 259
Kern, John 252
(1) Kerr, John 107, 119, 123, 155, 157
(2) Kerr, John 128
Kerr, William M. 111
Kibbe, G. E. 114
Kiger, George R. 199
Kiger, George W. 199
Kiger, J. A. 259
Kilingsmith, I. C. 114
Kines, J. Shirley 264
King, Alexander 53, 156
King, Charles 114
King, Horatio C. 114
Kingan, John 155
Kinsley, Joseph H. 114
Kinzel, Henry 114, 122, 126, 155, 243
Kinzel, George H. 134, 157, 195, 202, 243
Kinzel, T. Y. 155
Kirwan, Y. A. 114
Klenfield, Joseph 114
Kline, Roger A. 137, 195
Klipstine, Philip A. 156, 179, 180, 203, 211, 212, 238
Klompus, Philip 153
Knapp, ———— (Professor) 109
Kneeland, Thomas D. 114
Knight, B. M. 153, 157
Knight, B. M., Jr. (Dr.) 259
Knorr, H. L. 114
Knowlton, George 114
Kohlhausen, B. F. 259
Krebs, Henry Clay 104, 126, 153, 155, 157, 201, 204, 242, 243
Krebs, Isaac 111, 111a
Kremer, Conrad 65, 71, 74, 76, 77, 79, 85, 152, 156, 221, 222, 227, 237, 252

Lacey, J. H., Jr. 137
LaFayette, Marquis de 81, 181
Lamb, George W. 115
Lamb, William R. 115

Laithe, W. B. 115
Lang, Abraham 237
Laningham, Earl C. 141
Lannis, William H. 115
Largent, Brady W. 154, 201, 242, 243
Larrick, F. J. 259
Larrick, Hugh S. 259
Larrick, Roy A. 154, 197, 201, 202, 241, 243, 259, 261, 264
Larson, Ralph H. 259
Lauck, Peter 59, 64, 65, 66, 67, 68, 70, 76, 78, 79, 81, 85, 152, 155, 162, 163, 165, 167, 169, 175, 178, 179, 200, 202, 222, 227, 230, 237, 247, 252
Lauck, Samuel H. 222, 227, 229, 237, 238, 252
Lee, Robert Edward (General) 236
Leen, Isaac 21
Legge (or Legg), George 101, 128, 157
Lemley, Fred M. 137
Lemley, Gervis E. 137, 259
Lennox, Hugh 21
Lewis, John 20, 21, 24, 25, 27, 28, 33, 47, 156,
Lewis, Warner 45
Lichliter, Dudley C. 154, 201, 242, 259, 261, 264
Lincoln, Abraham 101
Lindsay, James 21, 22, 23, 24, 26, 28, 33, 34, 35, 155
Lineburg, P. E. 259, 261, 264
Linquist, George F. 114
Little, John P. 249
Little, William 23
Lloyd, George 115
Lloyd, John Willie, Jr. 259
Logan, Clyde 259, 261, 264
Logan, Lloyd 101
Louderback, Page G. 259
Love, Williams S. (Dr.) 110, 121, 122, 123, 134, 150, 153, 157
Loving, John J. 253
Lupton, John L. 114
Lupton, John S. 111a
Lupton, Thomas N. 157

Lutz, Wallace J. 259
Lynn, William H. H. 191

MacNamara,, Thomas 264
McBride, ———— 47
McCann, C. R. 150, 259
McCann, Harry L. 154, 259
McCarroll, Archibald, Jr. 115
McCaw, Thomas D. 188
McChesney, William B. 236
McConaughty, Frank 115
McCormac, Hollie B. 134, 153, 157, 241
McCormick, F. N. 259
McDonald, Angus 21, 28, 29, 30, 32, 35, 37, 47, 59, 152, 155, 167
McDonald, J. B. 100
(1) McDonald, John 152
(2) McDonald, John 148
McElroy, Robert 115
McFaden, Frank T. (Rev.) 139, 140, 143, 145, 146, 196, 235, 240, 241
McGee, J. Lowry 111, 115
McGraw, P. M. 115
McGuire (or Maguire), Edward 21, 33, 34, 36, 44, 45, 47, 48, 155, 156
(see also Maguire)
McIllwaine, John 115
McIlwee, Delmar P. 259
McKele, William H. 115
McKericher, James N. 115
McKinley, William (President) 14, 102, 104, 115, 118, 131, 132, 138, 139
McMurray, R. K. 115
McQuarrie, Hector 195
McVicar, Charles P. 241, 243, 259, 261, 264
McVicar, Charles P., Jr. 140, 259
McVicker, George W. 115

Maes, Frederick 115
Magaw, Samuel (Dr.) 51
Magill, Archibald 49, 50, 58, 62, 68, 69, 74, 75, 78, 143, 144, 148, 156, 174, 175, 176, 200

Index of Names

Maguire, William 50, 148, 155, (*see also* McGuire)
Mahon, Edward 115
Mallery, William A. 115
Maloney, Robert 228, 237
Malory, Thornton 111
Manuel, Robert F. 253
Maphis, J. Alan 137, 259, 261
Marmaduke, Presley 238
Martin, H. A. 259
Martin, Stanley W. 194
Mather, Myron D. 115
Mathews, J. Leonard 264
May, Samuel 21, 26, 28, 30, 33, 35, 36, 39, 45, 47, 48, 65, 152, 155
Mayer, Augustine 76
Mead, A. B. 115
Mead, Isaac N. 115
Meredith, F. E. 115
Miles, O. M. 197
Miller, Benjamin 155
Miller, George F. 140
Miller, Henry 115
Miller, J. Lee 154, 201, 243, 259, 262, 264
Miller, J. P. 259
Miller, Paul L. 259, 262
Minton, Allen C. 259, 262, 264
Moffett, James W. 111
Montfort, Joseph 161
Montgomery, ——— (General) 47, 85
Moore, Alexander 115
Moore, L. T. 89, 92, 153, 183, 200
Moore, R. W. 118
Moore, Thomas B. 107
Moore, Thomas W. 115
Morgan, Daniel (General) 13, 85
Morgan, Lester H. 259, 262, 264
Morley, Thomas 111
Morris, John P. 115
Morris, Theodore 259, 262, 264
Morris, William T. 111
Morse, Frank C. (Rev.)
Moseley, William L. 111
Moss, L. 98
Murrin, L. 115

Naphier, Andrew 115
Nash, Norman (Rev.) 237
Neat, Thomas C. 115
Newby, William 165, 202, 203
Newman, ——— 165
Noonan, Vincent M. 140, 259
North, George H. 116
Norton, Daniel 49, 65, 152, 156
Novick, A. J. 137, 259, 262
Nowland, N. M. 115
Nunsbach, James N. 115

Oates, Patrick 116
O'Loughlin, Cornelius 56
Omps, Voyne B. 259
O'Neal, Sam D. 259, 262, 264
Ott, Cloice J. 262, 264

Packard, L. F. 116
Page, Thomas (Dr.) 116
Page, William Byrd 80, 81
Palavid, M. J. 259
Palmer, Richard 259
Parker, R. E. 116
Parker, Richard (Judge) 9, 29, 103, 107, 110, 121, 122, 123, 124, 125, 126, 127, 143, 144, 145, 153, 187, 190, 201
Parrott, ——— 232
Patch, Nahum W. 222
Patten, William 95
Patrick, Charles W. 116
Paydon, Thomas E. 264
Payne, ——— 165
Pearis, George 31
Pearsing, H. W. 116
Pease, M. J. 259
Peck, Lewis M. (Colonel) 116
Pendleton, Edmund 75, 76, 155, 156,
Pendleton, Philip 33
Penn, James 211
Penticost, Dorcy 21, 23, 26, 47, 155
Perkins, William B. 116
Petrie, Richard 259, 262
Peyton, John 152, 156, 162, 165, 170, 200, 203
Pifer, H. I. (Dr.) 259

Pillett, Elias P. 116
Pine, Charles A. 259, 262
Pine, Lazarus 71
Pingley, H. R. 259, 262
Pitcher, George C. 116
Plundeke, W. C. 259, 262, 264
Polk, James K. (President) 91
Pollard, H. M. 116
Pommeroy, George B. 116
Poore, Mark 111
Pope, Richard Hunter 137, 138, 154
Porter, William B. 116
Porterfield, Archibald 72
Post, William H. B. 116
Potter, O. C. 116
Powell, Alfred H. 79
Powell, William 155
Preston, Byron I. 116
Preston, Sam D. 259
Price, James Hubert 139, 240
Purdy, Stephen D. 116
Purse, Thomas 162, 163, 167, 169, 170, 200, 202

Radford, German E. 259, 262, 264
Randell, Augustro 116
Randolph, Edmund 19
Randolph, J. T. 152
Randolph, Peyton 22
Randolph, W. F. 116
Raworth, Francis 156
Rawpe, Francis 76
Ray, John 128, 132, 155
Ray, Robert 117
Reakirk, Harvey R. 111
Reck, ——— (Rev.) 76
Reed, C. W. 243
Reed, George (Rev.) 79, 177, 178, 179, 181, 200, 210, 211, 213, 222, 227, 228, 231, 237, 238, 243, 252, 253
Reed, George A., Jr. 156, 199
Reed, John B. Tilden 88, 91, 93, 96, 97, 100, 102, 119, 126, 128, 152, 183, 185, 199, 200, 234 242
Reed, Robert W. 153, 200
Reed, Theodore 116
Rehart, H. K. 118

Reid, Hugh 141
Renalds, Marvin W. 264
Rhame, Charles C. 259, 262, 264
Rice, Beverly N. 259
Richard, J. W. 259, 262
Richard, Wyatt H. 259
Richards, William M. 259, 262, 264
Richardson, Mrs. ——— 104
Riddle, George W. 116
Riley, Hoye L. 259
Robertson, David 247
Rittenburg, Henry 116
Robinson, C. Arthur 259, 262, 264
Robinson, C. L. 150, 202
Robinson, Fred A. 259
Robinson, H. Delmer 137, 259, 262, 264
Rodgers, W. E. 262, 264
Rolf, Byron L. 117
Rooker, William Y. 152
Root, William W. 116
Rootes, George 21, 38
Rorapaugh, Uriah 116
Rose, Duncan 42
Rose, Hugh T. 70
Rosenberger, Thomas B. 259, 262
Ross, H. G. 264
Roszel, B. M. 137
Russell, B. E. 259, 262
Russell, Robert 21, 33 36, 47
Russell, William, Jr. 117

Sachs, Simon J. 197
Sachse, Julius 20
Salomon, Ralph 259, 262
Sampsell, S. E. 259
Samsell, E. Barr 264
Sartelle, R. Ray (Dr.) 259, 262
Sawyer, Charles C. 117
Schenk, C. H. 153
Schermerhorn, N. W. 117
Schumacher, F. Eugene 259, 262, 264
Schwalb, A. L. 259, 262
Schwartz, T. E. 191
Scofield, John 117
Scott, Hugh 152
Seabright, Harry M. 154, 259

Index of Names

Searcy, C. L. 259
Seaton, ———— 165
Seevers, Henry 72, 74, 93, 152, 221, 222, 228, 237
Seevers, Nathaniel 84, 152
Seibert, George W. 117
Sempeles, John P. 259
Service, John 56
Sexton, John 23, 26
Sexton, Joseph 65
Shade, E. Earl 259, 262, 264
Shade, Walter M. 154, 201, 242, 243, 259, 262, 264
Shaffer, John D. 264
Shannon, James 264
Sheetz, Harold C. 153, 201, 242, 243, 259, 262, 264
Sheetz, Harold C., Jr. 201, 243, 259, 262, 264
Shegoge, Alfred M. 117
Shelley, Percy Bysshe 137
Shepherd, William 156
Shepherd, W. P. 199
Sheridan, Philip (General) 100, 101, 102
Shiley, Wesley L. 259, 262
Shirey, P. M. 196, 242, 264
Shroeler, John C. 117
Shull, E. C. 137
Sibley, Hiram L. 111
Sigourney, Dan P. 197
Silver, William 64, 65, 66, 68, 170, 175, 247
Simpson, Taylor F. 259, 262, 264
Singleton, Washington G. 81, 182, 200
Sirbaugh, Carl W. 259, 262, 264
Sittler, Daniel 156, 203
Sittler, Joseph 65
Slater, Edward (Sr.) 80, 156, 162, 163, 165, 168, 170, 200, 203
Slifer, Edgar P. 259
Slocum, John W. 117
Slonaker, A. C. 133, 134, 153, 157, 201, 242
Slonaker, Dailey R. 154, 201, 242, 259, 262, 264
Slonaker, R. Bruce 259, 262, 264
Smidt, E. 117

Smith, A. Douglas, Jr. 141, 142
Smith, E. Lee 182
Smith, George 199
Smith, J. Clinton 132, 153, 191
Smith, J. Worthington 90, 92
Smith, John G. 259, 262
Smith, Paul Asa 260
Smith, Sebert J. 154, 260, 262, 264
Smith, W. Ray 134, 151, 153, 201
Smyth, J. I. 88
Snapp, R. B. (Dr.) 260
Snoke, Martin Van Buren 154, 201, 242, 260, 262, 264
Snyder, Frank W. 260
Snyder, George H. 140, 260, 262, 264
Solenberger, Ansel B. 260, 262, 264
Spencer, H. B. 117
Spring, Denver P. 260, 262
Steele, Arnold (Dr.) 117
Stephens, Alexander 72
Stephenson, John 111
Stevenson, Levi L. 83, 86, 91, 210
Stewart, William I. 117
Stickley, Claude B., Jr. 154, 201, 242
Stickley, Omar P. 264
Stickley, William M. III 262, 264
Stivers, B. F. 111
Stone, Charles B. 117
Stone, George E. 117
Stover, B. F. 118
Streit, Christian (Rev.) 60, 61, 67, 169
Swearingen, ———— 72
Swift, Elijah 117
Swift, Theodore M. 117
Swink, D. M. 243
Sybert, Paul W. 260

Tarleton, ———— (Colonel) 14
Taylor, Edmund 21, 33, 35, 47, 156
Taylor, George S. 140, 242, 260, 262, 264
Taylor, J. Howard 260, 262
Teeters, Albert B. 111a
Terry, ———— (Captain) 96
Thiel, John 117
Thomas, Daniel Walker 65, 66, 71, 72, 73, 74, 75, 76, 79, 156, 175, 176,

203, 218, 220, 221, 222, 223, 224,
225, 226, 227, 228, 229, 231, 233,
235, 237, 238, 241, 242, 252
Thomas, Jacob R. 221, 237
Thomas, Joseph P. 237
Thomas, Matthew 69
Thomas, R. W. 117
Thomas, Townsend W. 79
Thomas, W. C. 117
Thompson, H. 117
Thompson, James 117
Thompson, Joseph C. 264
Thompson, William 117
Thorpe, Henry W. 153, 200
Throckmorton, Warner 221, 229, 237
Thruston, ———— (Colonel) 47
Timberlake, George Washington 59, 72
Timberlake, John 21, 48
Timberman, J. E. W. 195
Titus, Richmond R. 117
Tooley, I. 81
Tower, Anson K. 117
Towers, William 157, 182, 203
Travers, William H. 106, 107
Tremain, A. F. 117
Trenary, C. W. 138, 243
Triplett, James H. 117
Trotter, Herbert 262, 264
Tucker, A. B. 200
Tucker, Charles 157
Turner, R. J. 264
Twain, Mark (Samuel L. Clemens) 108

Url, Walter 117

Vaile, E. E. 117
Van Meter, Isaac 13
Van Meter, John 13
Volker, Frank 117

Waddell, Julius 128
Wagner, W. B. 153, 201, 242
Wallace, L. W. 260
Wallis, J. P. 118
Walter, Gervin J. 260, 262

Warner, Russell S. 260
Warrick, John B. 118
Washburn, James 111a
Washington, George 12, 15, 44, 55, 59, 60, 61, 72, 83, 139, 161
Watkins, Maurice 118
Watson, J. Carson 153
Watson, Leon V. 260, 262, 264
Weatherall, Anthony 162, 163 (*see also* Whitehall *and* Witherall)
Weaver, A. G. 150
Webb, Thomas Smith 207
Webber, Charles E. 141, 197
Weekes, G. D. 118
Weidenstine, W. A. 118
Welch, John F. 111a
Wender, L. S. 260, 262
Wetzel, Christopher 74, 202
Wheeler, Victor W. 243, 260, 262, 264
Whitacre, John W. 260
Whitaker, Herman B. 264
White, ———— 165
White, Alfred P. 98, 111a, 157
White, Charles W. 111a
White, Elisha M. 118
White, James M. 118
White, John F. 118
White, Robert 83, 152
White, Roland S. 260
White, William 51
Whitehall, Anthony 71 (*see also* Weatherall *and* Witherall)
Whitehead, ———— 27
Whitemer, B. F. (Rev.) 118
Whitmer, George R. 118
Whitmire, Gilbert R. 260, 262
Whitney, William B. 81, 221, 228
Whitten, Robert A. (Rev.) 242, 260, 262, 264
Wicks, George S. 118
Widener, Perry W. 240
Wildes, Thomas S. 111a
Williams, ———— 73
Williams, A. W. 111a
Williams, John S. 66
Williams, R. C. 260
Williams, R. Gray 138

Index of Names

Willis, M. H. G. 128, 153, 191, 193, 202, 243
Willman, James M. 118
Wilson, C. W. 133, 157, 204, 243
Wilson, Frank T. 118
Wilson, John 156, 238
Wine, R. Samuel 260
Wingert, Asa K. 262
Wingert, Harold E. 260
Winn, William H. 260
Witherall, Anthony 77 (*see also* Weatherall *and* Whitehall)
Witherly, Artemus 118
Withers, Robert E. 249
Wolfe, Lewis 61, 62, 63, 64, 66, 68, 69, 91, 155, 174, 200
Wood, James 12
Wood, John 20
Wood, Thomas B. 105, 106, 157
Wood, William L. 201

Wooding, W. Crews 240
Woodrow, Alexander 23
Woolfolk, John C. 260
Wordsworth, William 137
Worthey, Thomas 118
Wright, Albert C. 118
Wright, D. E. 140, 260
Wright, George W. 139
Wright, John H. 118
Wright, Reubin W. 260
Wroe, Original 167
Wyndham, Thomas C. 72, 156

Yancey, John G. 193
Yeakley, H. E. 260
Yeatras, Stephen 260, 262, 264
Yost, E. C. (Dr.) 137, 260
Yost, Jacob H. 260

Zeigler, John J. 260

INDEX OF SUBJECTS

(Location of all places, Lodges, and other organizations listed is Virginia unless otherwise indicated. West Virginia localities are noted only after 1861.)

Acca Temple, A. A. O. N. M. S. 146
Alexandria 10, 19, 139
Alexandria Lodge No. 39 20
Alexandria-Washington Lodge No. 22 19
Alleghany City (Pennsylvania) 188
Alleghany Mountains 47
Allied Masonic Degrees 199
America, Grand Master of 41
"Antients" 25
Apple Blossom Festival (Winchester) 15
Arlington Chapter No. 35, R. A. M. 197
Aurora Lodge No. —— (Vermont) 101

Ballotting, Method of (Winchester) 89
Baltimore (Maryland) 34, 97, 101, 107, 108, 109, 208, 229, 232
Bank of the Valley (Winchester) 97
Benjamin B. French Lodge No. 15 (D. C.) 123
Berryville 86
Blandford Lodge No. 3 (Petersburg) 41
Blue Ridge Mountains 11, 12, 19
Book of Constitutions 51
Boston (Massachusetts) 85, 219, 253
British Isles 133
Bunker Hill, Battle of 13
By-Laws (Chapter) 164, 165, 168, 169, 181
By-Laws (Lodge) 24, 25, 29, 32, 38, 56, 58, 69, 78, 79, 82

Cabin Point Royal Arch Lodge 41, 161
Canada 13

Canton (Ohio) 138
Capon Springs 93
Carolina 32, 47
Cedar Creek, Battle of 100
Charity Box (Chapter) 188
Charity Box (Lodge) 124
Charlestown 86, 106, 144
Charlottesville 132
Charlottesville Commandery No. 3, K. T. 230
Charters:
    Winchester Hiram Lodge No. 21 247, 248
    John Dove Chapter No. 21, R. A. M. 249-251
    Winchester Encampment No. 1, K. T. 252, 253
Christ Church, (Philadelphia) 51
Christ Church, (Winchester) 15, 144
City Hall (Winchester) 15
Clandestine Masonry 25, 32
Clarksburg 111, 228
Columbia City (Indiana) 100
Common Council (Winchester) 77, 79, 86, 104, 119, 120
Common Hall (Winchester) 67
Concord (Massachusetts) 38
Confederate States of America 14
Connecticut 81
Cornerstone (Market House—Winchester) 237, 238
Cornerstone Laying 68, 79, 82, 92, 93, 106, 126, 129, 132, 133
Corporation Court (Winchester) 119, 120
Corporation of Winchester 67
Cowpens (The), Battle of 13
Culpeper 228
Culpeper County 57

279

Danville 194, 240
District of Columbia 107
Dove Lodge No. 51 (Richmond) 145, 151
Dumfries 161, 162, 208, 211, 212
Dumfries Council No. 2, R. & S. M. 208, 211
Dutch Presbyterian Church (Winchester) 60

Eagle Lodge No. 431 (Ohio) 138
Elks' Home (Winchester) 101
Elkton 195
England 41, 42
English Settlers 12
Excellent and Super-Excellent R. A. Masons 167, 168

Fairfax Commandery No. 25, K. T. (Culpeper) 239
Falmouth 35
Fees (Chapter) 182, 190
Fees (Lodge) 29, 34, 35, 36, 37, 45, 54, 57, 58, 77, 83, 88, 104
Fort Loudoun 13
Fort Sumter 95
Frederick County 12, 20, 22, 32, 102, 144, 148, 228
Fredericksburg Commandery No. 1, K. T. 230
Fredericksburg Lodge No. 4 33, 161
Fredericktown 12
Fredericktown (Maryland) 24
Freemason's Monitor 167
Front Royal 59, 76, 190, 239

General Assembly (Virginia) 14, 78, 143
General Grand Chapter, R. A. M. 207
General Grand Encampment, K. T. 217-226
German Settlers 12
German Lutheran Church (Winchester) 61
Gettysburg (Pennsylvania) 111
Glen Burnie (Winchester) 12

Grand Chapter of Pennsylvania, R. A. M. 178
Grand Chapter of Virginia, R. A. M. 145, 161, 170, 171, 173-178, 182, 183, 187, 191, 194, 195, 197, 207, 210, 211, 212
Grand Charity Fund 83, 85, 86
Grand Commandery of Virginia, K. T. 10, 65, 145, 217-241 (*see also* Grand Encampment of Virginia)
Grand Council of Maryland, R. & S. M. 208
Grand Council of Virginia, R. & S. M. 182, 210, 211, 212
Grand Encampment of Pennsylvania, K. T. 220
Grand Encampment, K. T. (U. S. A.) 233, 235, 239, 240
Grand Encampment of Virginia, K. T. 217-241 (*see also* Grand Commandery of Virginia)
Grand Lodge of England 11
Grand Lodge of Ireland 57
Grand Lodge of Missouri 92
Grand Lodge of Pennsylvania 56, 57, 59, 62, 63, 64, 147, 148, 177 (*see also* Provincial Grand Lodge of Pennsylvania)
Grand Lodge of Virginia 9, 19, 29, 30, 40, 41, 42, 43, 57, 58, 60, 63, 64, 65, 66, 72, 73, 76, 78, 80, 83, 84, 87, 88, 90, 92, 93, 110, 124, 126, 137, 138, 141, 145, 147, 148, 149, 150
Great Britain 39

Hall, Masonic (Winchester) (*see* Masonic Hall)
Hamilton 190
Handley Library (Winchester) 133
Harpers Ferry 14, 218, 228, 230
Hill City Lodge No. 183 (Lynchburg) 145
Hiram Lodge No. 21 (Winchester) (*see* Winchester Hiram Lodge No. 21)

Index of Subjects 281

Holy Royal Arch Chapter (Winchester) 71
How To Live at the Front 195

Indians 11, 47
Innocents Abroad 108
Investment (Reserve Fund) Committee 127, 134, 135, 158
Ioa Hill Lodge No. 63 (location unknown) 111b
Ireland 41, 42, 47, 77
Irish Ritual R. A. M. 163
Isle of Man 133

James River 161
John Dove Chapter No. 21, R. A. M. (Winchester) 145, 146, 186-197, 204, 234
Josiah Legend, Royal Arch Degree 179

Keller Building (Winchester) 140
Kentucky 72
Kilwinning Port Royal Crosse Lodge (Port Royal) 41
Knights of Constantinople 199
Knights Templar 73, 74, 79, 81, 92, 176, 190, 217-241

Lancaster (Pennsylvania) 23, 24
Lexington 95
Lexington (Massachusetts) 38
Lodge No. 479 (Ireland) 57
Lodge No. 105 (Maryland) 98
Lodge No. 2 (Philadelphia) 98
Lodge No. 32 (South Carolina) 168
Lodge No. 39 (Alexandria) 57
Louisiana 107
Love Lodge No. 311 (Winchester) 149-151
Luray 80, 81, 196
Luray Commandery No. 19, K. T. 239
Lynchburg 86, 145, 209, 211, 240
Lynchburg Council No. 6, R. & S. M. 211

Marion 145

Marion Lodge No. 31 145
Mark Master, Degree of 180, 182, 198, 212
Marshall Lodge No. 39 (Lynchburg) 86
Masonic Benefit Association 110
Masonic College of Missouri 93
Masonic Hall (Winchester) 67, 68, 73, 74, 75, 77, 79, 82, 86, 87, 98, 119, 120, 176, 186, 190 (*also called* Mason Hall *and* Masons' Hall)
Masonic Home of Virginia 127
Masonic Tablet (Dr. Robert Jonston) 15, 16
Masonic Tablet (Revolutionary War Heroes) 47, 139
Masonic Temple (Winchester) 103, 104, 105, 122, 131, 138, 139, 140,
Martinsburg (West Virginia) 110
Maryland 35
Maryland Lodge No. 120 (Baltimore) 108
Meridian Lodge No. 284 (Richmond) 145, 151
Methodist Episcopal Church (Winchester) 93
Millwood 82
Mineral Lodge No. 311 151
"Moderns" 25
Most Excellent Master, Degree of 180, 181, 182, 198, 212
Mt. Carmel Encampment No. 3, K. T. (location unknown) 218, 220, 221, 222, 223, 225, 230
Mt. Vernon Lodge No. 3 (New York) 114
Mountain City Lodge No. 67 (Lexington) 95

National Lodge No. 12 (D. C.) 116
New Jersey 13, 73
New York City 208
Norfolk 161, 162, 173, 209, 211, 212
Norfolk Council No. 3, R. & S. M. 211
Norfolk Lodge No. 1 41

Norfolk United Chapter No. 1, R. A. M. 162, 173, 175
North Carolina 56, 161
Northern Neck 13

Ohio County 232
Opequon 13
Orange County 12
Order of High Priesthood 193, 194

Pack Horse Ford 12
Paintings (Winchester Hiram Lodge) 108, 109
Past Master, Degree of 37, 72, 73, 180, 182, 212
Peabody Institute (Baltimore) 109
Philadelphia (Pennsylvania) 10, 16, 20, 21, 22, 50, 51, 53, 62, 98, 239
Piedmont Commandery No. 26, K. T. (The Plains) 239
Pennsylvania 10, 12, 13, 16, 19, 20, 21, 23, 29, 65, 127, 139, 164, 165, 186, 218, 247
Petersburg 209, 211, 212, 232
Petersburg Council No. 5, R. & S. M. 211
Polemic Society (Winchester) 77
Pomeroy (Ohio) 111
Portraits:
  Williiam McKinley 132, 133
  John Dove 189
Portsmouth 10, 19, 209, 211, 212, 231
Portsmouth Council No. 4, R. & S. M. 211
Portsmouth Encampment No. 5, K. T. 226
Portsmouth Lodge No. 41 19
Portland (Maine) 212
Potomac River 12
Presbyterian Church (Winchester) 139 (*also called* Loudoun Street Presbyterian Church)
Provincial Grand Lodge of Pennsylvania 10, 16, 19, 20, 21, 22, 25, 27, 28, 29, 30, 36, 41, 43, 44, 51, 52, 53, 247

Provincial Grand Lodge of Virginia 22

Quebec 13, 47, 85

Red Men (Winchester) 105
Reserve Fund 128, 134, 135, 158
Reserve Fund Committee (*see* Investment Committee)
Revolutionary War 13, 14, 38, 45, 47, 48, 139
Richmond 143, 144, 145, 146, 161, 162, 193, 207, 208, 212, 218, 226, 248, 251
Richmond Chapter No. 3, R. A. M. 162
Richmond Council No. 1, R. & S. M. 208, 211 (*same* as Hiram Council No. 1)
Richmond Encampment No. 3, K. T. 225, 230 (*later* Richmond Commandery No. 2)
Richmond Theatre Fire 143
Rockbridge Grays (War Between the States) 95
Romney 228
Rosters:
  Winchester Hiram Lodge No. 21. 257-260
  John Dove Chapter No. 21, R. A. M. 260-262
  Winchester Commandery No. 12, K. T. 263-264
Royal Arch Degree 161-197, 212
"Royal Arch Lodge" (Winchester) 62
Royal Master, Degree of 182, 207-213

St. George's Lodge (London) 91
St. John the Baptist's Day 26 (and *passim*)
St. John the Evangelist's Day 23 (and *passim*)
St. John's Rising Star Encampment, K. T. (Richmond) 218, 219, 220 (*see also* Richmond Encampment No. 3)
St. Peter's Church (Philadelphia) 51

Index of Subjects

Salisbury, (Maryland) 145
Saratoga, Battle of 13
Scotland 41, 42
Scottish Rite 146
Secret Monitors 199
Select Master, Degree of 182, 207-213
Sharpsburg (Maryland) 98
Shenandoah, Department of (War Between the States) 14
Shenandoah Valley 9, 11, 12, 19, 138
Sheridan's Ride 100
Shepherdstown (West Virginia) 13, 228
Sketches of the Magill Family 143
Sons of Temperance 91
South Carolina 33, 168
Standing Committee 58
Staunton 92, 161, 162, 174, 191, 209, 210, 211, 212
Staunton Council No. 7, R. & S. M. 211 (*same as* Valley Council No. 7)
Staunton Lodge No. 13 19, 92, 93
Stella Diana Lodge No. 4 (Italy) 76
Stephens City 12
Super-Excellent Royal Arch Mason, Degree of (*see* Excellent and Super-Excellent Royal Arch Masons)
Supreme Grand Chapter of Virginia, R. A. M. (*see* Grand Chapter of Virginia, R. A. M.)

Temple Lodge No. —— (Pennsylvania) 23
Temple, Masonic (*see* Masonic Temple)
Trenton Lodge No. 5 (New Jersey) 73
Trustees, Legal (Winchester) 132, 133, 134, 140, 157, 158

Union Chapter No. 2, R. A. M. (Staunton) 162

Union Lodge No. 66 (Winchester) 68, 69, 71, 74, 79, 84, 85, 87, 88, 89, 90, 91, 92, 144, 147-149, 154, 169
United States of America 11, 12
Universal Masonic Library 93
University of Pennsylvania 51
University of Virginia 137, 144

Valley Council No. 7, R. & S. M. 211
Valley Fire Insurance Company 92, 94, 96
Valley Lodge No. 109 (New York) 116
Valley of Virginia (*see* Shenandoah Valley)
Valley Royal Arch School 195
Vermont 101
Virginia, Colony of 19, 20, 40
Virginia, Commonwealth of 11, 40, 41, 161, 173, 207
Virginia Currency 55
Virginia, Grand Chapter of, R. A. M. (*see* Grand Chapter of Virginia)
Virginia, Grand Commandery of, K. T. (*see* Grand Commandery of Virginia)
Virginia, Grand Council of, R. & S. M. (*see* Grand Council of Virginia)
Virginia, Grand Lodge of (*see* Grand Lodge of Virginia)
Virginia Theological Seminary (Alexandria) 144
Visiting Brethren ("V. B.") 31, 56 (and *passim*)
War Between the States 95-103, 110, 144, 145, 185, 186
War of 1812 72
Warren Encampment No. 2, K. T. (Harpers Ferry) 218, 220, 221, 222, 223, 230

Washington College 236
Washington Monument (Richmond) 91
West Virginia 10, 212
Wheeling Encampment No. 1, K. T. 229, 230, 233
William McKinley Lodge No. 431 (Ohio) 138
Williamsburg 22, 23, 40, 41, 42, 43, 44, 209, 211, 212
Williamsburg Convention (1777-1778) 40-45
Williamsburg Council No. 8, R. & S. M. 211
Williamsburg Lodge No. 6 41
Winchester 9 (and *passim* throughout this volume)
Winchester (England) 12
Winchester and Potomac Railroad 14
Winchester Commandery No. 12, K. T. 107, 110, 123, 146, 194, 234-241 (known as Winchester Commandery No. 11 from 1861 to 1871)
Winchester, Confederate Occupation of 96, 100
Winchester Council No. 9, R. & S. M. 207-213

Winchester Encampment No. 1, K. T. 65, 73, 74, 92, 217-234
Winchester, Federal Occupation of 14, 97-104, 111-118
Winchester, Founding of 12
Winchester Hiram Lodge No. 21 9, 49, 64, 65-151, 183, 185
Winchester Lodge No. 12 19-64, 144, 145, 148, 162, 163, 169, 173, 217 (warranted by Pennsylvania)
Winchester Lodge of Super-Excellent Masons 198
Winchester Mark Lodge 198
Winchester Chapter No. 12, R. A. M. 62, 66, 71, 106, 110, 120, 161-186, 192, 196, 197, 204
Winchester Union Lodge No. 66 (*see* Union Lodge No. 66)
Woodstock 86
World War I 137, 195 196, 240
World War II 140, 241

York County (South Carolina)
Yorktown 46

Zerubbabel Legend of Royal Arch Degree 179